THE UNIVERSITY OF
WINCHESTER

Martial Rose Library
Tel: 01962 827306

CRIMES OF WAR

CRIMES OF WAR

Guilt and Denial in the Twentieth Century

OMER BARTOV, ATINA GROSSMANN,

MARY NOLAN

THE NEW PRESS

NEW YORK

Published in the United States by The New Press, New York, 2002.
Distributed by W. W. Norton & Company, Inc., New York.

LIBRARY OF CONGRESS CATALOGING-IN-PUBLICATION DATA
Crimes of war: guilt and denial in the twentieth century /
edited by Omer Bartov, Atina Grossmann, and Mary Nolan.
p.   cm.
Includes bibliographical references and index.
ISBN 1-56584-654-0
1. War crimes—History—20th century.   2. Holocaust, Jewish (1939–1945)
3. Prisoners of war—History—20th century.   4. Atrocities—Europe—History—
20th century.   5. Atrocities—Japan—History—20th century.
6. War—Moral and ethical aspects.   I. Grossmann, Atina.   II. Nolan,
Mary, 1944-   III. Bartov, Omer.
D803.C75 2002
940.54'05—dc21   2001044112

The New Press was established in 1990 as a not-for-profit alternative
to the large, commercial publishing houses currently dominating the
book publishing industry. The New Press operates in the public interest
rather than for private gain, and is committed to publishing, in
innovative ways, works of educational, cultural, and community
value that are often deemed insufficiently profitable.

The New Press, 450 West 41st Street, 6th floor
New York, NY 10036
www.thenewpress.com

Printed in the United States of America

2   4   6   8   10   9   7   5   3   1

Contents

Acknowledgments

W e wish to thank the many people without whose help this volume and the conference from which it came could not have happened. The Cooper Union and especially the Dean of the Art School Robert Rindler committed themselves enthusiastically to hosting the exhibition. At Cooper, we also received important support from Professor of Art Hans Haacke and Dean of the Faculty of Humanities John Harrington. Special thanks are due to Liselot van der Heijden, the extraordinary on-site curator for the planned Cooper exhibit. Her commitment and insight were indispensable to the entire project. The New School University and its Dean Judith Friedlander supported the conference with facilities, funds, and unstinting moral support even when the exhibition was canceled. The generous contribution of the Goethe House in New York helped fund travel for the conference and later translation costs, and its director, Stefan Nobbe, was a vital part of the conference planning committee. Reinhard Maiwurm played an early key role in initiating efforts to bring the exhibit to New York City. The Remarque Institute of New York University, directed by Tony Judt, contributed generously to the conference. Vanessa Khublall of the Goethe House, Sonia Salas of New School University, and Jair Kessler of the Remarque Institute ably handled administrative tasks. Anson Rabinbach was a central figure in the organizing committee. At a difficult time for them, the Hamburg Institute for Social Research contributed funds for the participation of the original exhibition organizers and other Institute researchers in the conference. Finally, we wish to thank

André Schiffrin of the New Press who supported and actively contributed to the conference, proposed doing this volume, and encouraged us as we put it together. We are grateful also to his assistant, Shomial Ahmad, who saw us through the production process with efficiency and good humor.

Introduction

OMER BARTOV, ATINA GROSSMANN, AND MARY NOLAN

Over a half century after the Nuremberg and Tokyo war crimes trials, the problem of defining and documenting war crimes continues to occupy a prominent place on the global political agenda. Nations across the world are haunted by controversies about crimes committed by their armies as they debate how those crimes should be remembered and represented. In the last decade many more crimes against humanity have been perpetrated by a combination of organized armies, militias, and ordinary citizens. In the complex politics of guilt and denial, nations strive to claim the status of victim rather than perpetrator. What is at stake is not merely commemoration or identity, but the lives of human beings, the enforcement of international law, and the setting of moral limits in a time of growing violence and lawlessness. And yet, as crimes against humanity and genocides multiply, the prevention of war crimes seems ever more elusive.

It is often difficult to distinguish between the kind of war that most nations recognize as legitimate under certain conditions and the growing potential of war in the modern era to produce a wide array of war crimes and crimes against humanity. For this reason scholars and others have tended to discuss these two closely related phenomena separately. While the anguished debates about war crimes have been framed by the memory of the Holocaust, they have rarely been explicitly connected to the conduct of the German army and its responsibility for war crimes and crimes against humanity perpetrated by Hitler's regime. The public perception of a clear distinction between the Holocaust and Germany's war was powerfully challenged in 1995 with the opening in Hamburg of an exhibition, "War of Extermination: Crimes of the Wehrmacht 1941–1944," devoted to exploring the legitimacy of this connection.

This controversial documentation of the German army's conduct in the Ukraine, Belorussia, and Serbia contained nearly 1,000 photos, some taken by army propaganda companies, others by soldiers to send home or save as mementos. The images were accompanied by extensive excerpts from army orders and reports, letters from the front, and diaries of officers and enlisted men. Photos and text detailed the shooting and hanging of civilians, the burning and pillage of villages, and the capture and starvation of POWs, all of which characterized this war fought outside the rules of war.[1] The exhibit was seen by over 900,000 Germans and Austrians in the four years it traveled throughout those two countries whose behavior it exposed so provocatively. This was the first time — or in the case of veterans, the first time since they witnessed such scenes in the war — that they confronted vivid photographs and personal accounts of the most gruesome and brutal aspects of the war. The effect was shock, dismay, disbelief, and rage. The exhibit produced an avalanche of reflection, both thoughtful and defensive, in newspaper articles, impassioned letters to the editor, and interviews. Within the German Bundestag it sparked a highly emotional debate about both personal and national relationships to and responsibility for the Third Reich. In Munich there were street demonstrations against the exhibit; in Saarbrücken the site was firebombed.[2] During 1999 charges circulated that some photographs actually depicted victims of the NKVD, the Soviet secret police, rather than those murdered by the Wehrmacht.[3] As the controversy escalated, some politicians, journalists, and scholars vociferously condemned the exhibit and called for its closing.

On December 2, 1999, the American version of the exhibit, entitled "The German Army and Genocide: Crimes Against War Prisoners, Jews, and Other Civilians, 1939–1944," was to have opened at The Cooper Union in New York City. Despite the fact that the planned New York exhibit had incorporated corrections and highlighted the problems of using photographic evidence, and despite the fact that the New Press in New York had published *The German Army and Genocide*, an English-language catalogue with corrected captions, the exhibit's sponsor, the Hamburg Institute for Social Research, felt compelled to cancel the exhibit two weeks before its scheduled New York opening and to suspend it in Germany.[4]

Bringing the Wehrmacht exhibit to the United States seemed important for many reasons. The events portrayed in image and text are central to the history of Germany, during the years of National Socialism and throughout the half century since its defeat. They are also central to the murder of millions of Jews, "Gypsies," and Russians. The exhibit did not portray the bureaucratically organized, industrial mass murder of the camps, about which so many Germans claimed not to have known at the time and from which they could more easily distance themselves later. The exhibit showed the beginning of the Holocaust: the face-to-face, day-to-day roundups and executions, hangings and shootings, forced marches and mass burials on the Eastern Front that preceded and later accompanied the atrocities at Auschwitz and the other death camps. It depicted the individuals and groups who participated, ordered, enabled, observed, and often photographed. It showed that the Holocaust was an integral part of the war on the Eastern Front.

"The German Army and Genocide," more provocatively entitled "War of Extermination" in the German version, spoke most directly to ongoing debates in Germany about "coming to terms with the past." It interrogated the nature of National Socialism and public knowledge about and complicity in the most horrendous Nazi crimes. Moreover, the exhibit confronted its viewers with broader questions that have dominated a century of unprecedented violence. What constitutes a war crime and are war crimes an inevitable part of war? What responsibility do "ordinary" soldiers bear for war crimes? For crimes against humanity? For genocide? And what precisely constitutes responsibility? Is it action or intention? Does knowledge imply complicity? Does passive observation mean legitimization? In the wake of Nazism's defeat and full knowledge of the Holocaust, these emerged as burning political and legal questions, as issues of national and personal history and memory.

Such questions are by no means relevant only to Germany. Other nations have been accused of war crimes—the Japanese for their conduct in China, the United States in Korea and Vietnam, the Turks against the Armenians, the Serbs in Bosnia, the Dutch in Indonesia, the Hutus in Rwanda. The list could be expanded, but the point is clear.

War crimes as an issue of history and memory, of individual complicity and national responsibility, haunt many nations.[5] The Wehrmacht exhibit, in short, spoke not only to German or European history but to American history as well; it raised troubling questions about the past and about present politics across the globe. It offered a controversial representation of the actions of the Wehrmacht in World War II and problematized issues of documenting and representing not only those war crimes but also the war crimes of other times and nations.

Thus, despite the cancellation of the Wehrmacht exhibit, the committee of American scholars that had prepared its New York opening (of which the editors of this volume were part) decided to go ahead with the conference that was to have attended its opening. That conference explored not only the history of the Wehrmacht on the Eastern Front but explicitly addressed issues of documentation and representation. It took a comparative approach to the study of war crimes, history, and memory, one still too politically charged to have been undertaken within Germany. This volume is drawn from that conference.

I

The twentieth century witnessed unprecedented military violence and war crimes as nations waged total war, with devastating consequences for civilian populations, and committed genocide against groups singled out for their religion, ethnicity, race, or political beliefs. But the twentieth century also saw the defining and defending of human rights and the delineation and punishment of war crimes and crimes against humanity. As Michael Ignatieff has argued, the project of moral universalism inherent in rights discourse and debates about war crimes and crimes against humanity is distinctly modern. It is also perpetually threatened by the seduction of utopian projects to create a world without enemies, a homogeneous and purified world.[6]

Germany played a leading role, but certainly not the only one, in the genocides and war crimes of the twentieth century. It featured prominently when concepts of crimes against humanity and genocide were established and when precedents for international law were set. The term "crimes against humanity" was coined after World War I in reference to the Turkish genocide of the Armenians. During the 1920s, in The Hague and in Geneva, efforts were made to regulate the new weapons of aerial bombardment and gas. The concept of genocide was invented by Rafael Lemkin, a Polish-Jewish refugee from Nazism, during World War II but before the horror of Auschwitz was fully known. Although the bulk of indictments at the Nuremberg Trials was for "waging a war of aggression," the trials represented the first effort to define and punish crimes against humanity under international law and to establish certain actions as criminal regardless of the laws of the country in which they were committed. Further steps to move crimes against humanity and human rights into a prominent position in international law were taken in 1948 when the United Nations passed the Genocide Convention and the Universal Declaration of Human Rights.[7]

Nazi Germany and its exterminatory policies thus featured centrally in international discourse about war crimes, crimes against humanity, and genocide; discourse that took on new forms as it gained greater visibility in the post-Holocaust decades. It proved much harder for post–World War II Germans, West and East, to understand their recent history in those terms. Even when they were able to acknowledge that "unspeakable crimes have been committed" (as Adenauer put it) they sought to delimit narrowly the circle of those responsible.[8] For several decades after the fall of Hitler's regime, both the official representations of Nazi crimes and popular opinion in Germany tended to draw a distinction between the criminal agencies of the regime, primarily the SS and Gestapo, and the professional and patriotic conduct of the armed forces. As early as the 1960s, however, scholars began to cast doubt over the myth of the "purity of arms" of the Wehrmacht, and for the next three decades evidence accumulated on the Nazi indoctrination of the Wehrmacht, the collaboration between its top echelons and the men in charge of the SS, the criminal orders handed out to the junior officers and the rank and file, and the mass involvement of military units in operations of extermination.[9]

Public perception of the army's role in the crimes of the Nazi regime was much slower to change, and not only because exposure to this specialized literature was relatively limited, filtered as it was through popular magazine and newspaper reports. Accepting the complicity of the army in the crimes of the regime had far-reaching implications. As long as the mass murders committed by the Nazis could be attributed to a relatively small group of perpetrators clearly identified as Hitler's and Himmler's evil agents, the bulk of the German population could not be accused of having known about the extent of the crimes or of having been in a position to stop them, let alone of having actually facilitated their perpetration. The growing evidence on the army's complicity now meant that millions of soldiers had been at least potentially involved in criminal actions, and that knowledge of these crimes must have been carried back to the rear by the troops who witnessed them or carried them out. The consistent and willing collaboration of the Wehrmacht in the destruction of lives and property meant that the Third Reich had relied on the complicity of its population. The Wehrmacht exhibit, coming to Germany and Austria as it did only in the 1990s, revealed that, for decades after the fall of Nazism, Germany had hidden this truth from itself. Indeed, it had built its postwar identity on the myth of a "pure" Wehrmacht as the embodiment of general public innocence. It was one thing to accept that crimes, even genocide, had been committed "in the name of the German people." It was quite another thing to accept that crimes, even genocide, had been committed by a national army of some twenty million Germans. This history, known to millions during the event, was hidden away in people's memories and dusty archives for another half century.

The controversy over the exhibition brought to the fore defense mechanisms that had characterized German discourse about the relationship of the army to the crimes of Nazism since 1945 (and, indeed, during the war and the Holocaust itself). Even as Germany repeatedly acknowledged its responsibility for the Holocaust, well-rehearsed obfuscations reappeared in the press and in the pronouncements of politicians. War is hell and therefore soldiers cannot be blamed for being brutal. The enemy was no better; perhaps it was even worse. Even if there were evidence of individual crimes, one could not generalize about an army of millions. Smearing the good name of the Wehrmacht was unpatriotic and an obstacle to German normalization. Despite these apologetic maneuvers, the Wehrmacht exhibition did change both public knowledge and discourse to a dramatic extent.[10]

The Wehrmacht exhibition forced the German public to revise its image of the military, whose legitimacy had survived war and the total collapse of the Nazi regime. It also shed light on the link between war and genocide in the twentieth century. Most important, the exhibition made public what scholars had long known, that there was a direct and

crucial link between the war and the Holocaust. The attempt to separate the two not only served apologetic purposes, but also created a false
understanding of the nature of modern genocide. The effort to distinguish between war and genocide was by no means the monopoly of
Germans. Most military histories of World War II written in the early
postwar decades devote little attention to the Holocaust, which was regarded as an entirely separate affair. Even today, many histories of genocide analyze events with little reference to their most immediate and
crucial context, war.[11] The Holocaust took place in a context of total
war and could be continued and expanded only as long as the war went
on. Moreover, it assumed many of the attributes of a military operation
and was legitimized and understood by its perpetrators as an essentially
military task that had a direct bearing on the security, or even the existence, of the nation.

In the last few years a growing volume of scholarship and journalism
has shown that genocide occurs normally under cover of war. This was
the case in the Armenian genocide in World War I, in the Cambodian
genocide in the 1970s, in the genocide in Rwanda, and in the mass
killing, rape, and ethnic cleansing campaigns in Bosnia—to cite the
most obvious cases.[12] This does not mean that genocide is the inevitable
consequence of modern war, but rather that it invariably occurs during
war or at least under the guise of a military threat. During the twentieth
century the ratio of military to civilian casualties in war shifted dramatically, so that civilians now comprise by far the majority of those killed,
mutilated, raped, and uprooted even when they present no conceivable
threat to the military adversaries. As war has come increasingly to target
civilian populations, so too has its potential for engendering genocide
grown.

Furthermore, the wars of the twentieth century, both in Europe and
elsewhere, often had a powerful ethnic element. They aimed to move
or eradicate entire populations that stood in the way of expansionist or
hegemonic goals, or were seen as a threat to the homogeneous character of the nation. And wars of ideology have always had an exterminatory potential. Hitler stated this quite clearly when he said that the war
against the Soviet Union would be a war of ideologies, and hence a war
of extermination (*Vernichtungskrieg*) where the conventional rules of
warfare would not apply and there would be no comrades in arms

("*keine Kameraden*").[13] But even when things were not stated in such brutal terms, the urge to cleanse, purge, depopulate, and eradicate was never far from the surface.[14]

Wars of nations are fought by national armies that tend to represent nations better than most other state institutions and organizations. Soldiers are recruited by universal male conscription and drawn from all walks of life and several age cohorts. They thus constitute direct links between the front and the rear, the civilian and the military sphere. Soldiers tell the home front about their experiences on the battlefront, experiences that may be the formative events in their lives.

Once the war is over, the soldiers, as young and virile elements of the population, are also expected to rebuild the nation. In cases of genocidal war, the relationship between veterans and postwar societies is particularly complex. For example, many "second-" and "third-" generation Germans—those born toward the end of the Nazi regime, and their children—saw the bulk of the "first" generation—those who were adults during at least part of the Third Reich—as mostly decent soldiers who did their duty. They saw them as having been victimized twice over, first by a fanatical leadership that persisted in fighting a losing war, and then by the victorious Allies. For these younger Germans it was a deeply personal and painful experience to discover that the veterans, their fathers and grandfathers, participated (willingly or reluctantly) in the regime's policies of genocide and destruction. The exhibit seemed to revive the long-dismissed assertion of collective guilt not as an amorphous notion but as a concrete understanding that the war waged by Germany was a criminal undertaking, and that the soldiers who fought in it were therefore directly or indirectly the perpertrators of innumerable crimes.[15]

Germany is an especially striking example of the link between war and genocide, but this should not obscure the extent to which war crimes have become an increasingly recognizable and massive component of war since the late nineteenth century. This raises a host of questions, some in the realm of history, others more relevant to judicial, political, and moral discourse. As historians we can say that while all sides committed war crimes in World War II, some of the combatant nations were far more criminal than others. In judicial discourse, we can ask how one makes distinctions between more and less criminal combatant nations. Is one allowed to commit crimes in the name of preventing or putting an end to greater crimes (as, for instance, in fire-bombing civilian populations as part of an effort to defeat Nazism)? Should one refrain from intervention against genocide for fear of losing one's own soldiers, or of harming civilian populations? Should a nation refrain from such intervention, despite its obvious humanitarian value, if it is not crucial to perceived national interest? (Think of American nonintervention in Rwanda or, conversely, the NATO bombing of Yugoslavia during the Kosovo crisis.) In political terms, should one adhere to a false representation of past or present actions in order to prevent internal strife or to maintain a nation's positive and optimistic self-perception (as in the American debate over the Enola Gay and the atomic bombing of Japan, or United States involvement in Central and South America)? In moral terms, can one support the idea of an international tribunal for war crimes if it is established by those who have superior power and selects those it indicts and tries from among groups it neither needs nor wishes to protect?[16] Can one defend the idea of international tribunals while accepting their inherent compromised position, or should one oppose the establishment of international justice in the name of absolute morality?

II

In order to reconstruct the complex issues of guilt and denial that surround the Wehrmacht exhibit and other discussions of war crimes and genocide, we need to understand the prominent place of national armies in societies and their histories. We also need to situate narratives of guilt and denial in terms of ongoing controversies about what a war crime is and when it is appropriate to stop or punish such a crime. Equally, we must view the controversies surrounding war crimes, guilt, and denial in context. For Germany, Japan, Russia, and the United States, the relevant contexts are two. The first is the domestic and international situations in the years immediately after a war (a theme that will be explored at length in subsequent essays). The second is the contemporary world of post–Cold War uncertainty about the future and preoccupation with the past, which has helped generate a particularly contentious politics of memory not only in Germany but in many other countries as well.

Since the mid 1980s Europe and America have witnessed an unprecedented memory boom. At its center stands the production and consumption of representations of the Holocaust and World War II and the bitter debate about who was a perpetrator and who a victim, who resisted and who collaborated, who knew what and saw what. This contemporary preoccupation with one of the most destructive episodes of the twentieth century has complex origins. The very violence of so much of the twentieth century makes it seem imperative to examine in depth this paradigmatic period of destruction, war crimes, and genocide. In the multiple catastrophes of genocide, war crimes, and nuclear weapons in Europe and Asia lay one possible outcome of modernity. Here we can find both compelling narratives of heroism and horrifying narratives of victimization with which many different groups seek to identify. And in contemplating war and genocide we may rethink conceptions of rights, international law, and humanity.

It was not only the nature of World War II but also the recent spate of commemorative events associated with it that has spawned such intensive and divisive memory work. The series of anniversaries associated with the war's beginnings and endings in Europe and Asia, far from providing closure to old conflicts among and within nations, reopened them. One thinks of Bitburg in 1985, for example, or the Enola Gay exhibit controversy in 1994–95.[17] The intensity of the ensuing debates marked not only a return of the repressed. It resulted as well from the fact that the generation that experienced the war as soldiers or civilians and the Holocaust as perpetrators, victims, resisters, or passive bystanders was dwindling. This was their last chance to recall the experience, to tell the story as they wished it to be told. Simultaneously, the gradual replacement of memory by postmemory, of experience by representation, has opened new debates about the reading of visual evidence, the memorialization of victims, and the purpose of historical museums.[18] The result is that we seem to have both a surfeit of memory and to be in a memory panic. On the one hand there is an (over)abundance of museums, memorials, films, plays, and memories as well as historiographical debates and restitution and compensation controversies. On the other hand, there is escalating fear, both about forgetting and about remembering the wrong things, as evidenced by the scandals about authenticity and the exposure of false memories.[19]

In the post–World War II decades Nazi Germany has occupied a place of prominence in the contemporary memory boom because its crimes are the paradigmatic case of genocide and crimes against humanity. But the Federal Republic has also received praise for the ways it has dealt with those crimes through the punishment of war criminals (however limited), through reparations to the state of Israel and to individual survivors, and through governmental statements, memorials, and ceremonies. Its postwar "politics of the past" (*Vergangenheitspolitik*) are said to have stabilized and legitimated the postwar democratic order, while its "coming to terms with the past" (*Vergangenheitsbewältigung*) has displayed a willingness to acknowledge crimes of war.[20] In comparison to Japan or the German Democratic Republic, the Federal Republic has been more open about its past actions and financially forthcoming to surviving Jewish victims. For both Germans and others it has been easy to overlook the silences in the practices and policies of memory. Crimes were acknowledged more readily than criminals; the focus was on Auschwitz, not the Wehrmacht, i.e., on industrialized mass murder by the SS, not the face-to-face mass murders by the army on the Eastern Front. Moreover, in their own memories of World War II, Germans preferred to count themselves among the victims rather than among the perpetrators.[21]

These public and private debates about the Wehrmacht, war crimes, and genocide were both intensified and reshaped in the highly charged political context marked by the disappearance of the Soviet Union and the reunification of Germany. Now that Germany has become once more a nation-state, there has been a sustained search for a usable past, one that would emphasize the normal rather than the criminal, the national rather than the post-national aspects of identity. After being discredited in the 1970s and 1980s, totalitarianism theory has gained a new respectability and, many argue, analytical purchase. With that has come a new emphasis on comparative history that puts the crimes of Nazism in the context of those of Stalinism or, in the case of *The Black Book of Communism*, the crimes of communism worldwide.[22] Whereas earlier debates focused on whether one could speak of fascism without speaking of capitalism, current ones ask whether one can speak of Nazism without speaking of communism. This has been reflected not only in the Wehrmacht exhibit controversy but also more broadly in debates about crimes against humanity and genocide that have recently taken place in the former socialist countries of eastern Europe as well as in France.[23]

These reshaped debates have been particularly complicated in Germany as witnessed by, among other examples, the enthusiastic public reception of Victor Klemperer's *I Will Bear Witness*, in the generally positive public reaction to Daniel Goldhagen's *Hitler's Willing Executioners*, and in the divisive debates about the Wehrmacht exhibit and the Memorial to the Murdered Jews of Europe in Berlin.[24] The diaries of Klemperer, a converted German Jew married to an "Aryan," who survived Nazism and the war in Germany, record the growing racialization of all aspects of everyday life, as well as economics and politics, from 1933 on. They detail moments of noncompliance with Nazi policies but depict more fully the humiliations and discrimination, profound and petty, to which Jews were constantly subjected and in which so many Germans engaged with such apparent ease and enthusiasm. Goldhagen's portrait of Germany is grimmer still. German society was permeated by exterminatory anti-Semitism, he argues, and under Nazism genocide became a "national project." The widespread praise for both these works seems to indicate a willingness to acknowledge the daily and visible terror to which Jews in Germany were subjected and a newfound focus on the perpetrators who supervised work camps, led the death marches, and, as members of police battalions, executed Jews on the Eastern Front. It seems to represent an admission of the pervasive knowledge of and complicity with the crimes of the regime. The recent decision of the German government, the city of Berlin, and a private foundation to construct a memorial to the murdered Jews of Europe (commonly referred to as the *Mahnmal*) on a site near the Brandenburg Gate seems to express recognition that there was no "community of victims" encompassing Germans and Jews, perpetrators and those they murdered. It was the effort to construct such a community (and thereby normalize German history) that had motivated the revamping of the Neue Wache memorial in Berlin in the early 1990s with its Käthe Kollwitz pietà and generalized dedication "to the victims of war and tyranny."[25]

The Wehrmacht exhibit exposed the limits of this willingness to confront the past honestly. Even as Germans of several generations recognized with horror the crimes of SS men and police battalions, many wanted to protect the reputation of the Wehrmacht. They seemed to read Klemperer's moving diaries without understanding its implications for questions about complicity in extermination. The decision to build the *Mahnmal* was taken only after a long and contentious debate, the project is still on the drawing board, and once built it will coexist uneasily with the Neue Wache, the two testifying to Germany's difficulty in resolving the question of who is a perpetrator, who a victim, and how each should be represented.

III

These questions of definition and documentation, representation, public exhibition, and memorialization that haunt recent German debates about war crimes are controversial in other nations as well. And they are the essential concerns of the essays in this collection, which explore the complexities of these questions and how particular war crimes are publicly represented or repressed.

The definition, documentation, and public discussion of war crimes, guilt, and denial have gone on in many arenas. Tzvetan Todorov provides an insightful categorization.[26] In the juridical arena, there have been trials and tribunals that seek to define crimes and punish perpetrators; in the political and legal realms there have been a variety of campaigns and contests over reparations, restitution, and compensation of both a material and symbolic sort. Efforts to claim some of what is owed have involved not only the Jewish survivors of the Holocaust, but the Japanese interned in camps in the United States during World War II, the Asian "comfort women" forced to service Japanese soldiers, Native Americans seeking the return of tribal lands, and slave laborers in Nazi Germany.[27] More recently, in South Africa and Latin America, truth and reconciliation commissions have aimed not at punishment but rather at confession, healing, and even amnesty.[28]

Deliberations in all these arenas have profoundly shaped definitions of war crimes and provided often painfully detailed knowledge about victims and perpetrators. They have strongly influenced the arena with which we are concerned: public memory, the public admission or denial of war crimes, and the public naming of or refusal to name war criminals. It is the intersection of historical research and debates with historical exhibitions and questions about representational strategies, challenges, and problems, as raised by the Wehrmacht exhibit, that intrigues us. What is a war crime and who is a victim? How can one document accurately not only the crimes but also the perpetrators and the victims? How should those documents be conveyed and displayed and in what narratives should they be embedded? What modes of representation are appropriate for crimes against humanity, their perpetrators, and their victims? Historical exhibits, such as the Wehrmacht and the Enola Gay, seem at once indispensable and impossible. They are essential for evoking and critically recasting public memory but it is extremely difficult to produce an exhibition that does justice to the complexity of the crimes. It is impossible to mount an historical exhibition on war crimes and war criminals that does not provoke an outcry from some or several political corners.

It is not so much the paucity of evidence that complicates the documentation, representation, and presentation of war crimes. Orders, reports, letters, memories, court testimony of a horrifyingly detailed sort exist in abundance. A perverse determination to count and catalogue is all too often operative when war crimes are committed. Rather, complications come from the nature of the evidence, from the use of photographs as a means of authenticating atrocity and the related difficulty historians, but not historians alone, face in reading photographic evidence. Photography has played a privileged role in documenting and memorializing the Holocaust and in indicting the Germans for their crimes.[29] Photography has also documented Hiroshima and Nagasaki and chronicled ethnic cleansing. Indeed, the absence of photographic evidence or of photos that fit the iconic forms tends to cast doubt on the possibility of war crimes or genocide. Photographs have a compelling and disturbing immediacy that the written word lacks. But photography has also been criticized for playing on emotions, simplifying complex situations, and attributing guilt and complicity without corroborating evidence. In the Wehrmacht exhibit, for example, the very identification of the victims and perpetrators in certain photos has been contested. The prominence of photographic evidence raises issues of how to identify correctly who and what is portrayed, for archival designations are often inaccurate and private photos untitled or inadequately titled.

The identification of the individual photo is only the first challenge. Into which narratives should the frozen moment of the photograph be inserted? These narratives are crucial in determining whether an act is a war crime or a crime against humanity and whether an apparent victim is really innocent. The prevalence of photographic evidence also forces historians to ask by whom and from whose perspective the photo was shot. Why was an atrocity photographed at all, especially when it was not a journalist or peacekeeper who took the picture but an official military photographer or soldier with his personal camera? How does the viewpoint of the photographer position subsequent viewers? What iconic images do we carry of the Holocaust and crimes against humanity and how do they influence our reactions to photographs of other war crimes?

Efforts at documentation invariably set off a competition to avoid being counted among the perpetrators and to secure one's place among the victims. Surely, one might object, even if the full circle of perpetrators may be hard to pinpoint with accuracy, the victims are an easily identifiable group — the shot, the gassed, the hanged, the beaten, the raped, the starved, and the displaced. But the politics of memory are precisely about contesting and confusing that seemingly self-evident category. Even when nations admit that crimes or, at any rate, very disturbing events like massacres occurred, they claim that no one intended to commit them — witness recent American responses to reports of massacres by U.S. soldiers at No Gun Ri in the Korean War and Thanh Phong in the Vietnam War.[30]

Those seen as perpetrators are most likely to insist that, on the contrary, they are victims. Turks accuse Armenians of insurrection and subversion, Wehrmacht soldiers cite their mistreatment as POWs in the Soviet Union, Serbs claim to have been persecuted by Albanians. This scramble reflects in part a simple desire to repress the consequences of one's own actions while dwelling on one's sufferings. In part it reflects a belief, held individually and collectively, that one's suffering and the suffering of one's nation were quantitatively and qualitatively greater than that of any others. The number of Germans expelled from the eastern territories by the Red Army has been compared to the number of victims of the extermination camps, for example, and the suffering of retreating German soldiers at war's end has often been depicted by Germans in anguished and empathetic prose of a sort not used for Jewish victims of those very soldiers.[31] Finally, the Holocaust has become the universal symbol of inhumanity, atrocity, and trauma. It provides the discourse and images through which and against which all other victims feel they must define themselves and the crimes against them.[32] The desire to be counted among the victims reflects what Todorov has described as "the usurpation of the narrative of heroism by the narrative of victimhood" in the late twentieth century.[33]

Although everyone may want to be among the victims, not every victim is accorded recognition. In the discussion about the United States massacre of Korean civilians at No Gun Ri, the American military, politicians, and commentators have repeatedly implied that those murdered were in fact North Korean soldiers disguised as civilians. Or if they were not, they might well have been—and how was one to know? The Wehrmacht exhibition displayed a broad spectrum of victims— Jews, POWs, and Russian and Ukrainian civilians—but critics labeled many of them partisans in an attempt to nullify their status as victims and justify the actions of the Wehrmacht. At each phase of definition, documentation, representation, and public exhibition, what was a war crime, who committed it, and who was a victim of it are contested. Tracing the convoluted processes by which crimes are disguised or transformed, guilt denied, and victims blamed for their suffering is essential to reconstructing the politics of memory that surrounds war crimes.

IV

Discussions of war crimes, war criminals, and their victims are inherently comparative and the Wehrmacht exhibition raised comparative issues in a way that exhibitions and museums on the Holocaust do not. Auschwitz and industrialized mass murder were unique but wartime massacres and atrocities are all too common. The participants in the conference, held at the non-opening of the Wehrmacht exhibition in New York, and in this volume insist on viewing the crimes of the Wehrmacht comparatively, even while recognizing that comparative analyses of Nazi crimes have had a politically problematic history. In the immediate postwar period, Germans downplayed their own crimes while loudly condemning those of the Soviets. In the Historians' Debate of the 1980s, liberal historians insisted on the uniqueness and incomparability of the Holocaust, while their conservative counterparts sought to historicize and minimize the Holocaust by comparing it to other twentieth-century genocides in Europe and Asia.[34] In the post–Cold War era, the comparative history of atrocities is once again on the agenda. If few are willing to go as far as Ernst Nolte did when he blamed Stalin for the crimes of Hitler, many insist that both regimes must be understood as manifestations of totalitarianism, that both were thoroughly criminal. Certainly while one practiced racialized genocide and the other oscillated between selecting its enemies on politico-social and ethnic grounds, both were extraordinarily destructive in their historically specific ways.[35]

Despite all the problems and potential pitfalls of comparison, we consider it essential to any analysis of war crimes, history, and memory. We do not, however, want to become embroiled in the politics of rating war crimes and ranking atrocities. We do not wish to compare genocides to see which qualifies or insist that any atrocity short of genocide does not need to be taken seriously or require intervention. Our interest in comparison is twofold. First, it is necessary to reconstruct and compare German voices on the actions of the Wehrmacht in order to get multiple perspectives on what soldiers did, what they remember doing, and how the public remembers both. Only through comparison can one construct narratives that show German crimes intersecting with the crimes of others. We need to include the voices of soldiers and their victims, Jewish and Russian. We need the views and actions of women on the front and at home. We need to recognize that one and the same German could be both a perpetrator and a victim, without thereby minimizing the horror of the crimes he committed.

Comparison also provides a way to break open what has been a self-enclosed German discourse. Just as debates about war crimes elsewhere have been profoundly informed by the German case, a more complex understanding of German war crimes and the way postwar German society remembered and repressed them can be arrived at by looking at other societies. How have other nations represented their war crimes in ways that admit and deny, acknowledge and distort them? How have those who are seen by outsiders as criminals come to construct themselves as victims or at the very least as innocent of intentional atrocities? And what happens to both the perpetrators and subsequent generations when denial is no longer possible?

Our comparisons concentrate on the first period of preoccupation with and contestation of war crimes, perpetrators, and victims—the period from the end of World War II through the 1950s. We also discuss the current wave of reconsiderations of those earlier memories with their partial recognitions and massive denials. While we bring in the United States with the example of the Korean War, we do not analyze colonial atrocities or those that were part of the wars of decolonization, such as in Vietnam and Algeria.[36] Nor do we examine the ways in which the metropole denied them. That omission reflects the Eurocentric nature of so much of the discourse about war crimes and crimes against humanity and limits our understanding of the circumstances under which they are committed and how the responsibility for them is denied. Nor do we touch on the recent war crimes in ex-Yugoslavia and Rwanda and the debates about definition, intervention, and criminal prosecution; they loom in the background of this work, reminding us of the ongoing urgency of these questions.[37]

While we do not in any way relativize the crimes of the Nazi regime and its numerous accomplices, we want to understand them within the larger context of war and war crimes in the past century. It is for this reason that we have chosen the wide-ranging essays that make up this volume. They discuss in detail both the facts and polemics of the Wehrmacht's crimes, a selection of other important war crimes, and the long-term process of coming to terms with their reality and memory.

V

The collection opens with two thoughtful reflections on the history of concern with and the definition of war crimes. Aryeh Neier, longtime human rights activist and head of the Open Society Institute, argues that World War II marked a turning point in how war was conducted, in ways that greatly increased the danger for civilians and the possibilities of genocide. In the wake of that war, however, great strides were made in defining and exposing war crimes and crimes against humanity. Technology, he notes, has played a double-edged role in this connection, facilitating knowledge of and action against war crimes but also facilitating their commission. Neier reminds us that the recognition and prosecution of war crimes are still very pressing issues on the international agenda.

Jan Philipp Reemtsma, head of the Hamburg Institute for Social Research, which produced the Wehrmacht exhibit, has a longer and considerably more pessimistic perspective on the discourse about war crimes. He chronicles centuries of crimes, denial, and, at most, grudging admissions quickly followed by exculpation on the grounds of necessity, defense of civilization, or the greater crimes of the enemy. He reminds us that debates about war crimes are inextricably linked with debates about the goals of the wars of which they are a part. He provides the first overview and assessment of why the Wehrmacht exhibit proved so controversial in Germany, and explains why the Institute decided to close the exhibition in Germany and not open it in New York in the fall of 1999.

What precisely happened on the Eastern Front? Were Wehrmacht soldiers complicitous and, if so, were they ambivalent or enthusiastic, were they motivated by conviction or were they indifferent? And was there widespread knowledge among Germans on the home front about the pervasive criminality on the Eastern Front? These questions are central to the studies of Saul Friedländer, a leading historian of Nazi anti-Semitism and the Holocaust, and Christopher Browning, who has reconstructed the murderous actions of German police battalions on the Eastern Front. Their analyses of two different areas and incidents during World War II illustrate the multiplicity of criminal acts, the ways the Wehrmacht was involved, and how aware German civilians were of them.

Friedländer unravels the interplay of criminality, complicity, and knowledge by reconstructing the murder of Jewish children in the Ukrainian town of Bjelaja Zerkow in August 1941. The Wehrmacht, he shows, cooperated extensively with the *Einsatzgruppen* (the murder squads of the SS and SD) in the murder of Jews, and soldiers often discussed these killings among themselves. Even those who objected to specific actions were caught up in the logic of war and extermination and accepted its dictates. Like Omer Bartov, Friedländer portrays an ideologically motivated army. But it was not only the army that knew about and accepted extermination. Those on the home front were aware and approved; ambivalence about or opposition to Nazi policies involved only those policies affecting Germans, not those singling out Jews or Slavs. Friedländer's essay, like recent work by Eric Johnson, suggests the need to revise our understanding of *Resistenz* or immunity to Nazism and to reassess assumptions about the widespread threat of terror.[38] Knowledge and acceptance were far more common than fear and opposition, Friedländer suggests, and this may help account for the vehement response to the Wehrmacht exhibit. Guilt and denial were as necessary for those on the home front as for those on the battlefront.

Browning's essay on the Wehrmacht in Serbia explores not the classic terrain of the "Final Solution," which aimed at destroying every last

Jewish man, woman, and child, but rather the landscape of genocide aimed at killing masses of people and destroying a culture. In Serbia, he argues, the Wehrmacht was very much in control and the SS were minor players. This sheds particularly stark light on the attitudes and responsibility of the former. Browning traces the interaction of pre-Nazi German prejudices, which saw Serbs as oriental others, emotional and uncivilized, with Nazi racial categories, which deemed Serbs racially inferior and on a par with Jews and "Gypsies." This suggests the need to examine the legacy of European imperialism and colonialism and how it affected conduct in World War II in Eastern Europe. Prejudice, old and new, and Serb resistance to the Nazi occupation provoked a harsh Nazi response. Browning analyzes deftly how labeling civilians as partisans justified a vicious reprisal policy, one which, like all Nazi policies was wielded with attention to Nazi racial hierarchies. If all Serb adult men were potential targets, preference was shown for Jewish and "Gypsy" ones.[39]

In the next section we turn from the Wehrmacht on the Eastern Front to the controversy around the Wehrmacht exhibit. Omer Bartov, who has written extensively on Hitler's army, offers a sweeping overview and rich critical analysis of the controversy surrounding the exhibition. Bernd Boll and Marianne Hirsch focus from quite different perspectives on the problems of reading photographic evidence, issues that played a central role in the critique of the exhibition.

Bartov was a member of the independent committee of experts set up after the closure of the Wehrmacht exhibition that was to assess the validity of the charges against it. That committee resoundingly rejected the claims of deliberate falsification and manipulation leveled by a few critics and disseminated widely by the German press. Bartov passionately affirms what historians have long argued: There is "overwhelming historical evidence regarding the criminal role of the Wehrmacht in the Third Reich." He reminds us that Germany defined the war against Russia as exceptional from the beginning. He constructs a multifaceted history depicting particular war crimes and their connections to others. "There was," he insists, "a direct link between NKVD executions, German-incited pogroms, SS and army massacres, mass murder by the *Einsatzgruppen*, and finally the construction and operation of the far more efficient extermination camps." Bartov refutes the argument of Bogdan Musial and Krisztián Ungváry about the limited number of Wehrmacht crimes in comparison to those of the SS, Ukrainians, and others.[40] He also critiques the myths they have revived in the post–Cold War era, myths about the ostensible Jewish collaboration with and benefit from Soviet occupation. His concluding remarks on the challenge of interpreting photographic evidence are taken up at greater length by Bernd Boll.

Boll, a co-producer of the Wehrmacht exhibition and a co-author of the accompanying catalogue, examines several of the disputed photos from the exhibit which depict the murdered corpses in the town of Złoczów (in the Polish region occupied by the Soviets in 1939 and the Germans in 1941). Boll explores why these photos were first identified as showing the murdered victims of the Wehrmacht. He acknowledges that, as critics have charged, several show victims of the NKVD, killed as the Red Army retreated before the Wehrmacht. But, he argues strongly, if these photos of NKVD murders are situated in the narrative of crimes and subsequent Wehrmacht activity, that hardly exonerates the German army. Far from it: the Wehrmacht used the NKVD murders to stir up hatred and encourage the murder of the Jews of Złoczów. Boll's essay illustrates the dangers of accepting archival designations of photos and the necessity of understanding photos in contexts that can only be reconstructed with written as well as photographic evidence. Finally, his essay reveals how much politics shape the reading and contextualization of atrocity photos and how persistent the critics of the exhibit and defenders of the myth of the clean Wehrmacht remain.

Marianne Hirsch, who has written extensively on photography and memory, examines the meaning of photography and the rhetoric and politics of representation and memory. Hirsch explores the peculiarities of "perpetrator images," a crucial issue in our context where most of the photos of the war on the Eastern Front and of the Holocaust were taken by perpetrators or liberators, not victims. In such iconic images as the photo of the boy from the Warsaw ghetto with raised hands, the victims "are shot before they are shot." Yet, paradoxically, these images also allow us as viewers to identify, oversimply, with these victims. Hirsch also explores how contemporary artists have incorporated these images and inquires about the idioms that are used to "redirect the genocidal gaze." In doing so she highlights, as is rarely done in the analyses of Holocaust photographs, the roles of gender and childhood in structuring the postmemory of those who were not in the Holocaust but have come to think of themselves as witnesses via the testimony and images left by those who were.

The essays in the next section take us back in time from the current controversy to the representations of and silences about the Wehrmacht's genocidal war in late 1940s and 1950s Germany. As many historians have demonstrated, silence did not characterize these years. Even as knowledge of the Holocaust was denied and guilt for it refused, there were noisy debates about perpetrators and victims, suffering and responsibility—but these debates took selective forms.[41] The essays by Gudrun Schwarz, Frank Biess, and Robert Moeller describe the ways war crimes were redefined and war criminals were either written out of history or written in as victims.

Gudrun Schwarz, a pioneer researcher on the role of women as perpetrators in the Third Reich, returns to the issues of complicity and knowledge raised in earlier essays. She explores them from the perspective of the hundreds of thousands of women who were not merely "mothers in the fatherland" but also soldiers of the "master race," active on the Eastern Front as Wehrmacht employees, members of the medical corps, and of auxiliaries in the SS, as well as colonizers in occupied Poland. Schwarz shows how the postwar memory and construction of German women as victims of war, bombings, expulsions, and rape by the invading Red Army effaced the active role of young single women in the war on the Eastern Front. That role has hitherto played no part in current debates about the Wehrmacht.

Frank Biess, who is writing a book about POWs in postwar East and West Germany, analyzes how German crimes on the Eastern Front were overlaid in German memory with the postwar consciousness of the victimization of German POWs in the Soviet Union. He focuses on the little-known history of veterans who were accused of collaborating with the antifascist enemy after the war on account of their actions in the POW camps. These *Kameradenschinder* trials, as Biess points out, were part of the ambivalent history of postwar justice and retribution.[42] What kind of culpability could be assigned to individual "ordinary" soldiers operating under the duress of war or captivity? Ironically, the very same groups who argued that the suffering German soldier on the Eastern Front had no choice but to obey orders insisted on the moral responsibility of the men who collaborated with the Soviets in the camps or somehow abused their comrades there.

Moeller, like Biess, traces the processes by which Germans effaced the memory of their victims and focused only on themselves as victims or perpetrators of crimes against other Germans. He also shows how West Germany dealt with the legacy of Nazism at home by focusing on communism abroad. Through displacement and equivalence Germans came to recognize the category of crimes against humanity but denied that Germans had committed any such crimes. Moeller and Biess contribute to a growing body of literature that links the war in the East and distorted memories of it to the construction and legitimation of the Federal Republic. But while Biess looks for these links in the courtroom, Moeller takes us to the cinema. Moeller analyzes how the epic battle of Stalingrad was depicted in postwar West German films. The chapter expands on his recent *War Stories: The Search for a Usable Past in the Federal Republic of Germany,* in which he analyzes representations of POWs and expellees from the East and how Germans came to see themselves as the true victims of World War II. Here Moeller pays particular attention to the 1959 film *Hunde, wollt ihr ewig leben?* (Dogs, do you want to live forever?), a film that summarized postwar understanding of the war in the East. It depicts innocent German soldiers sent to Stalingrad to be killed or captured, due to the brutal fanaticism of the Nazi leadership. An antiwar film that insisted that peaceful coexistence and an army of citizen soldiers were possible, *Hunde* is nonetheless marked by stunning silences. It starts in 1942 and never asks why or how the Germans got to Stalingrad. It depicts war as a tragedy but has Germans as the primary victims, part of the community of victims suffering from National Socialism. This kind of rehabilitation of the fathers in which Jewish victims hardly figure was repeated in later films on Stalingrad, including Kluge's *Die Patriotin* (1979) and Vismaier's 1993 *Stalingrad.* The total indictment of the German army presented in the Wehrmacht exhibition thus encountered entrenched popular representations of the Eastern Front and the established notions about who was a victim and who a perpetrator. Moeller concludes that it is time to overcome binary depictions of victims and perpetrators and to construct the sort of complex story that Vasilii Grossman, the Soviet novelist of World War II, does in his epic *Life and Fate*.[43] Such a history would move from Germany to Stalingrad, showing all the horror and extermination of that invasion. But it would also follow the soldiers from Stalingrad to the POW camps. It would give voice to Jews and Russians and allow Germans to be both perpetrators and victims.

The last section of the collection presents three cases of how other societies have dealt with war crimes, guilt, and denial. Amir Weiner examines the interaction of Nazi war crimes and Soviet purges and ethnic cleansing, as well as the Soviet memory of the war in the immediate postwar years. John Dower reflects on the contested memories of Japanese war crimes and the ways in which Japanese, like Germans, have both acknowledged past crimes and reconstructed themselves as victims. Marilyn Young looks at American war crimes, not in the extensively debated cases of Hiroshima and Nagasaki or Vietnam but in Korea.

Weiner, author of *Making Sense of War: The Second World War and the Fate of the Bolshevik Revolution*, takes us to the other side of the Eastern Front, examining not only what the Germans did to the Soviets, but how the Soviets responded with increasingly racialized thinking and practices that encouraged purges, discrimination, and population transfers of Jews and ethnic minorities. Social class was never fully eclipsed by biological categories, Weiner insists, and Soviet policies had inconsistencies and loopholes that meant people could be persecuted and then redeemed in ways unimaginable under National Socialism. Still, Jews were affected particularly strongly by both the more racialized policies of the war years and by the official ethos and postwar memory of the war as characterized by "hierarchical heroism and universal suffering." Jews were written out of public representations of the war, the myth of their refusal to fight became pervasive, and the Holocaust was subsumed as part of the epic suffering of the Soviet people. Enemies of the state and nation could be particularized, but not victims. The victims of German war crimes could victimize each other and memory proved just as selective for the victors as for the defeated.

John Dower's exploration of Japanese memories of war and war crimes challenges the prevalent view that Japan has refused to acknowledge its transgressions, critique nationalism past and present, or consider reparations to its victims. Dower details the kinds of memory that have coexisted and competed since World War II—denial, evocations of moral (or immoral) equivalence, victim consciousness, U.S.-Japanese sanitizing of responsibility for war crimes, and acknowledgments of guilt and responsibility. The conservative state, the Emperor, businessmen, and nationalist academics and writers have indeed minimized Japanese crimes, denied responsibility, and rejected reparations while vociferously condemning the atrocities of Japan's enemies. The Japanese public, by contrast, has shown a notable willingness over the decades to admit guilt and acknowledge responsibility. "It is precisely this general receptivity to such 'unpatriotic' notions," he concludes, "that has given a desperate edge to the rise of a new wave of reactive neonationalism in the last decade."

In the concluding essay, Marilyn Young, who has also written extensively on the Vietnam War, explores how Americans learned to forget the massacre of civilians at No Gun Ri when it happened in July 1950 and again when it was rediscovered by Americans in 1999. Through a careful analysis of media coverage, she shows how atrocities are redefined as "incidents," and how the government and military, when pressed by overwhelming evidence, make partial concessions but only in the service of a larger denial of intentional war crimes. It is a pattern all too common in the history of war crimes. She also reminds us of the need to view No Gun Ri in the context of a war in which, as in World War II, the majority of casualties were civilians, and civilians were often targeted as supporters of the enemy.

Even as Germany and Japan continue to come to terms with their pasts, the last century has seen a horrendous increase in the incidence and scale of war crimes, crimes against humanity, and genocide. Since the end of World War II the loci of such crimes has moved away from the heart of Europe to its fringes, from the colonial empires to decolonized states. The West has shifted from directly perpetrating or legitimizing war crimes to pointing them out as the best manifestation of its own superiority over ostensibly "primitive," "barbarous," and "uncivilized" parts of the world—while supplying the arms, political framework, and vocabulary for those crimes and reaping huge economic benefits from its collaboration with genocidal regimes.

The present volume hopes to contribute to the growing discussion—in academic, media, educational, and political circles—on the nature of modern war and its links to crimes against humanity and genocide.

CRIMES OF WAR

Chapter One

War and War Crimes

A Brief History

ARYEH NEIER

Since World War II, there have been two periods of great advance in the adoption of international rules against combatant abuse of civilians: in the immediate aftermath of the war when the world confronted the full record of Nazi atrocities and the nearly comparable crimes committed by Japanese forces in Asia, and in the 1990s, after the end of the Cold War, in response to ethnic cleansing in ex-Yugoslavia and genocide in Rwanda. The post–World War II advances included the establishment of the international criminal tribunals at Nuremberg and Tokyo; the designation of certain offenses as crimes against humanity; the adoption by the United Nations of the Genocide Convention; and the adoption by virtually all the governments of the world of the Geneva Conventions of 1949, which designated certain violations as "grave breaches," or war crimes and, for the first time, applied certain prohibitions to internal armed conflicts. The conflicts in ex-Yugoslavia and Rwanda inspired the establishment of the first international criminal tribunals since Nuremberg and Tokyo; extension of the concept of war crimes to certain offenses committed in internal conflicts; the first international prosecutions and convictions for genocide; and the adoption of a treaty for the establishment of a permanent international criminal court (likely to come into existence by 2003 after the treaty has been ratified by sixty governments).

Although rules against abuse of civilians were not as clearly delineated prior to World War II, their existence was well recognized by political and military leaders of the period. All sides during the war periodically denounced their antagonists for violations. When atrocities were committed, it was predominantly as a consequence of deliberate decisions by those who exercised command responsibility.

The rules of warfare are of ancient origin and it is possible to identify their roots in the ethical precepts of civilizations in many parts of the world. In the West, they developed in Greek and Roman times, are discussed in the writings of Christian philosophers such as St. Augustine and St. Thomas, and were refined in the chivalric codes of the late medieval era. As the legal scholar Theodor Meron has shown, several of Shakespeare's plays, particularly *Henry V*, demonstrate a sophisticated grasp of the laws of war as they evolved up to his time. In the seventeenth century, the Dutch scholar Hugo Grotius undertook the first comprehensive codification.

It took until the second half of the nineteenth century before agreements were negotiated between governments to make the rules of warfare binding through treaty law as well as in customary international law. It appears that a technological revolution helped to bring about this development. The invention of the telegraph by Samuel Morse made it possible for newspapers to deploy war correspondents to provide contemporaneous accounts of the conduct of armed forces, starting with the Crimean War of 1854–56. Previously, reports of warfare were published long after the events they described. Often, these were self-serving narratives by military commanders. Much of the emphasis was placed on their own skills and tactics and those of their opponents, and on deeds of bravery. The pain and suffering inflicted on combatants and noncombatants largely vanished from these glorifying accounts. War correspondents changed this. William Howard Russell's articles in *The Times* of London inspired Florence Nightingale and twenty-four British nurses to sail for Crimea to treat the sick and wounded. His reports and those of other correspondents also played a part in the adoption of the first Geneva Convention in 1864 by twelve European states (among them four—Baden, Hesse, Prussia and Württemberg—that subsequently became part of a unified Germany). That convention focused on care for the wounded and provided that the neutrality of ambulances, military hospitals, and their staffs be respected by belligerents.

Across the Atlantic, war correspondents also played a major role in the American Civil War. Their accounts were a factor in President Abraham Lincoln's decision in 1863 to promulgate the "Lieber Code," a detailed set of rules with 157 articles drafted by a German immigrant, Francis Lieber, who became a professor of law at Columbia University. The Lieber Code governed the conduct of Union forces during the war. It provided, among other things, that "the unarmed citizen is to be spared in person, property, and honor as much as the exigencies of war will admit" and that "All wanton violence committed against persons in the invaded country, all destruction of property not commanded by the authorized officer, all robbery, all pillage or sacking, even after taking a place by main force, all rape, wounding, maiming, or killing of such inhabitants, are prohibited under the penalty of death, or such severe punishment as may seem adequate for the gravity of the offense."

Thereafter, many agreements were negotiated among the nations of the world to regulate warfare, of which the most important before World War II were the Hague Conventions of 1899 and 1907 and the Geneva Conventions of 1929. These were based on two fundamental principles: the principle of necessity and the principle of humanity. Under the principle of necessity, that which must be done to prevail militarily may be done. Under the principle of humanity, that which causes unnecessary suffering is forbidden.

Much of the focus of the agreements adopted before World War II was on protecting prisoners of war and respecting the neutrality of medical personnel. In addition, the Hague Conventions barred the bombardment of undefended locations; required respect for the lives, liberties, religious convictions, family honor, and private property of civilians in occupied territory; and prohibited seizure, destruction, or intentional damage of religious, charitable, educational, artistic, or scientific property. The Hague Convention of 1899 on Laws and Customs of War on Land also included a provision known as the Martens Clause for the Russian jurist who proposed it. It stated:

Until a more complete code of the laws of war is issued, the High Con-
tracting Parties think it right to declare that in cases not included in the
Regulations adopted by them, populations and belligerents remain
under the protection and empire of the principles of international law, as
they result from the usages established between civilized nations, from
the laws of humanity, and the requirements of the public conscience.

When German and Japanese military and civilian leaders were
prosecuted at the end of World War II for crimes against humanity,
in essence the charge related to violation of "the laws of humanity"
referred to in the Martens Clause. That is, aside from the specific violations of the laws of war enumerated in the Hague and Geneva Conventions, the belligerents were bound by customary international law as
both countries repeatedly acknowledged, including through their ratifi-
cation of the Hague Convention.

In the First World War, German troops, along with those of the other
combatants, largely respected the laws of war. As the military historian
John Keegan has written, the First World War

imposed on the civilian populations involved almost none of the deliberate disruption and atrocity that was to be a feature of the Second. Except
in Serbia and, at the outset, in Belgium, communities were not forced to
leave their homes, land and peaceful occupations; except in Turkish Ar-
menia, no population was subjected to genocide; and, awful though the
Ottoman government's treatment of its Armenian subjects was, the
forced marches organized to do them to death belong more properly to
the history of Ottoman imperial policy than to that of the war itself.
The First, unlike the Second World War, saw no systematic displacement of populations, no deliberate starvation, no expropriation, little
massacre or atrocity. It was, despite the efforts by state propaganda
machines to prove otherwise, and the cruelties of the battlefield apart, a
curiously civilized war.[1]

That the Second World War would be different was signaled early on
as Hitler's Condor Legion and Mussolini's Aviazione General took part
in the terror bombing of Guernica in 1937 and Barcelona in 1938. Jap-

anese troops committed the Rape of Nanking in 1937 and deliberately bombed civilians in Chongqing in 1938. These were condemned at the time. Prime Minister Neville Chamberlain, who sympathized with Franco, denounced the killing of a thousand residents of Barcelona in a speech to the House of Commons in which he said,

> In the first place, it is against international law to bomb civilians as such and to make deliberate attacks upon a civilian population. That is undoubtedly a violation of international law. In the second place, targets which are aimed at from the air must be legitimate military objectives and must be capable of identification. In the third place, reasonable care must be taken in attacking those military objectives so that by carelessness a civilian population in the neighborhood is not bombed.[2]

And, on September 30, 1938, by unanimous vote, the League of Nations adopted a resolution condemning indiscriminate bombing.

Though Western leaders issued numerous statements in the early years of the war castigating the Axis powers for their bombardments of civilian communities, after a time they fell silent as American and British planes retaliated in kind, and then some. The firebombing of Berlin, Hamburg, Dresden, and Tokyo, and the atomic bombs dropped on Hiroshima and Nagasaki reflect abandonment of "the usages established between civilized nations" by the Allied side during the war.

The controversy that erupted in the United States in 1995 when the Smithsonian's National Air and Space Museum organized an exhibit displaying the "Enola Gay," the plane that dropped the atomic bomb on Hiroshima, demonstrated the sensitivity that Americans still feel when the actions of their troops during World War II are questioned. The exhibit called attention to Japanese suffering and implicitly questioned use of the bomb by providing a lower estimate than usual of the number of American military casualties had Japan been invaded. Many Americans, recalling that Japan started the war by bombing Pearl Harbor, were unwilling to accept that any conduct toward Japan was illegitimate. The exhibit had to be canceled as a result of the furor and the museum's curator was forced to resign.

The usual estimate of the number of persons killed during the First World War, a period of unspeakable carnage, is about ten million. A significant majority of the million British, the two million French, the two

million Germans and those of other countries who died in the war were
young men killed in combat. Among the other dead, most died as a
consequence of privation and disease caused by the ravages of war. In
World War II, the number killed was probably about five times as great.
Though millions of them were belligerents—and disease and hunger
took a huge toll then too—many millions were civilians intentionally
murdered because of who they were, not because of what they did, or
indiscriminately killed because of where they lived.

Unfortunately, the war set the pattern for the conflicts worldwide in
the five and a half decades since it ended. In our time, we have come to
expect that the vast majority of those who will die in armed conflicts are
noncombatants. Although our international legal prohibitions against
atrocities are more specific and more comprehensive than at any time
in the past, and although we are creating new mechanisms for their enforcement, we have barely reached the point where we can see that
these are making a difference.

As World War II was the turning point in the way war was conducted,
it is crucial to establish as clearly as possible how genocide took place
and who was responsible. The question of whether the German army
committed atrocities is especially significant as is illustrated today by a
debate that is still waiting to take place in Serbia. There, to the extent
there is any acknowledgment that Serbs committed crimes in Kosovo,
these are blamed on paramilitary forces. Accusations that the Yugoslav
army itself took part in pillage, forced deportations and murder have
resulted in a long prison sentence for a Serbian journalist, Miroslav
Filipovic, who raised the issue, and a national campaign of vilification
and harassment against a doughty Serbian human rights leader, Natasa
Kandic, who has painstakingly collected evidence. (Filipovic was freed
after President Milosevic was ousted from office in October 2000.)
The army, in Serbia as in Germany, represents the people; if they are
criminal, Serbs must face up to their own political responsibility for
criminality.

Some of those who wrote about the exhibit "The German Army and
Genocide," organized by the Hamburg Institute for Social Research,
used such words as "devastating" and "shocking" to describe it. As one
who has spent much of my career investigating atrocities, I can understand the use of such terms, but they are not what come to my mind
when I think about the exhibit. Rather, I wonder about its impact in

deepening what I believe has already been a profound acceptance of political responsibility for Nazi crimes by many Germans. Though the great majority of Germans today were not even alive when genocide was committed by other Germans, and only a small minority were old enough to take part or to have a say in political affairs, many Germans are mindful of the burden they carry because of their country's history. My hope is that the exhibit and the controversy it inspired will add to their grasp of the nature of that burden. I trust that it will also assist Americans and others to understand their political responsibility for the atrocities that have continued around the globe in the decades that have passed since the genocide of World War II.

Chapter Two

On War Crimes*

JAN PHILIPP REEMTSMA

Why are we so concerned about war crimes? Are we really? Hasn't there been and isn't there a lot of denial when war crimes become an issue in public debates? Very often we hear the famous words of General Sherman—"War is hell"—and people use this quotation to tell us that there are no laws and no rules in hell. Michael Walzer had to reject explicitly Richard Wasserstrom's words "war, in some important ways, makes psychopaths of [all soldiers]." "This is," says Walzer, "simply not true." But this is not a question of psychology—although if you're going to analyze cases of war crime in detail you have to use the vocabulary of psychology too—but of historiography and moral theory.

When someone says that the issue of war crimes is not important, they are either someone who believes that there is no right or wrong when you fight for your country, or someone who believes that war as such is a crime, and there should be no distinction between "lawful" and "unlawful" killings. If we are confronted with those kinds of atti-

* Slightly revised version of the talk given by Jan Philipp Reemtsma at the Conference on Military War Crimes: History and Memory, New York, NY, December 1999.

tudes, we should remember that they are in sharp contrast to the way all cultures we know of look at war. No matter whether a certain culture loves war, adores warriors, gets its collective values and ideals from the battlefield, or whether it is peace loving, is skeptical about the virtues of the warrior and has more respect for the pen than for the sword—both cultures will, in their own way, be proud of the fact (or the supposed fact) that there is something they would not do or allow to be done, even in war.

This is one of the most common ways cultures try to prove that they are "more civilized" than others or that some other cultures are not civilized at all. Barbarians have no rules: they do things a knight, a gentleman, a disciplined soldier—one of "us"—would never do. And if we occasionally do things of the we-never-would-do-that kind, we are forced to do so by the barbaric behavior of others. We maintain a fragile self-image. Remember the reality behind Shakespeare's *Henry V*, the Battle of Agincourt. Because of their "superior" strategy (which was not regarded as gentlemanly by the French, by the way), British troops had to guard a lot of prisoners behind the lines—but they did not have enough soldiers to do so and protect their fighting troops against an attack from the rear. So Henry gave the order to kill the prisoners. His knights refused to obey the order because it was against the rules of war. So Henry gave the order to the bowmen, who were not "of name" and felt no obligation toward the rules of knightly warfare.

What happened at Agincourt could not be denied—it was common knowledge. So Shakespeare had to give an interpretation that saved the British self-image and fitted with the image of King Henry he had designed: hence the words "use mercy to them all" about the citizens of Harfleur; and about civilians, "we would have all such offenders so cut off." It is not in the heat of battle: The order is given in cold blood with no specific justification but "necessity." Killing seems something that has to be done to survive—and conquer: "But hark! what new alarum is this same? / The French have reinforced their scattere'd men: / Then every soldier kill his prisoners: / Give the word through." This is the end of the sixth scene of the fourth act. The seventh scene starts with the discovery of a French war crime that can't be justified on the grounds of necessity. The French have attacked the train and killed unarmed and underage people: "Kill the boys and the luggage! / 'tis expressly against the law of arms." Then Henry's words: "I was not angry since I came to

France / Until this instant." And so the order to kill the prisoners is mentioned but gets lost somehow in comparison with the obvious crime (of which there is no historical evidence, as far as I know).

Shakespeare proposes the model that war crimes are discussed when they can't be denied any longer. Yes, crimes have been committed, but there was no way to avoid them, and all in all "we" have been less barbarous than "them." People who argue this way think that an unavoidable crime is not a crime anymore, and need not be discussed in terms of guilt and responsibility. But a murder even for a good cause is—to quote Michael Walzer again—murder: "They have killed unjustly, let us say, for the sake of justice itself, but justice itself requires that unjust killing be condemned." Replace the word "justice" with "civilization" and the quotation fits in my argument.

The problem is that societies confronted with their own armies' war crimes often try to get rid of the problem, first by denying the existence of the crimes (it's unjust and insulting to be accused of having committed such crimes), or, if the crimes cannot be denied any longer, by lowering the standards. In both ways people try not to give up the correspondence between reality and self-image in order to be a "civilized" society, even in war time. Denial is a way to preserve the self-image by transforming the reality; lowering standards is a way to preserve the correspondence with reality by transforming the self-image. A public debate about war crimes is always a debate about the whole society's moral standards—what we are, what we want to be, how we want to look, and how we really look.

So public debate about war crimes is often painful. It can be a debate in which a lot more is at stake than just a war and crimes committed during it. It can become a debate about different political views. The ongoing debate about the My Lai massacre is and has always been not only a debate about what happened in that one place in South Vietnam, but a debate about the Vietnam War, whether it was justified or not, about American foreign and military policy, and about the self-image the American people have, want to keep, or want to transform.

This debate is not easy and that is why it is still going on after all these years. It is hard to understand why the debate about German war crimes is still going on nearly fifty-five years after the end of World War II, creating so much public noise and so many emotions. Apart from a very small minority of right-wing extremists there is no controversy about the character of the Nazi regime. Among serious historians there is no tendency to excuse the crimes of Nazi Germany by pointing out the crimes of other nations, such as the Soviet Union. One would think that mentioning German war crimes among the other crimes committed by Nazi Germany would not cause much trouble. But it does.

To explain why it does, it would be necessary to tell a long and complicated story. Let me mention the most important chapters of this story. After 1945 there seemed to be a clearer view of the *Vernichtungskrieg* (war of extermination)—the title of the exhibition by the Hamburg Institute for Social Research on the crimes of the Wehrmacht. In 1946, Konrad Adenauer wrote:

> The German people . . . allowed themselves to be forced into line— without resisting and partly enthusiastically. This exactly constitutes its guilt. And besides, it was known . . . that the Gestapo, the SS, and in part our troops also terrorized civilians in Poland and Russia with unprecedented cruelty. . . . Therefore there is no way of claiming public ignorance of the fact that the Nazi government and military leadership constantly violated the rights of man, the Hague convention, and the simplest demands of civility and humanity. (Author's translation)[1]

After the founding of the Federal Republic and the rearmanent of West Germany, experts were needed and taken where they could be found. In the fifties, very few people wanted to take a closer look at "the German past." So something like a pact of silence was made: You keep silent about heroism, we keep silent about crimes. There was no official or semiofficial veteran's movement in Germany after World War II, although there had been one after World War I.

The second chapter to be mentioned is a legend. The Hamburg Institute was often confronted with the statement that the Wehrmacht was declared not guilty at the Nuremberg trials. It is true that neither the Wehrmacht, nor the high command, nor the general staff was defined as a criminal organization as the SS was. The Wehrmacht, like other armies, was not an organization that could be joined voluntarily, and the high command and the general staff were defined not as groups or organizations but as "an aggregation of military men, a number of individuals who happened at a given period of time to hold the high-ranking military positions." But then the judges at Nuremberg declared,

Although the Tribunal is of the opinion that the term "group" in Article 9 must mean something more than this collection of military officers, it has heard much evidence as to the participation of these officers in planning and waging aggressive war, and in committing war crimes and crimes against humanity. This evidence is, as to many of them, clear and convincing. They have been responsible in large measure for the miseries and suffering that have fallen on millions of men, women and children. They have been a disgrace to the honourable profession of arms. Without their military guidance the aggressive ambitions of Hitler and his fellow Nazis would have been academic and sterile. Although they were not a group falling within the words of the Charter they were certainly a ruthless military caste [. . .] Many of these men have made a mockery of the soldier's oath of obedience to military orders. When it suits their defence they say they had to obey; when confronted with Hitler's brutal crimes, which are shown to have been within their general knowledge, they say they disobeyed. The truth is they actively participated in all these crimes, or sat silent and acquiescent, witnessing the commission of crimes on a scale larger and more shocking than the world has ever had the misfortune to know [. . .] Where the facts warrant it, these men should be brought to trial so that those among them who are guilty of these crimes should not escape punishment.[2]

There have been some trials, but they didn't play a role in the collective consciousness about the crimes of the Wehrmacht.

The third chapter of this story is about the way the Holocaust became part of collective consciousness in Germany. In this regard, too, the fifties were a decade of silence. But after the Eichmann trial in Jerusalem the policy of silence was no longer tenable. The Auschwitz trials in Frankfurt followed. After this, the mass murder of the European Jews was more or less identified as what happened in the extermination camps. What happened outside the barbed wire, what was done not by SS guards but by SS army units, by the so-called *Einsatzgruppen*, by policemen, alone or in cooperation with the Wehrmacht, by ordinary soldiers of the Wehrmacht, and by auxiliary troops under the command of the Wehrmacht—this was no longer present in the collective consciousness. Academic research on those topics—and on the mass murder of Soviet POWs, and the systematic killings of non-Jewish civilians—fell outside the bounds of the common knowledge of Nazi crimes.

Historiography about National Socialism first concentrated on the regime, its major figures, and the bureaucracy. Later, different parts of the population became the subject of historiographical research: the doctors, the lawyers, the role of the industry, the banks and so on. The relationship between the regime and the *Volksgemeinschaft* (national community) became a topic of academic research and public debate only in the nineties. For example, the question of what happened to the furniture of deported Jews was not posed (or answered) until 1993. There were three public events that made the relationship between regime and *Volksgemeinschaft* the issue of a broad and highly emotional debate: the publication of Daniel Goldhagen's *Hitler's Willing Executioners*, the publication of the diaries of Victor Klemperer, and the exhibition about the crimes of the Wehrmacht by the Hamburg Institute for Social Research.

The Hamburg Institute wanted to bring the exhibit to New York. We did not. I have to explain why. From the beginning there was controversy about the exhibition. Although the title "war of extermination" stood for the war the Wehrmacht conducted in the East, and although the exhibition had only three parts (Serbia, Belorussia, and the path of the Sixth Army before Stalingrad), the exhibition was reproached for making general statements about the Wehrmacht, and saying that every German soldier had been a war criminal. Other critics said that the exhibition intended to create wild emotions by showing pictures of cruelty, emotions that would not allow for the necessary academic discussions. And from the beginning a lot of critics said that the definition of crime used by the exhibition was far too broad. They insisted that only a small percentage of the photographs showed real Wehrmacht crimes. I will come back to that point later.

The exhibition was on display for four and a half years and was seen by about 900,000 people. In 1997 the German parliament had a debate about it. During this time something like a public appropriation (or usurpation) of the exhibition took place. The title *Vernichtungskrieg, Verbrechen der Wehrmacht 1941 bis 1944* (War of Extermination: Crimes of the Wehrmacht 1941 to 1944) was replaced by *Die Wehrmachtsausstellung* (The Wehrmacht Exhibit). Even though a lot of people said during its first incarnation that the exhibition could only fail because visitors had to read too much and the photographs were too small, the exhibition was later called an exhibition of photography. There was a debate about the "real intentions" of the Institute. Some people called the exhibition the last battle of the Generation of '68 and said that the hidden agenda was to discredit the Bundeswehr (army of the Federal Republic). Others said that, on the contrary, the hidden agenda was to get rid of the German past and make the Bundeswehr fit to fight in the Balkans again.

Some documents, expecially some photographs, were especially contentious. For example, there was a photograph of a group of naked Jews. This photograph was interpreted by the Institute—as by others before—as a photograph of Jews facing their execution. A German magazine discovered that the source of this photograph was a Nazi propaganda brochure about the war in the East, and that the original caption was "Jews taking a bath." Further investigation revealed that there was indeed no other source for the photograph, so nobody could really prove that the picture showed an execution—although the context of anti-Semitic hatred was obvious. We had to take the picture out of the exhibition.

Then two historians from Eastern Europe announced that some of the pictures, which show dead bodies and German soldiers, do not show victims of German crimes.

In the first months of the war between Germany and the Soviet Union, the Soviet secret service killed political enemies in order to prevent their forming an alliance with German troops. Those victims were exhumed and photographed as proof of the cruelty of the Soviet system (which was regarded as Jewish). The response was a massacre of the Jews living in those cities—a massacre executed by the local population and not only tolerated but encouraged by the local command of the Wehrmacht units. It is still not clear how many German soldiers took part in this pogrom.

The news that there were photographs showing victims of the Soviet secret service revived memories of the Cold War fifties. People suddenly saw the Institute as working in the tradition of the Soviets, as in their efforts to pass off the massacres of Polish officers at Katyn as German crimes. The curators were called liars and falsifiers. Everyone who had ever criticized the exhibition was triumphant. Supporters stated that the thesis of the exhibition was not affected by mistakes . . . but, they said, and they were not wrong, every mistake could be seen by the public as a falsification of the story the exhibit wanted to tell.

It became impossible to discuss the questions in an appropriate manner. There was one week in which literally every newspaper in Germany had an article about the exhibition—every day. Statements about the photographs of victims of the Soviet secret service were mixed with the statement that only 10 percent of the photographs had anything to do with war crimes at all. It was no longer possible to distinguish between mistakes that had to be admitted and corrected, different interpretations of what happened in a given place, and different concepts of what should be called a war crime.

The exhibit mentioned many crimes in which the Wehrmacht was involved—but Wehrmacht soldiers did not do the actual killing. Sometimes Wehrmacht units blocked off the area and SS units, policemen, or *Einsatzgruppen* executed the massacre, or the Wehrmacht gave further support. Sometimes the murders were executed by auxiliaries of the Wehrmacht under its command. To ask "Who did the killing?" is only one part of the war-crime question. You also have to ask who was responsible and what kind of responsibility was shared by whom.

But all this couldn't be discussed anymore. If someone saw a certain sort of helmet in the catalogue, worn by Finnish auxiliaries, even though the photo had long been removed from the exhibition, there was a headline somewhere alleging that the exhibition wanted to pass off Finnish crimes as German ones. Attempts to discuss the questions were dismissed as attempts to change the subject. The exhibition and the Institute lost credibility. So we had to suffer the consequences and close the exhibition, declare a moratorium, and say that every document in the exhibition would be checked and the results presented to a group of external experts. Then we would reopen a redesigned exhibition, to give some new answers to old critics. This was and is the only way to regain credibility and control the damage to the exhibit's thesis about the extent of Wehrmacht crimes toward the Jewish population in Eastern Europe and the Soviet POWs, and about the terror and hunger used as weapons to decimate the non-Jewish population.

To close the exhibition in Germany and to open it in the United States at the same time was not possible. The attacks would have gone on and the critics would have said that we were not serious in our intention to check the accuracy of the materials of the exhibition and make the outcome public if we persisted in publishing doubtful documents. If we said that only a small part of the documents on display were in doubt, they would say that we intended to prejudice the outcome of the review.

This is why we have to write about an exhibition you can't see, an exhibition you will see again in Germany—and perhaps in New York. What we can do now is talk about what it means for a society to talk about war crimes—what it means in general, and what it means in Germany.

Chapter Three

The Wehrmacht, German Society, and the Knowledge of the Mass Extermination of the Jews

SAUL FRIEDLÄNDER

By early August 1941, some six weeks after the German attack on the USSR, the murder of the Jews in Soviet territory had expanded from the killing of men to that of entire communities. In the small town of Bjelaja Zerkow, south of Kiev, occupied by the 295th Infantry Division of Army Group South, the Wehrmacht area commander, Colonel Riedl, ordered the registration of all Jewish inhabitants and asked the SS *Sonderkommando* 4a, a subunit of *Einsatzgruppe* C, to murder them.

On August 8, a section of the *Sonderkommando*, led by SS *Obersturmführer* August Häfner, arrived in the town.[1] Between August 8 and August 19, a company of *Waffen* SS attached to the *Kommando* shot all of the 800 to 900 local Jews, with the exception of a group of children under the age of five. What followed has often been described;[2] when closely examined, however, it may lead to some new insights.

First, I shall dwell upon the events of Bjelaja Zerkow and, as a corollary, recall the widespread presence of members of the Wehrmacht at the sites of the massacres, as well as the participation of many of them in the mass killing of the Jews in occupied Soviet territory. This will lead to a reassessment of the German people's knowledge and attitudes about these exterminations. Finally, the description of the horror, the agony of the children of Bjelaja Zerkow, confronts the historian with a peculiar challenge that transcends the concrete issues dealt with in the presentation; it will be evoked in the summation.

BJELAJA ZERKOW, AUGUST 19–22, 1941, AND THE PARTICIPATION OF THE WEHRMACHT IN THE EXTERMINATION OF THE JEWS

As mentioned, one group of Jewish children was not immediately killed. They were abandoned without food or water in a building at the outskirts of the town near the Wehrmacht barracks. On August 19, many of these children were taken away in three crowded trucks and shot at a nearby rifle range; ninety remained in the building guarded by a few Ukrainians.[3]

Soon, the screams of these remaining children became so unbearable that the soldiers called in two field chaplains, a Protestant and a Catholic, to take some "remedial action."[4] The chaplains found the children half naked, covered with flies, and lying in their own excrement. Some of the older ones were eating mortar off the walls; the infants were mostly comatose. The divisional chaplains were alerted and, after an inspection, they reported the matter to the first staff officer of the division, Lieutenant Colonel Helmuth Groscurth.

Groscurth went to inspect the building. There he met *Oberscharführer* Jäger, the commander of the Waffen SS unit who had murdered all the other Jews of the town; Jäger informed him that the remaining children were to be "eliminated." Colonel Riedl, the *Feldkommandant*, confirmed the information and added that the matter was in the hands of the SD (*Sicherheitsdienst*) and that the *Einsatzkommando* had received its orders from the highest authorities.

At this point, Groscurth took it upon himself to order the postponement of the killings by one day, notwithstanding Häfner's threat to lodge a complaint. Groscurth even positioned armed soldiers around a truck already filled with children and prevented it from leaving. All of this he communicated to the staff officer of Army Group South. The matter was referred to the Sixth Army, probably because *Einsatzkommando* 4a operated in its area. On that same evening, the commander of the Sixth Army, Field Marshal Walter von Reichenau, personally decided that "the operation . . . had to be completed in a suitable way."[5]

The next morning, August 21, Groscurth was summoned to a meeting at local headquarters with Colonel Riedl, Captain Luley, a counter-intelligence officer who had reported to von Reichenau on the course of the events, *Obersturmführer* Häfner, and the chief of *Einsatzkommando* 4a, the former architect SS *Standartenführer* Paul Blobel. Luley declared that, although he was a Protestant, he thought that the "chaplains should limit themselves to the welfare of the soldiers"; with the full support of the *Feldkommandant*, Luley accused the chaplains of "stirring up trouble."

According to Groscurth's report, Riedl then "attempted to draw the discussion into the ideological domain. . . . The elimination of the Jewish women and children," he explained, "was a matter of urgent necessity, whatever the form it took." Riedl complained that the division's initiative had delayed the execution by twenty-four hours. At that point, as Groscurth later described it, Blobel, who had been silent up until then, intervened: he supported Riedl's complaint and added "that it would be best if those troops who were nosing around carried out the executions themselves and the commanders who were stopping the measures took command of these troops. . . . I quietly rejected this view," Groscurth wrote, "without taking any position as I wished to avoid any personal acrimony." Finally, Groscurth mentioned Reichenau's attitude: "When we discussed what further measures should be taken, the *Standartenführer* declared that the Commander-in-Chief [Reichenau] recognized the necessity of eliminating the children and wished to be informed once this had been carried out."[6]

On August 22, the children were executed. On the following day, Captain Luley reported the completion of the task to Sixth Army headquarters and was recommended for a promotion.[7]

In terms of criminal behavior, the dividing line did not run between the SS and the army but, as the Bjelaja Zerkow case shows, within the Wehrmacht itself. In this particular instance, alongside the SS, the police battalions and the Ukrainian auxiliaries, there were many soldiers and officers, including Field Marshal von Reichenau, Colonel Riedl, Captain Luley, and their kind; other soldiers and officers like Groscurth were shocked by what they witnessed. All in all, however, it was not the second group that characterized the behavior of the Wehrmacht. As we shall see, even Groscurth's position is troubling.

The first Germans with any authority to be confronted with the fate of the ninety Jewish children were the four chaplains. The field chaplains were compassionate, the divisional ones somewhat less so. In any case, after sending in their reports, the chaplains were not heard from again.

The killing of the Jewish adults and children was public. In a postwar court testimony, a cadet officer who had been stationed in Bjelaja Zerkow at the time of the events, after describing in gruesome detail the execution of a batch of approximately 150 to 160 Jewish adults, made the following comments: "The soldiers knew about these executions and I remember one of my men saying that he had been permitted to take part. . . . All the soldiers who were in Bjelaja Zerkow knew what was happening. Every evening, the entire time I was there, rifle fire could be heard, although there was no enemy in the vicinity."[8]

Similar things occurred all along the Eastern Front. Regular Wehrmacht soldiers were often ordered to assist the *Einsatzkommandos* in their task or they volunteered to do so. The eager participation of regular troops in the extermination campaign, for example, during the advance of the Sixth Army into formerly Soviet-occupied areas of Poland — particularly in Lvov and Tarnopol — and then into Soviet territory, is well established.[9] In some areas, divisional commanders took it upon themselves, without any prodding, to fill the role of the Sonderkommandos or of the police battalions when these units were not immediately available. Thus in the *Generalkommissariat* of Belorussia, the commander of Infantry Division 707 decided in the early days of October 1941 to act on his own. The division murdered rapidly and efficiently; its men shot 19,000 Jews, mainly in villages and small towns. In larger towns, the task was divided between Reserve Police Battalion 11 reinforced by Lithuanian auxiliaries and SD units from Minsk.[10]

Military commanders did not bother to explain the killings of women and children to their troops. Nor did Field Marshal von Reichenau in his notorious Order of the Day of October 10, 1941: "The soldier must have complete understanding for the necessity of the harsh but just atonement of Jewish subhumanity."[11] Hitler praised the Order of the Day and demanded its distribution to all front-line units in the East.[12] Within a few weeks, Reichenau's proclamation was imitated by the commander of the Eleventh Army, von Manstein, and the commander of the Seventeenth Army, Hoth.[13]

The number of Jews who fell victim to the participation of the Wehrmacht in murder operations is hard to evaluate and an estimate of the number of soldiers and officers who took part in the massacres is impossible. It is no less difficult to evaluate the reactions of Wehrmacht members who witnessed the killings but we know, from the most diverse sources, that vast numbers of soldiers and officers did attend and often photographed full-scale massacres. "Why these Jews were beaten to death," a lance corporal of the 562nd Baker's Company testified about the massacres in Kovno, "I did not find out. . . . The bystanders were almost exclusively German soldiers who were observing the cruel incidents out of curiosity . . ."[14]

A selection of soldiers' letters shows how widely Nazi anti-Semitic stereotypes and ideological statements about the Jews had been internalized.[15] Many of these soldiers were probably young enough to have been educated under the new regime and to have spent some time in the Hitler Youth, whose anti-Jewish brutality had been openly demonstrated during the prewar years.[16] The anti-Jewish violence of the Wehrmacht rank and file was already manifest during the Polish campaign, but it has often been overlooked by historians due to the well-known protests of General Johannes von Blaskowitz and some other high-ranking officers against SS atrocities.[17]

The traditional military elites were less rabidly anti-Semitic than the Nazi von Reichenau, but their attitude regarding the Jews was nonetheless hostile. After a conversation with General von Roques, the commander of Army Group North, Field Marshal Wilhelm von Leeb noted: "On July 8, 1941, Roques complained about the wholesale shooting of the Jews in Kovno (thousands) by local Lithuanian auxiliary police at the instigation of the German police. We have no control over these measures. All that remains is to keep one's distance. Roques correctly pointed out that the Jewish Question could hardly be solved in this manner. It would most reliably be solved by sterilizing all Jewish males."[18] In his study of the Axis and the Holocaust, Jonathan Steinberg, after quoting the violently anti-Semitic remarks of a German counterintelligence officer in Lybia added: "In many years of intensive research in German army archives, I have found fewer than five examples of German officers expressing anything other then the opinions quoted above."[19]

Some of the soldiers and officers were repelled by what they had witnessed in Bjelaja Zerkow. The cadet officer who has already been quoted also declared in his postwar testimony: "It was not curiosity which drove me to watch this, but disbelief that something of this type could happen. My comrades were also horrified by the executions."[20] Such comments were not infrequent. Thus, on December 9, 1941, Rudolf-Christoph von Gersdorff, the intelligence officer at Army Group Center headquarters, noted in his diary that the facts regarding the murder of the Jews were known to their full extent; they were discussed everywhere and considered by the officers as violating the honor of the German army.[21]

Let us now turn to the central personality in the Bjelaja Zerkow events: Lieutenant Colonel Helmuth Groscurth. A deeply religious Protestant, a conservative nationalist, he did not entirely reject some of the tenets of Nazism and yet became hostile to the regime and close to the opposition groups gathered around Admiral Wilhelm Canaris and General Ludwig Beck. He despised the SS and in his diary referred to Heydrich as a "criminal."[22] His decision to postpone the execution of the children in Bjelaja Zerkow by one day, notwithstanding Häfner's threat, and then to use soldiers to prevent an already loaded truck from leaving, is proof of courage.

Moreover, Groscurth did not hesitate to express his criticism of the killings in the conclusion of his report: "Measures," he wrote, "against women and children were undertaken which in no way differed from atrocities carried out by the enemy about which the troops are continually being informed. It is unavoidable that these events will be reported back home where they will be compared to the Lemberg atrocities." [This is probably an allusion to executions perpetrated by the NKVD.][23] For these comments, Groscurth was reprimanded by Reichenau a few days later. Yet his overall attitude is open to many questions.

After mentioning Reichenau's order to execute the children, Groscurth added, " 'We then settled the details of how the executions were to be carried out. They are to take place during the evening of August 22. I did not involve myself in the details of the discussion."[24] The most troubling part of the report appears at the very end: "The execution could have been carried out without any sensation if the *Feldkommandantur* and the *Ortskommandantur* had taken the necessary steps to keep the troops away. . . . Following the execution of all the Jews in the town it became necessary to eliminate the Jewish children, particularly the infants. Both infants and children should have been eliminated immediately in order to avoid this inhuman agony."[25]

Groscurth was captured by the Russians at Stalingrad, together with the remaining soldiers and officers of the Sixth Army. He died in Soviet captivity shortly afterward, in April 1943.

SPREADING KNOWLEDGE AND ITS IMPLICATIONS

Groscurth's attitude, examined according to the standards of the time, falls into an in-between category that was supposedly shared by the bulk of the German population in the Third Reich: "*Resistenz*." The term, coined as a historical concept in the 1970s, literally means immunity in a biological sense. It was used to define the attitude shared by a vast majority of Germans who, for various reasons, went along with Nazi policies and initiatives, but who, nonetheless, were at least partly immune to the ideology of the regime and even slightly defiant in some cases.[26]

Indeed, *Resistenz* found expression, as we know, in small everyday occurrences but also in more fundamental domains, as in the attitude of part of the Church to confessional schooling or the keeping of crucifixes in classrooms in Bavaria. An even more significant form of *Resistenz* was manifested in the growing anger of parts of the population about the murder of the mentally ill, leading to Bishop von Galen's public protest, which compelled Hitler to abandon the major euthanasia action in August 1941. Was any form of *Resistenz* also expressed in regard to attitudes about other, more extensive, criminal activities, such as the extermination of the Jews?

The answer to this last question has usually been that only during the final three years of its existence did Nazi Germany live in the shadow of "Auschwitz," and even then very few Germans were aware of the full scale of its horror; therefore, the majority remained blatantly passive.

Indeed, knowledge of "Auschwitz" was limited until late in the war, but information about the mass atrocities and wholesale extermination of Jews spread to the Reich soon after the beginning of the campaign against the Soviet Union.

Already in July 1941, for example, Swiss diplomatic and consular representatives in the Reich and in satellite countries were filing detailed reports about the mass murders perpetrated on the Eastern Front; their information all stemmed from German or satellite sources.[27] Senior and even mid-level officials in various German ministries had access to the reports of the *Einsatzgruppen* and to their computations of the huge numbers of Jews they had murdered. Such information was mentioned in Foreign Ministry correspondence in October 1941 and not even ranked "top secret."[28]

Among the German population, even in small towns in the westernmost part of the Reich, rumors about the massacre of Jews in the East were rife before the end of 1941. Thus, on December 6, 1941, the SD reported comments voiced by the inhabitants of Minden, near Bielefeld, about the fate of the Jews from their own town, deported to the East a few days beforehand. "Until Warsaw," people were saying, "the deportation takes place in passenger trains. From there on, in cattle cars. . . . In Russia, the Jews were to be put to work in former Soviet factories, while older Jews, or those who were ill, were to be shot . . ."[29]

The information was first and foremost disseminated by soldiers on leave in the Reich, through letters and snapshots sent home as mementoes from the Eastern Front. It was also transmitted through many other channels. Margarete Sommer, in charge of relief work at the Berlin Archdiocese, was informed in early 1942 by Lithuanian Catholics and also, it seems, by no less an official of the Ministry of the Interior than Hans Globke, of the mass killings in the Baltic countries of Jews deported from the Reich.[30] After meeting with Sommer, Bishop Wilhelm Berning of Osnabrück noted on February 4, 1942, "For months no news has arrived from Litzmannstadt. All postcards are returned. . . . Transports from Berlin arrive in Kovno, but it is doubtful whether anybody is still alive. No exact news from Minsk and Riga. Many have been shot. The intention is to exterminate the Jews entirely (*Es besteht wohl der Plan die Juden ganz auszurotten*)."[31] *Schutzpolizei* Captain Salitter, who accompanied the December 11, 1941, transport of 1,007 Jews from Düsseldorf to Riga, was told that the Latvians wondered why the Germans "bothered to transport the Jews to Latvia and didn't annihilate them right there."[32] As for the mass extermination of Jews in Bukovina and Transnistria, it was openly discussed in Bucharest society.[33] As Groscurth had warned in his memorandum, "It is unavoidable that these events will be reported back home."

In summary, there was indeed Resistenz in many domains, but—and this is the crucial point—in the face of the awareness of Nazi crimes, it found expression mainly in various degrees of protest in regard to measures taken *against Germans*, as in the case of the euthanasia.

Personal expressions of sympathy towards individual Jews, such as the greeting of Jews wearing the yellow star, were not uncommon. Victor Klemperer also writes about recurring words of encouragement from his foremen or passersby as he and a few other elderly Jews shoveled snow in the streets of Dresden in February 1942.[34] Even the warning of Jews by individuals involved in the killing system is known.[35]

Such initiatives sometimes demanded courage. But the only popular protest regarding the fate of the Jews was initiated in the spring of 1943 by the "Aryan" wives of a group of Jewish men about to be deported from Berlin. The Jewish husbands were released. As for the proposal made in August 1943 by Archbishop Konrad von Preysing of Berlin to protest the extermination publicly, it was turned down by his fellow bishops on the instigation of the head of the German episcopate, Cardinal Adolf Bertram of Breslau; it was also ignored by Pope Pius XII.[36]

Preysing himself ultimately chose to remain silent and it was the lonely voice of the prior of St. Hedwig's Cathedral in Berlin, Berhard Lichtenberg, that expressed the outrage of a segment of Christian society, in a sermon. Betrayed by two women parishioners, Lichtenberg paid for the protest with his life.[37] The discrepancy in attitudes regarding the victimization of Germans and that of "others" is even more striking when one turns to the actual oppositional groups. This is not the place to dwell on this issue but explicit anti-Semitism among leading members of the conservative civilian and military opposition to Hitler is well established.[38]

Until recently, the *prevalent* historiographical interpretation of German attitudes toward the extermination of the Jews was based mainly on an argument well summed up by the Israeli historian David Bankier:

> The lack of committed opposition to the persecution of the Jews largely explains why so many deliberately sought refuge from the consciousness of genocide and tried to remain as ignorant as possible: because it salved their conscience. Knowledge generated guilt since it entailed responsibility, and many believed that they could preserve their dignity by avoiding the horrible truth. This deliberate escape into privacy and ignorance did not save the public from being aware of the Third Reich's criminality. Knowledge of the mass shootings and the gassing filtered through to it, increasing the concern about the consequences of the Nazis' criminal deeds. [39]

What Bankier states, in other words, is not that the Germans could not have known about the extermination, but that they did not want to know. The same argument has been presented by the German historian Hans Mommsen, albeit in slightly different terms. Mommsen suggests that knowledge of the "Final Solution," easily accessible to those willing to face it, was repressed at all levels of German society in order to avoid an untenable dissonance between faithfulness to the regime and the knowledge of its massive criminality. [40]

As is perhaps already clear, I am trying to argue that such psychosocial constructs are hardly convincing or necessary. The information about the massacres was abundant precisely because of the massive involvement or presence of hundreds of thousands of members of the Wehrmacht at the killing sites. And, as we have seen, the fate of the deported Jews was openly discussed by the population. The reactions to the information that reached the Reich during the summer and fall of 1941 seem to have ranged from explicit compassion for the Jews to fear of expressing comments, to various forms of rationalization or even outright support of anti-Jewish crimes and, most commonly, to indifference. I stress explicit compassion, even if it was limited, because the reactions of the population taken as a whole did include all nuances. Some examples of such compassion have already been mentioned; furthermore, in Minden, after commenting on the deportation of the town's Jews, some of the inhabitants quoted in the SD report did express their disapproval, declaring that Jews too were "God's children." [41] Yet it is indifference to the fate of the Jews—by its very nature such indifference was not recorded by the diarists—that prevailed.

Consider the second clandestine leaflet distributed in early July 1942 by the "White Rose" resistance group, in which the murder of some 300,000 Jews in Poland was mentioned. The Munich students immediately added a disclaimer: Some people could argue that the Jews "deserved their fate," but then what about the murder of "the entire Polish aristocratic youth?"[42] In other words, these militant enemies of the regime were well aware that the mass killing of Jews would not impress all readers of the leaflet and that crimes committed against Polish Catholics had to be added, particularly in Bavaria. We cannot generalize on the basis of this example; we can only suggest that for many Germans the mass extermination of Jews was not of deep concern.

Knowledge about huge massacres is different from that of total annihilation but is the difference between the two as radical as many historians suggest it is? Is knowledge of "Auschwitz" really the decisive question? In terms of the protest against or the acceptance of mass criminality, we cannot, it seems to me, establish an insuperable divide between awareness of the murder of hundreds of thousands of victims, among them one's own neighbors, and that of the total extermination of an entire people. It should be added at this point that knowledge about the extermination centers was probably more precise than was thought until recently. Sybille Steinbacher has now shown that every summer hundreds of women visited their husbands who were camp guards in Auschwitz, and stayed for long periods of time. Moreover, among the Reich German population of Auschwitz there were complaints about the odor produced by the overloaded crematoria.[43]

In any case, the widespread indifference of the German population does not demand any unusual interpretation. The basic divergence in attitudes toward the members of the community and "others" suffices. Moreover, the constant spewing of anti-Jewish propaganda and the permanence of various forms of milder traditional anti-Semitism added, undoubtedly, to the scant interest in the fate of the Jews and to the absence of any significant countervailing forces.

A peculiar dimension has to be added. Furniture, rugs, clothes, household items, and even houses that belonged to deported Jews became available to deserving *Volksgenossen* (national comrades). Furthermore, personal belongings could be bought at dirt-cheap prices at the *Judenmärkte* (Jew markets) of major cities, or were distributed by the *Winterhilfe* (winter aid), often without the original tags having been removed. Material benefits reinforced the advantages of silence in the face of mass murder.[44] Whether under these circumstances one can speak of the normality of everyday life under National Socialism is a moot question. Differently put, the everyday involvement of the population with the regime was far deeper than has long been assumed, due to the widespread knowledge and the passive acceptance of the crimes, as well as the crassest profit derived from them. A massive repression of knowledge, if it existed at all, took place after 1945, and probably much less so beforehand.

SUMMATION

This presentation raises a basic question of narration (and also of interpretation) that often challenges the historian of the Holocaust. Does the historian have to choose the killing of children as an example for a murder campaign that could be described in less horrendous terms? Does writing about the extermination of the Jews of Europe have to include a narration of the horror as such? Finally, do these descriptions impinge upon the historian's ability to remain objective in regard to the Nazi era in its more general terms?

The choice of the Bjelaja Zerkow case was not haphazard. The children's execution illustrates in several ways the nature of the Nazi murder system and the Wehrmacht's function within it. The children were not killed on the spot: The issue was passed on from one level of authority to the next, from the field chaplains at the very bottom of the hierarchy to the commander-in-chief of the Sixth Army at the very top. Then, Reichenau's decision was transmitted through regular army channels of command. In other words, we are facing a major characteristic of the regime: utter inhumanity within a perfectly functioning military administrative structure. Moreover, as we saw in Riedl's comments, the killing of the children was considered an ideological necessity.

The precise recording of the horror is necessary if we are to grasp some of the peculiar characteristics, motivations, and attitudes of various groups of perpetrators. All the killings were mass murder, but not all mass murders were the same. The killings perpetrated by the Latvians, the Lithuanians, the Romanians, the Ukrainians, the Poles, or the Croats were identical to those perpetrated by the Germans in terms of collective criminality. Yet each of these groups left an imprint of its own: The anthropology of mass murder may lead the historian to traits and trends that will have to be taken into account in understanding the deeper strata of this extraordinary collapse of Christian and Western civilization. Such an anthropology must often rely on minute details, and, at times, on the description of the most horrifying behavior. Thus, apart from any other considerations, recording the horror is an outright historical imperative. How this should be carried, however, can only be left to the historian's sensitivity and judgment, in each specific case.

The question remains whether stressing the criminality of the Nazi regime and dwelling upon its horrors, and particularly the Holocaust, hinder the historian's ability to remain detached and objective. In the early 1980s it was strongly argued—by Martin Broszat among others—that the emphasis put by historiography upon the political and criminal dimension of the Third Reich offered a false or incomplete picture of its overall social dynamics and everyday reality.

It seems possible, a priori, to consider the full criminal dimension of the Third Reich and, at the same time, to perceive, describe and analyze the domains of social activity that escaped the impact of Nazi ideology and criminality. For the historian, the main challenge is to find the "right balance" between the two, both in terms of interpretation and narration. There is no way of avoiding this challenge and no formula for resolving it. But deleting a precise rendition of the horror may lead to a skewing of the overall picture and also to a distortion of the history of a society that was more tainted by the criminal dimension of National Socialism than has been assumed for a long time.

The final sequence of the events at Bjelaja Zerkow was described by Häfner at his trial.

> I went out to the woods alone. The Wehrmacht had already dug a grave. The children were brought along in a tractor. The Ukrainians were standing around trembling. The children were taken down from the tractor. They were lined up along the top of the grave and shot so that they fell into it. The Ukrainians did not aim at any particular part of the body. . . .

The wailing was indescribable . . . I particularly remember a small fair-haired girl who took me by the hand. She too was shot later. . . . [45]

Häfner, let us remember, was in charge of the killing.

In this fleeting last scene, in this total absence of any trace of humanness, it is possible that, beyond all theories, we may intuitively grasp, as minute symbol and terrifying reality, the peculiar evil of National Socialism and the quintessential core of the events that we call the Holocaust, the extermination of the Jews of Europe.

Chapter Four

The Wehrmacht in Serbia Revisited

CHRISTOPHER R. BROWNING

I would like to make clear at the onset that my focus on the Wehrmacht in Serbia is not meant to eclipse or obscure the fact that the vast majority of deaths in wartime Yugoslavia were inflicted in the course of civil wars within and conflicts between indigenous ethnic groups. German policy contributed greatly to the unleashing of these conflicts, but the Wehrmacht was not the direct instrument of these deaths. However, another look[1] at the role of the German military in occupied Serbia during the Second World War is useful in view of some of the criticisms that have been made of the recent exhibit on the crimes of the Wehrmacht. In addition to the issue of mistaken attribution of photos, criticism has been aimed at the lack of a wider context or historical background, the insufficient distinction between "war crimes" on the one hand and anti-partisan actions and executions permitted under international law on the other, and the commingling of Wehrmacht and SS crimes. Serbia is an important case study because of the predominant position held by the Wehrmacht vis-à-vis a relatively minor and subordinate SS presence in 1941. Moreover, as Serbia was a minor theater not at the center of Hitler's "war of destruction" and quest for *Lebensraum*, military commanders there had greater latitude to act according to their own inclinations, attitudes, and values. Both the dovetailing of military and Nazi attitudes and the autonomous behavior of the Wehrmacht can be seen with considerable clarity in Serbia.

Military occupation is scarcely an environment conducive to moderation under any circumstances. A Nazi political culture exulting in unfettered power, violence, and racial superiority could only aggravate the situation in which German troops found themselves in conquered Europe. Everywhere the troops were exhorted to be "tough" and to act like true *Herrenmenschen*. Among Slavic populations, deemed low in the racial hierarchy by Nazi ideology, the devaluation of the local population and the corresponding predilection for violence and atrocity were even greater.

In Serbia, however, the negative stereotypical image of the native population held by many Germans, particularly within the military, predated and anticipated National Socialism. For many German occupiers, Serbia was not part of the European community of nations. In their view European civilization ended at the old borders of the Austro-Hungarian empire, and the uncivilized Orient began in Serbia. There German occupiers could behave in the same uninhibited way that nineteenth-century European imperialists had behaved in their African and Asian colonies.

Several anecdotes illustrate this continuity of attitude. In one of his infamous marginalia, Kaiser Wilhelm II had proclaimed in 1914 that Serbia is "not a nation in the European sense, but a band of robbers." [2] In 1941 Field Marshal Wilhelm List became German occupation commander in the Balkans. He was a highly cultured man, a lover of classical music, especially Mozart, and a deeply religious non-Nazi from Bavaria. When asked at his postwar trial in Nürnberg if the Serbs were different from other people, he replied that they were "far more passionate, hot blooded, and more cruel." His explanation invoked an indiscriminate mixture of racial and historical factors. "The individual in Serbia is obviously like every other peasant under normal conditions, but as soon as differences arise, then, due to the hot blood in his veins, the cruelty caused by hundreds of years of Turkish domination erupts." [3]

To the notions of Serbs as "hot blooded" and "cruel," and more "Turkish" than European, were added several other stereotypical images. First, the Serbs were alleged to be "treacherous" by nature. In 1914 their complicity in the Sarajevo assassination had set Europe aflame. In March 1941, they had again betrayed Germany by rejecting an offered alliance, thereby delaying the invasion of the Soviet Union and thwarting early victory. Many Germans, therefore, blamed Serbia for not just one but now two generations of misfortune. A second stereotypical characteristic that many Germans attributed to Serbs—as part of a wider so-called "Balkan mentality"—was the alleged devaluation of human life. As Harald Turner, head of the military administration, wrote: "With the people of the Balkans, the life of others means nothing, one's own life only very little."[4] This notion that life was cheap in Serbia would be invoked frequently by the Germans to rationalize the magnitude of their reprisal policies.

The proclivity among the German occupiers toward racial stereotyping proved quite contagious. From the beginning of the occupation, the widely held negative stereotype of the Serbs was quickly mixed with other racial stereotypes. Of course, the Jews were assumed to be communists and would hence bear the murderous brunt of the Germans' anti-partisan policies even before the "Final Solution." "Gypsies" in turn were equated with Jews in the basic racial legislation decreed by the military commander.[5] When the partisans were characterized as "outlaw bands," the "Gypsies" faced double jeopardy, for they were also seen as criminally inclined nomadic bands. When the partisan resistance in Serbia reached its peak in 1941 and was perceived as a national uprising involving the entire population, then all Serbs faced the same fate as communists, Jews, and "Gypsies." One stereotype merged into another, creating a widening circle of victims.

The only mitigating factor to slow this potential spiral of violence was that the German occupiers were not agreed upon Serbia's ultimate role in the Nazi "New Order." For many Germans the Serbs were Balkan *Untermenschen* whose anti-German behavior from Sarajevo to the Belgrade putsch proved them so unreliable that only a vengeful policy of total subjugation and even population decimation held out the prospect of eventual pacification. For some Germans, however, at least selected Serbs, if properly cultivated and offered the prospect of a future role in the Nazi "New Order," had the potential to become useful junior partners and collaborators in the German war effort. The priority given to the Eastern Front and the chronic German manpower shortage in Serbia made necessary a pragmatic though limited experimentation with this latter approach even by those Germans who had advocated and implemented horrific policies of mass killing.

In analyzing the evolution of Wehrmacht policies in Serbia, it is important not to treat the Wehrmacht as a monolith but rather to dissect the layers of command and influence. Within Serbia itself, a military commander (*Militärbefehlshaber in Serbien*) was the highest authority. This position was held in succession by two Luftwaffe generals—first Ludwig von Schroeder, then Heinrich Danckelmann. Under him were both the army troop commander, General Paul Bader, of the 65th Corps, and the administrative staff (*Verwaltungsstab*) under State Councillor and SS *Gruppenführer* Harald Turner, the son of a professional soldier whose own aspirations for a military career had ended with severe wounds in the First World War. Turner supervised the activities of the provisional Serbian government, the four *Feldkommandanturen* (district commandants), the Sipo-SD *Einsatzgruppe*, and Reserve Police Battalion 64 from Cologne. The *Militärbefehlshaber* received his orders from *Wehrmachtbefehlshaber im Südosten* (Armed Services Commander Southeast), Field Marshal Wilhelm List, in Greece, and from the OKW (Supreme Command of the Wehrmacht) of Wilhelm Keitel. In addition to Danckelmann, Bader, Turner, List, and Keitel, a sixth Wehrmacht player was added in September 1941 with the appointment of army general Franz Böhme as *Bevollmächtigten Kommandierenden General in Serbien* (Plenipotentiary Commanding General in Serbia). Wehrmacht policy in Serbia would be produced at times by a consensus, at other times as a result of conflict, among these men.

There was initial consensus not to use army troops to combat the communist uprising in Serbia that followed the invasion of the Soviet Union, for the three divisions of Bader's 65th Corps were the dregs of the German army—understrength, overaged, poorly equipped, and still in training. Instead the uprising was to be countered with police measures (both German and Serbian) and terror—which meant above all reprisal shootings of "communists and Jews." The identity of the two was assumed from the beginning, and the number of reprisal victims reached 111 in one month.[6]

By order of General von Schroeder, the pool of "communist and Jewish" hostages vulnerable to reprisal shooting was swelled by the inclusion of any of the local population near the site of partisan attacks who were deemed "co-responsible" by virtue of passively resisting German investigation or offering fertile soil to anti-German activity.[7] The potential of this policy for indiscriminate slaughter was first realized on

July 28, 1941, when Serbian police were forced at gunpoint to shoot eighty-one harvest workers rounded up near the site of an ambushed German motorcycle.[8]

Neither police measures nor reprisal terror stemmed the rising tide of the insurgency, but the Germans could not agree on subsequent countermeasures. The OKW exhorted more drastic terror, especially hanging (rather than shooting). List not only urged greater terror but also wanted the army troops to take a more active role. Germans in Belgrade preferred to rely on strengthening the Serbian police.[9] All three policies in fact failed. By August the collaborating Serbian police force was demoralized and disintegrating.[10] The organization of army pursuit commandos to combat the insurgents militarily was ineffective, for the troops were too few and too immobile.[11] And reprisals, which increased nearly tenfold in August, also proved to be ineffective. As one German report noted, "Even with the most unrestrained reprisal measures—up until the end of August a total of approximately 1,000 communists and Jews had been shot or publicly hanged and the houses of the guilty burned down—it was not possible to restrain the growth of the armed revolt."[12]

In a desperate attempt to stem the growth of the partisans and prevent the nationalist Chetnik movement from joining the communist insurgency, the Germans in Belgrade tried to install a credible Serbian puppet regime under General Nedic. This move was ridiculed by List and his staff in Greece and produced no immediate results. On the contrary, the German position continued to deteriorate. In all of August the German army in Serbia had suffered 30 dead, 23 wounded, and 1 missing. Suddenly in the first three days of September, 175 German soldiers were captured in two villages. In short, the poor-quality German troops in Serbia had lost control of the countryside and were now threatened with piecemeal defeat and capture. In this crisis-ridden atmosphere of looming defeat and professional embarrassment, List dispatched newly arrived frontline troops to carry out a punitive expedition into the partisan-controlled Sava Bend region around Sabac. The guiding principle of the expedition was simple: "The entire population had to be punished, not only the men." All men were to be interned, all resisters were to be shot, and all women and children were to be driven off the land and into the mountains. Once cut off from their food supplies, the insurgents (to say nothing of the general population) would face a "food catastrophe." List also appointed the Austrian general Franz Böhme *Bevollmächtigten Kommandierenden General in Serbien* to bypass the despised Luftwaffe General Danckelmann. Böhme exhorted his troops: "Your mission lies . . . in the country in which German blood flowed in 1914 through the treachery of the Serbs, women and children. You are the avengers of these dead. An intimidating example must be created for the whole of Serbia, which must hit the whole population most severely."[13]

The decisions and orders of List and Böhme represented a major change in Wehrmacht policy. Not only was the policy of terror to be significantly expanded to indiscriminately target the entire civilian population, but implementation was now placed directly in the hands of Wehrmacht troops instead of the German and Serbian police. Between September 23 and October 2, 1941, troops of the newly arrived 342nd Division cut a swath of destruction through the Sabac region, executing 1,127 suspected communists and interning over 20,000 men. They relented from driving off the women and children only at the last moment when it became clear that no one would be left to care for the cattle and harvest, which the Germans intended to requisition.[14] The division then undertook a further punitive sweep through the Cer mountains and reported another 1,081 executions beyond enemies killed in combat.[15]

Rather than deter resistance, the punitive expeditions merely provoked counter-atrocities. The Germans knew that guerrilla units held more than 300 German prisoners, and military intelligence assiduously tracked their whereabouts. On October 2, however, insurgents ambushed a communications unit near Topola and killed 21 German soldiers, including 14 after surrender.[16] Though this was a small fraction of what the Germans had just done in Sabac, and although the other 300 German prisoners remained alive, Böhme escalated his reprisal policy yet again. The head of the OKW, Wilhelm Keitel, had recently ordered that for every German soldier killed by insurgents in occupied territory, 50 to 100 "communists" were to be executed in retaliation. He justified this order on the grounds that "a human life in these countries often counts for nothing and a deterrent effect can be achieved only through unusual harshness."[17] Böhme's response to Keitel's order was neither minimal nor reluctant. In an order drafted by his quartermaster, Captain Hans Georg Faulmüller, and initialed by his chief of staff, Colonel

Max Pemsel (both of whom subsequently enjoyed successful careers in the Federal Republic), Böhme immediately authorized the maximum ratio of 100:1 rather than the minimum 50:1. Moreover, entirely on his own initiative, he expanded the order to cover Jews as well as "communists," and explicitly targeted for execution 2,100 men, "predominantly communists and Jews" interned in camps in Belgrade and Sabac. In fact these camps held only Jews and "Gypsies" long-interned and hence totally uninvolved in the insurgency.[18] At Sabac the executions were particularly absurd and grotesque, in that predominantly Austrian troops gunned down central European refugees mostly from Vienna in retaliation for Serbian guerrilla attacks on the German army.

The 100:1 reprisal ratio was then established as the standard operating procedure for all subsequent casualties. As Böhme explained in a document, again drafted by Faulmüller and initialed by Pemsel, "In Serbia it is necessary because of the 'Balkan mentality.' . . . to carry out the orders of the OKW in the sharpest form." An adequate hostage pool was to be created by arresting all "communists," all "suspects," and *all Jews* as well as selected democrats and nationalists.[19] To Major General Hoffmann of the 717th Division, this order for a 100:1 reprisal quota was a veritable hunting license. Between October 15 and 21, his division shot 1,736 men and 19 women in Kraljevo and 2,300 males in Kragujevac.[20] One result was that Lieutenant General Doctor Hinghofer of the frontline 342nd Division was deemed "too slack" (*"nicht so straff"*) and demoted to command the inferior 717th, while the "butcher" of Krajelvo and Kragujevac, Major General Hoffmann, replaced him in command of the coveted 342nd.[21]

What advanced Hoffmann's career did not improve the Wehrmacht position in Serbia. In fact, List and Böhme now reaped what was sown by their constant incitements to "ruthless" terror. The two massacres at Kraljevo and Kragujevac had immediate repercussions, especially as the Kragujevac victims included students of the local high school and the workers of an airplane factory producing for the German war effort. The OKW was dismayed at the destruction of the armaments workers, and the increasingly helpful and needed collaborator Nedic pleaded for an end to arbitrary shootings. Böhme agreed.[22]

The Germans now sought to fashion a somewhat less indiscriminate reprisal policy. List had already ordered that Serbs caught in battle were to be executed immediately, while men merely encountered in the area of operations were to be interned and investigated. Those proven to be partisans were to be executed; those suspected were to be held as hostages for reprisal shootings; and those not suspected were to be released.[23] In short, List was willing to concede the existence of "innocent" Serbs who—unlike insurgents and "suspects"—were not to be shot.

Böhme's staff picked up on this notion. "Arbitrary arrests and shootings of Serbs are driving to the insurgents circles of the population which up to now did not participate in the insurrection. . . . It must be avoided that precisely those elements of the population are seized and shot as hostages who, being nonparticipants in the insurrection, did not flee before the German punitive expedition." Reprisal victims were henceforth to come from specific categories: those found in the vicinity of guerrilla attacks or villages considered focal points of the insurgency, those deemed suspects as the result of police investigation, and "as a matter of principle" *all adult male Jews and "Gypsies."* [24]

If the Wehrmacht in Serbia could conceive that not all Serbs were communists and that the random shooting of innocent Serbs would damage German interests, they displayed no doubt that all Jews and "Gypsies" were anti-German and deserving of death. Indeed, the military administration had already singled out Jews and "Gypsies" for legal discrimination in the spring of 1941, followed by mass internment. And reprisal shootings had been carried out collectively against "communists and Jews" since June. Once the partisan resistance drove the Germans to inflict upon themselves the obligation to fulfill the maximum reprisal quota, all interned Serbs were at great risk but the interned male Jews and "Gypsies" were doomed. Indeed, if more care had to be exercised in selecting Serbian reprisal victims, and actual communist partisans remained elusive, then the pressure to find hostages elsewhere—particularly among the interned Jews and "Gypsies" already conveniently at hand—was that much greater. Moreover, past experience demonstrated that their elimination involved no political cost, for in contrast to Kraljevo and Kragujevac, no one had protested the shootings of Jews and "Gypsies" in Sabac and Belgrade.

With totally random reprisal shootings now excluded, the supply of adult male Jews and "Gypsies" was quickly exhausted. Wehrmacht reprisal policy had in fact guaranteed their elimination, after which the horrendous 100:1 quota simply could not be met. A December 1941 statistical study of the reprisal program concluded that at least 11,164 reprisal shootings had been carried out, 68 percent by army firing squads and 32 percent by police units. But this figure was admittedly too low, for the compilers of the report had not received data from all units. The real number was approximately 15,000, of which 4,500 to 5,000 had been Jews and "Gypsies." Calculating German casualties and adjusting for insurgents reported killed in battle, the report concluded that there was still a staggering quota shortfall of 20,174 reprisal shootings to be fulfilled.[25]

By December 1941 the military situation in Serbia had in fact changed significantly. With the reinforcement of two frontline divisions, the German army had managed to chase the bulk of the partisan forces out of Serbia and into Bosnia, Croatia, and Montenegro. In Serbia itself, fighting by large-scale units came to an end until 1944. Henceforth, reprisal policy was generally in response to small-scale resistance, and a modified reprisal policy was adopted. The reprisal quota was lowered from 100:1 to 50:1 for each German soldier killed, and a more complex classification system was introduced. Nonetheless, one feature remained the same. Among those automatically "earmarked to atone for German lives because of their attitude and behavior" were not only communists but also "Gypsies" and Jews.[26] Thus if the Wehrmacht in Serbia did not fulfill its reprisal quota, it was because insufficient numbers of communists could be found, the political cost of randomly killing Serbs was too high, and the supply of Jews and "Gypsies" was exhausted. There is very little reason to believe the quota would not have been met, if only enough Jews and "Gypsies" had been available.

In light of the criticisms of the Wehrmacht exhibit, let us be very careful and precise about making distinctions. In two ways the attitudes and policies of the Nazi regime and the Wehrmacht in Serbia differed significantly. First, the Nazi "Final Solution" aimed at the extermination of all Jews within the German grasp, down to the last man, woman, and child. In contrast, the Wehrmacht in Serbia considered itself too chivalrous to execute women and children and thus killed only the adult male Jews and "Gypsies." Second, for the Nazi regime there were too many Jews and "Gypsies" in Serbia. For the Wehrmacht, once Jews and "Gypsies" had become the preferred targets of the 100:1 reprisal quotas, there were too few. If the policies of the Wehrmacht in Serbia did not yet constitute the "Final Solution," the massive and indiscriminate killing of Serbian noncombatants constituted a war crime of major proportions, and the killing of the adult male Jews and "Gypsies" simply because of their ethnic identity was quite simply genocide.

Chapter Five

The Wehrmacht Exhibition Controversy

The Politics of Evidence

OMER BARTOV

Between 1995 and 1999, the exhibition "War of Extermination: Crimes of the Wehrmacht 1941 to 1944" traveled to thirty-four cities in Germany and Austria and was seen by an estimated 850,000 visitors. Renamed "The German Army and Genocide," a slightly modified version of the exhibition was scheduled to open in New York City on December 2, 1999. Yet a few days before the official opening, the exhibition was closed down as the result of a massive public and media campaign that cast doubt over the accuracy or veracity of the photographic and documentary evidence the exhibition presented.[1] Shortly thereafter, the director of the Institute for Social Research in Hamburg, which had originally organized the exhibition, appointed an independent commission of experts to evaluate the historical validity of the photographs, captions, and documents shown at the exhibition in light of the charges. The commission submitted its report in November 2000, precisely one year after the exhibition was closed. While noting that a few photographs were indeed mislabeled, and that some of the explanatory texts that accompanied the historical evidence occasionally made sweeping and therefore not entirely accurate statements, the commission rejected all charges of falsification and manipulation. Moreover, the commission stated in no uncertain terms that

> the basic assertions of the exhibition regarding the Wehrmacht and the war of extermination conducted in the "East" remain in this respect correct. It is incontrovertible that in the Soviet Union the Wehrmacht not only became "entangled" in the genocide perpetrated on the Jews, in the crimes against Soviet prisoners of war and in the war against the civilian population, but that it participated in these crimes partly in a leading and partly in a supporting capacity. Hence this was not a matter of isolated "infringements" or "excesses," but of actions emanating from decisions made by the highest military authorities and by the troop commanders at the front and behind the front.[2]

The debate that led to the closing of the exhibition in 1999 was unleashed by several young scholars whose most powerful argument was that some of the photographs shown in the exhibition and its catalogue did not depict victims of the Wehrmacht but rather the bodies of men and women executed by the NKVD (the Soviet secret police). The critics also asserted that many of the photographs were irrelevant to an exhibition on crimes of the Wehrmacht since they depicted members of other German agencies or even of other armies allied with the Third Reich.[3] This sustained critique in turn allowed those who had always tried to defend the lost honor of the Wehrmacht not only to discredit the exhibition as such, but also to challenge the scholarly consensus about the deep complicity of the German army in Nazi crimes.[4] The commission of experts, for its part, noted that "out of the 1,433 photographs of the exhibition fewer than 20 photographs do not belong in the exhibition. Among them," it added, "are to be found also those photos which depict victims of the NKVD, as well as those in which one can see non-German soldiers (Hungarians, Finns)." Conversely, the commission insisted that

> Photographs, which depict Waffen-SS units, Einsatzgruppen of the Security Police and the SD, indigenous militias, Order Police, etc., do belong to an exhibition on "crimes of the Wehrmacht," as long as one can establish in concrete cases that such units were attached to or collaborated with Wehrmacht formations.[5]

Now that the dust is beginning to settle over the debate, it is time to take a more balanced and detached view of the issues it raised. In what follows, I will first attempt to explain what compels significant sectors of the German public, media, academe, and political establishment repeatedly to cast doubt on the overwhelming historical evidence regarding the criminal role of the Wehrmacht in the Third Reich. Second, I hope to show that much of the debate over the Wehrmacht exhibition revolved around the assertion or repression of conflicting national and ideological narratives on crime and victimhood in World War II. Finally, considering the remarkable public success and eventual debacle of the Wehrmacht exhibition, I will offer a few comments on the relationship between textual and photographic records as historical evidence.

I. THE OLD STORY

A German historian contradicts the common thesis that the Wehrmacht had nothing to do with the murderous policies of the *Einsatzgruppen* in Russia. The army was deeply involved. . . . [This historian and his collaborator] offer new documentation on "the shocking extent of the army's integration in Hitler's extermination program and extermination policies" . . . In a book about the history of the *Einsatzgruppen* they correct the by now much-loved notion of the "purity" of the Wehrmacht.

This passage was not written in the wake of the controversy over the Wehrmacht exhibition. Rather, it appeared in the popular German weekly *Der Spiegel* in 1981, in a review of the important study by Helmut Krausnick and Hans-Heinrich Wilhelm, *Die Truppe des Weltanschauungskrieges* (Soldiers of the Ideological War).[6] That same year, the prominent historian Andreas Hillgruber argued in an article published in the *Frankfurter Allgemeine Zeitung* that German memories of the war in the East tend to linger on the desperate battles of the latter part of the war, the massive expulsions of millions of Germans, the horrendous violence perpetrated by Red Army troops, and the ultimate separation of East Germany. The early phase of the war, asserted Hillgruber, in which the Wehrmacht stormed deep into Soviet territory, is remembered much less vividly. Moreover, what is especially repressed is the memory of

the systematic murder operation that took place behind the army's advancing units in the occupied territories of the Soviet Union, whose
goal—motivated by the racial doctrine of National Socialism—was to
uproot "Jewish Bolshevism" and its biological basis in order to win a
new "*Lebensraum*," making this "campaign" into "the most terrible war
of conquest, enslavement, and extermination" (E. Nolte) of the modern era.[7]

Not only were these articles published almost two decades before the
recent debate over the crimes of the Wehrmacht, they also preceded the
Historikerstreit, the German historians' controversy, by a few years. By
the mid 1980s, Andreas Hillgruber had been transformed into a vigorous *proponent* of the German memory of the war's last months, which
he characterized as a desperate struggle by the Wehrmacht and local
Nazi officials to delay and limit the extent of the "orgy of revenge" perpetrated by the Red Army on the innocent German population of the
Eastern Provinces. Similarly, Ernst Nolte, whom Hillgruber had cited
approvingly for emphasizing the unique barbarism of the war in the
East, distinguished himself during the *Historikerstreit* by insisting that
Auschwitz was a mere copy of the Soviet Gulag and that its only claim
to uniqueness was the introduction of gas as a means to mass murder.[8]
The *Historikerstreit* thus revealed a pattern that has continued to characterize public historical discourse in Germany until the present. On
the one hand, since the 1960s tremendous progress has been made in
uncovering the darker aspects of the Wehrmacht's history; on the other
hand, this accumulation of historical knowledge has been accompanied by strong negative reactions, both public and scholarly, against the
obvious implications of such findings. For the involvement of the Third
Reich's largest and most representative institution in mass crimes and
genocide implies a much greater complicity of Germans in Nazi policies than one is often willing to concede.[9] For this reason, for the past
several decades the crimes of the Wehrmacht have been repeatedly
"discovered" and "rediscovered" in ever greater and more horrifying detail, and each time such revelations have appeared to tell the German
public something it had not known before, and to arouse a great deal of
opposition, anger, and astonishment.

The strength and pervasiveness of the defense mechanisms that are
put to work whenever the complicity of the Wehrmacht in mass crimes

is invoked in Germany are by any account quite remarkable. The most obvious reason for this reaction is the difficulty in reconciling the fact that the Wehrmacht was both Hitler's army and the army of the people; that it represented all layers of German society during the Third Reich and a vast proportion of its male population (between 17 and 19 million soldiers served in the Wehrmacht) and that at the same time it was Hitler's main tool of conquest and destruction. For without the willing, indeed, often enthusiastic cooperation of the army, none of the Führer's plans would have come to fruition. From this perspective, it is clear why German conservatives pleaded that the Wehrmacht's name not be besmirched: its veterans went on to build up both postwar Germanys.[10] That the men of the Wehrmacht managed to create a democratic society after the war is indeed a remarkable and praiseworthy accomplishment. But this should in no way obscure the fact that the same men had spent the best—and worst—years of their lives in a criminal organization. For the Wehrmacht *as an organization* was involved in a variety of ways in the perpetration of war crimes and crimes against humanity, especially, but not exclusively, during its war in the Soviet Union and Yugoslavia. This is not to say that *every individual German soldier* committed crimes, but that the Wehrmacht *as an agency of the German state* was involved in the implementation of criminal policies. In this sense, we can say that the Wehrmacht was a criminal organization, rather than an organization of criminals. It is, however, also true that numerous individual soldiers were involved in committing crimes willingly and in many cases on their own initiative. The extent of such willing and/or voluntary participation is probably impossible to establish, as is the extent of resistance or of unwilling or coerced participation.[11] But all attempts to "save" the honor of the Wehrmacht must be seen as directed at erasing the heavily documented fact of mass German complicity in government-organized criminality.

The triumphal chord that was heard among conservative circles in Germany during the assault on the integrity of the exhibition and following the decision to close it in November 1999 was thus hardly surprising. In a certain sense, the debate over the Wehrmacht exhibition was the revenge of the *Historikerstreit*, itself a belated manifestation of a struggle that began with the fall of the Third Reich over the complicity of the Germans in the Nazi regime's crimes, the singularity of those crimes, and, by extension, the impact of Nazism on postwar German society and its prospective role in Europe. During the *Historikerstreit*, the "revisionists" argued that the Third Reich had essentially tried to protect Europe from the "Bolshevik hordes" and that, while Adolf Hitler may have been no better than Joseph Stalin, he did have the considerable merit of pursuing German national interests. Thus, for instance, Hillgruber bemoaned the fact that with the destruction of Nazi Germany Europe had come under the control of the two "flanking" superpowers, the Soviet Union and the United States. The disappearance of the Third Reich, he wrote, created a "hole" in the heart of Europe that relegated the entire continent to a secondary role in international politics.[12] Moreover, if such "revisionists" as Nolte claimed in the mid 1980s that the origins of Nazi extermination policies should be sought in Communist Russia, some of the Wehrmacht exhibition's critics claimed that the German army's murderous actions were not only comparable, but in a sense were engendered by previous Soviet crimes.[13] The main difference is that in the latter debate the conservatives won, at least temporarily; the exhibition was closed and, despite the commission's verdict that the fundamental assertions of the exhibition were accurate, it will never reopen.

The conservative victory in the debate is all the more significant in that most of the influential critics, who have challenged the very involvement of the Wehrmacht in genocide, no longer belong to the old generation (as was still the case during the *Historikerstreit*). They are, much like the rest of the political, intellectual, and academic elite in post-reunification Germany, men and women born after the war. Horst Möller, director of the highly respected *Institut für Zeitgeschichte*, and Rolf-Dieter Müller, of the similarly distinguished *Militärgeschichtliches Forschungsamt*, are good examples of the new conservative elite (whose Social Democratic generational equivalents in the political arena are Chancellor Gerhard Schröder and Foreign Minister Joschka Fischer) that has taken the arguments of the 1950s and given them new flair.

The larger context of the debate is possibly even more significant. Ten years ago some observers expressed concern that Germany's reunification would let loose its old strident nationalism in the most powerful country in Europe. This has not happened, and Germany remains a responsible member of the European and international community. But while some historical events (such as Germany's reunification) can happen with extraordinary speed, their deeper repercussions may be grasped only over a greater period of time. Thus it is possible that the recent debate over the Wehrmacht is not only the tail end of half a century of repression, revelation, and controversy, but also that it reflects the emergence of a new national sentiment in Germany, whose impact goes well beyond the conservative right and reaches the center and the left in German politics, academe, and the intelligentsia. This is not to deny that some German historians came out in defense of the exhibition. But with a few important exceptions, such expressions were rather halfhearted.[14] This obviously had to do with the fact that the exhibition was organized by an independent research institute—a highly uncommon phenomenon in Germany—and that its organizers were not members of the professional historical guild. It also reflected both the problems that characterized the exhibition and the occasionally unwise and tactless manner with which its organizers responded to criticism. Nevertheless, while fifteen years ago many distinguished members of the academic and intellectual community mobilized to stop what they rightly perceived as a revisionist trend, they and their successors manifested far less eagerness to do so this time. One feels compelled to suggest that both in academe and in the political arena, the rebels of the 1968 generation have not only become respectable members of society, but in the process they have also acquired a sense of patriotism that cannot be divorced either from their often justly gained status or from the extraordinary transformation in the German state. In other words, the last decade has seen both the reemergence of the German nation-state and the coming to power of the postwar generation. It is this context that explains a degree of anti-American sentiment (with roots both in left- and right-wing German traditions), a certain antipathy toward perceived foreign interference in German domestic affairs and the manner in which Germany deals with its past (even if this past involved the fate of innumerable foreigners), and some impatience with a self-imposed yet often resented preoccupation with the implications of past evils for present self-perceptions and visions of the future.

This type of nationalism and parochialism is of course part of the "normalization" of German history, society, and culture. Unfortunately, it also enforces a degree of conformism, especially in academic discourse, and forces some of the brighter and more original minds either to toe the line or to transplant themselves into more open-minded and liberal scholarly environments. Conversely, to a certain extent it may be precisely the kind of outside interference bemoaned by some Germans that will help prevent in the future, as it had done often enough in the past, blind spots and repression, the resurgence of nationalist rhetoric and xenophobia, the erosion of civil courage, and the diversion of attention from the heart of the matter. For, as even such harsh critics of the exhibition as Bogdan Musial and Krisztián Ungváry (who are themselves outsiders) seem to have belatedly grasped, the focus of criticism of the exhibition was quickly transformed into an attempt to undermine the assertion that Germany had conducted a criminal war.[15]

In fact, the debate over the Wehrmacht exhibition pitted two perspectives on the war against each other: the first insisted on the honor and sacrifice of the German soldier, the second stressed the criminality of the soldiers and the fate of their victims. Interestingly, despite the rivers of ink spilled during the controversy, some of the raw figures most pertinent to the discussion were hardly mentioned. Of the 4 million German dead in World War II, the vast majority were soldiers, along with some 500,000 civilian victims of bombing and shelling. Conversely, the Germans killed between 20 and 27 million Soviet citizens, 3 million non-Jewish Poles, 6 million Jews, and hundreds of thousands of Sinti and Roma ("Gypsies") (along with many more civilians of other nationalities and ethnicities)—almost all of whom were civilians.[16] We can understand why the exhibition aroused such passion. When we look at the photographs of the exhibition we must keep in mind that each figure, each mutilated and decomposing corpse, was once a human being with parents, a spouse, children. Some were killed by the NKVD; most were killed by the Wehrmacht, the SS, the SD, or their local collaborators. Their history became part of German history because they were murdered by or under orders of Germans. This is what the exhibition was about.

II. THE OTHER STORY

The extraordinary photographic evidence presented at the Wehrmacht exhibition attracted a large audience and a great deal of media interest, an unprecedented phenomenon in terms of German public confrontations with the past. Yet the historical perspective employed by the organizers followed a highly conventional thematic, focusing strictly on the German side of the event. In this respect, the exhibition was closely related to the bulk of German scholarship on the Third Reich. This rapidly growing literature is concerned with the vantage point of German perpetrators. In large part, this has to do with the fact that the documentation used for these studies comes mostly from German archives, and was originally generated by contemporary German agencies. Hence, however critically this material may be viewed by scholars, it is nevertheless predicated on a German perspective. Even when foreign documentation is used, as is sometimes the case in more recent German scholarship, it usually serves the purpose of providing greater depth to the German narrative.[17]

This kind of one-dimensional single perspective on history is, of course, inherently problematic. Its limitations are especially obvious in situations with conflicting views and interpretations of events. During the Wehrmacht's war in the Soviet Union, moreover, things were further complicated by the changing circumstances, difficulty in identifying perpetrators, and assertions of victimhood which, in themselves, motivated violence and destruction and distorted contemporary perceptions and subsequent views of the past. Consider the complex history of Eastern Galicia, for example, populated for centuries by a number of antagonistic ethnic groups and occupied in quick succession by the Red Army, the Wehrmacht, and once more by the Soviets. Indeed, this region has produced a variety of distorted, biased narratives; it is only by juxtaposing them that one can hope to glimpse objective reality.[18] No wonder that the debate over the exhibition was started not by a German historian but by two East European scholars, a Pole and a Hungarian, whose perception of the events differs significantly from that of either German or Jewish scholars, let alone Jewish victims.

The Communist narrative of World War II left no room for the crimes of the NKVD and the Red Army; it also refused to acknowledge the specific fate of the Jews under Nazi occupation.[19] And yet, the crimes of the Communists remained deeply embedded in the memory of many East European nations, and their official repression was associated with the loss of national sovereignty and the imposition of Soviet-controlled Communist rule. Hence the rapidity with which this memory resurfaced after the fall of Communism. It is with this context in mind that one should examine Bogdan Musial's criticism of the exhibition, whose subtext was manifested with greater clarity in a book he published less than a year later.[20] For the main thrust of Musial's work is a reassertion of Polish and Ukrainian victimhood during the Soviet occupation between 1939–1941. While he has no interest in white-washing the Wehrmacht, Musial nevertheless feels that an excessive emphasis on German crimes against the Jews has obscured the crimes of the Communists against his own compatriots. Recent scholarship has in fact demonstrated the extraordinary extent of collaboration with the Nazi perpetrators by the occupied Slav populations.[21] Such studies hardly increase one's sympathy for these nations' own suffering under the Nazis, let alone for their prior victimization by the Soviets.[22] It is because he wanted to resurrect an episode of Polish and Ukrainian vic-timhood under the Soviets, and to provide some explanation, if not apology, for their subsequent collaboration in the Nazi genocide of the Jews, that Musial chose to go back to the two-year occupation of Eastern Galicia by the Russians. By implying that the Jews of Eastern Galicia suffered less than the rest of the population, indeed, to some extent ben-efited from and collaborated with the Soviet occupation, Musial has resurrected the old Nazi assertion that the anti-Semitic furor of the local Gentiles and the similarly brutal conduct of the occupying German forces originated in Soviet criminality (with alleged Jewish support and assistance). This is a highly skewed narration of events. Most of the Jew-ish population actually suffered just as much, if not more, under Soviet rule, not least because the Jews were better represented in the middle classes, which the Soviets were out to suppress.[23] Indeed, many of those deported or murdered by the NKVD were Jews. Musial's version, how-ever, is highly useful not only for Polish apologists, but also for German revisionists who return to the contemporaneous Nazi argument that Jews and Bolsheviks were synonymous, and that therefore the Jews had to be eradicated.[24]

The use of Jewish sources in German reconstructions of the Holo-caust is especially sparse, haphazard, and limited, underanalyzed and serving primarily to test assertions about perpetrators' narratives. This is lamentable partly because simplistic uses of Jewish sources can distort their meaning. For instance, Bogdan Musial's critique of the exhibition rightly points out that a photograph presumably taken by a Wehrmacht soldier in the Galician town of Borysław depicts events in early July 1941 rather than in May 1942, as stated in the exhibition catalogue; he also correctly indicates that this photo includes victims of an NKVD mass shooting of political prisoners, ordered by Stalin to prevent them from falling into the hands of the rapidly advancing German forces (although it is difficult to tell whether these are the only victims shown). It should be noted, however, that Musial is relying on a series of photographs exhibited by the Polish Central Commission for the Investigation of Crimes Against the Polish People in Warsaw (AGK), which was replaced in January 1999 by the Institute for National Commemoration (Institut Pamięci Narodowej). Labels given to such photographs by a Polish institute, either under the Communist regime or after the fall of Communism, made it possible to blame the NKVD for crimes against the Polish people (although most of the victims were Ukrainian nationalists), and are obviously not entirely reliable. Furthermore, Musial refers to a memoir by Irene and Carl Horowitz, *Of Human Agony*, that "documents" the executions in Borysław carried out by the NKVD. Musial even claims to have spoken with Irene Horowitz and received her confirmation of his assertion. All that Musial has to say on this event is that "Following the entry of the Germans [into Borysław] the bodies [of the estimated 100 people executed by the NKVD] were exhumed and laid out for purposes of identification in the large courtyard in front of the NKVD building. This scene is described, inter al., by Irene Horowitz, an eyewitness, in her memoirs. Her father was forced at the time to bury the corpses."[25] However, anyone who actually reads the memoir will see that it documents a German-organized pogrom by local Ukrainians and Poles against the Jews, immediately following the exhumation of the NKVD victims by the Jewish population ordered by the military and SS authorities in the town. It was at that point that hundreds of Jews were murdered in the most heinous manner over the bodies they had been forced to exhume. Irene Horowitz writes:

> The Germans were always clean-shaven and well groomed, while the Russians' appearance was primitive and untidy. However, aside from their secret police, the Russians were warm-hearted, friendly and cheerful. On the other hand, the Germans were as cold as ice. Their gaze communicated hatred of Jews. . . . The Germans, in collaboration with the Ukrainian population, organized a pogrom immediately. When they went through the prisons and found the bodies of victims of the Russian secret police, they held innocent Jews responsible; this infuriated the

gentile population. Terror fell on our city. German actions against the Jews were unleashed with full force, abetted by local gentiles, mostly Ukrainian, whose bestiality and thirst for Jewish blood were reminiscent of the pogroms of Chmielnicki and his Cossacks centuries earlier. . . . [26]

The same holds for Musial's critique of the photographs from Złoczów, another town in Eastern Galicia. Musial must be credited both with identifying the locality and with pointing out that some of the photographs clearly depict exhumed victims of NKVD executions.[27] Yet Musial mentions only in passing that "the Jewish victims, who previously had to carry out the exhumation, were murdered by Ukrainian extremists and units of the *Einsatzgruppe* C in the mass graves that had meanwhile been emptied within the Citadel [of Złoczów] and subsequently were buried there."[28] As Bernd Boll has shown in excruciating detail using German evidence, the Jews were indeed forced to exhume the bodies of some 600–700 Ukrainian, Polish, and Jewish victims of the NKVD, and were then shot into the same mass grave. He adds, however, that at least 3,000 Jews were butchered at the same time by the local population, the SS, and the army on the streets of Złoczów (see also chapter by Boll in this volume).[29] That the local eyewitnesses interviewed by Musial seem to have "forgotten" the massacre of the Jews is hardly surprising in view of the role played by the population in the pogrom that took place there half a century ago. Musial is more concerned with Polish and Ukrainian victims of the Soviet regime than with the Jewish victims of the Nazis and their local collaborators, indicating the national biases built into this type of scholarship. But this has little effect on the contemporary record as it is reflected in the German documents of the time. The war diary of the 295th Infantry Division contains the following entry for July 3, 1941: "Unpleasant circumstances prevail in Złoczów. Mass murders of Jews and Russians by Ukrainians. Jews are being shot directly on the street. In the citadel lie some 900 corpses of Ukrainians murdered by Russians and of Russians and Jews murdered by Ukrainians."[30] Since July 1, 1941, the city was occupied by German troops, many of whom were taking photographs of these events. And yet, according to Musial, these days one can visit a small exhibition in Złoczów (now renamed Solotshiv) entitled "NKVD Mass Murder in the Citadel of Złoczów, Summer 1941." Apparently, the mass murder of the Jews, the majority of whom were women, children, and old men (unlike the political prisoners killed by the NKVD, who were all adults), has no place in local memory.[31]

Just as German military documentation can reveal aspects of the genocide of the Jews that local sources may be reluctant to concede, so can Jewish sources serve for more than condemnation. Here oral testimony sometimes helps to upset the stereotypes that have allowed each group to enclose itself in its own shelter of memories. One instance of this "gray zone," as Primo Levi called it, was related to me by Ilona Karmel, a survivor of many camps and the author of two novels based on her experience.[32] Some time in the winter of 1942–43 (she remembers hearing news about the battle of Stalingrad) she and other female inmates of a labor camp linked to the infamous Płaszów concentration camp near Kraków, Poland, were sent on a long march to the showers, with only wooden clogs on their bare feet. Although exhausted, they were glad to have this rare opportunity to wash. But as they stood naked under the showers, they realized that a group of Wehrmacht soldiers was sitting on a bench facing them. Initially terrified, they soon realized that the soldiers were looking down, perhaps out of embarrassment. As the women walked out of the showers, one of the soldiers motioned them to come closer. They froze in fear. But one of the young women ventured forward. As she reached the soldier, he took out a first-aid kit and dressed her bloody feet. And so they did with all the other women. This too happened; and although the same soldiers may have had plenty of Jewish blood on their hands, for one sacred moment in that war of genocide and destruction, they reached deep into their own humanity and helped to heal the wounded bodies and souls of a few doomed young women.

III. THE STORY RECORDED

Local SS and army commanders, Wehrmacht propaganda companies at the front, and Nazi propaganda agencies in the rear all made ample use of photographs depicting German heroism, Slav "subhumans," and "Judeo-Bolshevik" criminals. Pictures of NKVD victims were thus immediately put to use in order to incite and justify mass murder of the Jews. These early massacres at the very beginning of the invasion of the Soviet Union evolved into what we now call the Holocaust. There was a direct link between NKVD executions, German-incited pogroms, SS and army massacres, mass murder by the Einsatzgruppen, and finally the construction and operation of the far more efficient extermination camps. The origins of this incremental development can be seen also in the allegedly questionable photographs from Tarnopol—which, incidentally, was not just another godforsaken East Galician town, as it appears in German reports from the war and in recent German commentaries on the Wehrmacht exhibition controversy, but rather one of the great centers of Jewish life and learning for centuries. Bogdan Musial rightly noted that some photographs seem to indicate exhumed bodies of NKVD victims, while others show bodies of Jews just shot or beaten to death lying in a pool of blood.[33] Indeed, it is quite possible that all four Tarnopol photographs in the catalogue depict both categories of victim.[34] But Krisztián Ungváry and Dieter Schmidt-Neuhaus are entirely wrong in saying these photos show NKVD victims only, as the commission of experts has confirmed.[35]

Taking his criticism to an extreme, Ungváry has argued that only 10 percent of the photographs in the exhibition depicted Wehrmacht soldiers directly involved in murder. He reached this conclusion by maintaining that the Wehrmacht's own secret field police and field gendarmerie, who carried out many of the executions, were not part of the army. This is obviously nonsense. Furthermore, he insisted that even where soldiers were seen to be directly involved in executions of partisans or in acts of collective punishment, their actions were considered legal under contemporary international accords.[36] As noted above, the commission of experts rejected this assertion outright.[37] But such arguments indicate how important it is to understand the context in which the actions took place. Only very few of the participants in the debate pointed out that the German army marched into the Soviet Union equipped with orders that defined the "Barbarossa" campaign as essentially different from any other war.[38] The Soviets were "no comrades in arms," but a "Judeo-Bolshevik" and "Asiatic" enemy. The infamous "commissar order" led to the execution without trial of hundreds of thousands of Red Army political officers. The agreement between the High Command of the Land Forces (OKH) and the SS led to tight collaboration between the troops on the ground and the *Einsatzgruppen*. The curtailment of martial law in the occupied parts of the Soviet Union legalized the murder of prisoners of war and civilians in breach of any existing conventions. Indeed, Germany rejected the authority of all international accords as far as its conduct in Soviet Russia was concerned. This attitude meant that the Wehrmacht was directly responsible for the death of some 3.3 million Soviet POWs out of some 5.7 million captured. Finally, soldiers were told to act with special brutality against partisans, "Asiatics," and Jews.

This was the context from which army brutality on all levels emerged. It has been said that while there can no longer be any doubt about the complicity of the army high command in the implementation of National Socialist policies, this does not mean that individual units and soldiers actually carried out criminal acts. Conversely, it has been argued that although some units were obviously involved in murderous activities, this not make the Wehrmacht as a whole a criminal organization. To be sure, many Wehrmacht soldiers may have avoided criminal actions. At the same time, the fact that 20 to 27 million Russians died under German occupation, the majority of them civilians, means that someone must have either killed them or created the conditions that led to their death — hunger, epidemics, exposure to the elements through deprivation of shelter and clothing, exhausting forced labor, and so forth. Similarly, while individual soldiers may have behaved decently, the Wehrmacht as an organization was the primary tool of a criminal, genocidal regime. If this does not make it into a criminal organization, what would?

It is in this context, too, that the honor, or ignominy, of the Wehrmacht has been invoked. Ulrich von Hassell, who had served the Third Reich in high positions and later turned against it, eventually paying for his actions with his life, formed a clear opinion on this issue even before the invasion of the Soviet Union. Following a conversation with Colonel Hans Oster and the former chief of the general staff, General Ludwig Beck, in early 1941, he noted in his diary that "one's hair stands on end" upon learning about the orders that would be read to the troops on the eve of the attack on Russia. These orders, known as the Barbarossa decree, would bring about a "systematic transformation of military justice vis-à-vis the civilian population" in the Soviet Union, making it into "what . . . under any law is a ridiculous caricature." Hassell concluded that "with this subordination to Hitler's orders [Walther von] Brauchitsch [the commander in chief of the army] is sacrificing the honor of the German army." [39]

Ungváry and other critics have rejected the exhibition's claim (and that of many scholars) that the Wehrmacht's "anti-partisan" campaign during the early months of fighting in the Soviet Union was a euphemism for the attempted liquidation of Jews and other "unwanted elements" in the occupied territories. For such critics, the radicalization of army policy was the direct result of increasing partisan activity rather than its cause. Hence, to their minds, photographs of the shootings and hangings of civilians indicate the strength of partisan resistance, not the brutality of the Germans. The commission of experts has dismissed such rhetoric. It has pointed out, for instance, that "from the very beginning" of the campaign in the Soviet Union, Field Marshal Walter von Reichenau, commander of the Sixth Army, operating in the Ukraine in the summer and fall of 1941, and his staff,

> implemented a policy of the most brutal intimidation, intended to prevent the population from taking part in the partisan war ordered by Stalin in November 1941. Even if the radical actions against the civilian population were repeatedly justified in [Sixth] Army orders by reference to the danger of partisans, the documents of the [Sixth] Army show that there can be no talk of a massive partisan threat in summer and fall 1941. When one speaks of "liquidation" of "partisans" or "guerrillas," it must be taken into account that such terms did not include only partisans in the sense of the Hague Convention, but also Jews, "wandering persons," soldiers in civilian clothes, separated military elements which continued fighting behind the front under a responsible military command, as well as Soviet citizens suspected of helping partisans (partisan assistants) or offering any kind of resistance, even if only passive.[40]

Reichenau has become notorious for his order of October 10, 1941, in which he urged his troops to recognize that

> The essential goal of the campaign against the Jewish-Bolshevik system is the complete destruction of its power instruments and the eradication of the Asiatic influence on the European cultural sphere.
>
> Thereby the troops too have *tasks*, which go beyond the conventional unilateral soldierly tradition [*Soldatentum*]. In the East the soldier is not only a fighter according to the rules of warfare, but also a carrier of an inexorable racial conception [*völkischen Idee*] and the avenger of all the

bestialities which have been committed against the Germans and related races.

Therefore the soldier must have *complete* understanding for the necessity of the harsh but just atonement of Jewish subhumanity. This has the further goal of nipping in the bud rebellions in the rear of the Wehrmacht which, as experience has shown, are always plotted by the Jews.[41]

Hitler thought very highly of this order and had it distributed to all other Wehrmacht formations fighting on the Eastern Front. Many of them were quick to follow suit with similarly worded orders, both in the hope of pleasing their Führer and with the aim of motivating their troops.[42] It is important to keep in mind both the terminology and the logic of these orders when we try to sketch the historiographical and ideological trajectory that stretches from the Third Reich to current polemics. For it was during the war in Russia that the Wehrmacht repeatedly claimed to be engaged in a vast *Vergeltung* (revenge) operation both for past and for anticipated "Judeo-Bolshevik" "crimes." It was the logic of Field Marshal Reichenau and his colleagues that dictated the need to treat Jewish infants "as partisans," and to provide partisans, or "bandits," with the kind of *Sonderbehandlung* (special treatment), that is, liquidation, accorded to Jews.

This is why the nature and the content of the attacks on an exhibition containing devastating photographic evidence of German soldiers' involvement in mass murder were so telling. Horst Möller has claimed that the exhibition had employed the same "hammering-in effect [*Einhämmerungseffekt*] . . . already invoked by Hitler: repeat the same thing over and over again and it will finally sink in. That is, that the Wehrmacht was involved in crimes to such an extent that one must describe it as an instrument of crime."[43] Möller angrily rejects this assertion, and no amount of evidence to the contrary will move him from his position: One cannot generalize about the Wehrmacht on the basis of specific criminal acts (no matter how many). The exposure of the German public to a mass of evidence of military crimes is, he suggests, merely a repetition of the "big lie" propaganda perfected by Joseph Goebbels. Möller's attempts to save the Wehrmacht's honor are reminiscent of German army rhetoric employed to justify its crimes by accusing its victims of even worse transgressions. Not only is this a misunderstanding of the exhibition's effect on most visitors—they soon see that the Wehrmacht had very little honor to lose—but it is an astonishing statement about Möller, who has great familiarity with the massive scholarship on Wehrmacht criminality (including studies written at the very institute he directs).[44]

In a deeper sense, the Wehrmacht exhibition illustrated not so much the limits of photographs as historical evidence, but rather the limitations of historians unused to integrating such materials into their work. Official documentation is no more reliable or any less misleading than photographs; both are biased sources that must be carefully examined. But the conservative German scholarly community is arguing that one might do best to avoid such evidence altogether. This is a lamentable conclusion, not least because most of the available photographic material on the crimes of the Wehrmacht, as well as crimes by other agencies of the Nazi regime, has not been tapped at all. The Federal Archives in Coblenz, for example, hold about a million photographs taken by the propaganda companies of the Wehrmacht during World War II. Hardly any of these photographs have been examined. Indeed, apart from one study on the activities of the propaganda companies in southern France and a forthcoming article on anti-Jewish propaganda by these units, this is still an entirely unused source.[45] The errors made in the exhibition should not deter scholars from using photographs. On the contrary, they should motivate them to make greater and more sophisticated use of such material, and to develop new methods of critical analysis as well as of combining photographic and filmic evidence with official documentation, oral history, memoirs, literature, and so forth. I would suggest that by providing powerful graphic details and by revealing the extent to which this still remains a highly sensitive topic, the exhibition has highlighted the importance of photography in the historiography of the twentieth century.

We still need to analyze the use and abuse of photographs.[46] As noted above, photographs have often been used as propaganda. But the same photographs can also be put to very different use: to uncover aspects of a reality that they were intended to distort. Conversely, amateur photographs, such as those taken by Wehrmacht soldiers for their private use (and what that use was is yet another important issue), were exploited for propaganda purposes by the Nazi regime even as it strictly forbade private photography (a ban never effectively enforced). But when we look at these photographs today, our perception differs from that of the original photographers, as when we see soldiers smiling at piles of corpses, or humiliating or killing their victims.

Furthermore, we must also wonder about the effect of such depictions of sadism and atrocity on the viewing public today, as they are repeatedly reproduced by the popular media. For the constant exposure to scenes of humiliation and violence does not necessarily generate humanist sentiments; it may also produce a view of certain categories of human beings (such as Jews, "Gypsies," Slavs) as contemptible victims, and of others (such as handsome, young, and conquering soldiers) as exemplary heroes. In other words, while an exhibition such as this one may have a positive educational effect, it may also produce, among some viewers, empathy with the perpetrators and contempt for the victims. This is especially the case when the conquerors who commit the atrocities happen to be one's actual or potential family members, while the tortured, humiliated, and butchered victims are nameless strangers. For this reason, it is crucial to provide some sense of the victims' own humanity by showing them as they were before the atrocity, namely, as normal, healthy human beings, no different from their killers. This way, the crime can be understood; not by stressing its magnitude, but by showing what was destroyed, the lives and culture of ordinary human being.

To be sure, photographs of victims can also become icons. Look at the hundreds of brochures, conference programs, invitations to fundraising events and lectures, donation pledges, and so on, that invariably feature one of a small number of iconic photographs that have come to symbolize victimhood: a frightened boy raising his hands, a mother carrying a child while being shot by a soldier, a group of naked women running to their death in a freezing field, an old man whose beard is being shorn by smirking troops. These photos may serve as icons of suffering and humiliation; they may also become icons of identification and empathy. Several recent novels have explored the theme of identifying with photographs; protagonists imagine themselves into the world of a photograph, even if, or precisely because, they could not possibly have been there. Such novels excavate the minds of those who have constructed an imaginary universe, who feel threatened by an evil that no longer exists, who long for a heroism they cannot display, a sacrifice they can no longer make.[47] Photographs have a power of immediate identification that texts rarely possess. They are powerful foci of emotion, and are therefore both dangerous and immensely important. They lack the cool, detached feel of an archival document, but are no less valuable for all that. Just as there is nothing objective about an SS document on Jews, there is nothing inherently false about photos depicting their suffering. We need to recognize that neither kind of document speaks for itself; each is subjective, biased, determined by the time and circumstances. That photographs can evoke powerful emotions and inscribe themselves on the mind is both their strength and their weakness. We, as historians, should learn to control them and use them, not to flee from them. If they bring a glimpse of the humanity of the victims onto the historical stage, so heavily populated by the documents of the perpetrators, then we have no right to put them aside.

Chapter Six

Złoczów, July 1941:
The Wehrmacht and the Beginning of
the Holocaust in Galicia

From a Criticism of Photographs
to a Revision of the Past

BERND BOLL

[*translated from the German by Margot Bettauer Dembo*]

CRITICS FIND FAULT WITH
PHOTOGRAPHS: THE CONSEQUENCES

On November 4, 1999, the director of the Hamburg Institute for Social Research announced to the press that he was temporarily closing the exhibit "*Vernichtungskrieg. Verbrechen der Wehrmacht 1941 bis 1944*" (War of extermination: Crimes of the Wehrmacht, 1941 to 1944). The Institute would reopen the exhibit only after a thorough examination of all documents by an independent commission of historians. This moratorium also affected the English-language version of the exhibit, which was to have opened in New York a month later.[1] The reasons for this step were stories in the press about three articles that had appeared in historical journals. The articles claimed that many of the photos in the exhibit did not show crimes committed by the German army in the Second World War.[2] These allegations were particularly explosive because they did not merely accuse the exhibit organizers of having made mistakes, but of having intentionally twisted the truth. A number of the pictures, in the opinion of the critics, showed crimes the Soviet secret service, the NKVD, had committed, and not German occupying troops. In some cases the press implied that this was a falsification of history following the example set by the Soviet Union in Katyn.[3]

The criticism focused on five photographs that were taken in early July 1941 by German soldiers in the East Galician town of Złoczów. There, as in many other towns and villages in the district, members of the NKVD had murdered political prisoners before their retreat. Subsequently, in the first days of the German occupation, thousands of Jews were the victims of pogroms lasting several days. The question that must therefore be answered is this: Whose victims are actually shown in the photos? We had already done additional research on such photographs for more than two years following earlier allegations of questionable attributions in the press.[4] This research—which we, the organizers of the exhibition, did independently of the critics (who had created this stir not with their own published articles but through newspaper stories)—resulted in a number of corrections being made in the exhibit. However, in several cases the conclusions we reached were different from those of our critics. This chapter will enable the reader to understand the controversy surrounding the disputed photos from Złoczów. To begin with, in order to explain the context in which the photographs were taken, I shall reconstruct the events that took place in Złoczów in the first days of July 1941. Next I shall trace the history and documentation we have available on the photos and interpret them against this background, replying to the points that have been raised. In conclusion, I shall outline just how controversy about the pictures in the exhibit fits into the current debate in Germany about the past.

ZŁOCZÓW, EARLY JULY 1941
Sovietization and
Ukrainian Nationalism

On July 1, 1941, the Wehrmacht marched into Złoczów. For the next four days this little East Galician town was the scene of one of the bloodiest and most extensive murder campaigns against the Jews in the beginning of the war against the Soviet Union. Before World War II about half of the town's 20,000 inhabitants were Jews, most of them poor shopkeepers or workmen, many unemployed; a quarter were Poles, and another quarter Ukrainians. Polish, Ukrainian, and Yiddish were the languages spoken.[5] Anti-Semitism was a virulent endemic phenomenon. When Polish and Ukrainian students came home for Christmas, they would call for a boycott of Jewish shops. And when Jewish soccer teams won a game, fights usually ensued. But since the Jewish community had its own institutions—a town committee, religious leaders, judges, hospitals, synagogues, schools, a system of social services, sports clubs, a theater, and political organizations—it did not depend solely on families for protection against the hostile environment. And consequently a precarious balance developed between the population groups.[6]

This equilibrium began to falter when the Red Army occupied Złoczów on September 17, 1939. Shortly thereafter southeast Poland became a part of the Ukrainian Soviet Socialist Republic as a result of a secret supplementary agreement to the Hitler-Stalin Pact. At first the mood in Złoczów ranged from restrained to optimistic. The Jews knew what would have happened to them under German occupation, and they shed no tears for the Polish state, given their experiences since 1919. On the other hand, many Poles were relieved not to find themselves under German rule, or at least they gave this impression to their new rulers. In contrast, the Ukrainians, especially the nationalists, seemed to be the real winners. They welcomed the Red Army with flags and flowers in the hope that their old dream of an independent state would now finally come true. But they quickly had to bury their illusions.[7] For instead of the hoped-for autonomy they were faced with rigid Sovietization, expropriations, dismissal from jobs, and deportations. This affected all those who were considered unreliable, or who did not accept their new nationality, whether Jews, Poles, or Ukrainians.[8]

In Złoczów the new ruling power made itself felt first and foremost through a stronger police presence. Instead of a dozen or so policemen, as was the case before, there were now many police officers and hundreds of militiamen who saw to the maintenance of socialist order. But above all it was the agents of the notorious NKVD who, supported by a tight information network, were omnipresent. After a short while the first arrests began. The mayor, judges, police officers, civil servants, prominent Zionists, and often just any town residents at random, were deported to the interior of Russia, to Siberia, or to Kazakhstan. The NKVD, which was in charge of the treatment of prisoners in the Soviet

Union, took over the Zamek, an old citadel still in good condition, from the Polish administration. The fortress dated to the end of the seventeenth century, when it was built by order of Polish King Jan III Sobieski, the victor in the Turkish Wars. It had already been used as a prison under Austrian and Polish rule.[9]

Scarcely had the Wehrmacht invaded the Soviet Union on June 22, 1941, when the arrests in Złoczów began anew. Hundreds of prominent citizens, the majority of them Ukrainians, but also Poles and Jews, were imprisoned in the Zamek.[10] On instructions from Moscow the prisoners were to be immediately evacuated to the interior of the country. But time ran out. On June 24, 1941, Lavrenti Beria, commissar of internal affairs and chief of the soviet secret police, instructed his regional branches to shoot the "political" prisoners—all those who had been arrested for "counterrevolutionary activities," economic sabotage, political sabotage, and "anti-Soviet activities."[11] Stalin enacted these measures with inhuman brutality. He saw, quite justifiably, a fifth column of National Socialist Germany in the separatist movement that existed in the western Ukraine he had occupied less than two years earlier. Meanwhile, the most radical of the Ukrainian nationalists had been backing the German side, especially the Organization of Ukrainian Nationalists (OUN), which, in 1929, had grown out of the merger between the anti-Polish Ukrainian Military Organization and various student organizations. Like its predecessors, the OUN considered terror a legitimate weapon in a political war. But that only partially explains why Stalin fought Ukrainian separatism with such extreme harshness.[12]

Since the late 1930s when Germany was preparing for war against Poland, there had been close contacts between the foreign intelligence office of the OKW (*Oberkommando der Wehrmacht* [High Command of the Wehrmacht]) and the OUN. Although its leader, Andreas Mel'nyk was a moderate and attempted to neutralize the radical trends in his organization, the OUN leaned toward integral nationalism and ideologically favored the fascist movements in Europe. With the occupation of East Galicia by the Soviet Union in the autumn of 1939, National Socialist Germany seemed to be the only serious hope for the realization of a Ukrainian national state. The policy of the OUN grew increasingly more radical, conflicts between the leadership and the grassroots membership became more frequent, and the young revolutionaries drifted more and more away from Mel'nyk's leadership. The conflicts were heightened as thousands of young emigrants from Soviet-occupied territory joined the organization, and by the release of the imprisoned leaders of the Galician group of the OUN shortly before the Wehrmacht occupied Warsaw.[13]

Ukrainian activists, supported by the German *Abwehr* (military intelligence), which at the same time also restrained them, had been involved in espionage and sabotage in the western Ukraine since December 1939 and were preparing an armed uprising. These preparations, but not their other conspiratorial activities, were discontinued in the summer of 1940 on the instructions of Admiral Canaris, head of German military intelligence. The OUN had been playing a role in the Wehrmacht's preparations for war against the Soviet Union since May, 1940, and in return for its willingness to collaborate, the OUN was given extensive leeway for its propaganda, which, however, fell far short of its leaders' expectations. In the autumn of 1940 conversations were held between representatives of the Abwehr, among them Lieutenant Colonel Helmuth Groscurth (an extensive discussion of whose role in the Holocaust can be found in Saul Friedländer's chapter in this volume), and such Ukrainian functionaries as Mel'nyk and Stepan Bandera, the young leader of the radical opposition in the OUN. In the 1930s Bandera had gained prominence as head of an OUN terrorist group that attempted to assassinate Polish politicians. Even without satisfactory concessions by the Germans, the Ukrainians declared themselves ready to join the fight against the common enemy.

The growing orientation toward National Socialism demanded by the grassroots membership of the OUN ultimately led to a split in the organization. This became public in March 1941 at a general meeting of the OUN-B in Kraków. This splinter group, named Bandera after their leader, challenged the legitimacy of the elected OUN leadership. To have trained personnel at his disposal in case of an emergency, Bandera formed three troop units *(Pochidne hrupy)*, each comprising 700 men under the leadership of Ivan Klymiv-Lehenda. They were to march with or directly behind the Wehrmacht serving as interpreters, medics, or as transport and repair personnel, and they were assigned to tasks in the administration, the police, and the press. The Mel'nyk faction, the OUN-M, had similar paramilitary groups available.[14] Bandera urged the Wehrmacht to give his followers political training. In the spring of 1941 the German army set up two of its own units of Ukrainians: the *"Nachtigall"* (Nightingale) and the "Roland" Batallions, who were trained in part in the Brandenburg Training Regiment (*Lehrregiment z.b.V. Brandenburg*). Shortly before the start of the war, they were given the task of occupying military and other important installations and protecting them from the departing Soviet troops.[15]

Germans as well as Ukrainians tried to use each other to further their own interests. For their future occupation policies in the East, the Nazis were planning to create a counterbalance to the Polish population and to optimize their own intelligence work in exchange for cheap and always retractable concessions to the Ukrainians in their cultural sphere. The Ukrainian separatists, on the other hand, were trying to persuade Germany to guarantee them their own national state, but in any case to provide their cadres with military and administrative experience. At the same time they linked that to the idea that Polish influence would be eliminated and the nationalism of their fellow countrymen would be strengthened.[16] The OUN was convinced they could put pressure on the Nazis and, by declaring an independent Ukrainian state in Lemberg (L'viv, Lvov) on June 30, 1941, they attempted to present them with a fait accompli. But the arrest of the OUN-B leaders on July 9th by a detachment of the SD (the security service of the SS) put a sudden end to these nationalist dreams.[17]

It is highly probable that the OUN, by arrangement with Canaris's office, triggered the fight between the nationalities through synchronized local putsches after the war started in order to weaken the Red Army in its hinterland. To accomplish this goal, militias were created throughout East Galicia. There is evidence that the OUN attempted to foment uprisings in Lemberg, Skole, Buczacz, Sambor, Podhajce, and Monasterzyska. The scenario was to shoot at retreating Red Army troops and hunt down Soviet stragglers. It has not been conclusively proved that the pogroms against the Jews were also planned from the start. However, it is striking that pogroms in similar form occurred all over the western Ukraine at the end of June and early July.[18]

OUN flyers of June 1941 defined the enemy unequivocally: "Don't throw away your weapons yet. Take them up. Destroy the enemy. . . . People!—Know this!—Moscow, Poland, the Hungarians, the Jews— these are your enemies. Destroy them."[19] In the first days of the war a pogrom mood prevailed, which had wide repercussions and in particular gripped the Wehrmacht's Ukrainian interpreters, whom Army Intelligence had recruited primarily from OUN circles. In the Seventeenth Army sector a group of the Secret Field Police reported that their interpreters thought "every Jew should immediately be killed."[20] The "War Program" of the OUN had provided for "hostile minorities": "During the fighting, especially those who defend the regime are to be destroyed: [they are] to be resettled in their territory, the majority of their intelligentsia are to be destroyed."[21] Measures for ethnic cleansing were also included from the start. Klymiv-Lehenda announced his intention in a flyer: "I am establishing herewith [a measure] by which I am holding the masses (races and ethnic groups) responsible for any crimes against the Ukr[ainian] state and the Ukr[ainian] army."[22] In a letter to Bandera dated June 25, 1941, Jaroslav Stec'ko, a member of the OUN-B leadership, openly declared that these measures would primarily affect the Jews: "We are setting up a militia that will help remove the Jews."[23] They carried out these intentions in Złoczów. According to a report by *Einsatzgruppe* C on July 16, 1941, the influence of the OUN-B (the Bandera group) was very strong in Złoczów. They had established a "revolutionary" Ukrainian administration that, in posters and flyers, welcomed the Germans as their allies.[24]

The Pogroms Begin

In the last days of June 1941 Złoczów was almost continuously under German fire; the *Luftwaffe* (German air force) bombarded the city without differentiating between military and civilian targets. The worst bombardment occurred the night of July 1st and ended abruptly early the next morning.[25] Shortly thereafter the first tanks of the German 9th Tank Division rolled into Złoczów; they were followed by *Sonderkommando* 4b (Special Detachment 4b) of *Einsatzgruppe* C. The *Einsatzgruppe* uses only vague language in describing what happened next: "Wehrmacht happily [showing] good attitude toward the Jews."[26] It was the OUN's big moment. Groups of young OUN members, recognizable by their blue and yellow armbands, fraternized with the German troops, waved Ukrainian flags, and roamed rowdily through the streets. Many houses were burning, entire streets lay in ruins, there were bomb craters everywhere. The synagogue was in danger too, as Szymon, the son of a local candy manufacturer, reported more than thirty years later to the Mannheim Public Prosecutor Barbara Just-Dahlmann:

My father and my two brothers and I ran to the synagogue which was only a few hundred yards from our house; we broke open the door; each of us took two Torah scrolls and ran back [to our house]. Meanwhile, all the houses along the street were burning. Broken telephone and telegraph poles lay on the ground, and German soldiers on motorcycles were riding eastward to Tarnopol and Brody. Only a single person—and this is something I will never forget till the end of my days—a legless cripple pushing himself forward on a little board with wheels raised his right hand in a Hitler salute. . . .[27]

Samuel Lipa Tennenbaum, the proprietor of a printing shop, recounts what he saw on the morning of July 1st while looking out of a window in his neighbor's house.

I saw a motley mob, perhaps a hundred people, rushing in and out of the government stores across the street. They were looters. There was a bearded Jew in the crowd, and a young, pretty peasant girl who was carrying a large bolt of flowered material that unraveled and fluttered like a huge flag. A German military vehicle drove up; two noncommissioned officers jumped out, and without a word of warning one of them pulled out a revolver and started shooting into the crowd. Several people, among them the Jew and the girl, fell to the pavement. I kept my eyes on the Jew, who whirled around like a dancing dervish until he collapsed like an emptying sack of flour. The girl was covered with the material she had been carrying.[28]

Then Tennenbaum saw young people pointing out the apartments of Jews to German soldiers. Around noon several soldiers forced their way into his home, rummaged through all the closets, and left again half an hour later with their booty: several suits, a Japanese silk coat, and two expensive cameras. In the early afternoon the first news of a pogrom began to spread. Germans and Ukrainians were roughing up Jewish men on the streets and in their houses, beating or shooting them to death; others were dragged to the Zamek fortress.[29] There, two mass graves[30] had been found in the inner courtyard and at least two others were discovered in the adjacent orchard. They contained 649 dead prisoners altogether. They had been murdered on Beria's orders by officers of the NKVD before they fled the town.[31]

Now the actions against the Jews began. The German town commander ordered that all Jews, including children from the age of six, would have to wear white armbands with a blue Star of David and bearing the inscription "Jew." Anyone violating the order would be shot. "A chill seized us," Samuel Tennenbaum recalls. "Does this mean that a child of six caught without an armband would be shot?"[32] Ultimately the spontaneous raids, maltreatment, and murders turned into organized pogroms. On July 2, members of the Ukrainian militia who were now serving the Germans as auxiliary police, put up placards ordering Jews to appear the following day at 8 A.M. in the Town Hall square. "Those refusing to do so will be shot."[33]

THE MASSACRE
OF JULY 3 AND 4, 1941

On the morning of July 3 fear and mistrust among the Jewish population were so great that in spite of the unambiguous threat for noncompliance many people stayed in hiding rather than obey this summons. But militiamen came and pulled them out of their hiding places. The Ukrainian auxiliary police forced their way into the apartment of the candy manufacturer. "Jews, get out!" they shouted and began to beat him brutally. After several hammer blows to his back Szymon lay unconscious. He lost four teeth and could scarcely move his limbs for weeks afterward. His father and brothers fared no better. A neighbor's beard was ripped off with the skin.[34]

Shlomo Wolkowicz, an eighteen-year-old high school student from Lemberg who was fleeing from the German troops, had arrived in Złoczów toward the end of June and was taken in by his uncle's family.[35] After a long discussion, they decided not to go to the Town Hall square. But at 9 A.M. a German SS officer and a Ukrainian came to their home and picked up Wolkowicz and the women and children—they missed the uncle who happened to be in the garden at the time. Wolkowicz and the women were taken to the fortress, where a long line of Jews was already waiting. SS men stood at the entrance gate and mercilessly beat the new arrivals with truncheons. Finally they reached the prison courtyard. There they saw a big pit full of countless dead bodies—victims of the NKVD. The Jews were forced to lift the corpses—some of them already badly decayed—out of the pit.[36] Another eyewitness reported later, "The corpses were recovered, washed and laid out next to each other in rows. Some victims were identified by relatives and were taken away with the permission of the Germans."[37] Some of the corpses, she said, were fresh, others were bloated and black.[38]

They were guarded by ten Ukrainian policemen and ten SS people. Orthodox Jews especially were tortured to death by the SS, Wolkowicz recalls: "They would beat their victim with sadistic pleasure until he lay on the ground unconscious, and then they would kick him back into the pit. Sometimes family members would try to help the poor souls, but then they were subjected to the same fate, often even worse. Several were pulled out of the pit and bludgeoned to death with incredible brutality. The murderers allowed the wounded who were in pain and agony to die slowly of their injuries."[39]

Toward evening the SS men set up machine guns and turned them on the pit. Wolkowicz goes on to say, "and it was obvious that this was the end for us. People were gripped by uncontrollable fear. They didn't know how they could save themselves from certain death. Panic broke out. I can still hear the screams and prayers of these helpless human beings. We had a feeling of complete helplessness, of having been caught in a trap that could slam shut at any moment. I was only waiting for a sign to look death in the eye. The tension was unbearable. All we wanted was for it to be over. Suddenly a German gave the order 'Fire!' and shots rang out, long, uninterrupted salvos." Wolkowicz was unhurt because he threw himself to the ground in time. But many of his fellow sufferers were dead or seriously wounded. Then, unexpectedly, a German officer appeared and ordered the firing to stop.[40] For three days the Wehrmacht had watched the pogroms and murders without doing anything. The third general staff officer (intelligence) of the 295th Infantry Division noted on July 3, 1941: "The situation in Złoczów is unpleasant. The corpses of nine hundred Ukrainians murdered by the Russians are lying in the citadel; currently they are being dug up by Jews and Russians using their hands. Right out in the open on the streets of the city and in the citadel there are mass shootings and murders of Jews and Russians—including women and children—by Ukrainians."[41] The Fourth Army Corps found out only two days later that soldiers of the Waffen SS Division "Viking" were also participating in these mass murders.[42] Only then, and only because of the intervention of Lieutenant Colonel Helmuth Groscurth, first general staff officer of the 295th Infantry Division, did the town commander step in.[43] He summoned Colonel Otto Korfes, the Commander of the 518th Infantry Regiment of the 295th Infantry Division, and directed him to "reestablish order."[44]

Korfes had learned of the plundering and murders in the town from a noncommissioned officer he had sent ahead to reconnoiter. He dispatched Lieutenant Colonel Patzwahl, a batallion commander in his regiment, to Złoczów with instructions to reestablish public order, if necessary by using force of arms.[45] But even though Patzwahl was authorized to act not only by his immediate superior officer but also by the town commander and his division headquarters, he was content merely to release the women and children from the citadel. They were not even out of sight, Wolkowicz reports, when the SS again opened fire. Once again he was not hit. He lay there, without hope, till evening, buried under several bodies. He was saved by a severe thunderstorm because the murderers sought protection from the rain and temporarily took their eyes off their victims. Wolkowicz finally succeeded in burrowing his way up through the corpses. Only a few other Jews besides him had survived the massacre. After dark, they crawled through a fence and returned to the town.[46]

As a result of Patzwahl's halfhearted intervention, the murders continued on the morning of July 4, again with the participation of the Waffen SS: "From Złoczów there are again reports of the most gruesome shootings by the retreating Russians as well as by the Ukrainians and the SS. At least 300 Ukrainians and 300 Jews [sic!] have allegedly been shot."[47] As soon as Korfes received this report from an ordinance officer, he and his adjutant drove to the citadel. There he found many German soldiers; hundreds of Jews were standing at the edge of a pit. Perhaps a dozen Ukrainian civilians armed with spades, axes, pickaxes, and hand grenades were under the command of the SS. Sixty to eighty people—men, women, and children—were standing in the pit. Many others had already been killed or wounded by hand grenades. Korfes gave the order for the killing to stop and sent the watching soldiers out of the citadel. He had noncommissioned officers close off the fortress entrances and sent his adjutant and Patzwahl into the town to fetch medical help. "Then," Korfes remembered later, "I asked the people in the pit to come out; they were now under the protection of the German Army and had nothing more to fear."[48]

While his soldiers were caring for the survivors, Korfes briefed the commander of the 295th Infantry Division, Lieutenant General Geitner, who had arrived toward noon with his aide, Major Bechly, and Lieutenant Colonel Groscurth.[49] Then Korfes inspected the area where the murdered Jews were lying. Korfes said in 1960,

> It had apparently once been a parade ground, an open square within the citadel which these gangs had used to pile up the dead. Evidently, in order to be able to count them better they had heaped them up in piles of five or six. As far as I can remember, there were about 500 to 600 lying there. I walked past the dead bodies with a doctor to ascertain whether any of them were still alive. But most had either received an additional pistol shot to finish them off, or, as in the case of children, were immediately torn to pieces by the hand grenades, while the rest had their heads split open. The civilians carried pickaxes, axes, and spades. They had used these to smash the skulls of the seriously wounded in the pit, and had then taken them out and piled them up for counting.[50]

A German soldier who accidentally entered the courtyard of the citadel at that time later confirmed this statement: "I saw corpses piled up in stacks taller than a man, and there were so many that I could immediately see there were several hundred corpses, perhaps 400, maybe even more."[51] He made a point of saying that the smell coming from the corpses was minimal: "This town had been occupied several days before by the German fascist Wehrmacht, yet the smell of this mountain of corpses was minimal. Therefore, as a physician I can [now] say that these murders must have been committed only a short time before, approximately a day before, if one takes into consideration that it was summertime and hot."[52] So the dead Jews were not being laid out in rows for identification by their relatives as was done before with NKVD victims, but rather they were first piled up for statistical purposes. We have photographs from Złoczów showing this.

Within four days thousands of people had become the victims of these killing actions in the citadel and in the town. The precise number is difficult to determine since, in addition to citizens of Złoczów, there were many Jews among the victims who had fled from the territories occupied by Germany in 1939 and who were therefore not registered. Almost every family had lost at least one of its members; in many families all the men had been murdered. The selection of the victims reveals that the purpose of the mass murders was the "ethnic cleansing" of Złoczów: Almost all the town's physicians, lawyers, pharmacists, and engineers were among the victims, in some cases even their half-grown sons. The entire Jewish leadership of Złoczów had been literally anni-hilated.[53] Altogether more than 12,000, by some estimates as many as 24,000, Jews lost their lives in the western Ukraine in dozens of pogroms during those days. The pogrom in Złoczów was one of the worst.[54]

RESPONSIBILITY FOR THE ZŁOCZÓW MASSACRE

In the final analysis, who was responsible for the mass murder of the Jewish population of Złoczów? The records and the testimony of eye-witnesses yield a contradictory picture. OUN activists participated in large numbers, many of them displaying above-average brutality. And from the outset the OUN leadership had certainly planned to murder their political and ethnic opponents. However, if one believes a report by *Einsatzgruppe* C, the Ukrainian militia, acting "on instructions of the Wehrmacht," had captured several hundred Jews—from 300 to 500—who were subsequently shot; it does not say by whom they were shot. The *Einsatzgruppe's* own units, on the other hand, were alleged not to have participated in the killings. *Sonderkommando* (Special Unit) 4b, which moved in with the Wehrmacht, had only "briefly dealt with" Złoczów.[55] Yet the war diary of the 295th Infantry Division reports that "Ukrainians" and "SS" carried out the shootings, and Korfes identi-fies these as members of the Waffen SS Division "Viking."[56] Still, that does not mean that the order for the murders came from this division. One must go back further to clear up the question of responsibility.

During the first weeks of the German occupation, the Reich Main Security Office (*Reichssicherheitshauptamt*) did not rely on mass shoot-ings of Jews and other "enemies of the Reich" but rather hoped for "ef-forts to achieve self-purification in anticommunist and anti-Jewish circles" within the local population. In his teletype message of June 29, 1941, Reinhard Heydrich, head of the Reich Main Security Office, in-structed the heads of the *Einsatzgruppen* to "unleash and intensify" pogroms "if necessary, and to direct them into the right channels so that these local 'self-defense circles' could not later claim they received orders or political assurances." To be sure, these measures were to take place "without leaving traces" and in a decentralized way, if possible directly after the occupation of a town or village by the Wehrmacht.[57] This required close consultation with military headquarters. General Karl Heinrich von Stülpnagel, commander in chief of the Seventeenth Army, which was responsible for Złoczów, immediately reacted to Heydrich's order with the supplementary suggestion that anti-Semitic and anticommunist Poles in the newly occupied territories be enlisted for these "self-purification measures."[58]

Of course Heydrich also had his eye on the "Polish intelligentsia" as a target group for persecution. Nevertheless, the prospect of being able to enlist anticommunist and anti-Jewish Poles as the "initiating element" for pogroms and as "informers" for the "purification actions" made him take up Stülpnagel's suggestion. And so he ordered the *Einsatzgruppen* to spare for the time being "any Poles disposed that way": The word to proceed "with regard to the Polish intelligentsia, etc." could just as well be given later on.[59] Apparently the *Einsatzkommandos* and their advance units which marched with or directly behind the Wehrmacht, had orders to remain in the background for the time being while the radical Ukrainians performed their murder operations against Communists and Jews. The Kommandos were to get involved only if the Ukrainians did not proceed as desired.

In accordance with these instructions issued by the Reich Security Main Office, *Sonderkommando* 4b under Günther Hermann held back at first in Złoczów and contented itself with searching out "agents and material."[60] That fits perfectly with the usual behavior of Kommando leader Hermann in those days. He had to be warned several times by the leader of *Einsatzgruppe* C, Otto Rasch, not to restrict himself to shooting convicted "enemies of the Reich" but rather to shoot Jews on principle as such "enemies."[61] In Złoczów too Hermann preferred to leave it to others to get their hands bloody. The Ukrainian "anti-Bolshevists" and "anti-Jewish circles" were sufficiently well represented anyway: They served as interpreters, drivers, and medics among the troops, and in Złoczów, they formed the "revolutionary Ukrainian administration" with its own militia who, as many contemporary witnesses recalled, were visible everywhere in the streets.[62]

Certainly the OUN is responsible for many cases of mistreatment and murder. But the recovery of the corpses in the citadel turned into a mass killing only because of the participation of the soldiers of the SS "Viking." This division was subordinate to the Fourteenth Army Corps of Panzer Group 1. Since July 1, 1941, it had been marching from Lemberg to Złoczów, following directly behind several other divisions, and it seems to have considered the first days of the war in the East a sort of hunting expedition, with people as prey. On July 2 and 3, it blocked the route of advance, apparently intentionally, while several members went "hunting for Jews" and in the process shot "everything and anybody that looked even the slightest bit suspicious, e.g. civilians with shaved heads (Russian soldiers)."[63] Shortly before his arrival in Złoczów, Helmuth Groscurth also reported to his superiors in the Fourth Army Corps "that the SS are randomly shooting great numbers of Russian soldiers and civilians who look suspicious to them."[64] The SS "Viking" continued the bloodbath in Złoczów. Otto Korfes was informed by a dispatch rider that "the SS, together with civilian bandits, were plundering, dragging people out of their homes, and had already killed quite a lot."[65] Moreover, he had seen two SS soldiers in the citadel and suspected that the hand grenades with which the OUN supporters were murdering the Jews in the mass grave came from the stocks of their own division.[66] Whether members of *Sonderkommando* 4a were also involved in the shootings is not clear, but because of the restraint they had exercised so far, it would seem rather unlikely.[67]

The plunder, mistreatments, and murders were apparently no problem for Seventeenth Army commander in chief Stülpnagel. They dragged on for days without the Wehrmacht—from the army on down to the town command—seeing any reason to intervene. It was not until the 295th Infantry Division arrived that someone appeared on the scene who felt they had gone far beyond the bounds of allowable behavior, namely First General Staff Officer Groscurth. Christian Streit correctly points out that Groscurth's intervention was possible only because at that time "in comparison with the usual conditions, an amazingly homogeneous intragroup agreement existed" in the 295th Infantry Division.[68] Even General Geitner, who usually turned a deaf ear to the political views of his first general staff officer, unconditionally approved his actions and made a personal appearance at the scene of the crime—to show symbolic support.[69]

On the other hand, Stülpnagel, who also was certainly no supporter of the Nazi party and had in fact belonged to the inner circle of the military resistance since 1938, showed sympathy for the measures against the Jews.[70] He was able to combine a critical detachment toward Hitler with an anti-Semitic attitude. As early as May 1935 he had written in a memorandum about the "snooping behavior and underhanded dealings of the commissars in the Russian army who mostly belong to the Jewish race." On July 30, 1941, three weeks after the murders in Złoczów, Stülpnagel ordered that in the future the murder units of *Einsatzgruppe* C should maintain constant contact with the intelligence officer of his army, through a liaison officer. Reprisal measures for sabotage, he ordered, should "first of all be directed at Jewish and Communist inhabitants," especially Jewish members of the Comsomol who were to be considered "supporters of sabotage and the formation of youth gangs."[71] So on principle he was prepared to let Himmler's death squadrons have their way.

And it wasn't only these death squads, but also the Ukrainian nationalists who were instigating anti-Jewish pogroms in the Wehrmacht's wake. Even though he could not have failed to notice this, Stülpnagel had authorized the local Ukrainian self-defense groups on July 7, 1941.[72] This measure had its origin in a July 2 suggestion from the subordinate Fourth Army Corps, which felt it was unable, because of "urgent tasks," to "cleanse" the territory to the rear of the corps of Red Army stragglers and to protect the civilian population from them.[73] Consequently, the army leadership was responsible, at least indirectly, for the murders committed by these local groups. Stülpnagel made the Jews into scapegoats to demonstrate to the rest of the loyal population that the Wehrmacht would react "severely but justly" in cases of hostile acts by civilians. Therefore, in a message to Army Group South dated August 12, 1941, on the subject of "The Position and Influence of Bolshevism" he demanded that the propaganda units "pointedly explain Jewry" to the Ukrainians "to elicit their unified and uniform rejection" and to make it impossible for the Jews to "become active as the center of a resistance movement."[74] He left no doubt that he himself was willing to pursue this line of action with the utmost severity. When, at the end of September 1941, three incidents of sabotaged telephone lines were reported, the Seventeenth Army asked *Sonderkommando* 4b for "reprisals" against the Jewish population—"reprisals" being a euphemism for murder.[75] On the other hand, the limits beyond which Helmuth Groscurth would not participate in such measures were much more clearly drawn. Streit defines these limits as "where murderous actions were directed against clearly innocent people, no matter whether they were enemy soldiers or civilians."[76]

The higher-ranking officer corps was quite prepared to support the "self-cleansing measures" introduced by the Reich Main Security Office against the Jews, even if it was only by not stopping them. Thus in Złoczów, *Sonderkommando* 4b could leave it to the local Ukrainian activists to successfully carry out measures against "enemies of the Reich"—primarily against the Jewish population, in part also against women and children. The Ukrainians found welcome help from the SS Division "Viking," which had made murder actions its specialty from the outset. This passive support of the killings by army leadership had been called into question only as a result of Groscurth's individual decision, and then only because his intervention found consent from divisional headquarters. Comparable intervention by the Wehrmacht would have been possible at any time in other locations and by other units before the massacres escalated.

From the end of June to early July 1941, thirty-five towns in the former Polish part of the Ukraine became the sites of mass murders comparable to the massacre in Złoczów. It is obvious that the reason given—namely, revenge on the Jews for crimes committed by the NKVD—was only a setup. For even though no corpses of Ukrainians were found in Sokal, for example, local militiamen and units of *Sonderkommando* 4a murdered 317 civilians there at the end of June 1941. Wehrmacht soldiers were always curious onlookers at these massacres, which took place in public; some soldiers even participated in the pogroms on their own initiative, as for instance in Lemberg, Niemirow, Sokal, and Tarnopol.[77]

In Lemberg the soldiers were "so fanaticized," a lieutenant reported to a Wehrmacht chaplain, "they only wanted to see the shooting of Jews. He had seen a Wehrmacht sergeant who had stabbed a Jew with his bayonet."[78] The town commander of Lemberg, Colonel von Prittwitz, allowed the killings to go on for four weeks, just as had General Karl von Roques, the commander of Army Sector South in the rear. Not until July 25, 1941, when "soldiers of the Wehrmacht participated in the worst possible way in a pogrom against Jews carried out in the local prison by Ukrainians lusting for revenge and retaliation" did von

Roques order the commanders to report to him and severely reprimand them. That seemed to have had the desired effect; after that he [von Roques] "never again heard of a similar case."[79]

In an order of July 29, 1941, von Roques made it clear to his troops that the jurisdictional decree (*Gerichtsbarkeiterlass*) covered participation in pogroms only in "the course of fighting," and henceforth not in the now "pacified territory." At the same time he advised his law enforcement units to end the pogroms by the locals.[80] This order was somewhat less successful than von Roques later claimed. In the weeks that followed there were renewed cases "of soldiers and officers shooting Jews or participating in such shootings," and on September 1, 1941, he once again was forced to forbid participation in executions, this time by SS and police organizations.[81]

The NKVD Murders in German Propaganda

The exhumation of NKVD victims and the murder of the Jewish population in Złoczów attracted numerous Wehrmacht soldiers as curious onlookers. Anyone who had a camera hurried to photograph the events. At least one of the bystanders recorded them with a movie camera.[82] A former infantryman who was among the onlookers recalls that the Wehrmacht military police had closed off the citadel and prevented him from photographing: "As I took my camera out from under my motorcycle coat to take a picture, a military policeman suddenly appeared at my side and told me to get out of there as fast as possible, otherwise he would confiscate my camera and report me. Taking photographs here was forbidden, and any involvement by the German Wehrmacht was not appropriate because this was a Ukrainian matter." He also said that the murder of the Jews of Złoczów was considered an act of revenge by the soldiers "because Jewish Commissars of the Red Army had killed hundreds of Ukrainian civilians who wanted to welcome the German liberators with a triumphal arch made of fir branches."[83]

In this respect his memory is mistaken, although it seems to have preserved a rumor making the rounds among German soldiers at the time. What it does show is that scarcely had the murders been committed when they were given a new context in a coordinated effort by the

OUN, the SS, the Wehrmacht, and the Ministry of Propaganda. On July 8, the 295th Infantry Division sent two press reports to the officer in charge of censorship at the deputy general command of the Eleventh Army Corps in Hannover.[84] The first report had been drawn up by a private first class in the division. He wrote about what had occurred in Złoczów: "The Jewish population of the town, embittered by our constant victories and the joyful reception accorded us by the Ukrainian populace, allowed themselves to get so carried away that they rounded up the poor people who were friendly to us, dragged them to the citadel, and brutally murdered them there. It is quite impossible to describe the horrible mutilation and tortures of the victims. The 500 people who became the victims of the sadistic frenzy of these Jewish sub-humans form a new link in the chain of evidence. A fire will burn in us until the last Jew has disappeared from Europe. This war signifies the end of Jewry in Europe."[85] The second report came from a war correspondent in Propaganda Company 666. In order to make the murders of Jews more acceptable, he promptly invented mutilated corpses of German soldiers: "Those Ukrainians who were still alive confronted the Jews with their disgraceful deeds and then punished these sub-humans as they deserved to be punished, harshly but justly. An air force lieutenant, a sergeant, and a private were murdered in that same place. The air force lieutenant and the non-commissioned officer had parachuted here, and even though they were taken prisoner, they were brutally murdered. These disgraceful acts will also be remembered and will be atoned."[86]

These articles were meant to be published in two regional newspapers *Niedersächsische Tageszeitung* and *Der Mitteldeutsche*. The division ordered 2,000 copies each for distribution to its soldiers. Enclosed with the articles were nineteen photos taken by a radio operator of the division.[87] In the days that followed, Wehrmacht newspapers published at the front repeatedly printed reports about the NKVD murders under sensational headlines. The intention to make the soldiers understand the need for ruthless retaliation is unmistakable.[88] The survivors never forgot seeing numerous German soldiers photographing the massacres. In his memoir, published in 1967, S. Altman described the cynical attitude of the photographers, and also the use Nazi propaganda made of the photos: "Many German officers watched the pogrom with calm cynicism, clicking their cameras all the time. A few months later I happened to come across some of these photographs in an illustrated German weekly. One of them depicted a scene at the citadel, with women weeping over a pile of corpses. Among these I definitely recognized Lusia Freimann, the daughter of Shyjo and Dziunka Kitaj. The photo bore the caption 'Ukrainian women mourning their husbands, who were murdered by Jews.' "[89]

Such atrocity reports came in handy for the German propaganda machine. After almost two years of restraint toward the Soviet Union, necessitated by the Hitler-Stalin Pact, Goebbels needed material with which he could make the German people fear for their lives, and at the same time draw a picture of the "Jewish-Bolshevist enemy."[90] Films of the discovery of corpses in the NKVD prison in Lemberg provided him with a model: "The Führer wants us to launch the big anti-Bolshevist campaign now," he wrote in his diary on July 6.[91] The German *Wochenschau*, the weekly movie newsreel, dealt with the massacre for an entire month, pointing to the direction policy would take: No mercy was to be shown to the authors of the crimes, the Jews. Reports by the security service on the mood of the people demonstrated that these films, shown with appropriate commentary, served their intended purpose among the public. On July 7, for instance, the report says that "the majority [of moviegoers] expressed the conviction that nowadays just such pictures illustrating the true nature of Bolshevism and the Jews in all their realistic horror ought to be shown repeatedly."[92] And from the report of July 31: "Here and there the question comes up whether these atrocities are being atoned for with the necessary harshness."[93]

The newspapers also focused on the subject. On July 5, 1941, in his instructions to the press, chief of the Reich Press Office Otto Dietrich issued the following watchword of the day: "In a way Lemberg shows the normal condition of Jewish-Bolshevism and is proof of the bloodthirsty frenzy of the Jewish-Bolshevist rulers." And he demanded this of the press: "The main emphasis must be on denouncing the criminal Jewish Bolshevist regime."[94] The massacres in Galicia—with the proper propagandistic emphasis—even came up in a collection of soldiers' letters from the Eastern Front being prepared for publication at that time.[95]

On July 9, 1941, Goebbels noted with satisfaction that his campaign had not failed to have an effect on high-ranking officers who had at first looked at "Operation Barbarossa" rather skeptically: "There is no one prominent in the Wehrmacht today who is not grateful to the Führer for having taken upon himself the responsibility for the war in the East, and for having struck at the right time, without waiting until the enemy attacked the Reich. In view of the horrendous atrocities the Bolsheviks have committed, and also because of the past history of this political trash which virtually cries out to heaven, no quarter will be shown in the East."[96] This view of the generals was apparently quite realistic. Many conservative officers, posted as commanders on the Eastern Front, issued orders similar to Stülpnagel's. Equating Jewry with Bolshevism was an obvious notion for them, and it governed their actions. Killing Jews in order to strike at Communism was the murderous but logical consequence of that. At the same time they didn't have to perceive the murder of the Jews as genocide, but could see it as a "strategic measure." This made it easier for them to deceive themselves into thinking that the disappearance of the Jewish population brought them closer to a military goal that they shared with Hitler: the annihilation of Communism.

INTERPRETING THE ZŁOCZÓW PHOTOGRAPHS

Some new photographs that were presented in the course of the critique of the exhibit or which turned up during a review of these criticisms have made it possible to interpret several photos that were previously not identified and to assign them a place in the sequence of events. The last German version of the exhibition shows a total of eight photographs from Złoczów, which were explained in the relevant caption. In the English-language version of the catalogue seven of these eight pictures are similarly arranged.[97] The nine pivotal photos of the sixteen known to exist of the Złoczów massacre are interpreted below in detail, including the respective history of their origins, documentation, and publication details.

Jews exhuming victims of the NKVD

Sources for Figure 1

1 GARF—State Archive of the Russian Federation, Moscow. Caption: "The Town Commander of Odessa, February 17, 1945. To the Chairman of the Special State Commission. I enclose two photos that were

Figure 1

found in July 1944 on a German soldier who was killed near Pila-
Podljaska, to the west of the city of Brest. From all appearances, the people in the photo are military people or civilians who were shot."
2 Yad Vashem, Jerusalem. Caption: "Lvov, Field with Jews near
corpses."
3 Yivo Institute for Jewish Research, New York.
4 Archiwum Wschodnie, Warsaw, photograph number 823. Caption:
"Soviet Crimes."

Reproductions of Figure 1

1 *Deutsche Chronik,* p. 394.[98] "In Winniza, victims [Soviet Jews] scoop
out their own graves with their bare hands."
2 Catalogue for the Wehrmacht exhibition, "Vernichtungskrieg," 1st
ed., p. 204, fig. 20. Caption: "Locality unknown."
3 Klee, Dreßen, and Rieß, *Schöne Zeiten* (Good Old Days),[99] p. 60.
Caption: "Lithuania, summer 1941. Jewish men and women are forced
to excavate a mass grave in a wooded section; in the foreground, Jews
who have been shot."
4 Catalogue for the Wehrmacht exhibition "The German Army and
Genocide," p. 195, fig. 31.
5 Musial, *Bilder,* p. 569.

The site was identified by eyewitnesses.[100] The individuals at top left must be Jews who are piling corpses of NKVD victims taken from a mass grave in the orchard of the Złoczów citadel, and laying them out—not yet in order—in the foreground, right. Since the grave is still relatively shallow, the photo could have been taken at the beginning of the exhumation on July 3, 1941. The photo in Musial, *Bilder*, shows the same subject and is probably a copy made from the same negative.

Sources for Figure 2

From the private collection of General Otto Korfes, Berlin (photographed by a soldier in then Colonel Korfes's regiment).

Figure 2

Reproductions of Figure 2

1 Catalogue, "The German Army and Genocide, p. 195, fig. 34.

2 The caption in the Korfes biography by Sigrid Wegner-Korfes reads "Mass murder of Jews, citadel of Złoczów, early July 1941." (Wegner-Korfes 1994, p. 91).

In General Korfes's private photo album three copies of this photo in postcard format are pasted on the front and back of cardboard. The sheet obviously comes from an extensive album and bears the page assignments "14–15" and "p. 15b." The sheets carry inscriptions in two different handwritings. In the smaller, more flowing handwriting it originally said under the two "14–15" photos "Złoczów citadel, July 3–5, 1941"; with cross-outs and additions this was later changed to "Złoczów, early July 1941." The photo of the Jews in the pit labeled "p. 15b" is captioned "Złoczów July 4, 1942" (obviously "42" was written in error instead of "41"). The second handwriting, according to Sigrid Wegner-Korfes, was that of Otto Korfes's widow, who supplemented this caption with information from her husband: "Mass murder of Jews, citadel, Jews murdered by the SS. Through his intervention, Otto was able to prevent further murders. What happened after the withdrawal of his Regiment?" This photograph was taken somewhat later, either late in the afternoon of July 3, when the mass grave was already almost empty, or the morning of July 4, when the killing resumed. It shows Jews standing in the pit; on the ground is the corpse of an NKVD victim, the body swollen as a result of decomposition. This condition is characteristic and can also be seen in other photos.

Murdered Jews lying next to bodies they have exhumed

Sources for Figure 3

Private collection of General Otto Korfes, Berlin (photographed by a soldier in the regiment of then Colonel Korfes).

Reproductions of Figure 3

Catalogue, "The German Army and Genocide," p. 195, fig. 32.

The exhumation is now finished. At the right in the middle distance: The exhumed bodies have been laid out side by side for identification.

Figure 3

Some are barefoot, their clothes have faded to a light gray without contrasts. The bodies of Jewish forced laborers who have since been killed are lying from front left and up to the pit in the left middle distance. They are lying on the ground as though thrown there any which way; their clothing still looks fresh and shows distinct contrasts. Contrast is a characteristic feature important in the identification of these photographs.[101]

Figure 4

Exhumed NKVD victims
laid out side by side for identification

Sources for Figure 4

Private collection of General Otto Korfes, Berlin (photographed by a soldier in the regiment of then Colonel Korfes).

Reproductions of Figure 4

Catalogue, "The German Army and Genocide," p. 195, fig. 33.

The caption in the biography by Wegner-Korfes reads "Mass murder of Jews, citadel of Złoczów, early July 1941" (Wegner-Korfes 1994, p. 91).

Because of the condition of the corpses (they are swollen, their clothing faded), their precise arrangement, and by comparing this photo with Złoczów-05, it can be assumed that these are not the corpses of Jews but rather of NKVD victims. They have been laid out in rows to be identified by their relatives.

Sources for Figure 5

Russian State Archive for Film and Photo Documents, Krasnogorsk. Caption: "Kiev Area. Soldiers and bodies. Reproduced from photos taken from a German noncommissioned officer, January 1944."

Reproductions of Figure 5

1 Catalogue, "Vernichtungskrieg," 1st ed., p. 205, fig. 30.
2 Catalogue, "The German Army and Genocide," p. 195, fig. 28.

This photograph, which shows only NKVD victims, was part of the exhibit from the start. It was removed from the fourth edition of the German catalogue on the basis of the organizers' previously mentioned research because, according to information from the German publisher, it was technically impossible to compose a series of photos with different captions—as was done in the exhibit and in the American catalogue.

Figure 5

Figure 6

NKVD victims in the foreground,
Jews in the background

Sources for Figure 6

Documentation Archive of the Austrian Resistance (*Dokumentations-archiv des Österreichischen Widerstands*), Vienna, photograph number 9003. Caption: "Concentration camp corpses after liberation as well as the opening of mass graves. (where?)"

The written attribution accompanying this photo in the Documentation Archive of the Austrian Resistance is completely incorrect. The fact that the civilian in the foreground seen walking between corpses—NKVD victims—has tied a cloth over his nose and mouth is an important indication that the smell of corpses pervaded the whole area. In the left background, in the corner between the house and the wall, near three other civilians, one can see corpses piled on top of one another. Everything indicates that this is a different group of corpses, which were not deemed worthy of being "laid out": the victims of the anti-Jewish pogroms. There are two close-up shots of this subject; however, they do not show the rotting corpses of the NKVD victims.

Figure 7

Sources for Figure 7

1 Kraków District Commission, photo number 1398. Caption: "Interior courtyard of the Złoczów citadel, exhumation of NKVD victims, July 1941."[102]

2 Wschodnie Archive.

In the foreground of this photograph one again sees the NKVD victims "laid out" in rows. In the background women are working with wheelbarrows. Evidently they are piling corpses on top of one another in the corner between the house and a fortress wall. These corpses can only be the Jews who were murdered a short while before.[103] The same corpses are also visible in the two photos that follow.

Figure 8

Piled-up corpses of Jews

Sources for Figure 8

1 Russian State Archive for Film and Photographic Documents, Krasnogorsk. Caption: "Kiev district. Soldiers and corpses. Reproduced from
photos seized from a German noncommissioned officer, January 1944."
2 GARF—State Archive of the Russian Federation, Moscow. Caption:
"February 12, 1944. To the Chairman of the Special St[ate] Comm[is-
sion]. I send you herewith photos that were taken from Noncommissioned Officer Richard Worbs (Army Postal Service number p/p 31102)
who was killed near the village of Winograd, and the soldier Heinz
Manke (Army Postal Service number p/p 1951e)."

Reproductions of Figure 8

1 Catalogue, "Vernichtungskrieg," 1st edition, 1996, p. 205, fig. 31.
2 Catalogue, "The German Army and Genocide," p. 195, fig. 30.

Figure 9

Sources for Figure 9

1 Russian State Archive for Film and Photographic Documents, Krasnogorsk. Caption: "Kiev District. Soldiers and corpses. Reproduced from photos seized from a German noncommissioned officer, January 1944."

2 GARF—State Archive of the Russian Federation, Moscow. Caption: "February 12, 1944. To the Chairman of the Special St[ate] Comm[ission]. I am sending you herewith photos taken from Noncommissioned Officer Richard Worbs (Army Postal Service number p/p 31102) who was killed near the village of Winograd, and the soldier Heinz Manke (Army Postal Service number p/p 1951e)."

Reproductions of Figure 9

1 Klee and Dreßen, *Gott mit uns*, p. 51, with the caption: ". . . probably taken in a prisoner of war camp."

2 Catalogue, "Vernichtungskrieg," 1st edition, p. 205, fig. 29.

3 Catalogue, "The German Army and Genocide," p. 195, fig. 29.

The entry for July 3, 1941, in the war journal of the 295th Infantry Division noted that "approximately 900 corpses of Ukrainians murdered by Russians, and of Russians and Jews murdered by Ukrainians" were lying in the citadel. A local eyewitness later recalled that the bodies of the prisoners murdered by the NKVD had been washed and laid out side by side in rows so that they could be identified by relatives. On the other hand, a German officer and his regimental physician recalled that the corpses of the recently murdered Jews were stacked in high piles. On the basis of the information from these three sources the probable interpretation is that these two photographs show dead Jews. Also, the corpses appear fresh and full of contrasts as compared with the corpses identified as victims of the NKVD. The facial features of the visible corpses are still clearly recognizable; there are no traces of distension; the clothing still seems intact and does not appear to be faded.[104]

FROM A CRITICISM OF PICTURES
TO A REVISION OF THE PAST

What I have shown in my analysis of the Złoczów photographs is also valid for the other exhibited pictures that have been criticized. In a few cases the criticism was justified. In considerably more instances, however, the necessary corrections had already been made at the time of their publication. And in most cases there are good if not compelling reasons to reject the critiques. All in all, the controversy about the photos has considerably broadened our view of the circumstances under which these photographs came into being and enriched our knowledge of amateur photography in World War II. This process, however, has not led to an improvement in the exhibit, but rather to its closing. This is an interesting phenomenon. In order to explain it, I must briefly outline the debate that has been raging in Germany about how to deal with the nation's past.

One thing all three of the above-mentioned critics have in common is that they are not content with questioning individual documents. Their objections also target the central thesis of the exhibit, and they do so with arguments that neither correspond to the latest research nor empirically substantiate interpretations that differ from the results of this research. One critic, for instance, claims that within the Wehrmacht only the military police and the secret military police carried out shootings—in other words, only a minute minority—1 percent—of all Wehrmacht soldiers.[105] Another critic insists that the mass murders of Jews

were committed exclusively by Ukrainians without any German participation, and that only those Jews were killed "who had been or were suspected of having been connected with the Soviet system in one way or
another, as functionaries, spies, or other accomplices." [106] And the third
critic complains that historians "speak of the Wehrmacht as a whole"
when, after all, it was made up of almost 18 million individuals, and
thus "innumerable decent soldiers would also see themselves accused
of" these crimes. [107]

What started as a debate about mistakes was now given a definite
twist that turned it into a debate about Germany's past. By proving the
existence of a few errors, the critics seemed to have called into question
the credibility of the exhibit as a whole. [108] For many people the question suddenly no longer seemed to be *how* the Wehrmacht participated in the National Socialist extermination policy, but *whether* it
did *at all*. Even critics who were well disposed to the exhibit began to
doubt that more than an extraordinarily small proportion of the soldiers
could be considered perpetrators. When it came to the Wehrmacht,
hitherto seemingly uncontested positions of research on National Socialism and the Holocaust were suddenly being put to the test again. In
the background was the unspoken claim that, despite their National Socialist past, Germans had a right to see their history as one of achievements and accomplishments without constantly having to think of
Auschwitz. [109]

In recent years an increasing number of people have voiced a similar
uneasiness with the form of the current debate about the National Socialist past. One of these is Rolf-Dieter Müller, a historian in the Research Office for Military History (*Militärgeschichtliches Forschungsamt*) of the Bundeswehr. In his foreword to an anthology about the
Wehrmacht published in 1999, Müller shifts the blame for the mass
murders of Jews to the local Ukrainians: The massacre of Babi Yar, he
wrote, was intentionally provoked by the Red Army through their
mining of the town; the Germans, for their part, merely counted on
Ukrainian anti-Semitism and selected those victims "destined for extermination anyway." Thus the murder of 33,000 human beings is turned
from a state crime into unavoidable fate. [110]

With the expressed intention of putting an end to the public discussion surrounding the participation of the Wehrmacht in National

Socialist crimes, Müller calls upon a concept that Martin Broszat introduced into the historians' controversy in 1985: "historization." But Müller trivializes the concept and uses it merely to take the debate about the Wehrmacht out of the public arena and into the terrain of the historians for their exclusive use as a strictly academic subject: "Our path must lead from the politics of history to historization, and even more directly to scholarship and away from thinking in ideological terms. History belongs in the hands of historians who will approach it with their own tools and their own ways of asking questions."[111] As far as Müller is concerned, any further debate about the Wehrmacht would be superfluous: The crimes of the Wehrmacht leadership are sufficiently well known; one *need not* continue that debate. On the other hand, not enough is yet known about the participation of ordinary soldiers; therefore one *must not* debate that. This is a simple rephrasing of Müller's demand for the historization of the Nazi period. To carry out this demand would result in more than just an undeserved intellectual privilege for the guild of contemporary historians, which in and of itself is presumptuous enough. At the same time, a gag order would be imposed on any individuals recollecting the war, as well as on any "laymen" expressing opinions. Thus the way an entire nation sees and debates its identity would be put on ice.

During the parliamentary recess in the summer of 2000 there was vigorous discussion of Bogdan Musial's book, mentioned several times here. Musial defines the concept of historization even more dubiously than Müller. For him it means the attempt "to understand something from its historical circumstances, to transport oneself into the period, instead of looking down on it from above. What matters is not being absolutely right, but rather to be aware of the facts. Certain events and participants should be judged by seeing them in their own time; that means in the historical context which must be reconstructed for that purpose—and this must be done without the moral superiority to which not a few of those uninvolved and unaffected are prone."[112]

Whether he means by this that a historian must assume the perspective of the National Socialists, his readers do not learn; the unclear formulations leave many interpretations open—which is probably done intentionally with the reading public in mind.

If one believes Musial, then the curators of the Hamburg exhibit have in the past prevented "an objective discussion" about the Wehr-macht in an "opinion war" against the "unteachables." And they suc-ceeded because "the Germans have difficulty in approaching certain things." The prevailing "climate of guilt" still keeps people from dis-cussing "this chapter of contemporary history substantively and objec-tively." According to Musial, the following are among the taboos that were set up in Germany by "so-called efforts to come to terms with the past"—the "moral creed" of the "secular religion" of bringing critical objectivity to the Nazi period: "the taboo against making historical comparisons between National Socialist crimes and other crimes," the taboo against the "thesis of a partial reciprocal effect between Soviet and National Socialist crimes," and the taboo against "presenting Jews as perpetrators."

For Musial, Jews no longer have the privilege of claiming "the role of chief victims," since this applies only "in the context of the National So-cialist period: Of course, in the context of the Soviet crimes, assigning the roles of victims and perpetrators on an ethnic basis is no longer so unequivocal. True, there were Jews among the victims, and yet there were also perpetrators of Jewish origin."[113] Musial defines perpetrators in the Stalinist apparatus in ethnic terms even though he knows that such affiliations didn't matter to the NKVD, either in its selection of employees or in its identification of enemies. This throws significant light on Musial's perceptions. To dispel the suspicion that he is moving the limits of revisionist views considerably forward, Musial hastens to as-sure us in the same article that his purpose is "not to change the per-spective but rather to broaden the perspective."

Such attempts at a revision of the historical picture occur especially frequently with regard to the Bundeswehr. In a review of the anthology Die Wehrmacht: Mythos und Realität (The Wehrmacht: myth and real-ity) that appeared in a magazine published for soldiers, the reviewer considers the same ideas. He demands that historians give a "complete picture" of the Wehrmacht and judge the National Socialist period from "inside." That is why, he says, one must not reconstruct history from the records but from the memories of those who were involved. An understanding of the Wehrmacht is possible only through an under-standing of individual officers and soldiers. Moreover, the period must be understood on in its own terms, which, he says, not all the collaborators in the volume under discussion succeeded in doing. Nevertheless, he says, the book is a counterbalance to "some German" generalizing and defamatory publications. But it was also necessary to deal with the crimes of the opposing side "without immediately being accused of equating [crimes]." [114]

The crimes of the opposing side are also a central theme in Klaus W. Wippermann's review of the same volume. Wippermann is editor of the journal *Aus Politik und Zeitgeschichte* (Politics and Contemporary History), which is published by the *Bundeszentrale für politische Bildung* (Federal Center for Political Education). It is a supplement to the weekly newspaper *Das Parlament* (Parliament). In the debate about the Wehrmacht he finds fault with "a picture of the self and of history that borders on the pathological," whose "most visible presentation," he writes, is to be found in "Mr. Reemtsma's so-called Wehrmacht Exhibit." Whereas he praises the aforementioned foreword by Müller, he reproaches the younger historians in particular, saying that often they did not even strive for the required scholarly differentiation in their contributions. Furthermore, he rails against political correctness, the nursing of guilt, taking the viewpoint of the victim, and making the older generation's war experiences taboo. The one-sidedness of the younger contributors, he says, shows up primarily in their silence about Versailles, in the refusal to consider the claims to power of Germany's European neighbors against Germany including their international law and human rights violations, and in the uncritical way they side with the anti-Hitler coalition, to which, after all, Stalin— except for Hitler the worst criminal of the twentieth century—had also belonged. This, he says, leads them to a sweeping indictment of the "institution of the Wehrmacht," which, in Wippermann's view, apparently took not the slightest part in Hitler's war and extermination policies. [115]

Nowadays such opinions rarely meet with direct contradiction. That is cause for reflection, if not yet for apprehension. Apparently revisionism is on the point of leaving the ghetto of the extreme right and applying for a place in the political center. For several years the exhibit channeled the debate about the crimes of the Wehrmacht and forced those expressing opinions in the mined border area of revisionism to put their cards on the table. To be sure, this caused the oft-lamented politicization of the debate, but it also essentially prevented the revisionists from using the public sphere as a podium for airing their opinions about National Socialism. This obstacle disappeared with the self-imposed scuttling of the exhibit by the director of the Institute for Social Research in Hamburg. Writers who have sometimes represented democratic consensus, but who at other times openly spouted revisionist positions, are becoming increasingly self-assured.

One example of this position of determined ambiguity is Meinrad von Ow, one of the eyewitnesses Bogdan Musial interviewed for his dissertation and the first to publicly question the Złoczów photos. In a newspaper article about the exhibit published in May 2000 he accused the Hamburg Institute for Social Research of "plagiarism, falsification, deception, selective choice of sources and expert witnesses, interference with freedom of research, defamation of critics, and concealment of bias." [116] Those whom he charged with bias were Omer Bartov, Manfred Messerschmidt, and Christian Streit, all members of the exhibit's review commission. A revisionist Web site has a more than twenty-page-long manuscript that presents what, in von Ow's opinion, should be the new evaluation of the Wehrmacht: the Commissar Order did not lead to the murder of commissars; the jurisdictional decree did not mean impunity for German soldiers; the Wehrmacht was not responsible for the deaths of more than 3 million Russian prisoners of war; Wehrmacht leaders avoided corruption by the Nazi regime and were not executors of the extermination policy. In conclusion, von Ow insinuates that not even the police and the SS committed crimes in the occupied territories in the East. [117]

When it comes to dealing with the past, the signs of a change in Germany's mood are unmistakable. But this is not simply about an attempt by conservative and rightist elements to influence the writing of contemporary history and the politics of historical debate. The front lines have become blurred; we are dealing with a complex discourse about the future of the past that is being carried on in public. After the end of military blocs, the reuniting of the two German states, and in view of the foreseeable dying-out of the war generation, there is a new need to secure our national identity. A relearning of history is taking place that is full of contradictions. In part it amounts to reconciling differing, often conflicting memories that overlap and contradict each other and in doing so also knit together divisions among the people of our country: the memories of former officers and ordinary soldiers; of perpetrators, victims, and the diffuse group of those forced to collaborate and to suffer; of the war generation and its children; and finally of East and West Germans. The new view of history that could emerge from this reworking of the past need not signify a return to the denial of National Socialist crimes, something the international research on National Socialism would certainly prevent in any case.

If the comments so far have shown a trend, it is this: A strict concept of crimes now recognizes only autonomous crimes and excludes those that were not committed on orders from above; that is, outrageous crimes by individuals—which "can happen in any army." In addition, crimes by allied armies and local auxiliary troops will no longer be attributed to the Wehrmacht. Violations of the conventions of war and human rights laws committed by the Wehrmacht in cooperation with the SS, police, and SD are chiefly attributed to the latter. But even there the tendency is to take responsibility from the lower ranks and shift it to the higher echelons.

Even if no one so far has demanded that victimology be examined for its usefulness as a subject complementary to the study of contemporary history, the share certain victim groups had in their own murder will surely be carefully studied. This channeling of responsibilities will certainly be embedded in a comprehensive antitotalitarian perspective: Whether the extermination actions in the East are balanced against the crimes of Stalinism or are simply put in context, these two options do not necessarily have to lead to different conclusions. Summing up, this trend can be reduced to the formula "Speak openly about the crimes, but be silent about the perpetrators."

Many contemporaries seem to be intellectually and emotionally overwhelmed by the fact that the National Socialist chapter of history is full of ambivalences that, for many generations to come, can be approached only with critical detachment. They comprise the audience for the historians and other intellectuals who are now demanding that the fractures in German contemporary history be made painless and invisible. Meanwhile, a great deal is expected of the Hamburg Institute for Social Research: It is supposed to become the driving force for a new antitotalitarian way of dealing with the past that will leave behind the "culture of guilt" of the '68 Generation.[118] At the same time, the Institute for Contemporary History and the Research Office for Military History are getting ready to regain their lost hegemony over the interpretation of Wehrmacht and Nazi crimes. It remains to be seen how all this will affect the long-nurtured plans for a completely new version of the exhibit about the crimes of the Wehrmacht.

Chapter Seven

Nazi Photographs in Post-Holocaust Art

Gender as an Idiom of Memorialization

MARIANNE HIRSCH

... he raised his eyes and looked at me. . . . that look was not one between two men; and if I had known how completely to explain the nature
of that look, which came as if across the window of an aquarium between
two beings who live in different worlds, I would also have explained the
essence of the great insanity of the third Germany.

Primo Levi [1]

Photography was a routine part of the extermination process in Nazi
Germany.

Sybil Milton [2]

I f you had to name one picture that signals and evokes the Holocaust
in the contemporary cultural imagination it might well be the picture of the little boy in the Warsaw ghetto with his hands raised (Figure
1). The pervasive role this photograph has come to play is indeed astounding. It is not an exaggeration to say that, having assumed the archetypal role of Jewish (and universal) victimization, the boy in the
Warsaw ghetto has become the poster child for the Holocaust. [3] In
Lawrence Langer's terms "the most famous photograph to emerge from
the Holocaust" has appeared in Holocaust films, novels and poems, and,

Figure 1. From the Stroop report on the destruction of the Warsaw ghetto. (Photograph courtesy of the United States Holocaust Memorial Museum Photo Archives.)

almost obsessively, on the covers of brochures advertising Holocaust histories, teaching aids, and popular books.[4] It serves as the cover image not only of such popular publications as *The Jewish Holocaust for Beginners* or the CD-ROM Holocaust history *Lest We Forget*, but also of recent scholarly texts.[5] Its international reach and recognizability is further emphasized by its prominent place on the cover of Yad Vashem's primary English-language historical booklet, *The Holocaust.* The photograph was featured in Alain Resnais's 1956 *Night and Fog*, Ingmar Bergmann's 1966 *Persona*, and in 1990 it became the subject of a documentary video examining the contention of Holocaust survivor Tsvi Nussbaum that he is the boy with his hands up. It was also the catalyst for Jaroslaw Rymkiewicz's novel *The Final Station: Umschlagplatz*, originally published in Poland in 1988,[6] and it inspired a number of poets and visual artists such as Yala Korwin, Samuel Bak, and Judy Chicago.

The picture's well-known history, however, remains mostly invisible in its contemporary representations, representations that actually enable viewers to forget, or to ignore, its troubling source. The picture of the little boy was originally included in a report by Major General

Jürgen Stroop, commander of the operation to liquidate the Warsaw ghetto. Entitled "Es gibt keinen jüdischen Wohnbezirk in Warschau mehr!" (The Jewish quarter of Warsaw is no more!),[7] the report collected the daily communiqués on the progress of the operation that were teletyped from Warsaw to Friedrich Wilhelm Krueger, Higher SS and Police Leader East in Kraków. The *Bildbericht*, consisting of 54 photos, was added to the communiqués and the whole was presented to Himmler as a memento. In the image, the young boy stands among a group of Jews herded out of underground bunkers toward the *Umschlagplatz* where they would await deportation. Surrounded by soldiers with pointed machine guns, they are photographed in the most vulnerable of poses. This photographic addition to the record of the ghetto's liquidation shows more than the details of roundup and deportation: It can show the particular ways that Jews were overpowered and humiliated by their captors. Stroop's caption, never included in contemporary reproductions of the image, reads: "Mit Gewalt aus Bunkern herausgeholt" (Removed from the ghetto bunkers by force). This photo thus illustrates well Sybil Milton's contention, cited in the epigraph to this essay, that "photography was a routine part of the extermination process in Nazi Germany." It also illustrates the broken look that shapes photography in the context of an eliminationist racism, a look that Primo Levi tries to understand when he faces a Nazi official during his chemistry examination in Auschwitz-Buna, "which came as if across the window of an aquarium between two beings who live in different worlds."

The little boy's picture is a perpetrator photograph, taken by perpetrators as an integral part of the machinery of destruction, and it can help us to understand the particularities of perpetrator images. But the enormous cultural attraction to it, the obsessive way that it appears just about everywhere these days, enables us to address a different question as well. How have perpetrator images — images shaped by the broken look Levi describes, and evidence of photography's implication in the death machine — come to play an important, even a prevalent role in the cultural act of memorializing the victims? How have contemporary artists — even Jewish artists of the second generation — been able to incorporate them so widely into their memorial work?

This paper concerns the politics of retrospective witnessing, the politics of the act of appropriating and recontextualizing archival images

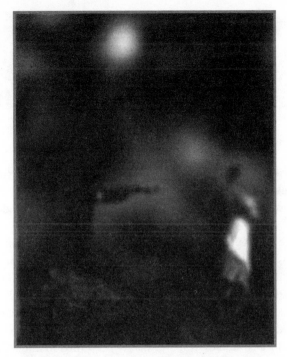

Figure 2. David Levinthal, from "Mein Kampf." (Courtesy
of the artist.)

in post-Shoah memorial texts. I will argue that if perpetrator images can
mediate the visual knowledge of those who were not there, it is only because their contemporary reproductions mobilize some very powerful
idioms that obscure their devastating history and redirect the genocidal
gaze that shaped them. In order to look closely at some of these mitigating idioms, I will examine several specific Nazi photographs
and their reproductions by contemporary artists: the little boy image,
several images of *Einsatzgruppen* killings in the East (Figure 2), and an
image of the execution of the famous partisan from Minsk, Masha
Bruskina (Figure 3).[8] The re-use of these images in contemporary works
serves to illustrate one such idiom particularly well: the *infantilization*
and *feminization* of victims and the concomitant *hyper-masculinization* and thus *depersonalization* of perpetrators. By making gender a determining if hidden idiom of memoralization, these artists, however
unwittingly, mythologize the images they use, obscure their sources,

Figure 3. Nancy Spero, "Masha Bruskina," from "The Torture of Women."
(Courtesy of the artist.)

and thus allow them to become appropriable. It is precisely this absence of mitigating recontextualizations, I will suggest, that fueled the controversy surrounding the exhibition "The German Army and Genocide."

Before developing these points, I would like to comment on the implications of highlighting gender in a reading of how these Nazi photographs are recirculated in post-Shoah art. In the last twenty years, feminists have complained about the overwhelmingly masculine story that has come down to us from the Holocaust, and have tried to unearth the forgotten and ignored stories of women. Thus, where gender has entered Holocaust studies, it has primarily been used as a lens through which to understand the particularities of women's testimonies and memoirs. I wish instead to explore the rhetoric and the politics of memory and representation. I see gender as a vehicle that mediates the ways certain images have been able to circulate in the visual culture of the postmemorial generation. A feminist analysis can thus illuminate the structure of memory, what stories are told, and what images are seen, as well as how those stories are told and how those images are constructed.[9] An analysis of gender is especially important in relation to a story as overwhelmingly masculine as that of the crimes of the Wehrmacht and other armed forces. At the same time, this essay illustrates another trend in recent feminist scholarship—the acknowledgment that, to be illuminating, gender as an analytic category need not radically supersede other categories of analysis. But neither can our understanding of the rhetoric and the politics of postmemorial representation be adequate without a gender analysis.[10] As we shall see, the more sophisticated our analysis of gender dynamics, the more responsible and subtle we can be in our memorial work.

PERPETRATOR IMAGES AND
THE NAZI GAZE

Most contemporary viewers confronted with images from the Holocaust do not readily distinguish their source or the context of their production. Indeed, in the vast archive of photographic images that have come down to us from the Holocaust (historian Sybil Milton calculated the figure at 2 million in the mid 1980s, before the opening of the Soviet archives and before the massive collections undertaken more recently) this information is often difficult to detect. Many images appear in collections with poor labeling and, when they are reproduced, some are identified by their present owner rather than the date and place of their production. Contemporary viewers tend to know a few images repeated over and over in different contexts and used more for their symbolic or affective than for their evidentiary or informational power. All images associated with the Holocaust, moreover—whether they are prewar images of destroyed Jewish communities, or images of bulldozers burying bodies at the moment of liberation—are marked by our retrospective knowledge of the total death that divides the people marked for extermination from us as retrospective viewers.[11] This knowledge shapes our viewing and thus one could say that the photographer's identity is immaterial.

And yet I want to argue here that the identity of the photographer—perpetrator, victim, bystander, or liberator—is indeed a determining, if often unacknowledged, element in the photograph's production, and that, as a result, it engenders distinctive ways of seeing and, indeed, a distinctive textuality. Perpetrator photos are ruled by what I have elsewhere termed a "Nazi gaze" that deeply shatters the visual field and profoundly reorients the basic structures of photographic looking.[12] These photos are fundamentally shaped by the history of their production and, since for many images that history is coming to be more thoroughly documented, its erasure in their current recirculation is extremely problematic.

There are, of course, many different kinds of perpetrator images, and many different kinds of uses to which they have been or can be put. The well-documented photographs I am looking at in this essay—all frontal images of victims looking at executioners in which the photographer, the perpetrator, and the spectator share the same space of looking—

illustrate particularly well the structure of the genocidal gaze of the
Nazi death machine. Thus, in the Warsaw ghetto image, guns are pointing at the boy from the back and side, even as the camera records the
encounters between perpetrators and victims. The camera thus embodies the gaze of the perpetrator who stands in a place identical with the
weapon of roundup and execution: it mirrors, head-on, the most visible
soldier's gun. This structure suggests, disturbingly, a conflation between
camera and weapon that constituted, until the 1980s, a dominant view
of the power differential between the photographer and his subject. Although more recent theories of photography have stressed instead the
multiplicity of looks structuring a photographic image, contesting the
idea of the monolithic and deadly power of the photographic act,
the use of photography in the context of Nazi genocide certainly recalls
this equation.[13] Thus the act of photographing the violent evacuation
of the ghetto and of using these humiliating images to illustrate the report merely underscores the cruelty and violence perpetrated by the SS.
The picture of the Warsaw boy and his compatriots, like all perpetrator
images, is deeply implicated in Nazi photographic practices.[14] It is evidence not only of the perpetrator's deed but also of the desire to flaunt
that deed. The Stroop report, for example, was just that: a letter addressed to Himmler, a gift of joyous and victorious violence. The act of
photographing the roundup is like the exclamation point in the title of
the report "The Jewish quarter of Warsaw is no more!" It is a sign of excess, connecting the perpetrator's gaze to the perpetrator's deed. Thus,
when we as spectators confront perpetrator images, we look at the
image as the implicit Nazi viewers did, under the sign of that exclamation point. What is often most astounding about perpetrator photographs is not what they show but that they even exist. That is, in fact, the
effect of the Wehrmacht exhibition and perhaps the cause of the controversy surrounding it. Here the identity of the photographer is in no
way ambiguous: the images included in the exhibit are clear and un-
mitigated manifestations of a Nazi gaze.

If, as Susan Sontag has so powerfully said, "all photographs are *memento mori*," then the negotiation between life and death is fundamental to the temporality of the photographic look.[15] Photographs freeze
one moment in time and if, as Roland Barthes has said, the photograph
proves the "having-been-there" of the subject, its past, then the viewer
situates herself in two presents—the moment of looking and the mo-

ment when the picture was taken. The power of the photograph derives from the effort, in looking at the person depicted, to reanimate the past by undoing the finality of the photographic take. The work of looking consists in the bodily act of connecting the past with the present. The retrospective irony of every photograph, made more poignant if death separates the two presents, consists precisely in the simultaneity of this effort and the consciousness of its impossibility. As we look at photographic images, we hope nothing less than to undo the progress of time.[16]

But in the context of the "total death" of Nazi genocide and its destruction not only of individuals but of an entire culture such an act of undoing seems doomed, and the photograph's finality hopelessly irrevocable. No retrospective irony can redeem or humanize the images produced in the context of Nazi genocide. The images can signify nothing less than the lethal intent that caused them—and that they helped carry out. The boy is held at gunpoint by a soldier who, with his helmet and uniform, is an embodiment of violent intent. The camera gaze mirrors the machine gun and announces the gas chamber. A system that reduces humans to "pieces" and ashes through mechanized genocide creates a visual field in which no look between perpetrator and victim can be exchanged or returned. The subjects looking at the camera are also victims looking at soldiers whose guns help herd them off to trains and extermination camps. As they face the camera, they are shot before they are shot.

But this image also qualifies such a monolithic definition of an overpowering determining gaze by showing that the perpetrators are *individual* soldiers, each with his own embodied, *individual look*, motivated by *individual* as well as collective desire. The notion of a *Nazi gaze* that is shaped by the forces of totalitarianism must not obscure the *looks* that operate under its shadow: the force of individual responsibility, the personal, human encounter between photographer and subject, executioner and victim. Of course, as Primo Levi makes clear in the epigraphical passage in this essay, the looks exchanged between victim and perpetrator in a racist Nazi universe are not subject to the same conventions as the looks of ordinary human interaction. And yet, if we discuss or reproduce perpetrator images in our memorial work, we have to acknowledge both the massive genocidal program of which they were a part and the individual choices that enabled the killing machine to function.[17]

I believe that this totalized notion of a Nazi gaze, qualified through a recognition of the individual soldier's broken look, helps to define the character of perpetrator images. The murderous quality embedded within them remains, even fifty years later, dangerously real. It continues to disable the retrospective irony that is so fundamental to the act of looking at photographs. Perpetrator images carry this excessive history—this double act of shooting—with them. How then has the picture of the boy in the Warsaw ghetto been able to assume its pervasive memorializing role? What enables viewers to identify with the boy despite the fact that his raised hands have become the sign of utter unredeemable annihilation?

INFANTILIZING/FEMINIZING
THE VICTIM

The most common reproductive strategy used by contemporary post-Shoah artists and publishers is cropping. Most reproductions and recontextualizations of the boy's picture not only leave out but actually deny the original context of its production by focusing on the boy himself, isolating him from the community within which he was embedded, and removing the perpetrators from view. They thus universalize the victim as innocent child and, through a false sense of intimacy fostered by the close-up, reduce the viewer to an identificatory look that disables critical faculties. If anyone else is included, it is usually the one soldier standing behind the boy, aiming his gun at the boy's back. This is how, for example, the boy appears in a painting by Rebecca Shope that is on the cover of *The Jewish Holocaust for Beginners.* Victim and perpetrator are enclosed in a large frame; the actual street scene is erased and all that remains of the Warsaw context is a mythic encounter between innocence and evil that removes the picture from both its greater and its more specific historical context.

Cropping is also a strategy used in a 1995 series of studies, mainly self-portraits, by child-survivor artist Samuel Bak, which are part of a larger and extremely successful project entitled "Landscapes of Jewish Experience" (Figure 4).[18] Bak best illustrates the boy's ready availability for viewer projection and identification. In these images the little boy's face is replaced by a number of other faces, including that of the artist himself. Bak multiplies the image and transposes it into a variety of well-

Figure 4. Samuel Bak, "Study F" from "Landscapes of Jewish Experience." (Courtesy of the Pucker Gallery.)

known iconographic motifs, ranging from the crucifixion to the felled tree of life to more specific representations of concentration camp life—the striped uniform, the essential shoes. Like his other images in this series, these "landscapes of Jewish experience" are ruined landscapes, populated only by the most obvious symbols of Jewish life and death—the star, the tree, the candle, the tomb, and, surprisingly, by Christian motifs as well—outspread arms, a cross and nails. The image is completely decontextualized, perpetrators are invisible, and thus the viewer is sutured into the image through a look of empathic identification with the archetypal victim. Bak's narrative becomes a mythic narrative of "Jewish experience" rather than the particular narrative of the Warsaw ghetto, or even the Shoah.

Like Bak, the Polish protagonist of Rymkiewicz's *The Final Station: Umschlagplatz* identifies with the boy: " 'You're tired,' I say to Artur. 'It must be very uncomfortable standing like that with your arms in the air. I know what we'll do. I'll lift my arms up now, and you put yours down. They may not notice. But wait, I've got a better idea. We'll both stand with our arms up.' " These are the empathic words of a fictional character, but even the Yugoslav writer Aleksandar Ţisma, himself a survivor, asked by the newspaper *Die Zeit* to send in a photo of himself that holds some particular meaning for him, sent this picture instead: "There are no photos of me that I connect to an important memory," he writes. "I send you instead the photograph of another that I actually consider as my own. . . . I immediately saw that the boy with his hands up in the right-hand corner of the picture is me. It's not only that he looks like me, but that he expresses the fundamental feelings of my growing up: the impotence in the face of rules, of humanity, of reality. . . . I recognize myself in him, in him alone."[19] Again Ţisma emphasizes the general—impotence in the face of rules—rather than a more specific history that, after all, he shares with the boy. Identification in itself need not necessarily be a form of decontextualization but, in these particular cases, the discourse of identification simplifies and distorts, becoming so encompassing as to foreclose a more oblique, critical, or resistant retrospective look. Neither does identification need to be as transparent or projective as it seems to be in these examples. Indeed those of us who have been working on the politics of postmemory have been trying to define a more complicated postmemorial aesthetic based on a mediated, non-appropriative, indirect form of identification that would clarify the *limits* of retrospective understanding, rather than make the past too easily available.

Bak's dozen or so studies and these other fictional and autobiographical acts of what one might call "transparent" or "projective" identification clarify some of the mediating discourses that have allowed this image to occupy the role of "most famous Holocaust photograph": It is of a child who "performs" his innocence by raising his hands, and it is of a child who is not visibly hurt or harmed or suffering. Images of children are so open to projection that they might be able to circumvent even the murderousness of the Nazi gaze. Geoffrey Hartman's suggestion that this image emblematizes Nazism as the loss of childhood itself underscores the power of the figure this image embodies, the figure of infantilization.[20] In the post-Holocaust generation we tend to see every victim as a helpless child and, as Froma Zeitlin has noted in a recent article on post-Holocaust literature, we enact a fantasy of rescuing one child as an ultimate form of resistance to the totality of genocidal destruction.[21] Images of children lend themselves to universalization. Less marked by the particularities of identity, children invite multiple projections. Their photographic images, especially when cropped and decontextualized, elicit an affiliative as well as a protective spectatorial look marked by these investments, a look that promotes forgetting, even denial. To achieve a more triangulated and non-appropriative encounter with images of children, they need to preserve some of their visual layers and their historical specificity.[22]

Judy Chicago's *Holocaust Project* incorporates the boy's cropped picture into a panel entitled "Im/Balance of Power" which illustrates well the gendered dimensions of the victims' infantilization (Figure 5).[23]

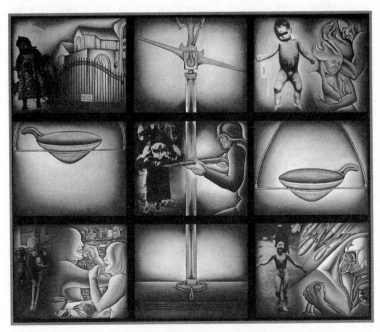

Figure 5. Judy Chicago, "Im/Balance of Power," from the *Holocaust Project*. (Courtesy of Through the Flower.)

Chicago surrounds the boy with other images of hurt or threatened or hungry children. The boy from Warsaw is at the center of the scale that will measure a universalized "im/balance" of power, and he shares the center panel with a caricatured Nazi soldier who, in Chicago's reversal, points his enormous gun right at the boy's chest. The boy is the only European child—the starving children in the other panels are Asian, African, or Latin American. In the lower right-hand corner, diagonally below the Warsaw boy, is the famous photograph of a Vietnamese girl burned by napalm, naked and running; in Chicago's reappropriation, painted bombs point directly at her head. Chicago's crude iconography shows here that infantilization is also, structurally, a figure of feminization: the running girl is overpowered not only by the crassly phallic bombs, but also by a cartoon figuration of a masked soldier who wears a badge marked "AGGRESS. . . ." Similarly, on the back cover of the Yad Vashem brochure, for example, there are three boxes with close-ups: the little boy's face, and the faces of two of the women in the image. If the victim is infantilized, then the perpetrator is hyper-masculinized, represented as the ultimate in masculine, mechanized, supra-human evil. In inscribing the perpetrator in as exaggerated a way as she does, Chicago also points to his absence in the cropped representations of the boy. In spite of her stated desire to raise the world's consciousness about the powerlessness and neglect suffered by today's children, she invites viewers to assume the subject position of victim, since it is the only position available. In inscribing themselves only into the place of the victims who are both infantilized and feminized, viewers are made to participate in the hyper-masculinization and depersonalization of perpetrators that allows for an erasure of the agency of perpetration—of the individual soldier who aims his gun, who takes a picture, who looks at it afterwards. The profound impact that the machinery of destruction has had on how we see is mitigated in Chicago's troubling representations. Her naive representation of children's images explains the despair she describes in her journal as she works on this panel.

But images separated from their original context can function on many different levels. It may not be surprising that Langer's "most famous photograph" of the Holocaust is an image from the Warsaw ghetto. The name Warsaw is associated with heroism and resistance and this boy can thus be both the ultimate victim and the archetypal hero; he can be feminized in the visual image even as he is remasculinized for those who know his connection to Warsaw. This image is reenacted in an Israeli play by Hanokh Levin entitled *HaPatriot*. Here a little Arab boy, Mahmud, stands with his hands up as an Israeli soldier holds a gun to his head. The soldier, Lahav, addresses his own mother as he aims the revolver: "He will avenge your blood and the blood of our murdered family, as then, mother, when your little brother stood alone in front of the German at night. . . ." [24] In this complex and politically charged passage the boy can be both victim and hero but the gender roles are clearly differentiated: perpetrators, whether Nazi or Israeli, are male whereas victims, whether Jewish or Palestinian, are children of grieving mothers. If the memory of the Holocaust is invoked to shape contemporary politics, it is by relying on familiar gender stereotypes that are facilitated by the use of readily available archetypal imagery.

"MEIN KAMPF"

The oppositionally gendered politics of representation becomes clearer still in the work of the American artist David Levinthal in his series "Mein Kampf" (Figure 6). [25] Levinthal is known for his installations of toys photographed with a 20 x 24 Polaroid Land Camera that, when the aperture is wide open, yields glossy, shallow-plane, blurry, and ambiguous images. In photographing toys, Levinthal exposes cultural myths and stereotypes. Searching for authentic Nazi toys in amateur shops, Levinthal came upon dolls of Hitler, of Nazi soldiers and Reichsbahn cars. In "Mein Kampf" he reenacted perpetrator images, some of which remain faithful to their originals, while others are reinterpreted or reimagined.

Most troubling, perhaps, are his reenacments of the frequently reproduced photographs of *Einsatzkommando* executions in Poland, Russia, Latvia, and Lithuania that show groups of victims, women and men, often undressed, sometimes cradling babies or small children, facing the camera just seconds before they are to be put to death. In the original photographs, the camera is located in the same place as the executioner, and perpetrators are visible in the image primarily through this disturbing co-implication. The presence of these images on museum walls and in Holocaust textbooks is troubling, especially since in most of these contemporary contexts, the role of photography in the act of genocide remains implicit and unexamined. In the context of the

Figure 6. David Levinthal, from "Mein Kampf." (Courtesy of the artist.)

Wehrmacht exhibition, in large part composed of such images, the context is indeed hyper-visible, and carefully elucidated, as is the pervasive presence and determinative role of the camera in the process of destruction. The blunt exposure such images get in the exhibition and their meticulous contextualization offer an important counterpoint to their reappearance in the work of contemporary second-generation artists such as Levinthal. Here they are made more tolerable through various strategies of mythification and mitigation.

Perpetrators are represented in each of Levinthal's pictures; they are never absent. And the victims are there, in their utter vulnerability and nakedness. Thus, if Levinthal's images circumvent the full impact of the Nazi gaze it seems to be primarily through their aestheticization since, in other ways, his use of perpetrator images appears to offer a counter-example to the work of Bak or Chicago. Unlike the writers and historians using the little-boy image, David Levinthal is as interested in perpetrators as he is in victims and, in reenacting the encounter between victim and executioner, he certainly underscores both the reality of the crime and the excess performed in photographing it. Levinthal's images do not enable us to forget that exclamation point in the title of Stroop's report: in fact, in his restagings, soldiers are moved to the front of the image and their guns, often the only items in clear focus, are pointing right at the victims.

In James Young's reading of "Mein Kampf," Levinthal's work is significant for post-Holocaust representation because it acknowledges that "when he sets out 'to photograph' the Holocaust, . . . he takes pictures of *his* Holocaust experiences—i.e. recirculated images of the Holocaust."[26] For Levinthal, the pictures are "intentionally ambiguous to draw the viewer in so that you make your own story."[27] The pictures' composition ensures that this intense imaginary projection on the part of viewers includes the role of the perpetrator as well as the victim. But in shooting the pictures, Levinthal himself occupies the place of the Nazi photographers; as in his title "Mein Kampf" he does not hesitate to claim the most abject space in this representational structure. As Levinthal retakes the image of the Nazi photographer and reenacts the perpetrator gaze, we as his viewers are invited to stand in the space of the Nazi viewers who were the addressees of the image. That space is disturbing in a number of ways. Looking is necessarily and, I believe intentionally, an act of revictimizing the victims, however miniaturized they are. The Nazi toy soldiers, like all such simulacra, are, like Chicago's constructions, hyper-masculinized—they are de-individuated, generalized, clichéd amalgamations of body and weapon. The soldiers are seen from the back as, disturbingly, we look over their shoulders. As recirculated toys they can embody the totalizing quality of the Nazi gaze, but they can also mitigate any consciousness we might have of the individual soldier's act of murder.

To stage the victims, Levinthal used naked sex dolls made in Japan for the European market. These busty female dolls with their nipples showing are the perfect demonstration for what happens in the insane logic of such representations: As the victims are infantilized and feminized, the perpetrators are hyper-masculinized and de-realized. In the encounter of such figures with one another, the radical power difference between them thus becomes eroticized and sexualized. As an alibi, and in response to James Young's and Art Spiegelman's personal objections to these female dolls, Levinthal maintains that he is only repeating the eroticization of Nazi murder in the popular imagination (*Night Porter, Sophie's Choice, The White Hotel, Schindler's List*).[28]

Levinthal is making us conscious of the uncomfortably tainted position we always occupy when we view images photographed by perpetrators. His photographs not only point out the defining role of gender in all of these relationships, but they reveal how gender can serve as a means of forgetting. Thus I would argue that his critique, or his reenactment of the perpetrator-photographer's position—for critique and reenactment are never easily distinguishable—is also a form of obfuscation. If there is blurring in these blurred images, it is the blurring between sexualization and "racialization": To the postmemorial viewer these *female* victims may have maintained their sexuality, but to the murderers, these *Jewish* victims were no more than vermin to be added to the statistics of extermination, indistinguishable by gender, class, age, or other identity markers. David Levinthal, in eroticizing the power relationship between perpetrator and victim, is also "deracializing" it. And in subjecting the scene of execution to a pornographic gaze, he moves it into a different register of looking altogether, circumventing the murderousness of the Nazi gaze that shapes the pictures on which his work is based.

Levinthal says, and surprisingly Young agrees, that sexual humiliation in the victims' last moments was one of the ways Nazis dehumanized their victims. Certainly Jewish women were more sexually vulnerable than men, and there was rape and sexual abuse in the ghettos and camps. (These are often repressed stories that feminist scholars have only begun to recover.) Yet there is no evidence in anything that I have read about the *Einsatzkommando* killings in particular that the killers in any way recognized their victims' sexuality, or that there was anything sexual in these murders. In fact, the opposite seems to have been the case: the victims were *dehumanized* precisely by being robbed of any subjectivity and thus also of their sexuality. Nazi killers were not perverts but "ordinary men" whose murderous work became routine.[29] In a recent article, "Pornographizations of Fascism," the art historian Silke Wenk analyzes contemporary visualizations of National Socialist crimes. She relies on Ruth Klüger's analysis of sentimentality, kitsch, and pornography as defenses against the memory of past violence and trauma. For Wenk, sexuality and perversion offer familiar explanatory paradigms, and thus pornography can mitigate the anxiety and discomfort caused by atrocity photos: It is a form of universalization, a transformation of discomfort into cliché. Femininity functions as myth or fetish for the threatened retrospective witness.[30]

Levinthal's hyper-masculinized and hyper-feminized figures and his pornographic gaze thus allow for much obfuscation and appropriation. A responsible and ethical post-Holocaust discourse needs to enable us to think about perpetators and victims in ways that take their relationship out of the realm of caricature and cliché. Images that enable us to read both perpetrator and victim, both gender and race, may not be as easily appropriable as these have become. Memorial work that is historically informed as well as self-conscious about its dynamics of gender and power would be more cautious about using perpetrator images than some of these contemporary artists have been.

BEYOND CLICHÉ

I would like to end these reflections with an alternative use of perpetrator images. American artist Nancy Spero's installations are based on the photographs of the execution of the seventeen-year old Russian partisan Masha Bruskina, the heroine of Minsk (Figure 7). The eight surviving archival photos of Masha were taken by a Lithuanian battalion member collaborating with the Germans. On October 26, 1941, Masha was one of three Communist resisters who were paraded through the streets of Minsk and publicly hanged. The gruesome photos of their humiliation and execution were made public just after the war, but only the two men were identified; the girl was denied an identity, and especially a Jewish identity, until 1968 when the Russian filmmaker Lev Arkadyev initiated an investigation about the "unknown girl." Eyewitnesses provided detailed descriptions and stories about this Jewish seventeen-year-old, who lightened her hair and changed her name so that her Jewish identity would not interfere with her resistance work. They not only identified Masha but told about her remarkable demeanor on the day of her execution.[31]

Spero has included the execution photos in a number of installations that are part of her series "The Torture of Women" and in work that focuses exclusively on the images and the story of Masha Bruskina.[32] The installations are built around the archival perpetrator photos, but here the images are presented through various alienation

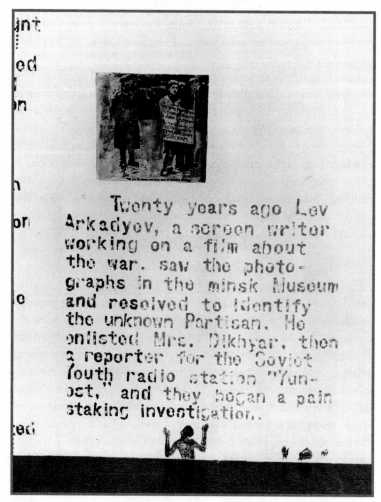

Figure 7. Nancy Spero, "Masha Bruskina," from "The Torture of Women."
(Courtesy of the artist.)

devices: they are surrounded with text, with other related images, with
figures from Spero's large corpus of goddesses and mythological characters. They are cropped, multiplied, reproduced at various angles
and in unexpected spaces, such as the bottom or the top of a gallery
wall, on the ceiling, in a corner. These strategies prevent the viewer
from simply looking at the perpetrator image head-on, repeating the
spectatorial Nazi gaze. Instead, Spero's installations make us conscious

of the looks that structure the image itself, of the screens and mediations that separate them from us in the present, of the artist's and our own compromised relation to them. The texts speak explicitly about the photographs, thus removing any simple transparence from them and restoring their original context. Significantly, Spero's photographic intertextuality enables the viewer to be conscious of the interaction between perpetrators, victims, and bystanders. Bystander testimonies are part of the texts and perpetrators are included in the images. The media through which these images have come down to us—newspaper articles, archival collections, documentary films—are explicitly foregrounded. Spero's installations are self-conscious, as well, about the gender dynamics that shape the heroization of Masha, about the "racial" dynamics that erased her Jewish identity, and about the politics of its reclamation. Masha herself, like the sign she carries, becomes a symbol but Spero needs to redirect the Nazi gaze in her installations and redefine the symbolization to which Masha has been subjected. Confronted with Spero's collages and installations, the viewer must read as well as look, thereby extricating herself from any unilateral identification with either victim or perpetrator. In one installation, Spero crops the image slightly, removing one of the men and thus highlighting Masha's heroic role. In another, she superimposes another picture, found in the pocket of a member of the Gestapo and showing a naked woman bound with a noose around her neck. Unlike the picture of Masha, this is a spare, almost classical image that emphasizes the mythicizing of the female victim or hero, especially when it is placed in relation to Spero's goddesses. This image of a bound woman also reveals the pornographic dimension of the perpetrator/victim relationship, which might seem to corroborate Levinthal's interpretation. Certainly, some Nazi killers did sexualize the act of murder, but while Spero shows this by reproducing an image that is already pornographic, Levinthal adds a pornographic dimension to images that exist in a different register altogether. And by confronting these two images, Spero multiplies feminine roles and complicates gender stereotypes.

In some installations, Spero surrounds these pictures with poems— Bertolt Brecht's ballad about Marie Sanders, who slept with a Jew, a poem by Nelly Sachs, another by Irena Klepfisz. Thus Spero's representations of Masha hover between mythicizing the resistance hero and individualizing the girl from Minsk. She makes it clear that surviving archival images cannot evade appropriative discourses of transmission and mediation. Those discourses have now become part of the images themselves, but Spero acknowledges this fact instead of reenacting it.

As she extricates the girl from the Nazi gaze, Spero nevertheless inscribes her in other mythic frameworks. By surrounding her image and story with some of her stock mythological figures, she comments on the monumentality of her own installations, on her own signature and relation to these haunting figures from the past. Masha becomes part of the story Spero herself tells about the torture of women, about war and the victimization of women in war, and about female resistance. This is also a gendered story that rests on binary oppositions between victims and perpetrators. But by including text, Spero highlights the historical specificity of Masha's victimization. She allows her to be both individual and symbol.

Spero may be no less appropriative, no less invested than Bak, or Chicago, or Levinthal. But I would say that in her layered images she reveals a greater level of consciousness and responsibility about her role as retrospective witness. Spero's imaginative aesthetic strategies allow her to resist a too-easy identification with the female victim, or a mere repetition of the perpetrator gaze, and to replace these with an act of denunciation. Spero refocuses our look without repairing what has been irrevocably broken. At its best, then, her use of Nazi photographs in her memorial artwork would allow us to be conscious of photography's implication in the dynamics of gender and race, power and powerlessness, seeing and being seen.

Chapter Eight

"During Total War, We Girls Want to Be Where We Can Really Accomplish Something"

What Women Do in Wartime

GUDRUN SCHWARZ

Seven months after the war ended, a remarkable story appeared in *Sie*, Berlin's largest women's magazine. The piece described the return of a young woman from prisoner-of-war camp. . . .

> "There lay the street along which she had strode, one long year ago, cheerfully, confidently, even a bit proud of the uniform that revealed to all that she belonged to the German Anti-Aircraft Service; . . . that was once the uniform that made every young girl so endlessly proud . . .
>
> "A million eyes still keep the daily watch for 'him,' the father, the husband, the brother, the friend, but few also discover among the released prisoners—the women. Do they no longer remember that they met women in uniform everywhere, with steel helmet, with backpack, at the searchlight, yes, even with guns? . . . ' " [1]

What this young woman could not know was that seven months after the collapse of the National Socialist system, a new model for women had already been established. Military-related work was not the only aspect of women's wartime experience that postwar Germany ignored.

"Women in uniform" and the Nazi activists and party members, the "perpetrators, followers, bystanders" had shucked off their past and been transformed into innocent women, women whose whole existence was devoted to loving their husbands and children and who had lived their lives in the private sphere of the family and were not responsible for the dictatorship or Nazi crimes. What remained in postwar folk memory for most Germans—and I will use the term German to refer to those men and women who were defined by the Nazis as "real Germans"—were memories of women's sacrifices, sufferings, and exertions in the absence of their men.

The symbol of this collective process of suppression was the *Trümmerfrau* (woman of the rubble), who cleared away the rubble in Germany and paved the way for reconstruction. Historians, whether men or women, have described National Socialism as an extreme form of masculine hegemony and have concentrated on male actors when they investigate wartime Germany as a society of perpetrators.

German women did not lose their innocence until the late 1980s, thanks to the work of an American colleague. The controversy between Claudia Koonz and Gisela Bock has entered the annals of women's studies in Germany as the female "version of the historian's debate (*Historikerstreit*)."[2] Claudia Koonz raised "issues of female agency and complicity in Nazism and the Holocaust" for the first time in her book *Mothers in the Fatherland*[3] (1987) and provoked sharp criticism from Gisela Bock, one of the most prominent specialists in women's history in Germany.[4] Bock responded to Koonz's thesis—i.e., that "most German women (like most German men), in a myriad of complex and ambivalent ways, collaborated with the regime"—with a counterthesis, according to which the majority of women, especially pregnant women, mothers, and housewives, were more resistant than men to Nazi propaganda, including its racist aspects.[5] In the following contribution, I will show how German women, whether on the home front or near the battlefield, were involved in the war, and how they supported and upheld the Nazi system.

I

The publicly organized involvement of German women was characteristic of both world wars. This is a fact that is all too often forgotten. War is thus removed from the analysis of society and becomes a masculine myth. In fact, war takes place not only at a single, easily surveyed front; war is a way of life for everyone living in the society waging war.

Since World War I, the term "home front" has been synonymous with the mobilization of an entire people and has pointed to a new relationship between the front and the hinterland, the two "war zones" that need to be mobilized. The introduction of the term "home front" during World War I unmasked the myth of war as the business of men who "go off to war" and leave women and children "at home" in a peaceful place, which must be defended. Home had become, to a great extent, a site of war and something very different from the image that reigned in the thoughts and longings of soldiers. During World War I, the mobilization of the female German population did not begin until war was actually declared; it was carried out under the auspices of the National Service, an organization established by the leaders of the Federation of German Women's Associations (*Bund deutscher Frauenvereine*). Under the Nazis, by contrast, various organizations of the National Socialist state began preparing girls and young women, the so-called HJ generation (the abbreviation for *Hitler Jugend*, Hitler Youth), for their active contribution to the war effort as early as 1933. The law reestablishing conscription in Germany, the *Wehrgesetz*, took effect on May 21, 1935, and required every German man and woman to "serve the fatherland" in the event of war.

The HJ generation was born during the Weimar Republic, the "postwar" period of World War I. After Hitler's successful takeover (in January 1933), children who were accepted as German were subjected to Nazi socialization and trained in paramilitary formations as "preservers of the future" of National Socialism.[6] With the establishment of the *Jungmädelbund* (Young Girls League, for ten- to fourteen-year-old girls), the *Bund Deutscher Mädchen* or BDM (League of German Girls, for fourteen- to eighteen-year-olds), the voluntary *Landjahr* (Agricultural Service Year, beginning in 1933), the *Pflichtjahr* (Year of Duty, beginning in February 1938), the *Arbeitsdienst* (Labor Service, created in August 1936), and the *Kriegshilfsdienst* (Auxiliary War Service, established in 1941), the Nazis created organizations and instruments of power designed to oversee the political training of German girls and co-ordinate their public service. In these organizations, girls were to be trained as loyal members serving the entire German community, the *Volksgemeinschaft*. They could also acquire skills and power in the pub-lic sphere, something earlier generations of girls and women had no op-portunity to achieve. Most girls who grew up between 1933 and 1945 joined the BDM voluntarily and were happy to serve there: the League had no lack of new members.

These organizations were especially attractive because they were an opportunity for girls to experience youth as an independent phase of their lives—the so-called *Mädelzeit*—which encompassed more than the traditional female sphere of *Kinder, Küche, Kirche* (children, kitchen, and church). Household and caretaking tasks were not elimi-nated, but supplemented with hiking, camping, athletics and games, social gatherings, competitions, and festive parades. The BDM ex-ploited those traits purported to be characteristic of young people, such as their desire for action and willingness to make sacrifices, their ambi-tion and will to achieve, their longings and search for meaning in life. The various social services kept them busy but also allowed them to feel part of a larger whole. By taking part in campaigns to collect anything from old clothes to potato bugs to herbs for tea, by participating in pub-lic information campaigns and doing handicrafts for organizations like the *Winterhilfswerk* (Winter Welfare Service), by joining the *Land-dienst* (Agricultural Service), the *Ernteeinsätze* (Harvest Force), and as baby-sitters in the harvest kindergartens, they served Germany and the Führer.[7]

As Sibylle Hübner-Funk notes in her study *Loyalität und Verblen-dung* (Loyalty and Illusion),

It is and remains a remarkable phenomenon that the transformation of female socialization, in particular, was efficient and successful in the Nazi state and that the transfer of soldierly values, attitudes, and behav-ior, which followed in the wake of Nazi organizations, was well received among female youths. The radical de-privatization of the daily lives of fe-male youths, their integration into the "higher" duties of the state pro-duced the feeling of "being needed" and thus imparted a sense of

meaning which transcended the individual. A new feeling of political—
or rather, "*völkisch*"—responsibility arose.[8]

Girls were so completely co-opted by the Nazi state that they rarely
found their individual roles within these collective lives in uniform con-
stricting. Instead, they often considered their positions an honor and an
increase in status. "You are nothing, your *Volk* is everything" was the
central tenet to which they voluntarily subordinated themselves. Renate Finckh, a former BDM leader, describes this experience:

> I sang about freedom with a "shining heart" and felt free while doing it;
> free from oppression by the father I feared, free from the constraints of
> old-fashioned methods for raising daughters, free from the pressure to get
> good grades from "politically unreliable" teachers, free of the imposition
> of having to think about people with different political opinions. The
> empty term "freedom" affected me, at the age of twelve to fourteen, like
> a drug, clouding its own sense-distorting content. That's how I could feel
> free and still be willing to obey every order.[9]

This state of mind, produced in the BDM, "stood the test" in
wartime. Conscious of their own importance and full of faith in the
Führer, the young women and girls "served . . . with heroic devotion on
the home front."[10]

II

Young unmarried women, in particular, were prepared to serve the war
effort long before the war began (as long as they were of the correct
racial type and as long as they conformed socially and politically). Before the war, young women's labor was harnessed into two programs:
the Year of Duty and the *Reichsarbeitsdienst—weibliche Jugend* (the
Reich labor service—female youth), understood as parallels to compulsory military service for young men. They wore gray "baggy, shapeless,
drab"[11] uniforms. Then, in the summer of 1941, a further six-month period in the Auxiliary War Service was added to the half year in the Labor
Service for Female Youth. Women spent the second half-year mainly in
armaments factories. The armed forces, Gestapo offices, public trans-

portation, and hospitals also used female workers from the Auxiliary War Service.

Even before the war, nearly 90 percent of all single women were employed, as compared to 36 percent of married women. These single women—and not married middle-class mothers—were the "reserve army," which the Nazi state (by way of the Nazi women's organizations) mobilized for functions considered vital to the war effort. Middle-class mothers were supposed to do volunteer service for the Red Cross or the Nazi Women's Movement, but there was no compulsory service for these women. As Elizabeth Heineman explains, "While allowances for dependents of military men allowed hundreds of thousand of wives to leave the workforce, single women's work not only expanded but also changed qualitatively. Most striking was the government's employment of millions of young, single women in the military and affiliated organizations."[12] As flak helpers, they took part in armed conflicts, as Wehrmacht auxiliaries and nurses' aides, they supported the army, air force, and navy.[13] Furthermore, many women volunteered to work in the occupied territories in the east or west and were employed as civilians in the offices of the German military administrations there or worked for German private companies in these regions.[14] As part of the military services, these young women traveled, found adventure—and participated in the domination of the non-German people in the countries occupied by the Nazis. And shortly before the Germans lost the war, BDM girls were drafted to build antitank lines along all borders. A former BDM leader wrote, in 1985, about such an assignment with undiminished pride: "Twenty-five thousand girls were in action. Although the operation was in vain and the completed fortifications could no longer be manned, that fact cannot reduce the admiration which I feel even today for the girls' achievements."[15] BDM girls from the western part of Germany were called up to construct the fortifications on the western border, the *Westwall*.[16]

Beginning in the summer of 1940, some 10,000 young women and teenage girls—members and leaders of the League of German Girls, the Women's Labor Service, and the Nazi Women's Movement as well as students, young teachers, and nursery school teachers—worked as so-called resettlement assistants in occupied Poland. They worked under orders from *Reichstatthalter* Arthur Greiser and in cooperation with the SS. Recruited for tasks related to the Germanization program, they "were working in a context that was structured by the power relations created by the Nazi-imposed 'racial' hierarchy and by the destructive dynamic of Germanization."[17]

In the western part of Poland, the provinces Poznán and Lódz (Litzmannstadt) had been incorporated into the German Reich and given the name *Reichsgau Wartheland,* or *Warthegau.* Nazi plans were to deport the Jews living in the conquered regions that were to be "Germanized" and to drastically reduce the non-Jewish population. Between December 1 and 17, 1939, about 90,000 Jewish and non-Jewish Polish families were driven out of the *Warthegau.* They were deported to the Lublin district, in eighty freight cars, and left there. About 40,000 Jewish and non-Jewish Poles were deported to the *Generalgouvernement* from February 10 to March 15, 1940, and again more than 135,000 by the end of January 1941. By late 1942, the total number of persons deported from these areas amounted to half a million. SS *Hauptsturmführer* Adolf Eichmann was appointed Special Official for the Evacuation of Jews and Poles in October 1939. His so-called Central Office for Resettlement was installed in Lódz. October 1939 also saw the beginning of the forced relocation of Poland's Jewish inhabitants to the ghetto camps. These operations were preceded, throughout Poland, by labeling people and shops as Jewish. Jewish Poles' freedom of movement was restricted, they lost their economic basis for survival, and thay had to registrater for forced labor.[18] At the same time, the ethnic German minority, together with ethnic Germans whom the Nazi regime had resettled within the Greater German Reich from areas outside of its borders, was to be "strengthened" and supervised according to National Socialist criteria. After a brief period of initiation by the SS settlement staff in Lódz, young women and girls following in the wake of the SS—which had forced thousands of Polish villagers to leave their homes—removed the traces of such expulsions by cleaning homes and preparing them for resettlement by ethnic Germans. This was the first opportunity to practice being a "*Herrenmensch,*" one of the master race. We can ascertain from a report entitled "Working Girls [*Arbeitsmädel*] written from the *Warthegau*" that the homes and apartments were cleaned by Polish women, not by German girls. "The Polish women must now scrub and scour the apartment under the direction of the *Mädel.*"[19]

As representatives of the "master race," they taught the new settlers

"German" values and Nazi virtues. But they also joined in these violent expulsions and plundered the intact farmhouses of Jewish and non-Jewish Polish families. That this behavior was not unusual but in fact "normal" is demonstrated by a letter written in 1941 by a leader of the League of German Girls: "Then we visited the last Jew still living in the neighborhood . . . There was not much to get. But . . . a wardrobe, three chairs, and a table were our 'spoils.' "[20] A former leader of the League of German Girls, Melita Maschmann, tells us in her memoirs that she not only participated in "evacuation" operations in the *Warthegau* but also fulfilled the function of the police in driving out the Poles.[21] Furthermore, Elizabeth Harvey notes that "kindergarten organizers and kindergarten teachers working in the Lublin district of the *Generalgouvernement* in 1941 also . . . were involved in the planning of expulsions of Polish and Jewish families from villages in the Zamosc area."[22] Thus, young women and teenage girls took an active part in this ethnic cleansing.

The story of Melita Maschmann illustrates the opportunities that the war provided for a young, ideologically committed woman. She became an activist in the League of German Girls in 1933 at the age of fifteen. The war opened up a new world to her: the occupied East. The sight of starving, begging Poles not only left her unmoved, it also gave her an almost enthusiastic feeling of superiority. She was even unmoved during her travels through the Lódz and Kutno ghettos. As the head of a Women's Labor Service camp, she supervised her group's operation to drive Poles from their ancestral homes and to confiscate their property.

Nearly "10,000 BDM-Girls served in the Eastern Action program during the course of 1941. While many of these girls remained in the East, another 16,022 went there during the course of 1942."[23] These women and girls made indispensable contributions to the Nazi's racist "Germanization" policies in occupied Poland. They accepted the suppression of the Jewish and non-Jewish Poles as a matter of course, just as they made use of the privileges of the German occupiers. For them, this was just normal daily life. They took advantage of the opportunity of participation that Hitler's state offered and enjoyed the fact that Nazi racist practices secured them a higher place in the gender hierarchy than that of ethnic groups defined as inferior. In the words of Melita Maschmann, "Our relationship was unproblematic: I gave the orders and these people carried them out."[24] Maybe this was one of the reasons the German government sent young women to the East, namely to deepen their racial education and to prevent them from crossing racial boundaries.

III

The *Osteinsatz* (Service in the East) of young women and girls was not limited to duty as resettlement assistants. Wherever a German administration was established in the occupied eastern territories, BDM leaders, leaders of the Nazi Women's Corps, and female members of the Nazi People's Welfare soon followed. The tasks performed by BDM leaders in the service of Alfred Rosenberg's *Reichsministerium für die besetzten Ostgebiete* (Ministry for the Occupied Eastern Territories) included organizing the daughters of local ethnic Germans and of the German personnel and administrative staff members as well as providing political instruction for these girls. Together with the SS, they also organized the so-called Hay Action and SS Helper Action. In other words, they assisted in abducting young girls and boys from the occupied territories of the Soviet Union to work as forced laborers in the German Reich.[25] Both in Rosenberg's Berlin headquarters and in the general commissions in the occupied territories—in Riga, Rovno, Tallinn, Kaunas, Minsk, Zhytomyr, Kiev, Nikolayev, and Dnepropetrovsk—youth departments had been established. BDM leaders also supervised the young female students who were sent to the occupied Soviet territories as part of their *Semestereinsatz* (Service Semester).

A student and BDM leader reports on her Service Semester in the fall of 1941: "I would also like to tell about all the people who came to the base to rest when darkness fell. . . . I will always find it a source of strength that I experienced again and again—no event can shake the German will to win and German faith, all difficulties are met with an even more adamant 'nevertheless'." For this young woman, being called up by the ministry was the "most interesting and wonderful job of my life."[26]

Women who had completed training at the Colonial Women's School in Rendsburg also volunteered for duty in the East. They were assigned posts as housekeepers on SS estates in Estonia and Latvia and as school assistants on SS estates in the Ukraine. When, in mid-August

1944, these women were forced "to leave the *Ostland*, due to the military situation," some of them were reassigned to the *Auskunftsstelle für Kriegsverluste der Waffen-SS* (Information Office for Wartime Losses of the Waffen SS) in Bamberg. Frustrated by this work, they wrote to the head of the *Rasse- und Siedlungshauptamt* (Main Office for Race and Settlement) on September 14, 1944:

> We feel completely superfluous here. . . . We therefore request that you send us back to our old posts. . . . According to what we've heard, Fräulein von F . . . is still in Estonia on the SS estate Krävavete. We are not afraid and anyway, it is not necessarily safe here in the Reich these days, either. Anyway, that is unimportant. During total war, we girls want to be where we can really accomplish something. In case duty in the East is at present still impossible, maybe we could be assigned as heads of the rations distribution points for those working on field fortifications. Mostly schoolgirls are employed there. There is a lack of qualified personnel. If we work there in SS uniforms, then there is no danger that the Labor Office will grab us and we will be lost for the SS. Of course, we want to avoid that at all costs. But this is only intended as a suggestion, in case we cannot go back to *Ostland* at the moment.[27]

One can read this letter as an illustration of the authors' loss of a sense of reality. By September 1944 Estonia had been liberated by the Red Army. Latvia, which they called "Ostland" and to which they longed to return, was no longer controlled by German troops. The fact that these young women nonetheless unwaveringly believed in the "final victory" is documented by a letter from another housekeeper.

Dora S. was hired in 1943 as a school assistant "for the female eastern camp of the SS for rural households and home economics" in Hegewald near Zhytomyr in the Ukraine. After she was also forced to leave the East "for military reasons," she worked until early February at the "SS Farm for the Disabled" in Chernovits and subsequently quit this position to begin an apprenticeship on a farm in East Prussia, "which she later hoped to take over herself." A letter dated February 2, 1945, rescinded her notice of termination and reinstated her in her old job. "Since the bank in East Prussia to which Fräulein S.'s pay was to be transferred no longer exists, we request that, for the time being, her pay be transferred to her address in Chernovits."[28]

All the young women who worked behind the lines for the Wehr-macht, the *Waffen* SS, and the police as staff assistants, signal corps as-sistants, secretaries, and translators also performed "service in the East." In such positions, as well as in the offices of the civilian administration, the Nazi Party, and in private companies, they were indispensable per-sonnel. They wrote and certified letters like the following: "Letter from the Commander of the Security Police and the SD, Riga, Latvia, from May 19, 1942, to the Registry Office [*Standesamt*] Riga. 'I herewith confirm that the 368 incurably mentally ill persons listed in the enclo-sure died on January 29, 1942.' Signed for: Kirste SS-*Sturmbahnführer*, certified [Käthe] Eckstädt, staff member." [29]

The increasing importance of these jobs in the course of the war is demonstrated in the following statement:

> Among the army's civilian employees, work done by women is becoming ever more important. The size and expanse of the area occupied and conquered by the German Wehrmacht, in particular in the East, makes an ever increasing deployment of supplementary female employees nec-essary. The signal corps helpers have been joined by staff assistants and hospital assistants. Almost like in olden days, albeit in a different fashion, women have become men's partners in battle and follow them, even when conditions are difficult, to the areas lying behind the front. [30]

The same was true of the nurses working in military hospitals and soldiers' homes. When the war began, 140,000 women were already employed by the army—50,000 white-collar workers and 90,000 blue-collar workers. At the end of the war, the Wehrmacht's female employees numbered 500,000. [31] A further 3,000 were members of the SS-Women's Corps, [32] and, as of January 1, 1945, 361,500 women belonged to the Wehrmacht medical corps—500 physicians, 48,000 nurses' aides, and 313,000 helpers, all of whom were members of the German Red Cross. [33]

These women were involved in the crimes committed by the Wehrmacht and the SS in various ways. They lived and worked in an atmosphere of murder and crime, were bystanders and, as such, wit-nesses. Many were profiteers, some became accomplices, and still oth-ers became perpetrators themselves. When employed as assistants to the military staff, female Wehrmacht, SS, and *Kriegshelferinnen* police helpers were charged with typing the reports of crimes perpetrated by these formations. Those who were signal corps helpers were responsible for communicating criminal orders by way of radio, telephone, or telex.

One can define witnessing a crime as an indirect form of committing a crime. To be witness to acts of violence and mistreatment is also to participate in these crimes. Being a witness can indicate a process of agreement, desensitization, and brutalization. Being a witness can mutate into being an accomplice, as in the case of the former SS employee Gerty Breiter. In a statutory declaration presented by the defense attorneys of the SD at the Nuremberg Trials, she declared:

> From about October 1943 until January 1944, I worked as an office employee for the commander of the Security Police and the SD for Central Russia and White Ruthenia in Minsk. I am acquainted with SS-*Hauptscharführer* Ruebe because of my work there. Ruebe was not a member of the SD, he was a Gestapo *Beamter*. I can state that with certainty. He worked in department IV B, which dealt with Jewish affairs. The SD in Minsk had nothing to do with Jewish affairs. The SD's activities were limited to writing reports about the general morale and public sentiments. The reports were sent to Department III RSHA [*Reichsicherheitshauptamt*, Reich Main Security Office] in Berlin. The General Commissar in Minsk received copies of selected parts. There was no SD prison in Minsk. The facts stated above are true. I have made this statement voluntarily and am not acting under duress.[34]

Numerous postwar trials have proven that this statement is false. Rübe, who was pronounced guilty of perpetrating atrocities by a West German court,[35] was a member of the staff of the commander of the Security Police and the SD and therefore a member of *Einsatzgruppe* B, as was Gerty Breiter. *Einsatzgruppe* B was deeply involved in the annihilation of the Jewish and Russian population following the German attack on the Soviet Union.

Gerty Breiter must have known about these crimes, since it was her job to type the relevant orders and reports. The historian Christian Gerlach reports on what the other women employed in Minsk—approximately 2,400 in number[36]—could have known:

Among the employees of the occupying powers, including those in lower positions, extensive information circulated about the dimensions of the crimes, about the number of those dying in the prison camps and about shootings of Jews, or about the former number of residents in cities destroyed by incendiary bombs. In front newssheets, the murder of Jews was mentioned in a joking way; the journalists of the *Minsk News* were informed, for the simple reason that a mass shooting of Jews took place in the courtyard of their office building. Newspapers reported on shootings of Jews, while scenes of the pogroms in Riga flickered from all the movie theater screens as part of the newsreels, the *Deutsche Wochenschau*. The German radio station in Minsk broadcast live reports from the campaign against partisans with only a short delay . . . [37]

But even when former Wehrmacht assistants decide to testify, the result is often lopsided. A case in point is the report given by Ilse Schmidt, a former staff assistant, about the deportation of the residents of the Jewish ghetto in Rovno:

Late summer 1942. The babble of voices, the sound of tin plates being thrown away and soldiers' commands wake me up one night. Ellen isn't there. I get out of bed, go to the window, and look out at the street. There is a movie theater across the street from our house. A crowd of people steps out of the open door of the movie theater onto the street and is led away, guarded by soldiers. It is [between] three and four in the morning. I can clearly see men, women, children, old and young. I can tell by their clothes that they are from the ghetto. Since September 1941, it was mandatory to wear a Jewish star. At first, I don't understand what is happening down there. What are all those people doing here? Why are they throwing their dishes onto the street with such vehemence? Then I understand: They want to make themselves noticed. Look here, what is happening to us! Don't let it happen! Help us! I stand behind the window and want to shout out: Do more! That is not enough! Resist! You outnumber them! A few of you can be saved! For these people—according to my estimate, about 300—I later learn that there were many more—are being led away by a handful of soldiers. But the prisoners shuffle down the dim street with their heads bowed, murmuring quietly, and submit without a fight. I watch them until they disappear behind a turn in the road. Then I lie down on my bed. I have a premonition, these people will be killed. What is going on inside the heads of the guards when they see their victims? Do they agree with what they are doing?[38]

She goes on to report that she falls ill the next day. Ilse Schmidt was a staff assistant in the office of the Commander of Patrol Duty, which, according to her explanation, fulfills "more or less the function of a police unit for the fighting troops."[39] Although she states that she cannot remember what her job was—"I don't remember today what exactly I did at the time"[40]—she does proudly declare that she brought order to the hopeless mess in the office and was soon working independently. Furthermore, she reports that she could look out of her office window into the courtyard of the SD building, a place where people were regularly shot. Her dramatically retold story of the deportation loses credibility.

On the night of July 14–15, 1942, all remaining residents of the Rovno ghetto, about 5,000 people, were liquidated. Herman Friedrich Gräbe, a German engineer who was in Rovno at the time, has a very different memory of what occurred. Testifying at the International Military Tribunal in Nuremberg, he stated:

> Since in most cases the Jews refused to leave their dwellings and resisted, the SS and militia both applied force. . . . All through the night, these beaten, chased, and wounded people dragged themselves across the lighted streets. Women carried their dead children in their arms, children hugged their dead parents and dragged them by their arms and legs down the road toward the train. . . . On the streets through which I passed, I saw dozens of bodies of people of all ages and both sexes.[41]

Bearing in mind this description of these horrible events, let us recall Frau Schmidt's description and her call to the Jews: "Do more! That is not enough! Resist! You outnumber them! A few of you can be saved!" We must conclude that her testimony reveals complicity and that, years later, her empathy goes to the perpetrators (the young soldiers) and not to the victims.

Schmidt remembered voluntarily and made these memories available to the public. Other women were called on by various district attorney offices to provide eyewitness testimony. In all the testimony I have read over the last few years, none of the former SS employees questioned proved to be cooperative. On the contrary, in all of these interrogations they demonstrated their solidarity with their former bosses, their unwillingness to testify, and thus their complicity. One example is Hildegard R., who worked for the commander of the Security Police in Riga beginning in October 1941. The district attorney who conducted the questioning noted this:

> During questioning of the witness, I could not help thinking that the witness was holding back information. . . . She also did not state the names of her female colleagues of her own initiative but named them only with reservations after I had once again informed her of the laws regarding acting as an accessory to a crime. Although it is difficult to remember names after so many years, I do not think it impossible that the witness would be able to say more about former members of the *Sipodienststelle* in Riga if she is confronted with other relevant information.[42]

The women who served in the East were not only witnesses of the crimes, they also profited from them. After the destruction of the ghettos and their residents, the property of Jews was plundered confiscated, sent to the Reich, or distributed to the German members of the occupation administration.[43] That women were among those who lined their pockets is documented in a report written in April 1943 for the commander of the Security Police and the Security Service for the district of Galicia: "One can observe that women are much more unhesitating in snatching up such valuables and know neither inhibitions nor scruples when it comes to acquiring a coveted object. The sense of one's own worth is often so weakly developed that they not only snatch up clothes, furs, and jewels, but also display all of this in an unsuitable way."[44]

Some of the women who worked in the East (we don't know the actual number) became perpetrators themselves. One example is the secretary of the commander of the Security Police in Bialystok, who participated in rounding up Jews during the February deportation operation in the ghetto. Another are the secretaries who appeared in the ghetto of Slonim to photograph the shootings. Gerlach notes that "Not a few of them had intimate relationships with members of the regional commissariat and some of them married them."[45] One of them was Gertrud Segel, who began working for the Gestapo in Vienna as a shorthand typist in 1938. In 1941, she volunteered for duty in the occupied eastern territories and reported for her new job, working for the commander of the Security Police in the Radom district, on February 1, 1941.[46] She effected her transfer to Drohobycz in the fall of 1941, where she worked as a secretary and lived with her future husband, SS man Gustav Landau, in a luxurious villa, in which she stockpiled confiscated valuable Jewish property, including furs, paintings, porcelain, and fabrics. This is where the following scene took place, as reported by Marjan Nadel, a survivor of the Holocaust. According to Nadel's recollection, Landau and Gertrud Segel were sitting on the balcony and watching the Jews working in the garden. Gertrud Segel had a hunting rifle in her hand and aimed at the Jews working below. Landau took the rifle from her hand and shot one of the Jews. Then, Landau and his mistress went back into the room, laughing out loud.[47] "Apparently, Landau wanted to show her how the lives of the Jews were in his hands and that he was authorized to shoot down a Jew like a dog."[48] Whether Gertrud Segel was involved in shooting the Jewish worker or not must be left up to speculation. As a secretary in Vienna, with the Gestapo in Radom and Drohobycz, she demonstrated that she reserved her sympathy and humane feelings for her "own race" and that she supported the racist policies of the SS. The shooting of a Jew amused her.

IV

In May 1945, Nazi Germany was defeated and occupied by Allied troops. Now astonishing things occurred. In no time, Germany was transformed from a society of perpetrators into a society of victims. Perpetrators, beneficiaries, supporters, and indifferent onlookers of both sexes turned into people who had merely done their duty or acted on orders and under duress, people who were unsuspecting and good, people who just got on the bandwagon or who had been seduced. Only a handful of perpetrators remained. Denazification and the escalation of the East-West conflict promoted this process of reinterpretation: The Germans now perceived themselves as victims of the Allies' war, victims of expulsion, victims of the Red Army, and victims of the "Nazis," now stylized as a fanatical minority. Women in the society of perpetrators also stylized themselves as victims. In an editorial published in 1946 in the first issue of the Catholic women's magazine *Der Regenbogen*, the argument reads as follows:

Men wage wars—women must endure them. For war is by its very nature foreign to women. She who carries life within herself and passes it on must hate him, the killer, as her most terrible enemy. Some will say that without women, without their efforts, the long continuation of this men's war, with all its horrifying consequences and effects, would have been impossible. That may be true, but only insofar as those very efforts of women were, deep down, endurance and suffering—cajoled, exacted, blackmailed from women by those who wanted this war and who abused the strength of the female heart for their own purposes.[49]

The lives of millions of women and girls who, as members of various Nazi and military organizations, contributed to the smooth functioning of the racist National Socialist system did not determine (self-) perceptions of women in Nazi Germany. Instead, the nonpolitical and therefore innocent German woman, living her life in the private sphere of the family and devoted to the love of husband and children, was to become part of the mythological narrative about "women's lives in the Third Reich."

Chapter Nine

Between Amnesty and Anti-Communism

The West German *Kameradenschinder* Trials, 1948–1960*

FRANK BIESS

In the summer of 1949, a West German Social Democratic news-paper bemoaned the fact that many a war criminal had escaped justice "by simply disappearing in their previous or in their new environment." The chances of identifying these criminals, the paper lamented, were slim unless they were identified by a former victim who insisted on calling them to task. Yet even in that case, the paper argued, prosecution and conviction would be difficult because potential witnesses were hard to identify or no longer alive and because there was no central agency in West Germany that could collect evidence in support of a conviction.[1]

The article, however, did not refer—as one might have suspected it

* An earlier version of this essay was presented to the 23rd Annual Conference of the German Studies Association in Atlanta. I would like to thank the commentator of the session, Jeffrey Herf, as well as Robert Moeller, Uta Poiger, Peter Schwartz, and Jonathan Wiesen for their helpful comments and suggestions. All names have been rendered anonymous.

would, in the aftermath of war, fascism, and genocide — to perpetrators of the Nazi regime. Instead, it commented on the case of Oskar S., a returned POW from the Soviet Union who had served as the commandant of a prison unit inside a Soviet POW camp near Leningrad between 1946 and 1947. Upon his return from captivity, several returnees charged him with beating and abusing fellow POWs in Soviet captivity. He was subsequently arrested and tried before the Wuppertal district court. During his trial, S. himself admitted to having beaten fellow POWs in two cases; he justified his behavior by saying he had to maintain camp discipline. In its verdict, the court, however, followed the testimony of several witnesses who had accused S. of systematically mistreating and abusing fellow POWs in his function as prison commandant. As a result, the court sentenced S. to ten years in prison for bodily harm in ten cases, one of which had led to the death of a German POW. Due to the "morally reprehensible" nature of S.'s offenses, the court also stripped him of his citizenship rights for six years.[2]

This case was the first in a series of so-called *Kameradenschinder* trials (trials of those who tormented their comrades) that took place in West Germany between the late 1940s and the early 1960s. These trials focused on former POWs who had collaborated with their Soviet or Eastern European captors by assuming official functions in the administration of the camps or by engaging in political reeducation efforts as "antifascist activists."[3] Upon their return, some of these POWs were then charged with criminal offenses such as denouncing their fellow POWs to Soviet authorities or beating and abusing fellow POWs in their function as camp officials. The legal construction was that denunciations to Soviet authorities had aided and abetted in the deprivation of liberty of POWs because they had often led to a prolonged period of captivity. Other returnees were convicted for causing "bodily harm" or "grave bodily harm" to fellow POWs. According to a 1956 statistic of the West German Ministry of Justice, West German courts convicted close to a hundred POWs, leading to prison sentences ranging from several months up to fifteen years for such offenses. The actual number of such legal investigations, however, must have been considerably higher since the majority of these cases were dismissed due to lack of conclusive evidence or because the defendants were acquitted of the charges.[4]

These trials have thus far received little attention from historians. Yet they represent an important case study for West German confrontations with the consequences of war and defeat in the context of the Cold War. They were also part and parcel of a European-wide effort to prosecute treason and collaboration during the Second World War. In both Eastern and Western Europe, courtrooms became the site of a protracted battle over the multiple and often ambiguous meanings of defeat, occupation, and liberation.[5] The *Kameradenschinder* trials, to be sure, occupied a rather peculiar place within this larger effort to address the legacies of the Second World War in the new context of the Cold War. While the bulk of postwar political trials on former Nazi-occupied European territory targeted indigenous Nazi collaborators, these trials focused on German collaborators with Soviet Communism. As such, the *Kameradenschinder* trials were inextricably linked to West German efforts during the 1950s to come to terms with the past, and they were decisively shaped by the new ideological parameters of the emerging Cold War. The trials represented a prime, if largely unknown, example of the displaced, selective, and indirect manner in which West Germans approached the ever-present consequences of war and defeat during the formative period of their postwar reconstruction.

The trials were shaped by two powerful tendencies. On the one hand, the trials and the legal investigations that preceded them sought to maintain the rule of law and the principle of individual guilt based on clear and sufficient evidence. For the new West German liberal democracy, these two principles served an important legitimizing function. These principles distanced the Federal Republic from the abuse of the rule of law in the Third Reich as well as from what was perceived as political justice in the Communist regimes in Eastern Europe and the Soviet Union, thus testifying to the "antitotalitarian consensus" of the Federal Republic.[6]

Yet at the same time, the trials were also strongly influenced by ideological and mental continuities among the West German judiciary beyond 1945. These continuities derived, above all, from the incomplete denazification of the West German legal profession. After a brief and quite extensive purge of the West German judiciary by the occupation authorities, most previously dismissed judges and prosecutors returned to their official positions in the late 1940s.[7] While older judges from the Weimar period often occupied the leading positions, former Nazi party members soon filled the lower and middle ranks of the West German judiciary. In the North Rhine—Westphalian district of Hamm,

76.6 percent of judges were former Nazi party members by 1947, a figure that increased to between 80 and 90 percent by 1948 for the entire British zone of occupation.[8] This does not mean, however, that the majority of West German judges and prosecutors continued to harbor National Socialist sentiments. Instead, the dominant attitude among the legal personnel of the early Federal Republic consisted of a largely conservative and bourgeois worldview that often derived from the Weimar years or even reached back to the imperial German era. This conservative mentality, however, also included features such as strong anti-Communism that had been highly compatible with Nazi ideology and that could easily be incorporated into the antitotalitarian consensus of the Federal Republic.[9]

This peculiar reconstruction of the West German judiciary goes a long way toward explaining not only the considerable unwillingness of West German courts to prosecute Nazi crimes during the 1950s but also their relative eagerness to prosecute former POWs who had collaborated with Soviet authorities. Against the background of these conditions among the judiciary, this essay seeks to place the *Kameradenschinder* trials within the two contexts of judicial confrontations with the Nazi past and of West German anti-Communism.

The *Kameradenschinder* trials happened precisely in the period when the legal prosecution of Nazi crimes came to a virtual standstill. After a brief period of a quite vigorous prosecution of Nazi war crimes under the auspices of the occupation authorities, West German judges and prosecutors became reluctant to call Nazi perpetrators to task. The legal confrontation with National Socialism reached a low point in 1955 when only 21 people were convicted for crimes committed under Nazi dictatorship. This number may have roughly equaled the number of returned POWs who were convicted for their actions in Soviet captivity in the same year.[10]

As recent research has shown, returning POWs from the Soviet Union assumed a crucial significance in West German memories of the Second World War. The experience of German POWs in Soviet captivity seemed to epitomize German suffering and served as the basis for widely accepted narratives of victimization that equated the suffering of Germans with the suffering of Germany's victims, especially victims of the Holocaust.[11] The *Kameradenschinder* trials added another twist to these patterns of postwar selective memory. While postwar German memory generally tended to focus on German victimhood rather than on German perpetrators, these trials actually targeted the latter. But these were perpetrators who had acted under the auspices of the Soviet dictatorship, not the Nazis, and who were accused of victimizing other Germans rather than non-Germans. The *Kameradenschinder* trials therefore displaced a legal, political, and moral confrontation with homegrown Nazi dictatorship through a confrontation with the foreign, Communist, and Soviet dictatorship.

This process of displacement manifested itself in the frequent equation of alleged *Kameradenschinder* with Nazi perpetrators. According to one judge, German officials in Soviet POW camps had operated within a "system that was also practiced in German concentration camps."[12] Some returnees were initially charged with "crimes against humanity," and some of the verdicts also referred to this offense.[13] Individual judges, to be sure, emphasized that Allied Control Council Law No. 10 applied only to those "inhumanities that were linked to National Socialist rule."[14] Yet this insight did not prevent another judge from characterizing the offenses of one former POW in Soviet captivity as "bordering on crimes against humanity."[15]

Like West German judges and prosecutors, contemporary public observers drew explicit parallels between accused returnees and Nazi perpetrators. The aforementioned comment on the trial of Oskar S., for example, celebrated this case as the first sentence of a "crime against humanity that had been committed under the auspices of Communism." The same article did not hesitate to put S.'s offenses in the same category as those of Ilse Koch, the infamous female concentration camp guard from Buchenwald.[16] Further strengthening the rhetorical link between alleged *Kameradenschinder* and antifascist activists, the weekly periodical *Christ and Welt* identified the problem of former antifascist activists as a "reverse SS complex" and argued against "collective justice" with respect to both groups.[17] In West German legal and public discourse, the *Kameradenschinder* trials offered an opportunity to create a common category for perpetrators of totalitarianism that included the "beasts of Auschwitz, Buchenwald, Ravensbrück, and Sachsenhausen" but also former German POWs who, in Soviet captivity, had become "pawns of a system that seeks to achieve its goals through forced labor."[18] By equating Nazi perpetrators and (German) perpetrators of Soviet Communism, the *Kameradenschinder* trials both contributed to and reflected the emerging totalitarianism paradigm as the foundational ideology of the Federal Republic.

Although these trials both reflected and shaped West German selective memories of the Second World War, they did exhibit some important similarities to trials of Nazi perpetrators. But these similarities did not so much derive from an ultimately invalid and cynical equation of crimes committed in Soviet captivity with those committed in Nazi concentration camps, as many postwar observers insisted. Instead, the trials raised a series of moral and legal issues that also featured prominently in trials of Nazi perpetrators. The *Kameradenschinder* trials addressed, for example, the problem of individual responsibility for offenses that had been committed under oppressive conditions, i.e. in captivity. The defendants frequently claimed that they had abused or denounced other POWs only as a result of intense physical or psychological pressure from Soviet authorities.[19] The courts thus needed to determine to what extent alleged *Kameradenschinder* could claim the "privilege of necessity." By defining the extent of individual moral, political, and legal responsibility under a dictatorship, the *Kameradenschinder* trials negotiated an issue that was to feature prominently in later trials of Nazi perpetrators, and one that assumed crucial symbolic significance for postwar Germans in general. As Peter Steinbach has argued with reference to the Nazi trials, the "question of diminished guilt simply as a result of external circumstances concerned, in essence, all Germans."[20] During the 1950s, however, it was easier for the West German public and for the West German judiciary to address these issues with reference to a foreign, Communist dictatorship rather than to an indigenous Nazi dictatorship.

How, then, did the courts evaluate the individual responsibility of German POWs in Soviet captivity? Because of the moral and legal complexity of this question, the courts did not arrive at a consistent position. In some cases, judges and prosecutors exhibited a remarkable empathy for the difficult position of German camp officials who needed to reconcile the conflicting demands of fellow POWs and Soviet authorities. Especially if witnesses confirmed the actions of German camp officials on behalf of other POWs or if camp officials had refrained from involvement with the antifascist reeducation effort, courts tended to exonerate the defendants of all charges.[21] In other cases, however, judges and prosecutors were less willing to grant the

privilege of necessity to alleged offenders. Instead, they held accused returnees fully accountable for their actions in captivity. In the case of a
former leader of a POW work company, the court cited alternative ways
of meeting work quotas than beating and abusing fellow POWs, such as
"friendly words" or "engagement on behalf of other POWs."[22] In another trial in 1951, the court emphasized that a German camp official
did not possess any disciplinary powers and that the defendant's erro-
neous belief that he held such powers did not exonerate him.[23]

In 1952, the problem of camp officials' individual responsibility for
their actions in Soviet captivity advanced to the highest legal authority
for criminal and civil offenses, the *Bundesgerichtshof* (BGH). In its ruling, the BGH denied the emergency privilege to a returnee who, as
leader of a work camp, had ordered and participated in the beating of
fellow POWs for the theft of food and clothing. The defendant in this
case had appealed his conviction by the Göttingen district court by arguing that these measures had been necessary in order to maintain
camp discipline. The BGH, however, rejected this argument and emphasized a variety of other means by which the defendant could have
contained the further spread of thefts within the camp. As a result, the
court argued that the defendant had not sufficiently evaluated whether
"infringement on the rights of others was necessary in order to escape
danger himself."[24]

The denial of mitigating circumstances to accused returnees also derived from the influence of pressure groups such as the Association of
Returnees (*Verein der Heimkehrer*, VdH). Returnee associations were
one of the driving forces behind these trials and they sometimes filed
charges on behalf of other POWs.[25] The VdH newspaper, *Der
Heimkehrer*, reported regularly on ongoing *Kameradenschinder* trials
and generally voiced harsh criticism if sentences appeared too lenient.[26]
The West German judiciary also cooperated closely with the VdH in
gathering evidence in the trials. Judges and prosecutors frequently
asked for the assistance of the VdH in identifying potential witnesses.[27]
The association, moreover, also maintained a special committee that
provided expert testimony on conditions in Soviet captivity. VdH functionaries tended to emphasize the possibility of free choice and argued
that any POW who had assumed an official function in captivity had
done so voluntarily and was therefore fully responsible for his actions.[28]
This rather uncompromising attitude stood in stark contrast to the ex-

tensive engagement of the same association and other pressure groups on behalf of a general amnesty for German war criminals who were detained by the Allies. As Norbert Frei has shown, large segments of West German public opinion tended to exonerate these convicted war criminals on the basis that they had simply "followed orders."[29]

Partly as a result of the considerable influence of outside pressure groups, West German courts thus frequently denied accused POWs the mitigating circumstances that were routinely invoked in trials of Nazi perpetrators.[30] Judges and prosecutors tended to afford a greater degree of individual agency and, hence, legal accountability to German POWs in Soviet captivity than to Nazi perpetrators. The available evidence suggests that West German courts applied harsher moral and legal yardsticks to crimes committed by Germans under the Soviet dictatorship than those committed under the Nazi dictatorship.[31] Some West German officials ultimately also became aware of this imbalance. In the case of Oskar S., mentioned above, the head of the Wuppertal prison pleaded with the chief prosecutor to grant parole to S. after he had served two-thirds of his sentence. He based his request on the considerably lower sentences that the same Wuppertal district court had meted out in the trial of former guards of the Kemmna concentration camp, which had taken place parallel to S.'s trial in 1949.[32] As a result, this prison official favored parole for S. "lest he get the feeling that he had been judged according to political criteria."[33] This rather different treatment of Nazi perpetrators and convicted POWs, moreover, was replicated in West German social policy. Whereas a conviction in a *Kameradenschinder* trial automatically disqualified returnees from receiving benefits according to the 1954 POW compensation law, these benefits were routinely extended to convicted war criminals who had been interned by the Allies.[34]

Some of these trials not only addressed violence perpetrated in Soviet captivity, but, at least indirectly, violent transgressions by German soldiers during the racial war of annihilation on the Eastern Front. These trials were often initiated by POWs who returned from Soviet captivity only in 1953 or even in 1955–56. Most of these returnees had been convicted by Soviet courts in a wave of war crimes trials that immediately preceded the end of mass repatriations of German POWs in the spring of 1950.[35] Upon their return, some of these returnees charged former fellow POWs with having denounced them to Soviet authorities

and, by doing so, with having caused their prolonged detainment in Soviet captivity. Legal investigations and trials were then needed to evaluate the factual basis of these allegations and the validity of convictions of
German POWs by Soviet war crime tribunals.

The problem of denunciations, to be sure, had constituted one of the
most contested problems of German criminal law during the occupation period. In the British zone of occupation, from which most of the
cases discussed here originated, the occupation authorities had handed
over most of the jurisdiction for the prosecution of Nazi crimes to German courts by 1946–47. As a result, German judges and prosecutors
were increasingly confronted with the problem of how to prosecute
those Germans who had denounced other Germans to Nazi authorities
during the Third Reich. There is evidence that courts in the British
zone were rather reluctant to employ Allied Control Council Law
Number 10 on "crimes against humanity" in such denunciation cases,
although they were entitled to do so, and that they tended to arrive at
rather lenient judgments of denouncers. Martin Broszat, for example,
concluded that "usually, convictions [in these trials] only occurred
when the consequences of the denunciations had been very drastic"
while acquittals in denunciation trials amounted to about 60 percent.[36]
It is difficult to establish how conviction rates in *Kameradenschinder*
trials compared to conviction rates in these Nazi denunciation trials.
Nevertheless, the *Kameradenschinder* trials demonstrated that the
West German judiciary invested considerably more energies in prosecuting denunciations to Soviet rather than to Nazi authorities. In a
1952 decision, the BGH claimed principal jurisdiction of West German courts for these cases due to the fact that "Russian military justice"
was incompatible with the "dominating legal sensibility in our cultural
sphere [*in unserem Kulturkreis herrschende Rechtsempfinden*]." Denunciations to Soviet authorities were considered illegal because they extra-
dited German POWs to a legal system that did not correspond to
German norms.[37]

Just as West German courts had become very familiar with denunciations as a legal problem, the social practice of denunciations was not
foreign to former Wehrmacht soldiers. In fact, the myth of comradeship
as a primary means of social cohesion within the Wehrmacht was also
based on the threat and the reality of denouncing those soldiers whose
views or behavior placed them outside of the National Socialist "na-

tional community." Denunciations among Wehrmacht soldiers thus became one of the driving forces for the murderous expansion of military justice within the German army.[38] It is therefore perhaps not too surprising that German soldiers resorted to denunciations after they fell into Soviet captivity. This was true especially for previously compromised soldiers such as officers, members of the SS, or military judges. These soldiers faced a higher risk of being prosecuted by Soviet authorities for war crimes and hence seemed to have been more susceptible to informing on their fellow POWs in captivity in order to escape prosecution themselves. Yet precisely because of their prominent role in the war on the Eastern Front, these former soldiers were likely to have witnessed, if not participated in, German acts of genocidal warfare. As a result, they were in a privileged position "to think and to narrate" stories of criminal transgressions on the Eastern Front, regardless of whether their testimonies to Soviet authorities identified the right culprits or not.[39]

The extent to which compromised soldiers had been willing to inform on their fellow POWs in Soviet captivity became apparent, for example, in the case of Fritz K. K. had volunteered for the "Armed SS" in the spring of 1940, had served as a member of the SS divisions "Viking" and "Deathhead" on the Eastern Front since 1941, and was then taken into Soviet captivity in 1945.[40] As a former SS member, he was at high risk of being subjected to reprisals by Soviet authorities. As a result, he ultimately cooperated with Soviet investigators and accused Bernd S., a fellow POW, of having executed 106 Jews in gas and torture chambers in the Kovno ghetto. Partly based on K.'s statement, Bernd S. was sentenced to 25 years in prison and did not return from Soviet captivity until 1955. Upon his return, he charged Fritz K. with having informed on him to the Soviet authorities. In the ensuing trial, Fritz K. admitted to having knowingly provided false testimony about Bernd S., but he also claimed that Soviet NKVD agents had coerced him. The courts, however, denied any emergency situation to K. and sentenced him to two and a half years in prison as well as to loss of citizenship rights for two years.[41]

Not all of these denunciation trials, however, ended with a conviction. In another *Kameradenschinder* trial, Heinz S., a high civil servant in Bonn, was accused of having denounced two fellow POWs, Erwin W. and Franz R., for their participation in the execution of 200 Russian civilians on the Eastern Front. When confronted with these charges, Heinz S. did not deny having testified to Soviet authorities. Yet he justified his actions by the fact that he had faced considerable danger in Soviet captivity due to his function as a military judge on the Eastern Front. In particular, he feared Soviet reprisals for the death sentences he gave thirty members of a Russian Cossack unit who had subsequently been executed. In his testimony, Heinz S. admitted that war crimes had occurred in the area of his division, but he claimed that these crimes had not been committed by army units.[42]

The Frankfurt district court sentenced Heinz S. to two and a half years in prison for aiding and abetting in the deprivation of liberty of two fellow POWs. In 1960, however, the *Bundesgerichtshof* overturned this verdict on the basis of a "putative emergency situation." The BGH argued that Heinz S. had sincerely believed that refusal to testify to Soviet authorities would inevitably result in his own deportation to Siberia and prolonged internment. As a result, the court argued, he could not be held responsible for his actions. Ironically, it was precisely Heinz S.'s rather compromised past on the Eastern Front that ultimately served as the basis for his acquittal by the highest West German court.[43]

Acquittals for returnees in these trials, moreover, did not necessarily derive from defendants' being granted the privilege of emergency. In some cases, the courts simply failed to establish that the denunciations were not true. In January 1956, for example, the returnee Anskar H. brought charges against Theo B. for having falsely accused him of a series of war crimes, including the execution of 125 Russian civilians in the village of Guljai, the execution of 120 "partisans" in the village of Naltschik, and the execution of a Jewish servant. These accusations, H. argued, had led to his detainment in Soviet captivity until January 1956. In his testimony, B. claimed that he had provided this information only based on third-hand accounts and under intense pressure by Soviet authorities, yet he did not say that it was untrue. After hearing several witnesses, the court cleared H. of all charges because it could not be proven that he had provided false testimony voluntarily and knowingly. Yet the court also determined that these allegations of war crimes were made at least partly on a "factual basis," even though it was not clear whether and to what extent Anskar H. had actually been involved in these deeds.[44]

The questionable methods used in the Soviet trials of German

POWs, to be sure, contributed significantly to discrediting any differentiated effort at assessing individual responsibility for criminal transgressions on the Eastern Front. By portraying thousands of German POWs as collectively guilty (largely based on mere association with certain army units), these trials led most West Germans to believe that returning POWs from the Soviet Union were collectively innocent.[45] Still, in at least one case, a West German court actually confirmed—based on the testimony of several witnesses—the conviction of a German POW by a Soviet court. In February 1950, a returnee organization brought charges against Rolf S. for having accused Rudolf M. before a Soviet court of killing three Russian "partisans" by tying them to his tank and dragging them to death. After hearing several witnesses, the West German court decided that Rudolf M. had actually committed this offense. As a result, the court cleared Rolf S. of all charges, even though the court considered it morally problematic that he had presented this evidence to a Soviet rather than to a German court.[46]

As these trials demonstrated, West German courts during the 1950s were unlikely to prosecute or even investigate criminal acts by German soldiers toward non-German victims on the Eastern Front.[47] There is no indication that any returning POW brought charges in a West German court against a former comrade for crimes committed during the war rather than in Soviet captivity.[48] Instead, the notion of "comradeship," which had facilitated German soldiers' participation in genocidal warfare, now served as an ideological means to cover up German soldiers' criminal transgressions.[49] German POWs who collaborated—for whatever reasons—with Soviet authorities had disqualified themselves as "comrades" and, if they had informed on fellow POWs, had broken the code of silence regarding war crimes on the Eastern Front. Several verdicts in the *Kameradenschinder* trials thus explicitly said that defendants had violated the bonds of "comradeship," which, according to one judge, had constituted the only "psychological support" for German POWs in Soviet captivity.[50] By juxtaposing treacherous denunciators with virtuous "comrades," the *Kameradenschinder* trials had clearly apologetic implications. The trials implied that the firm allegiance to previous beliefs and attitudes was the only ethically correct stance for German POWs in Soviet captivity. By so doing, the trials confirmed the widespread assumption in postwar society that German soldiers had remained aloof from National Socialist ideology all along, that they had served their country bravely and honorably, and that there was therefore no larger ideological, political, or moral need to rethink one's previous allegiances in Soviet captivity.[51]

Nevertheless, what was remarkable about these trials was that they actually brought the violent transgressions on the Eastern Front into West German courtrooms during the 1950s, and thus had the potential of undermining the myth of the "clean" Wehrmacht. In this context, it is perhaps not of primary importance whether the stories of mass murder on the Eastern Front, as they were presented in the *Kameraden-schinder* trials, were based on false denunciations or true offenses. Instead, it is significant that these stories were based on an experiential basis that both the accusers and the defendant had shared on the Eastern Front. In several cases, moreover, the trials revealed that these stories did not lack a "factual basis," as one judge put it, thus at least hinting at the reality of criminal transgressions toward Russian civilians, POWs, and Jews on the Eastern front. For much of the 1950s, however, West German judges and prosecutors largely failed to capitalize on the availability of this kind of evidence. The court's attitude in the case of Anskar H. seems to have been representative for the West German judiciary as a whole: despite the availability of witnesses, it explicitly decided not to pursue further allegations that Anskar H. had murdered his Jewish servant, because this offense had not been part of his conviction by Soviet courts.[52] The *Kameradenschinder* trials thus documented the rather comprehensive effort of the West German judiciary to collect evidence regarding violence that had been done to Germans while signaling, at the same time, a virtually complete neglect of the violence that Germans had meted out to non-Germans. Or, as one judge declared: "Further investigations [in Theo B.'s case] are superfluous and do not promise much success. They could only be based on a clarification of the actual events during the German occupation [of the Soviet Union]."[53] As this and other cases made abundantly clear, West German courts during the 1950s were not interested in such a "clarification." The *Kameradenschinder* trials documented, however, that the courts' failure to prosecute German war crimes during the 1950s did not so much derive from a lack of evidence but from a profound unwillingness on the part of the legal system to draw on the existing evidence.

These trials, however, did more than displace West German confrontations with the past from the Nazi to the Soviet dictatorship. They also indicated the extent to which the ideology of anti-Communism shaped West German confrontations with the consequences of war and defeat. The trials raised the question of West German political justice at the height of the Cold War.[54] That the trials were strongly influenced by the political climate was the suspicion of at least one contemporary observer. Writing in a West German law journal in 1951, this commentator was concerned that the *Kameradenschinder* trials, "which have become increasingly frequent over the last year," were provoked "by political antagonisms" and were based on the "agitation of returnees, especially lawyers among them" against former comrades.[55] I am not, however, primarily interested in whether or not verdicts were justified; as we have seen, there was sometimes strong evidence for actual criminal offenses. Instead, what interests me is the ways West German courts and the West German public at large interpreted and evaluated deviant behavior in Soviet captivity.

The difficulty of reconstructing past events in faraway places opened up the *Kameradenschinder* trials, as it did the Nazi trials, to subjective interpretations and value judgments by judges and prosecutors.[56] In the case of the former camp doctor and antifascist activist Dr. Rolf T., the prosecutor admitted that as far as individual punishable offenses were concerned, "the prosecution had to confront problems that were already familiar from other trials of returned POWs. In many cases, conclusive evidence could not be established, partly because important witnesses were not available, partly because witnesses were unable to provide exact information due to the length of time that had passed since then."[57] As a result of these difficulties, the outcome of the trials depended largely on how the judges evaluated the available testimony of witnesses. In the case of Rolf T., however, the judge exhibited a clear bias toward middle-class witnesses for the prosecution. The verdict stated that "witnesses testifying in favor of the defendant had been, to a large extent, rather simpleminded people whereas most witnesses who compromised the defendant belonged to professions that could be called 'bourgeois' and who can be considered—due to their education and their responsible professions—as men of particular maturity, experience and of an independent way of thinking. They have exposed the defendant's guilt."[58] As a result of this evaluation of witnesses, the court sentenced Rolf T. to three and a half years in prison and the loss of citizenship rights for five years. Courts, to be sure, generally sought to question as many witnesses as possible in collecting evidence.[59] Yet in substantiating their verdicts, judges relied "to a particular extent" on "life experience, knowledge of human nature, and inference" in determining this sentence.[60] In other trials, judges employed legally questionable constructs such as the "moral principles of the general public" as the basis of their judgment.[61] These statements indicated that judges and prosecutors sought to compensate for lack of evidence with fuzzy legal concepts that eerily resembled the "healthy public sensibilities" that had often served as the basis of National Socialist judicial practice.[62]

It would be misleading to assume, however, that the courts pursued an explicitly political agenda in the *Kameradenschinder* trials. In fact, after 1945, the West German judiciary embraced a legal positivism that claimed to be distinctly apolitical. By doing so, it hoped to counter what was perceived as an extreme politicization of justice both during the Nazi period and during the period of Allied occupation.[63] This impetus manifested itself in the courts' tendency to portray the collaboration of POWs with Soviet authorities as an outgrowth of pathological personality structures rather than the result of political choices. The trials, in other words, resorted to psychological explanations in order to depoliticize the actions of the alleged *Kameradenschinder*.[64] Several verdicts were explicitly based on the "characterization" or the defendants' "personalities."[65] According to most verdicts, German POWs had collaborated with Soviet authorities solely for opportunistic reasons and in order to improve their living situations in captivity. Defendants in the *Kameradenschinder* trials were thus described as having exhibited a "weak character" as well as "mean" and "reprehensible" behavior. They had followed "low urges" and had pursued "reprehensible goals."[66] Occasionally, however, courts also charged collaborators with excessive political activism that "went far beyond anything that was permissible among civilized peoples."[67] In the case of Rolf T., who had served as a camp doctor in Soviet captivity, the prosecutors linked the charge of political fanaticism to homosexuality and to possible morphine addiction, thus further underlining the alleged pathologies of the defendant's personality.[68]

The courts also portrayed the accused POWs as lacking masculine virtues. In Rolf T.'s case, the judge suggested that T.'s behavior stood in stark contrast to that of POWs who had exhibited an "upright, manly attitude" and had resisted collaboration.[69] The verdicts, moreover, indicated that the courts continued to subscribe to soldierly ideals of mas-culinity.[70] West German judges and prosecutors, for example, described the avoidance of military service as indications of defendants' flawed characters. In the case of Oskar S., the court held it against the defen-dant that he had managed to stay on the homefront during the First World War and had also managed to assume positions in the rear of the front up until the end of the Second World War, even though "every available man was needed for front service in the last months of the Russian campaign."[71] The *Kameradenschinder* trials, however, also in-dicated a shift toward more refined ideals of militarism that differed sig-nificantly from their traditional Prussian antecedents. While the court considered lack of military service as a liability for S., the verdict in S.'s case also cited excessive militarism as one source of the defendants' transgressions in captivity. It was therefore S.'s "militaristic behavior" and his "militaristic inclinations" that were partly responsible for his abuses of fellow POWs.[72]

This ambivalent attitude toward military service became especially apparent in the case of Hans Peter T., who had been a highly successful career soldier in the German army. He had entered the Wehrmacht in 1937 as a volunteer, earned a distinguished military record in the French and Russian campaigns, and even served for some time as an aide in Hitler's headquarters. When he fell into Yugoslav captivity in 1945, he initially withstood considerable pressure to collaborate. In 1949, however, he began to interrogate German POWs on behalf of the Yugoslav authorities. He forced a number of German POWs to make false confessions through intimidation and violence; these prisoners were then held in Yugoslavia until the early 1950s. T. himself returned to West Germany in 1951. But in 1955, his past caught up with him. He was charged for offenses committed in captivity and sentenced to 18 months in prison for aiding and abetting in the deprivation of the liberty of fellow POWs.[73]

In determining the verdict, the court granted T. mitigating circum-stances due to his successful military service. According to the court, it was "considerably in the defendant's favor that he had proven himself in his profession as soldier on the front for many years." A psychological evaluation, moreover, granted T. a generally "positive moral attitude," which had manifested itself especially in his "soldierly career and qual-ification as a brave and eager officer."[74] As these statements indicated, military service remained an essential component of the courts' notions of respectability and ideal citizenship. The same psychologist, however, found T.'s successful military career partly responsible for his transgressions in captivity. As a "young professional soldier," according to his evaluation, T. had been "destined to receive orders" from Yugoslav authorities. Due to his "inflexible character," he continued to live in a "military dream world" and did not develop the "kind of thoughts that more complex and more sensitive human beings would have."[75]

While the court embraced the Wehrmacht tradition represented in T.'s successful military career, the case also exposed its dangerous potential: blind obedience to authority. The case indicated the ease with which traditional military virtues could be used for totalitarian purposes. The collaboration of a successful officer such as T. with Yugoslav authorities was also a metaphor for Wehrmacht collaboration with the Nazi state. The West German state was in the process of building up a new defense force and T.'s alleged failure in captivity had important lessons for the new West German army. It confirmed the efforts of military reformers such as Count von Baudissin to instill the new soldiers of West Germany with a firm set of moral and democratic principles that would prevent these new "citizens in uniform" from ever again becoming an instrument of totalitarianism.[76]

On a more concrete level, the behavior of former Wehrmacht soldiers in captivity also became a critical yardstick in evaluating them for service in the new Bundeswehr. Officials at the *Dienststelle Blank*, the agency in charge of creating a West German defense force, were deeply concerned about former antifascist activists infiltrating the ranks of the West German army. The Ministry of Expellees, which was formally in charge of POW affairs, compiled several lists for the *Dienststelle Blank* with the names of officers suspected of having compromised themselves in captivity. They were described as "uncomradely egoist[s]," "unclean in terms of character and appearance," or as "always having received better posts from the Soviets" while in captivity.[77] One employee of the *Dienststelle*, moreover, was actually charged with displaying a "Communist attitude" and with becoming "an instrument of the Soviet system," thus undermining the "reputation of the officer corps."[78] It is not clear to what extent these concerns were based on actual facts. They demonstrated, however, that loyal conduct in Soviet captivity was an important precondition for service in the new West German armed forces.

The *Kameradenschinder* trials clearly pathologized any kind of collaboration of German POWs with Soviet authorities. The defendants in these trials appeared as callous opportunists, merciless ideologues, and excessive militarists. They therefore represented the exact opposite of the ideal liberal-democratic West German citizen. The accused POWs, by contrast, were charged with having displayed a totalitarian personality structure compatible with both Nazism and Stalinism. Public commentators also emphasized that former Nazis had been more likely to collaborate with Soviet authorities so that the "local NS leader" (*NS-Zellenleiter*) had become the "political educator" (*Politbetreuer*) in Soviet captivity.[79] Some postwar observers, moreover, were deeply concerned that these specific character traits, this "psychology of the *Kameradenschinder*," seemed not to be limited to "criminal natures" but was also displayed by "fathers, sons, and brothers of our own people, by colleagues at our workplace and by people with whom we interact in daily life." According to this commentator, the collaboration of the POWs in Soviet captivity had exposed the "inhuman in us."[80] In West German public discourse, the secret informer in Soviet captivity, whose "name remained unknown" and who could not be detected by "physiognomic guessing," was equated with the elusive totalitarian enemy within who stood for both the Nazi and the Communist threat to postwar society. This totalitarian enemy often assumed the devious character traits that Nazi propaganda had previously associated with Jews.[81] Postwar commentators, however, no longer advocated racial purification as the "Final Solution" to these elusive threats. Instead, they sought to distance the Federal Republic from both Nazism and Soviet Communism by evoking the liberal values of democracy, freedom, and the dignity of the individual as the most important defense mechanism against the "missionaries of totalitarianism from the Left and from the Right."[82]

By portraying collaboration as a kind of psychopathological disorder, West German commentators replicated, in a somewhat different form, contemporary American concerns about Communist brainwashing of American POWs during the Korean War.[83] The refusal of twenty-one "turncoat GIs" to be repatriated after Chinese captivity was so incomprehensible to U.S. commentators that they resorted to notions of psychopathological deviance to explain it. At the same time, however, the case prompted widespread discussions of the perceived ills within American society that had allegedly rendered the POWs incapable of resisting Communist indoctrination. In particular, commentators blamed overprotective mothers for what they perceived as the feminization of American male youth.[84] Such a general discussion about the deeper causes of the POWs' collaboration in captivity, however, never emerged in West Germany. With very few exceptions, public commentators tended to explain the POWs' behavior in terms of individual pathology and not in terms of larger societal problems. This recasting of collaboration with Soviet authorities in psychological terms, however, does not seem too surprising. Any extended discussion of the larger societal and political factors that had led the POWs to collaborate with the Soviet dictatorship might have all too easily turned into a debate over ordinary Germans' "collaboration" with the Nazi dictatorship. Instead, in the context of the Cold War, the steadfastness of ordinary POWs, their refusal to collaborate with Soviet authorities and hence to become disloyal to the armies of Nazi Germany, appeared as the only ethically correct behavior and as a model of post-totalitarian citizenship.

This was especially true since former antifascist activists were celebrated as ideal citizens of the new "antifascist democratic" republic in East Germany.[85] The different reception of these POW collaborators in East and West Germany illuminated how one German society became the exact mirror image of the other: while these returnees were pathologized and criminalized in West Germany, they were considered model citizens in East Germany. The *Kameradenschinder* trials therefore also supported West German efforts to delegitimize the other German state across the border. The leaders of the East German "Socialist Unity Party" (SED), for their part, clearly recognized the potentially negative propagandistic impact of the trials. The SED denounced the trials as being driven by "reactionary" and "fascist" returnee associations and as targeting primarily those POWs who had displayed a "progressive attitude" in Soviet captivity. As a result, the SED even sought to prevent the release of the last POWs from the Soviet Union because the Party was concerned that this would expose former antifascist activists to criminal prosecution in West Germany.[86]

It was this specific German/German "communication" concerning the past that rendered any more differentiated assessment of behavior in Soviet captivity all but impossible.[87] The tendency to ascribe POWs' collaboration to deficient character or pathological personality ignored the question of whether they had had good moral and political reasons to be disloyal to Nazi Germany. Judges and prosecutors were therefore not prepared even to consider more explicitly political arguments in defense of collaboration with Soviet authorities. The courts' refusal to address these moral and political dilemmas became especially apparent in the case of one Gustav J. He had been captured in Stalingrad in 1943, and while in captivity he became a member of the Soviet-sponsored antifascist organizations of German POWs, the "League of German Officers" (BdO) and the "National Committee for a Free Germany" (NKFD). Gustav J. returned to West Germany in 1950. But in 1953, Hans S., a former fellow POW, reported him to the police as an informer and collaborator. Hans S. questioned the legitimacy of Gustav J.'s involvement with the BdO and the NKFD and accused him of helping Soviet authorities to prolong the internment of "German POWs because they have fulfilled their self-evident duty towards their fatherland."[88]

Gustav J. defended his choices. According to him, he had participated in the League of German Officers for two major reasons. He wanted to engage in resistance against Hitler and work for a quick termination of the war. He had arrived at this attitude as a result of his Catholic upbringing as well as the realization that "rarely have human beings been abandoned so shamelessly by their leadership as the German soldiers in Stalingrad." Secondly, he knew that Soviet authorities would try to reeducate the POWs and he saw the League of German Officers as a way to gain some influence in these reeducation efforts, so that they would not be left completely to the control of more radical German and Soviet elements. While he admitted that he had underestimated the constraints imposed by Soviet authorities as well as the resistance among ordinary POWs to reeducation, he never doubted that it was essential to foster a "democratic transformation and a distancing from the existing political system [in Germany]" among German POWs. He vehemently denied that he had received any better treatment in Soviet captivity than ordinary POWs and he cited his refusal to be repatriated to the Soviet zone of occupation in 1948 as evidence of his resistance to Soviet indoctrination efforts. As a result, he interpreted the charges against him as a "consequence of the war" and a vendetta against political dissidents that aimed at destroying his "honor," his "professional life," and his "family."[89]

The West German prosecutor, however, refused to address any of J.'s political arguments. Instead, the prosecution declared that J. had become a "willing instrument in the hands of the Russians," a "servant of the Russians" in Soviet captivity who did not "refrain from making more difficult the life of his fellow inmates for purely egoistic reasons." According to the prosecution, J. had therefore acted "extremely abominably." Despite this moral condemnation, the prosecution, however, failed to collect enough evidence that Gustav J. was actually guilty of denouncing other POWs to Soviet authorities. As a result, the prosecution dismissed the case. Despite this outcome, this case demonstrated the judiciary's unwillingness to recognize collaboration with Soviet authorities as a legitimate form of resistance against Hitler—whether there was enough evidence for actual criminal offenses or not. Instead, the courts tended to portray any kind of disloyalty toward Hitler's army as a moral if not legal offense and equated it with treason and betrayal.[90] As such, the *Kameradenschinder* trials also fostered the negative reception of the National Committee for a Free Germany.[91]

Nevertheless, while these larger considerations undoubtedly influenced the conduct of the trials, it is significant that the majority of legal investigations actually ended—as in the case of Gustav J.—with a dismissal or—if a trial actually took place—with an acquittal. Some cases had to be dismissed simply because witnesses provided contradictory testimony or prosecutors failed to marshal enough evidence for an indictment or a conviction.[92] In other cases, judges concluded that defendants had been guilty of criminal offenses but acquitted them on the basis of the 1949 amnesty law. This law nullified all offenses that could be expected to be punished with less than six months in prison and thus served to exonerate tens of thousands of small and not-so-small Nazi offenders who had committed bodily injuries and even manslaughter during the Nazi dictatorship.[93] The same law, however, also applied to POWs,[94] even though the *Bundesgerichtshof* had decided against the application of this amnesty to former POWs since their offenses were not directly related to the "political collapse" of Nazi Germany.[95] The courts confronted the legal, political, and moral problems raised by the

Kameradenschinder trials with confusion and considerable insecurity. The trials demonstrated a strong impetus within the West German judiciary toward rigorous prosecution and harsh sentencing of these offenses, and they were clearly driven by strong anti-Communist attitudes among judges and prosecutors. On the other hand, the frequent acquittals and dismissals of these cases also suggest that judges and prosecutors believed more generally in amnesty and in limiting or ending *any* legal confrontation with the past.[96] The trials were thus located between the contradictory tendencies of anti-Communism and amnesty.

The trials, therefore, present an ambivalent picture. On one level, the trials were part of a wave of political justice that swept Eastern and Western Europe alike during the early Cold War. They reflected the limitations of ideological pluralism in postwar West Germany. They served to minimize and relativize Nazi crimes by associating them with crimes committed in Soviet captivity, they limited the range of politically acceptable POW experiences, and they helped to prevent a more general debate on loyalty and resistance during National Socialism by associating any form of cooperation with Soviet authorities with treason and betrayal. As such, the *Kameradenschinder* trials had important similarities with the East German purges of former POWs who had attended political reeducation courses while in Western captivity.[97] While political trials in Eastern and Western Europe exhibited numerous differences, they both, in Charles Maier's words, "inhibit[ed] dissent, narrow[ed] the limits of political discussion, and by ritualized confrontations under oath and confessions, dramatiz[ed] the conflict between the faction ruling in the name of public virtue and its enemies."[98] In that sense, both the trials and the purges sought to eliminate behavior during the Second World War that did not fit into the ideological parameters of the Cold War. Moreover, both the trials and the purges were driven by widespread fears of ubiquitous "enemies within" who were suspected of undermining the respective reconstruction efforts.

But at the same time, there were important differences between East and West Germany. The East German purges were state-sponsored prosecutions of political enemies whereas the *Kameradenschinder* trials were conducted by a formally independent judiciary that—despite clear ideological biases—by and large upheld the rule of law. As we have seen, many of the *Kameradenschinder* trials ended in acquittals, which was a rather unlikely outcome for the East German purges. West German judges and prosecutors psychologized and marginalized politically deviant behavior but refrained from prosecution for mere political reasons. The *Kameradenschinder* trials thus also illuminated the institutional obstacles to blatant political prosecution in West Germany. As such, they mirrored the limitations but also the achievements of West German democracy in the 1950s.

Chapter Ten

"In a Thousand Years, Every German Will Speak of This Battle"

Celluloid Memories of Stalingrad*

ROBERT G. MOELLER

On February 2, 1943, the German Sixth Army surrendered to the Red Army, ending the battle of Stalingrad, one of the fiercest and most deadly conflicts of the Second World War. Estimates place German casualties at around 60,000. Another 110,000 Germans were taken captive, of whom only some 5,000 would straggle back to Germany in the next twelve years. This tally does not include Rumanians, Croatians, Italians, or Russian collaborators with the Germans.[1] Victory came at an extraordinarily high price. Between November 19, 1942, and February 2, 1943, nearly 155,000 Red Army soldiers lost their lives at Stalingrad and over 330,000 more were left seriously ill or wounded.[2]

On the day the German army conceded defeat, the *Völkischer Beobachter* published the full text of an address delivered three days earlier in Berlin at a mass meeting of the Nazi faithful. The occasion was

* My thanks to Heide Fehrenbach, Temma Kaplan, Lynn Mally, Klaus Naumann, Ulrike Strasser, and Marilyn Young, who helped me make this a better article.

the tenth anniversary of Hitler's seizure of power. Even before the German surrender, Hermann Göring, designated by Hitler as the man who would succeed the Führer, was ready to treat Stalingrad in the past tense, an event to be interpreted, understood, endowed with meaning, and incorporated into the German present; he promised that "in a thousand years, every German will speak of this battle in reverence with hallowed awe." Locating Stalingrad in a mythological firmament that included the "battle of the Nibelungen," part of that misty Teutonic past that loomed so large in the National Socialist imagination, and the successful repulsion of Xerxes's armies by a handful of Spartans in a battle that predated Stalingrad by two and a half millennia, Göring insisted that the "*Opfer*" of the Sixth Army would not be in vain. The German word can denote both passive victimization and sacrifice—suffering in service of a higher cause. For Göring, the *Opfer* of the Sixth Army should be an example to inspire all Germans to rededicate themselves to mobilization for the "final victory" (*Endsieg*) in the winter of 1943.[3] All Germans should take pride in emulating the heroic example of those who had fought at Stalingrad. Every soldier would feel "even prouder and more joyful" to be a part of such an army, guaranteeing "that Germany and Europe can continue to exist."[4]

Sixteen years later to the day, West Germans could see newsreel footage of the 1943 rally and hear Göring's words not at a meeting of a neo-Nazi organization or a right-wing veterans' reunion, but in movie theaters. On the silver screen, Göring's voice rang out from a radio, precariously perched on a wall in a basement filled with badly wounded Germans. For these near delirious celluloid soldiers, Göring's bombastic comparisons are no substitute for medical attention; not awe and reverence, but despair and anger are the responses the Reichsmarschall provokes. Still, this depiction of Stalingrad at the movies, many years after the shooting stopped, indicated that Göring was right about one thing: Germans would long continue to speak of this turning point in the war, determined to find in it a set of meanings that would be appropriate for the present.

The scene that included Göring's speech was part of *Hunde, wollt ihr ewig leben?* (Dogs, do you want to live forever?), a film directed by Frank Wisbar. Wisbar, drawing on historical research and interviews, took his title and some story elements from a novel by Fritz Wöss, published in 1958 after it had been serialized in a popular illustrated weekly. Many West Germans knew one version of *Hunde* before they saw it in movie theaters.[5] Nor was Wöss's page-turner the first account of Stalingrad on offer in postwar West Germany. The war on the Eastern Front in general and the defeat at Stalingrad in particular had been the subject of other novels and movies, which had begun to appear almost as soon as the war was over.[6]

Wisbar's movie thus did not move into uncharted territory, but he claimed to be traveling eastward via a bold new route. In Germany, Wisbar opined, "it was senseless to make senseless movies," a category that included a range of accounts of the war in the East that treated it as militaristic adventure, exaggerated melodrama, or tragicomedy in which the good-hearted everyman in uniform confronted not only the Soviet enemy but also the bungling incompetence of his German superiors. In contrast, Wisbar claimed to keep company with Schiller, Kleist, and Shakespeare, writers who understood that "the important themes come from contemporary history." The leitmotiv of his era was war. "In order to resist it, you have to show what it is really like" — something, in his view, that no other film account of war on the Eastern Front had accomplished. He hated "nothing more than war" and sought only to "lend artistic form to this hate."[7] A background story on Wisbar explained that the starting point of this "Bard of the Second World War" was "inferior and morally dubious novels from the illustrated magazines" but his commitment to objectivity allowed him to translate pulp into solid foundations for his antiwar message.[8] He was driven to Stalingrad by his "need to investigate the truth about one of the greatest tragedies of our time."[9]

Aimed at a mass audience, *Hunde* heralded no cinematic breakthrough, nor was it in any sense a precursor to the "Young German Cinema" that would announce its agenda only three years later in the "Oberhausen Manifesto," demanding an end to "Papa's Kino" and boldly proclaiming that "The old film is dead. We believe in the new one."[10] Had the proponents of the "Young German Cinema" ever produced a list of the movies they most abhorred, *Hunde* might well have been on it. However, if Wisbar's movie offers testimony to the abject state of cinematic innovation in the 1950s, it also has much to say about how postwar West Germans had come to understand Stalingrad and create a public memory of the Second World War. Linda Schulte-Sasse writes of Nazi historical films that they "assume a foreknowledge on the part of the . . . viewer, and their pleasure generally derives less from teaching new material than in affirming the audience's foreknowledge, allowing it to savor what it already 'knows.' "[11] Wisbar did not create a completely new framework for understanding the "sacrifice" of the Sixth Army; rather, *Hunde* clearly expressed meanings that had evolved since 1943, telling movie audiences what they already knew and were eager to hear again. An analysis of the movie also suggests how reflections on the Second World War could become a medium through which West Germans could better understand their present. In *Hunde*, Wisbar focused on the "tragedy of Stalingrad," but his movie also commented critically on the triumph of the "economic miracle" and the geopolitical status of the Federal Republic a decade and a half after the end of the Second World War.

The story *Hunde* offers begins not in Stalingrad but Berlin, with black-and-white Nazi newsreel footage of a military parade. Hitler greets the cavalry and goose-stepping soldiers as a sober voice-over intones: "It is magnificent to watch a parade. To the tune of stirring music, brightly polished boots hit the asphalt. In perfect unity, they march on."[12] The film will be no celebration of the Prussian military tradition, however; the narrator fast-forwards to where the story will end "when snow and wind blow away the shrouds and cover up what at first was so radiant and certain of victory." Now the newsreels show frozen corpses, German soldiers victimized by the Red Army and the Russian winter. Hitler, an intermittent presence throughout the film, usually filmed with his back to the camera, gazing out the window of the chancellery, negates this future. In November 1942, when he learns that the Sixth Army has been stopped just short of Stalingrad, he continues to insist that his army must take the city. The line between living and dead has been drawn. The order to fight on, the narrator explains, "would be the death sentence for the Sixth Army," the path that will lead to "gravestones on the hill of Calvary in Stalingrad." "A dead soldier doesn't care who won or lost the war," the narrator philosophizes, insisting, however, that it is necessary to "create a monument without gilding it," to tell the truth of the "life and death of the Sixth Army." Shot in black and white, Wisbar's movie picks up where the newsreels leave off.

As the film progresses from these solemn incantations to action, the truth is revealed through the experience of a bright-eyed young Wehrmacht lieutenant, Gerd Wisse (Joachim Hansen), fresh from training in the *Ordensburgen*, the elite Nazi schools where the "Führers of the future" were taught sports, racial science, and the Third Reich's version of history.[13] Still bubbling over with optimism and enthusiasm, Wisse has no doubts that he has come to fight the good fight and create order in a land where none reigns. It is the fall of 1942, and he has just arrived in Kharkov where he awaits his assignment. In a world that is otherwise virtually free of any female presence, it is more than coincidence that brings Wisse together with a Russian woman as he registers his arrival with the local German command. Katja, played by Sonja Ziemann, one of the biggest box office stars of the decade and familiar to audiences from a host of *Heimatfilme* including the smash hits *Schwarzwaldmädl* (Girl of the Black Forest) and *Grün ist die Heide* (The heath is green), appears here not in a dirndl nor does she break into song; rather, she is a Russian, seeking work with the occupying forces lest she be deported to the Fatherland and an uncertain fate.[14] Wisse quickly determines that Katja, a university student until the war interrupted her plans, speaks his language fluently; her father had a "weakness for the Germans" and insisted that she learn from their culture. Pressed for time because his departure for the front is imminent, Wisse exploits his connections to Lieutenant Fuhrmann (Gunnar Möller), an old friend from back home, a concert pianist who is recovering from a wound that has not diminished his ability to offer an elegant rendition of Beethoven's *Appassionata* Sonata. The best of German culture provides momentary solace from the harsh reality of war. Wisse appeals to his mate on Katja's behalf. "We can't deport someone like that," he exclaims, and his friend agrees to help; Katja will find temporary refuge working in the base library. Eager to express her gratitude, Katja shows up at the train station to see Gerd off; their intimacy extends no further than chaste handholding, but it seems clear that some German men in uniform can melt a Russian heart.

The train carrying Wisse eastward is filled with predictable companions—the battle-weary tank commander who complains that Hitler is celebrating victory at Stalingrad before the fighting is over and the pastor (Alexander Kerst) whose silence suggests that he senses what is to come. Their journey is interrupted because partisans, apparitions who never appear in the film, have blown up the tracks, but they find shelter for the night with a Russian family, absent a father dead in the war, but still filled with the great Russian soul. The widowed mother graciously accepts the impromptu dinner that the Germans throw together from their own provisions, food brought from the *Heimat*, not pillaged from the homes of the people whose land they occupy. Three adorable children who stare with wide, admiring eyes at their visitors do not confuse them with the evil beasts portrayed in Soviet propaganda. Their evening prayers before an icon on the wall are another indication that in the heart of Mother Russia, the *narod* (folk) has found ways to survive Stalin. Wisse, surprised to find religion in the godless East, is reminded by the pastor that "they tried to get rid of it in Germany too, but they failed, despite *Ordensburgen* and the Hitler Youth." It is clear that Wisse has much to learn. Wisse, so close to Wöss that the autobiographical quality of the novel seems apparent, is also close to *wissen*, to know, but at this point, Wisse still does not know much.

Wisse's next lessons will be at the front, where he has been assigned as a liaison officer to Rumanian troops. His German superior, Major Linkmann (Wolfgang Preiss), is identifiable immediately as the bad Nazi in this story; he distrusts the Rumanians, questions their ability as soldiers, and believes that Hitler plans to let them be "*verheizt*," the German word that can mean both "sacrificed in vain" or "incinerated." When the shooting starts, Linkmann will seek refuge in his bunker. Like the Führer in Berlin, this little Hitler at the front is confident that the Germans will be victorious but he will let others do the shooting.

And the shooting is soon to start. It is November 19, 1942, and the Red Army is mounting the attack that will leave the Sixth Army encircled. General Frederich Paulus (Wilhelm Borchert), the commander at the front, knows that the attack is imminent, but in the capital of the Third Reich, Hitler delays sending reserves. At 6 A.M., Soviet artillery shown in newsreel footage, not the dawn, is lighting up the sky. Wisse fights bravely, showing what stuff he's made of by charging to the front and single-handedly taking out a Red Army tank. If his men have worried up until now that this product of elite training will wilt when things get tough, their fears are now allayed.

Wisse has proven himself, but neither he nor the Sixth Army can hold off the Soviets. With the Red Army to the west, the only way to retreat is eastward. As Wisse and his men withdraw, they pass a provisions depot about to go up in flames, so that nothing will remain for the enemy. Wisse takes charge, overriding the quartermaster's orders and distributing supplies to his men. Blind obedience may have worked in the *Ordensburg*, but Wisse is responsible to a higher order in Stalingrad.

In the field post of the military leadership, there is a similar awareness in some quarters that not all commands from Berlin should be carried out. General Walter von Seydlitz (Carl Lange) believes that the army must attempt to break out of the "cauldron," despite the Führer's insistence that they hold out for victory. Seydlitz's superior at the front, Paulus, shares his fears, but Paulus, the symbol of the Prussian military tradition, still believes that an order is an order; his disillusionment is not yet complete.

Transferred to an artillery post near Stalingrad, Wisse rediscovers his arch nemesis, Linkmann, once again his superior officer. The lieutenant's spirits briefly rise at the news that a tank battalion is on its way to break through the Soviet lines and carve out a path for the retreat of the Sixth Army. However, once again Paulus refuses to disobey an order; the Führer has forbidden him from pushing out to meet the oncoming relief forces, and Wisse and the others trapped at Stalingrad soon learn that their rescuers have been stopped well short of the mark.

Christmas brings little occasion for celebration, but even Wisse is drawn to the makeshift tree and the sweet sounds of "Silent Night" coming from a chorus that huddles around the pastor. "I lost my parents when I was young," Wisse confesses to him, "and you know that the people who raised me allowed no room for God." The spiritual shepherd of this flock reassures him that it's not too late: "Sometimes it's only in hell that God finally reveals himself." Wisse has completed another chapter in this bildungsroman.

In charge of an artillery post, Wisse discovers that his old friend Fuhrmann, the pianist from Kharkov, is now part of the same detail. Wisse moves into the ruins of Stalingrad to determine where the shells from his guns are landing and in no time is engaged in a firefight with the Red Army. Bodies are dropping left and right, but Wisse and his men dodge the bullets, downing Russians and holding their position. When one of Wisse's men threatens to kill a Russian he has taken prisoner, Wisse not only intervenes but also releases the enemy and sends him back to his troops.

When the shooting stops, an exasperated Wisse rhetorically asks:

"Whatever are we doing in this part of the world?" Fuhrmann, the pianist, responds, "I can understand that the Russian wants us out of here—even factory workers, women and children are fighting for that. We have not really lost anything." This spirit of sympathy and understanding invades Wisse as well, and he orders a thirty-minute cease-fire so that both sides can clear away the dead and wounded. A piano, miraculously spared by the bombs and street fighting, allows Fuhrmann to provide background music—more Beethoven—for this somber scene. Russian eyes meet German eyes, grins and smiles are exchanged, even women and children peek out from surrounding buildings . . . and then the shooting starts again.

On January 10, 1943, the Russians renew their offensive, and newsreel footage offers vivid testimony of how things can go from bad to worse. Hitler has refused to surrender, and the answer seems clear when Seydlitz asks Paulus, "Will an army be sacrificed for no cause [*verheitzt*]?" Short of all supplies, Wisse and his sidekicks make a last attempt to find food and fuel at a nearby depot. When a member of Wisse's unit sees a plane preparing to take off, carrying officers and wounded men back to Germany, he makes a break for it. Kicked at the last minute from his perilous perch on the wing, he dies as the plane's tail snaps his neck. When Linkmann receives this news, he has no sympathy for Wisse and sends him to a makeshift hospital to find shirkers to fill out his squadron. Wisse finds not malingerers but his friend Fuhrmann, who is near death, both piano-playing hands blown away. Here he also listens to Göring's eulogy to the brave men at Stalingrad, until the pastor smashes the radio and one of Wisse's mates angrily rejects "any premature funeral orations."

Wisse could not be more disillusioned, but his battle is not yet over. Finding himself alone, cut off from his men, he picks a Red Army hat off the head of a fallen comrade and uses the disguise to enter the enemy's midst, even lining up to receive his ration of soup. Doling out calories and encouraging smiles is none other than Katja. Their eyes meet, and there is no question that she also knows how to disobey an order. Taking Wisse aside, she shows him the way to return to his side of the fight. There is romance in the air, but the moment is not right. When Wisse moves in for a kiss, Katja responds: "You cannot do that. We cannot be friends; we must be enemies. What has this war done to us?" This is a question the film seeks to answer.

When Wisse returns to Linkmann's command post, he lets him know what he has long believed: "You are no superior officer, you are a coward and a *Schwein*." With the Red Army three houses away, Linkmann has run out of time. Wildly rummaging through his trunk, he unearths a leaflet issued by the Red Army that promises those who surrender "life, good treatment, and a return home after the end of the war." When he emerges from his bunker, white handkerchief above his head, taking off for the enemy lines, Kraemer (Peter Carsten), a rough-and-tumble corporal who accompanies Wisse from the start, executes summary justice: "That is not our major; that is a deserter and a traitor."

The end is nigh. A dejected Paulus learns that Hitler has promoted him to general field marshal, an unambiguous signal that he should fall on his sword, but he declines this "invitation to suicide." "They lied to us," he tells his assistant. "I will never rid myself of the doubt that everyone made unbelievable mistakes." The attempts by other officers, now lined up to be marched off by the Soviets, to shift all the blame to Paulus triggers a forceful response from the cynical tank commander, who reminds them, "Don't fool yourselves. Everyone who could have prevented this disaster and cooperated anyway is guilty. And you, dear sirs, with your important careers, you kept your yaps shut, you obeyed and you demanded obedience. That's the source of all this evil [*da liegt der Hund begraben*]." Wisse, nearing rock bottom, but also wiser with every passing moment, wonders if "anyone will ever thank us. I don't know—it isn't really that important." Back in Berlin, Hitler does not miss a beat when he learns that "the Sixth Army is dead." Brusquely, the Führer responds, "Leave that pathos behind: it is only an army. Create a new one!" Newsreel footage of Germans trudging off to Soviet POW camps is interspersed with a final benediction from the pastor. His faith has also been tested, but he is still hopeful that "perhaps we can learn something from all this." Wisse has the last word: "Or perhaps not."

Hunde, wollt ihr ewig leben? was a film that many West Germans saw. Judged the second-best movie of 1959, it was awarded a National Film Award (*Bundesfilmpreis*) and a cash prize of DM 100,000 by the Interior Ministry.[15] Most reviewers joined in praising Wisbar for his extraordinary accomplishment. There could be no doubt that *Hunde* was an antiwar movie that "represented a monument to the innocent victims of the war," the soldiers who had given their lives in battle or in Soviet prisoner-of-war camps. Even critics who had become skeptical about "militaristic . . . still quite brown movies of rehabilitation" or were numbed by "the entire industry that seems to exist to produce an incessant stream of war movies" gave Wisbar high marks for making a movie that "honored not war, but the dead, constructing a monument that was not gilded." [16] With this movie, the "German film industry had delivered a contribution to the historical theme of the Second World War that should be taken seriously." [17]

Background stories on the making of the film emphasized that Wisbar's personal history equipped him to illuminate this national past. An officer in Weimar who had surrendered his commission in 1927, he had immigrated to Hollywood on November 9, 1938, *Kristallnacht* (the night of broken glass), "when I'd finally had enough." He returned to West Germany only in 1956. Interviewed by the weekly news-magazine *Der Spiegel*, Wisbar claimed that his commitment to bring-ing Stalingrad onto celluloid dated back to February 3, 1943, when he heard the news of the German defeat. In the drama of Stalingrad, he had seen from the start a "transnational tragedy, the tragedy of a nation that loses its freedom." [18] Wisbar had even started a screenplay, but his plans were interrupted by a lucrative career churning out over 300 tele-vision shows for an expanding American market. By the mid-1950s, the magazine reported, he was ready to return to Germany and to more se-rious topics. Unlike war movies made in the United States, which treated their subjects like "veiled Wild West movies," there was no room in Germany for "useless movies" about the Second World War; Stalin-grad deserved better.[19] Who could question the intentions of such an objective observer who counted on research and historical documenta-tion, not blurred memory, to tell his tale?[20]

A highly favorable review in the *Frankfurter Rundschau* echoed the pastor's closing words and praised *Hunde* as a "new chance to learn from Stalingrad." [21] The insertion of Göring's January 1943 speech was an explicit indication that old lessons would not be revived. At least some of the film's curriculum, however, was long since familiar. Like other movies that depicted the shooting war, *Hunde* was part of the restoration of German military honor in the face of Allied charges at Nuremberg of war crimes and crimes against humanity and claims that Germany could rid itself of the virus of National Socialism only if thoroughgoing demilitarization accompanied denazification and de-mocratization. By the early 1950s, creating the myth of the "clean"

Wehrmacht was a project that involved not only West Germans but also the western allies, who readily reversed their postwar condemnation of the German army once Germans in uniform were needed to fight new battles against old enemies, this time on the front lines of the Cold War.[22]

The careful distinction between good Germans and bad Nazis was one that had evolved quickly after the war. In 1945, Dwight D. Eisenhower, the Supreme Allied Commander in Europe, previewing the charge of the prosecution at Nuremberg, publicly maintained "that the Wehrmacht, and especially the German officer corps, had been identical with Hitler and his exponents of the rule of force,"[23] perpetrators of the same crimes, subject to the same penalties. Less than six years later, Eisenhower and the Allies had moved dramatically away from this global indictment; soldiers and Nazis could not be lumped together. In an official statement, hammered out by West German representatives and the U.S. High Commission, Eisenhower now averred that "there is a real difference between the regular German soldier and officer and Hitler and his criminal group." "The German soldier as such," Eisenhower assured West Germans, had not "lost his honor;" the "dishonorable and despicable acts" committed by a handful of individuals should not reflect on the overwhelming majority of Germans in uniform.[24] The same strategic inclination to forgive was also apparent in U.S. High Commissioner John McCloy's decision to pardon a number of Germans sentenced for war crimes, a move that embodied what historian Thomas Schwartz terms the U.S. policy of combining "moral compromises and political expediency" to integrate West Germany into the Western alliance.[25]

Like Eisenhower and almost all West Germans, *Hunde* drew clear lines between heroes and villains. The film offered reassurance to domestic critics of rearmament that Germans in uniform in the 1950s were changed, like Wisse, by their experience—they were not the unrehabilitated products of the Hitler Youth and the *Ordensburgen*. Sixteen years after Stalingrad, reviewers lauded Wisbar's success at not presenting a "puffed-up picture of blood and fire for the edification of those who had not experienced a battle,"[26] or copying the heroic shoot-'em-ups on offer in the illustrated magazines and the serial publications devoted exclusively to the glorification of the common soldier (*Landserhefte*).[27] The film's opening sequence of goose-stepping soldiers and stirring march music was a reminder of the susceptibility of the masses who failed to realize that the parade could lead to a "battle of destruction" (*Vernichtungsschlacht*). Wisbar's message was that, equipped with such hindsight, the army of the 1950s would not return to the patterns of the army of the late 1930s and early 1940s.[28]

Critics noted that Wisbar identified a problem that lay even deeper in the Prussian military tradition: the source of the goose step and codes of unquestioning military obedience that were not Hitler's invention. Wöss had taken his title from an apocryphal story of Friedrich the Great, who was said to have exhorted his troops to fight to the bitter end rather than die a coward's death. By understanding this past, West Germans could avoid repeating it. Like Wisse, the "citizens in uniform" of the newly constituted Bundeswehr could shed the legacy of Prussian militarism.

Franz Josef Strauss, West German Minister of Defense, did not agree that *Hunde* effectively communicated this lesson. He rejected Wisbar's request to make equipment or soldiers available for battle scenes in the movie, arguing that the "time is not yet ripe for a convincing representation of this fateful event." Should Wisbar proceed, he ought to know that he ran the risk of "unleashing heated public discussions." "Precisely for this reason," Strauss argued, he could not sanction the participation of German men in uniform as extras in *Hunde*. Seconding Strauss's refusal to cooperate with Wisbar, Adolph Heusinger, the commander in chief in the defense ministry, questioned whether it was "in the general interest once again to dig up this greatest tragedy of the German military," a move that threatened to open many "old wounds."[29] Strauss's refusal even led to a debate in the West German parliament, where the defense minister insisted that prudence was particularly important with films that addressed "the still unmastered past of our most recent political and military history."[30]

For the film's advocates such objections were proof positive that the time was right for such introspection, the healing balm that might help to close still open "wounds of battle."[31] *Hunde* could demonstrate the "meaning of war" to West Germany's youth, and for "today's young soldiers" it offered invaluable lessons about the "naked horror of the character of war."[32] Although Strauss might argue that the film inadequately illuminated the "moral bases for defensive preparedness,"[33] Wisbar's defenders argued that his message was precisely what the soldiers of the new Bundeswehr needed. The sympathetic portrayal of Seydlitz was another indication of the complex lessons Wisbar sought to draw from Stalingrad. Seydlitz, whose repeated requests in the film for reinforcements or the opportunity to break out of the "cauldron" of Stalingrad are rejected by Berlin, surrendered after the German defeat and remained in Soviet captivity until October 1955. Well known in the Federal Republic as a founder of the League of German Officers and a leading member of the National Committee for a Free Germany, organizations that had recruited antifascist forces among German POWs, Seydlitz was viewed by many West Germans as little more than a traitorous collaborationist who had abetted the cause of the Soviets and the Communist leaders of the "Soviet zone of occupation"[34] when he returned to the Federal Republic in 1955. Wisbar offered a far more sympathetic view, and in *Hunde*, Seydlitz appears as a tragic figure, seeking the good of his men and resisting irrational commands from Hitler. Precisely because it offered such a nuanced approach to the past, enthusiastic reviewers advised, recruits and officers in training should not shy away from this film, rather, for the next generations of leaders, it deserved the designation "particularly valuable."[35]

Neither Wisbar nor reviewers confused antipathy toward war with advocacy of complete disarmament. *Hunde* did make clear, however, that the soldier representing Germany in a reformed army would be freed of the symbols, ceremonies, and mystification that had characterized the German military in the past.[36] Wisse was proof positive that this new model of the military man had been forged in the crucible of Stalingrad. In late 1955, as the first recruits prepared to enter the Bundeswehr, the liberal weekly *Die Zeit*, describing the simple, unadorned uniform of the new West German army, observed that the pre–World War I hit song "The Soldier, The Soldier, He's the Handsomest Man in the Parade" would have no fans in a democratic Germany. It was time to take off the highly polished "boots . . . the symbol of a form of domination that the best representatives of the German army never wanted."[37] Wisse was plenty handsome, but he also provided evidence that good looks, valor, and honor could be packaged differently; he was the "citizen in uniform," who was ready to serve in the new West German military.

Many reviewers emphasized that this message was one that younger audiences in particular should take to heart. Because of Strauss's refusal to provide Bundeswehr troops, the extras used in battle scenes were students. Representatives of the postwar generation "that knows little of what happened in that winter of 1942–43 between the Volga and the Don,"[38] they learned from former military consultants about the technicalities of warfare.[39] However, one reviewer stressed that the film illuminated for young viewers not only the face of battle, but also the faces of their fathers, too often buried beneath the "prosperity of the years of the economic miracle [that] has drawn a layer of fat over our hearts so that we have forgotten the victims."[40] *Hunde* and other war movies were reminders to sons of their fathers' pasts. Concerns about "rebellious youth" in the second half of the 1950s focused on the fact that for many postwar young people, there were no adequate role models. Alexander Mitscherlich employed the categories of popularized psychoanalysis to describe the "Divided Father" and "generational conflict in the modern world"—products, Mitscherlich explained, of the "invisibility of the father." Fathers no longer had work that allowed them to demonstrate their abilities, leading to the "removal of the father" (*Entväterlichung*) from society. Distant or altogether absent fathers produced rebellious sons.[41] *Hunde* made fathers present, heroes, capable of exerting an influence, even from the "mass grave" of Stalingrad.

War movies like *Hunde* also offered a response to Americanized versions of sexuality and gender that bombarded West Germans in the second half of the 1950s. The wildly enthusiastic reception of American movies like *Blackboard Jungle*, featuring Bill Haley's "Rock Around the Clock," and the youth riots that accompanied Haley's appearance in Berlin in 1958, awakened fears about young people, particularly young men, who were defined by disaffection and rebelliousness.[42] West German descriptions of Elvis Presley as a "talented female striptease dancer," a performer who could transport his audiences from "Disneyland to Kinseyland," registered concerns about models of masculinity that were not only openly sexual but dangerously androgynous. By 1958, West German commentators referred to a "tame" Presley, now on West German soil in a U.S. Army uniform, but *Hunde* offered still other conceptions of a proper, homegrown, youthful man, capable of resisting authority when it took the form of a fanatical Nazi and able to win the girl with respect, decency, and a firm jaw line, not sideburns or gyrating hips.[43]

In 1959 Wisbar's moral prescription was aimed not only at revealing the corruption of Prussian military traditions and preventing battles like Stalingrad. As one reviewer noted, his film was a cautionary tale about battles in which atomic bombs, not tanks and machine guns, were the weapons of mass destruction. Only a year before *Hunde* premiered, the parliamentary ruling coalition of the Christian Democratic Union and the Christian Social Union outvoted opposition Social Democrats and pushed through final acceptance of NATO plans to station nuclear weapons on West German soil. Debates of the "March Resolution" coincided with the twenty-fifth anniversary of the "enabling act" that had left the Nazis securely in power in 1933, and the Social Democrat Fritz Erler evoked a "frightening time in the past, when a man—whom we all now consider the destroyer of our nation—stood before a huge crowd in our former capital city and said: 'Do you want total war?' "[44] *Hunde* underscored that Hitler, not the Germans, had destroyed Germany, but it also reminded West Germans of the devastating effects of "total war" and offered a warning to those superpowers whose fingers were on the nuclear button, capable of staging a nuclear "incineration." The bombed-out landscape of Stalingrad in Wisbar's movie evoked the bombed-out landscapes of Hiroshima and Nagasaki and suggested how sadder but wiser West Germans could admonish the nuclear superpowers to remember war's consequences. Wisbar hoped his film would have an audience outside Germany because, on one level, his story had universal meaning: "If you change the uniforms, then they are your soldiers, your generals, your men."[45]

Hunde also revealed a Russia with which West Germans could peacefully coexist. Although critical reviewers questioned whether the romance between Wisse and Katja was more than an "erotic concession" to the viewing public,[46] Ziemann's bilingual character represented possibilities for German-Soviet understanding that had existed even under Stalin. Embodied in Katja, Russian womanhood has nothing in common with the Communist "pistol-packing mamas" (*Flintenweiber*) that inhabited the imaginations of the World War I veterans described by Klaus Theweleit.[47] The choice of Ziemann for the role of Katja left no doubts on this score. Few actresses would have been more familiar to West German moviegoers in the 1950s, and probably none would have more readily evoked an image of unvarnished femininity. Katja's cultural compatibility with Wisse only further domesticates Russia/Russians in the film. She is armed only with a soup ladle. The same compassionate Russia peeks out from the religious peasant household where Wisse and his sidekicks find temporary shelter on their way to the front. If mutual understanding was possible in the midst of Stalingrad, then it was surely within reach over a decade after the war's end.

In West German political culture of the late 1950s, the Soviet Union no longer harbored the "Judeo-Bolshevik" threat of Nazi propaganda, nor, for that matter, the Asia that "began on the Elbe," demonized by Adenauer in the early postwar years.[48] In the second half of the 1950s, Soviet–West German relations steadily improved. In September 1955, Adenauer traveled to Moscow to negotiate an exchange of ambassadors with the Soviet Union, receiving in return Soviet promises to release the last German prisoners of war, including Seydlitz and some other Stalingrad veterans. The return to West Germany of the "Last Soldiers of the Great War," as the returning POWs were called, allowed the West German press to proclaim that "Now the War Is Over." It was time to recognize that good Germans had survived Hitler, just as good Russians had survived Stalin.[49] By 1957, a year after Nikita Khrushchev's revelation of Stalin's crimes, N. A. Bulganin, the Soviet minister president, was encouraging Adenauer to entertain "a decisive shift from mutual distrust and even a certain enmity to trust and friendship," based in part on the recognition that "in the last war the Soviet and the German people made the greatest sacrifices."[50] Even the "Berlin Crisis," triggered in 1958 by Soviet demands that western Allied forces leave West Berlin and threats to incorporate the city as an "independent political entity" into the German Democratic Republic, did not reverse this trend.[51]

In *Hunde*, Wisse and Katja cannot be lovers; whatever their affinities, a gulf divides them. Russia was no longer a deadly enemy, however, and for Russia and the Federal Republic—as for Katja and Wisse—peaceful coexistence is a distinct possibility. One enthusiastic reviewer recommended that the movie's antiwar theme was an "admonition for Germans, but for other countries too, even for Russia! With purity and fairness, it will become a connecting link between the German people and erstwhile enemies, and it is suited to replace coexistence with friendship."[52] Press reports emphasized that the Soviets concurred. The positive Soviet reception of the film contributed to Wisbar's ability to obtain rights to shoot parts of his next movie on location. This drama revolved around the end of the war in East Prussia, an area occupied by the Red Army in the winter and spring of 1945, transforming Königsberg into Kaliningrad. A news report recounted Wisbar's meeting with the head of the Soviet film industry who responded, when asked why he had not yet purchased *Hunde* for circulation in his country, "Do you have any suggestions for how I should explain to my staff that the best Stalingrad film was made not by a Soviet Russian but by a German?"[53] It was time to engage in collective reflection on the senselessness of war as a basis for mutual understanding, not mutual recrimination.

Some critical responses in the popular press emphasized not what Wisbar offered but what he failed to include. The movie did not answer "the question of why in fact the Germans marched to Stalingrad,"[54] and the Social Democratic Party's weekly *Vorwärts* questioned whether it was possible to understand the "crazed and criminal plans of the brown 'master race' to conquer the world" without critically examining the origins of Hitler's war, not just Germany's single most momentous defeat.[55] Stalingrad, added Hans-Dieter Roos, writing in the *Süddeutsche Zeitung,* was no sad, isolated case; the "laws of war" that could explain the "origins of this particular misery" were left unexamined by Wisbar.[56] Still, for most reviewers, the significance of Stalingrad as a symbol of the "crimes of Hitler's war" and a reminder to the "broadest German public" of the things that "can happen in their name"[57] made *Hunde* a film worth seeing. A review in the influential *Frankfurter Allgemeine Zeitung* concluded that it was an "objective presentation of the front, the common soldier, and his horrifying suffering," an important contribution to "the theme of the unmastered [*unbewältigte*] past of the war."[58]

In the year that the philosopher Theodor Adorno won the literature prize from the "League of West Berlin Critics," Wisbar won the film prize from the same group for *Hunde.*[59] While Wisbar's movie was showing on West German movie screens, Adorno was commenting on Germany's "unmastered past"—but that past was one of "deportations and . . . mass murder" of Jews, not the "senseless sacrifice" of Germans in uniform at Stalingrad.[60] For Adorno, what was missing in West Germany's attempt to "come to terms with the past" was a serious effort to eradicate all traces of National Socialism and restructure the capitalist system that had called forth fascism, condemning the majority of the population in the 1950s, no less than in the 1930s and 1940s, to a "condition of political immaturity." West Germans had tried to "master" the past—to put it behind them and lay it to rest—not confront their accountability for the horrors of National Socialism.[61]

Hunde is one indication that for West Germans there were other "unmastered" pasts in the 1950s, pasts of "innocent victims of the war"[62] who were not Jewish and who conformed fully to the expectations of the "racial state." They had been sacrificed by fanatical Nazis in Berlin and abandoned by fanatical Nazis at the front. *Hunde* was praised as an attempt to give meaning to the "huge sacrifice" they had made.[63] Critics took Wisbar to task not for dwelling on that sacrifice but for understating it, depicting soldiers who "remain freshly shaved and in tidy uniforms to the very end." The film's shortcoming was not that it displayed German suffering, but that it failed to display that suffering in all its glory.[64] If the simplistically "black-white characterization of its characters [was] disturbing" fourteen years after German capitulation, the film was nonetheless a necessary reminder that the "name Stalingrad is associated with one of the greatest tragedies of the war." The film's "resonance with the public" meant that West Germans should move beyond the "shameful silence" that had too long surrounded this "perfect example of the horrible, final consequence of the authoritarian principle, built on the bases of absolute power and slavish obedience," the "greatest tragedy of German history."[65] As one reviewer put it, perhaps Germans still shared with the Führer an inability to confront "defeat, guilt, and fate;" perhaps "the ghost of Hitler still survives within us."[66] Wisbar returned from America to serve as the exorcist of this German past. Packed movie houses, noted one reviewer, proved that "even movie audiences were now ready to contribute to the so-called 'mastering of the past,'"[67] a past in which the victims wore Wehrmacht uniforms.

According to a reviewer for a Hamburg daily, Nazi excesses included a crime that Germans should never forget had been committed "in their name,"[68] the same passive formulation that Chancellor Konrad Adenauer had used in September 1951 when he acknowledged that "unspeakable crimes have been committed" against Jews, prompting him to seek a reparations agreement with the state of Israel.[69] In the categories of West German public memory in the 1950s, both in concentration camps and at Stalingrad, a handful of crazed Nazis had sent innocent victims to their deaths.

The parallels ran deeper. The Sixth Army had been *verheizt*—subject to the "horrors of Dante's inferno."[70] The image of incineration and infernos evoked memories of other crimes of National Socialism, other victims meaninglessly sacrificed. Since the middle of the 1950s, public discussion of these other victims had intensified in the Federal Republic. As Harold Marcuse writes in his superb study of postwar West German confrontations with the Holocaust, the history of the Nazi period "was gradually broadened from the vague conception of the concentration camps as nebulous places where awful things had taken place, to include anecdotes about repression, deportation, exploitation, and, finally, murder in extermination camps." Key markers of this heightened awareness included a popular paperback edition of *The Diary of Anne Frank* in 1955, soon followed by a staged version in 1957. In the same year that West Germans could first see *Hunde*, an American film based on the play reached an audience of millions of West Germans.[71] In the last third of the 1950s, a growing number of acts of anti-Semitic vandalism against synagogues and Jewish cemeteries also raised fears domestically and abroad that a troubling phoenix was arising from the ashes of National Socialism.[72] One mode of combating the threat of neo-Nazism and anti-Semitism in the present was to confront its manifestations in the past. The creation of a "Central Office of the State Judicial Authorities for the Prosecution of National Socialist Crimes of Violence" in Ludwigsburg followed the highly publicized trial of a number of SS men who were charged with carrying out mass executions in occupied eastern Europe. And as *Hunde* played in movie theaters, Gustav Sorge and Wilhelm Schubert, SS sergeants charged with brutal crimes at the concentration camp Sachsenhausen, were nearing the end of a trial that had lasted five months and would result in life sentences.[73]

Against this backdrop, *Hunde* was a powerful reminder that National Socialism had also claimed countless victims who wore not the striped uniform of the concentration camp but the field gray of the Wehrmacht. Like the newspaper accounts of the homecoming of the last German POWs in 1955, labeled war criminals by the Soviets, *Hunde* emphasized that it was completely misguided to equate a tiny group of true "concentration camp beasts with the millions of honest German soldiers."[74] The film was also powerful evidence that in the West German popular culture of the 1950s, there was much more room for some victims than others. Wisbar's movie represented a "German Requiem"[75] but the film industry in West Germany offered no kaddish. When Anne Frank appeared, she was an American, speaking dubbed German.

Writing in 1959, Erich Kuby anticipated the critique of those who have looked back on *Hunde* and other war movies in the 1950s as part of the rehabilitation of the German military in the context of rearmament.[76] Kuby, a gadfly journalist and writer, acerbically noted that movies filled with heroic survivors offered a means to retell war stories with different outcomes. Writing specifically of *Hunde*, he reflected that "our life in West Germany since 1950 can only be comprehended if we understand that, this time around, every single German wants to win the war he lost. A German man cannot tolerate having a lost war in his past."[77] For Kuby, *Hunde*, though no propaganda for West German rearmament, nonetheless delivered the message that, armed with only a few more antitank weapons, air power, and a division or two, Germans could have trounced the Soviets at the city on the Volga. "Every German man who leaves this movie can feel that he has been exculpated. He can tell himself, right, if they had only given us more, we were really pretty terrific guys."[78]

But *Hunde* was not only about winning the war the second time around; it was also about winning the peace, establishing a moral high ground. From there, Germans could look back on National Socialism as part of a community of victims that included others who had been "incinerated" by the Nazis. In *Hunde*, the past also offered commentary on the present. The young men in Wisbar's film presented modes of masculinity that were untainted by the influence of Americanization and uncorrupted by the potential excesses of the "economic miracle." Compassionate and emotional, they were models for other young Germans who could once again put on the uniform.[79]

By the late 1970s, West German historians had put in place a far more complicated version of what the Sixth Army and other Wehrmacht units had done in the war in the East, unearthing a past in which Germans were perpetrators, not victims. Their account, however, did not register in Alexander Kluge's cerebral homage to Stalingrad, the 1979 movie *Die Patriotin*, a film doubtless seen in theaters by audiences much smaller than those Wisbar commanded two decades earlier.

Kluge was a representative of the "Young German Cinema," the progressive artistic movement that had only harsh words for the West German cinema of the 1950s. However, *Die Patriotin* indicated that the Left also believed it was necessary to offer empathetic reflections on what fathers in uniform had suffered, as they attempted to find an adequate description of the Second World War and offered alternatives to the accounts that had dominated the 1950s.[80]

Stalingrad had long preoccupied Kluge, and in the 1960s he produced multiple accounts of the battle.[81] In *Die Patriotin*, the war in the East, particularly the German defeat at Stalingrad, is also at center stage, weaving in and out of the story of a West German high school teacher "who has sympathy with the dead of the Reich" and who searches for ways to present German history to her students. Like Wisbar, Kluge makes much use of documentary film footage of the battle of Stalingrad.[82] He also evokes memories of the aftermath of German defeat by making the narrator of his movie a German knee, what remains of a soldier killed at Stalingrad in late January 1943.[83] The knee, borrowed from a poem by Christian Morgenstern, was also an allusion to other dramatic narratives of the Second World War. In Wolfgang Borchert's 1947 drama *The Man Outside*, a play widely known in the 1950s and 1960s, the central character is a veteran from the Eastern Front, a POW, "one of the many" returning from the Soviet Union who has "waited outside in the cold for a thousand days. And as entrance fee he's paid with his kneecap."[84] In the play, the confused survivor, Beckmann, is tortured because he followed orders, set out on an impossible mission, and led the men under his command to their death. Kluge goes a step further, suggesting that Germans also killed others by opening his film with the background music composed for the movie *Night and Fog*. This 1955 documentary on the concentration camps by the French director Alain Resnais had been seen by some West Germans in movie theaters in the second half of the 1950s, but it was available to many more when it was premiered on West German television a year before the opening of Kluge's film. In his analysis of *Die Patriotin*, Anton Kaes suggests that this choice "may hint at a consciousness that does not want to exclude Auschwitz from the patriotic *Trauerarbeit* [work of mourning]" in the film. However, as in Borchert's play and Wisbar's movie, it may also suggest an equation of the war's victims. And even for Kluge, depicting the war from the enlightened perspective of the late 1970s, Jews killed by Germans are present as a subtle musical reference, while the fallen dead at Stalingrad and bombed German cities are vividly portrayed.[85] The presentation of postwar Germany as a nation of victims was by no means the exclusive preserve of the Right.

Stalingrad became "big box office" again with the fiftieth anniversary of the battle in 1993, when Joseph Vilsmaier's version of the event attracted nearly one and a half million German viewers in that year alone. Vilsmaier's *Stalingrad* begins in August 1942 in Italy, where Wehrmacht soldiers lounge on the beach with Italian beauties who playfully rub them with olive oil, an intimacy that suggests that they have exchanged fluids of other sorts. This idyll is ruptured as the Germans are mustered to battle in colder climes. The narrator explains that the war is "moving into its fourth year. Hitler's armies occupy nearly all of Europe and parts of North Africa." The Third Reich is at the peak of its power, and the Sixth Army is close to securing the Caspian Sea and the oil fields of the Caucasus. What follows will be "the most horrifying battle of the century: Stalingrad." But in Italy, an enthusiastic young lieutenant, Hans von Witzland (Thomas Kreischmann), scion of an aristocratic military family, knows nothing of this future. He is off to earn his spurs — or his Iron Cross — on the Eastern Front.

Once the lieutenant arrives at the front, his disillusionment is rapid. He is completely unprepared for the brutality of the war in the East. Horrified by the mistreatment of Soviet POWs and the Soviet civilian population, he is soon at odds with his jaded, ideologically crazed superiors who cynically advise him that if he has complaints, "the best thing to do is to go straight to the Führer himself." Witzland is quickly identified as a "goddam Russian-symp [*Russenfreund*]," out of place in a war against subhumans.

Witzland's battle-weary men know better than to share his initial enthusiasm but the ruins of his idealism form the foundation on which they create a community of survivors. In battle scenes that anticipate the ferocity and horror of war for which Steven Spielberg's *Saving Private Ryan* received such praise, the lieutenant soon learns that his men, not the Führer or the incompetent leadership at the front, offer the only chance to escape death.[86] This is not the innocent Wehrmacht of Wisbar's movie. Vilsmaier depicts Germans killing not only Red Army soldiers but also civilians, even when their number includes a beardless youth who has aided Witzland's squad. He and his men know that these innocents are not "saboteurs—there is just nothing more to eat, that's why" they will be shot. Witzland is no criminal, and his men, exhorted to "cease this playing around with the Jews," join the firing squad only because they know that if they refuse, they will be lined up next.

Even more than in *Hunde*, these Germans are unwilling soldiers and certainly no murderers. When they flagrantly violate military discipline, requisitioning a doctor at gunpoint to minister to a wounded comrade, they are sentenced to a penal battalion (*Strafbatallion*) clearing minefields, until massive casualties and the need for additional men at the front justify their amnesty. When the shooting briefly ceases, they dream of home, longing to know if the crops have come in or if their favorite soccer team has won. And when one learns that "while I risk my ass for the *Heimat*, my wife is carrying on with a Frenchie, a POW," the others do their best to provide comfort and understanding.

Like film re-creations of the war in the East from the 1950s, Vilsmaier's movie cannot resist introducing the eternal feminine into this homosocial world; the lieutenant's ability to preserve a sense of honor in the midst of chaos and moral collapse is symbolized by his valiant protection of a female Red Army fighter, found bound to a bed in an abandoned officers' quarters. Raped by Nazis, she is protected by this noble German, and the lieutenant guarantees that his men will not add insult to injury. Daughter of a German mother, the comrade also realizes a strange kinship with her enemies and joins them in their vain attempt to escape through Soviet lines, until she is shot dead by her own troops in the midst of a desolate, snowbound landscape. Snow and cold claim the Wehrmacht soldiers. The good Russian and the good Germans transcend ideological systems to join forces, but both are ultimately victims of the insanity of war.

Vilsmaier's film is no simple remake of the visions of Stalingrad that circulated in the 1950s. The movie graphically presents the horror of a war that claims countless Soviets, including civilians and unarmed POWs, and alludes to Nazi anti-Semitism, a topic that Wisbar altogether avoids. The church is not a source of solace. Rather, when a pastor appears, he reminds the soldiers that their belt buckles carry the reassurance that "God is with us." On the eve of battle, they should remember that "There is no more beautiful duty than the defense of the Christian values of the Occident against the Bolsheviks of the East."

However, Vilsmaier's telling of the past presents some fascinating

parallels with the version of Stalingrad offered by Wisbar nearly thirty-
five years earlier. This time it is not Göring's eulogy to the Sixth Army of
late January 1943 that provides an ironic measure of the gap between
Nazi visions and war's reality, but Hitler's November 8, 1942 speech
commemorating his failed coup attempt, where he proclaims that only
isolated pockets of resistance separate the Wehrmacht from victory in
the city that bears the arch enemy's name. The jarring scene from
Hunde in which soldiers scramble to board a plane leaving for the
Heimat with the wounded appears again as Vilsmaier's heroes miss the
last flight out on January 23, 1943. If Vilsmaier allows organized religion to join the Nazis, that ur-German holiday, Christmas, does not
turn brown. As in *Hunde*, soldiers for whom home is now the front comfort one another with a spontaneous Christmas carol. Vilsmaier offers
no imagined vision of a Führer gazing from his Berlin window onto
falling snow, and at the front, the high command is absent. But no more
than Wisbar does he explore what brought Germans to the Volga. And
like Wisse, after a particularly bloody firefight, Witzland calls for a
cease-fire to allow both sides time to clear away their wounded, while
Red Army and Wehrmacht forces exchange understanding glances and
scarce supplies.

Nor does Vilsmaier shy away from implicit comparisons between
victimized soldiers and other victims of the war, a message familiar from
the 1950s and delivered again in 1985 by Ronald Reagan, who joined
West German chancellor Helmut Kohl at Bitburg to proclaim that the
Waffen SS dead buried there were "victims of Nazism also . . . They
were victims, just as surely as the victims in the concentration camps."[87]
The same theme was explicit when Andreas Hillgruber triggered the
Historikerstreit (historians' debate), a protracted scholarly controversy
over the meaning of the National Socialist past for the Federal Republic, by juxtaposing "the destruction of the German Reich and the end
of European Jewry."[88] If anything, Vilsmaier draws the parallels even
more clearly. As soon as Witzland and his men leave their seaside
refuge in Italy, they travel by train through a dark tunnel, and the music
turns somber and ominous. They become another group of deportees,
sent by fanatical Nazis not to the killing fields of Sobibor, Majdanek,
Treblinka, Auschwitz, and Chelmno, but to another equally hellish
destination. Witzland and his men arrive by *Nacht und Nebel* (night
and fog) in a huge factory-like hall, a train station that evokes images of

other final destinations, other victims in Eastern Europe. The battle scenes are all filled with flames. The "incineration" of the Sixth Army is depicted even more vividly than in Wisbar's black-and-white film, evoking other fiery hells that consumed other victims. The movie's closing scene depicts Witzland, dead, cradled in the arms of one of his men, also a casualty of the cold. This pietà appeared on the screen as Germans debated the appropriate form for a memorial in Berlin that would commemorate victims of Nazi terror alongside German victims of the war. Selected to symbolize this range of victims was a replica of Käthe Kollwitz's sculpture *Mother with Her Dead Son*, the "Kollwitz pietà," as it was called in the popular press.[89] Like Kollwitz, Vilsmaier presented a memorial, a movie that, in the words of *Die Zeit* columnist Andreas Kilb, "shows the Germans just as they most like to see themselves: as victims"[90]—victims of crazed Nazis, the Russian winter, the Red Army, and a war they never wanted to fight.

Two years after the debut of Vilsmaier's *Stalingrad*, Hannes Heer and Klaus Naumann marked another commemoration, the fiftieth anniversary of the end of the war. They published a volume that accompanied the opening of *Vernichtungskrieg*, a traveling exhibition of photographs portraying German army troops brutally murdering partisans and other civilians, many of them Jews, in Eastern Europe. Although the crimes of the Wehrmacht had long been known to the scholarly public that studied the Second World War, here documents were on public tour along with an impressive collection of essays summarizing what was already known and also including new archival sources. The result was a hair-raising record of the Wehrmacht's complicity in mass murder.

Stalingrad figured in Naumann and Heer's volume as well. In an article that described the Sixth Army's route to the Volga, Bernd Boll and Hans Safrian demonstrated that to begin the army's story in November 1942—the real starting point for Wisbar, Kluge, and Vilsmaier, and, as the authors note, virtually every other German student of the "end of the Sixth Army"—was to leave the worst unsaid. Like many other Wehrmacht units, the soldiers of the Sixth Army could unequivocally be designated perpetrators, "agents of the policies of conquest and destruction of the NS-Regime as [it] marched through the Soviet Union to the East . . . , actively involved in genocide and not only when following orders."[91] Four years after the exhibition opened, it came under attack by critics who established that some of the photos had been incorrectly identified; what some pictures documented were Soviet, not German, atrocities.[92] However, no serious scholars questioned the devastating archival record on which Boll and Safrian based their account. They provided irrefutable evidence that on its way to Stalingrad the Sixth Army took time to round up and murder Jews and other civilians. Its route went through Babi Yar where Sixth Army soldiers cooperated actively with the SS in the mass murder of some 33,000 Jews, and by the time Wisse arrives at Kharkov in late 1942, soldiers from Paulus's army had assisted in the murder—by shooting or in gas wagons—of some 22,000 Jewish men, women, and children in that city. Wisbar and Wisse exempt their heroes from this carnage by allowing them to arrive at the front only in late 1942, and the men they join are battle-weary victims, not mass murderers.

Ultimately, however, Boll and Safrian's account of the Sixth Army's progression toward Stalingrad is no more adequate than the versions that repeat with endless variation the "mythology of victimhood" first propagated by the Nazi state.[93] The story of Stalingrad cannot begin with the German army's encirclement by the Red Army and abandonment by the Nazi leadership in Berlin any more than it can end with the Sixth Army as an accomplice in crimes against humanity. Understanding the power of each of these variants is important; each marks a phase in the development of public memory in Germany since the end of the Second World War.

One phase was characterized by an unwillingness on the part of West Germans to confront their complicity in Nazi crimes. Adorno identified this tendency in his 1959 essay, and it was echoed in Alexander and Margarete Mitscherlich's 1967 charge that Germans demonstrated an "inability to mourn." Using Freudian categories to analyze the postwar German psyche, the Mitscherlichs argued that after 1945, Germans should have come to an understanding of their deep identification with Hitler and the "national community" (*Volksgemeinschaft*), thus acknowledging their responsibility for crimes committed by the regime they had overwhelmingly supported. The only way to leave this difficult history behind was to invest in the "expansion and modernization of our industrial potential, right down to the kitchen utensils."[94] In the psychic economy that the Mitscherlichs described, creating for the future was a way to avoid the past.

At a 1983 conference to commemorate the fiftieth anniversary of the Nazi seizure of power, Hermann Lübbe offered a variation on the theme of German silence, arguing that in the 1950s, West Germans had necessarily maintained a "particular quiet" around memories of National Socialism. There was no easy way to judge and condemn a small group of leaders when the unavoidable truth was that the majority of the German people had enthusiastically supported Hitler. According to Lübbe, keeping quiet about the past was not the same as repressing it. A deliberate distancing from National Socialism was the prerequisite for moving beyond painful memories and creating a unified, democratic Federal Republic.[95] More recently, Jeffrey Herf has presented another version of this thesis. He argues that for Adenauer, "Economic recovery and political legitimacy, not additional purges [of National Socialists], were the proper medicine. Democratic renewal went hand in hand with silence and the forgetting of a dark past. Too much memory would undermine a still-fragile popular psyche."[96]

Hunde is a good indication that silence about the past was only part of the therapy West Germans required in the 1950s to move beyond National Socialism. There were other "dark pasts" best treated with the talking cure, and other memories that circulated in excess. The transformation of the Sixth Army into victims was another mode for confronting the past that allowed the millions of men who had put on military uniforms, in many cases engaging in extraordinarily brutal forms of warfare and mass murder, to return to civilian life as heroic survivors. The devastating outcome of the war allowed West Germans to remember selectively, to tell stories of a past in which they, not others, were the war's most tragic victims.[97] Trauma and suffering are among the most powerful forces capable of shaping "communities of memory." In the 1950s, most West Germans created such communities by focusing on their own experiences.[98] West German public memory was selective; some stories of the Sixth Army were told again and again, others were not.

The reiteration in Vilsmaier's film of the theme of German victimization suggests the abiding power of this account of the war on the Eastern Front. But by the early 1990s, Boll and Safrian's stunning indictment of the Sixth Army made clear that there was more than one version of the past available to the citizens of a unified Germany. Their work built on nearly two decades of scholarship that established what West Germans in the 1950s had systematically denied. A generation of sons and daughters called for a history in which the Wehrmacht was fundamentally racist as it set out to confront the "Judeo-Bolshevik" menace. How difficult it is for some Germans to accept this alternative is apparent in the controversy that continues to surround the exhibition for which Boll and Safrian provided a solid scholarly underpinning.[99]

Perhaps there are ways to tell the story of Stalingrad that move beyond worlds of absolute good and evil. A year after the premier of *Hunde, wollt ihr ewig leben?* Vasilii Grossman completed the manuscript of *Life and Fate*, a sprawling novel that revolves around the battle of Stalingrad. In *The Bones of Berdichev*, John Garrard and Carol Garrard's gripping account of Grossman's life and work, Grossman appears as an eyewitness to the battle, reporting on it for the *Red Star*, the Soviet military's daily newspaper. Grossman also knew the route by which the Sixth Army had arrived at the Volga. In January 1944, he visited Berdichev, his own birthplace and the site of his mother's death on September 15, 1941. Grossman, like fifty percent of Berdichev's population, was Jewish, and his mother was killed by the same SS special commando that trailed the Sixth Army eastward, stopping next at Babi Yar.[100] In Grossman's stunning tale, Ukrainians too are anti-Semites, loyal comrades are sent to the gulag, some Germans commit crimes against humanity but other Germans suffer, Hitler presents Paulus with impossible alternatives, and in the clash of two totalitarian regimes neither is without blame.

When Grossman sought a publisher for his work, he discovered that even eight years after Stalin's death *Life and Fate* told a story too complicated for the Soviet Union. Despite the "cultural thaw" that accompanied Khrushchev, Soviet authorities were not ready to explode the myth of the "Great Patriotic War" or to undermine the official memory that allowed no room to "divide the dead" by emphasizing that Ukrainians had assisted Germans in killing some Soviets because the Soviets were Jews. A kinder, gentler Soviet state did not move to eliminate Grossman, but on February 14, 1961, three KGB agents did "arrest" all copies of his manuscript. Grossman died in 1964, but his words lived. A copy of the manuscript was smuggled out of the Soviet Union, and *Life and Fate* appeared in French translation in 1980. It was finally available in Russian at the end of the decade in a Soviet Union transformed by glasnost.[101]

It is difficult for Germans to describe such a nuanced past. In the early 1990s, Vilsmaier's frozen martyrs confronted Naumann and Heer's cold-blooded murderers, and in neither account did Soviets have life or breath. Perhaps when we reflect on Stalingrad sixty years after the German defeat on the Volga, it will be possible to provide a cinematic—and historical—account of the battle that describes the Sixth Army's murderous route to Stalingrad *and* the death or consignment to Soviet captivity of thousands of Germans and their allies. The objective would not be a "balanced" account nor an account that denies that the German army appeared as an uninvited aggressor in the Soviet Union in June 1941. Nor would the purpose be to equate the suffering of German soldiers with the suffering of those they victimized. In the midst of the *Historikerstreit* of the 1980s, Jürgen Habermas questioned the motives of "whoever insists on mourning collective fates, without distinguishing between culprits and victims."[102] No account of Stalingrad should blur that boundary.

A tale of Stalingrad that follows the Sixth Army to the Volga *and* describes their fate once they arrive, an account that describes German soldiers as both subjects and objects of extraordinary violence and in which Jewish and other Soviet victims speak, however, would come closer to capturing the complexity of this historical moment. This is superior to a binary world of "victims" and "perpetrators" in which victims are innocent and speak an unassailable truth and perpetrators, brought to justice, get what they deserve.[103] Grossman's layered alternative makes clear that telling the story in this way can reveal much about how people behave under extraordinary circumstances; it is a historical account that has profound ethical and moral implications. And without taking seriously both how the Sixth Army arrived at Stalingrad and what happened between November 1942 and February 1943, it is impossible to understand how Germans came collectively to remember themselves as victims. This memory emerged even before the Sixth Army's surrender and after 1945, it facilitated the reconstruction of civil society in the Federal Republic and the reintegration of millions of German men who came home with horrifying visions of the war on the Eastern Front. Without addressing the defeat of the Sixth Army, it is impossible to understand how collective memories from the late 1940s and early 1950s of an army of innocents sacrificed at Stalingrad have survived for more than five decades.

The violent political response to the Wehrmacht exhibit raises questions about whether citizens of a unified Germany will ever achieve such a complex view. There are, however, other indications that Germans are eager to revisit a "past that will not pass."[104] Although the reception in Germany of Daniel Goldhagen's *Hitler's Willing Executioners* could be interpreted in several ways, the discussion it generated—crossing generations and involving historians and the lay public—indicates that many Germans are ready to acknowledge the enormity of the Nazis' crimes against humanity and accept a broadly defined national responsibility for these crimes.[105] Although some commemorations of the fiftieth anniversary of the war's end were characterized by renewed insistence that German victims be recognized, huge numbers of ceremonies and exhibitions not only alluded to Nazi crimes but also took care to remember the names and faces of the victims of the Third Reich.[106]

No single position dominates the politics of memory in contemporary Germany. Continued distance from the event may also facilitate the move toward a more complicated understanding of the war in the East. As the generation of '68 turns gray at the temples and the generation who marched east in 1941 dies off, revisiting Stalingrad will no longer trigger a battle between fathers and sons. And the end of the Cold War allows historians to view Russian-German enmity in the past without implicit reference to Russian-German enmity in the present.

Perhaps in this changed context it will be possible for Germans to move beyond the quasi-religious categories of sacrifice and atonement that have so long dominated popular representations of Stalingrad, to provide an account of the battle and its postwar representations that does not confuse history, mourning, moralism, and commemoration and to offer an injunction to remember that does not make memory the responsibility of Germans alone. From this perspective, it might be possible to follow German soldiers east via Babi Yar and Kharkov without denying the enormity of their suffering at Stalingrad, to tell a story of the war in the East that includes the Jewish "bones of Berdichev" as well as the bones of the German dead that still litter the brown steppes surrounding a city on the Volga that once bore Stalin's name.[107]

Chapter Eleven

When Memory Counts

War, Genocide, and Postwar Soviet Jewry

AMIR WEINER

Ordained as the Armageddon of the Bolshevik enterprise, the Second World War precipitated major changes in both the Soviet state and in popular ideology and practices. Nowhere were these changes more noticeable than in the perennial cleansing drives. The war signaled a qualitative and quantitative shift in a polity already consumed by constant campaigns to eradicate internal, elusive enemies that hampered the pursuit of sociopolitical harmony. During the prewar era, the regime maintained differentiation and the prospect of reform and rehabilitation of groups targeted as internal enemies, but in the war's wake it considered such groups undifferentiated, unreformable, and irredeemable collectives.

The result was the unprecedented deportation of entire ethnic communities charged with harboring sympathy for the invading Germans or actively collaborating with them. Internal enemies were no longer differentiated according to their alleged degree of hostility toward the Revolution and the Soviet state, or because of the presence of family members with the proper politico-ideological background. Deportations that hitherto had been confined to term sentences now meant permanent exile. In essence, these acts constituted severe challenges to what was previously a sacred tenet of the Soviet enterprise, according to which individuals and groups were considered sociological constructs, prone to transformation via Soviet acculturation.[1]

Consecrated as the climactic clash of the Revolution that would usher in the era of Communism, the war was also viewed as a final cleansing of the human "weeds" who had survived previous cycles of purges. There was little hope for those stigmatized as having failed to rise to the occasion. The Soviet regime and citizenry may not have possessed the exterminatory impulses and institutions that made the Nazi regime unique. But after the war, they displayed a willingness to discuss and operate on the very same assumptions as their archenemy, if only temporarily. And this was the position in which Soviet Jews found themselves during the last decade of Stalin's reign, when the antifascist regime to which they pledged loyalty began flirting with racial thinking and practices.

Conventional wisdom points to the establishment of the state of Israel and the unfolding Cold War as primary causes for the deterioration in the status of the Jewish community within the Soviet polity. Indeed, the creation of the Israeli state transformed Soviet Jewry overnight into a diaspora nation with a highly active external homeland. In the 1930s, a similar situation cost Polish and German minorities in the Soviet Union dearly. Often glossed over, however, is the centrality of the living memory of the war and the Jewish genocide in shaping the course of Soviet-Jewish relations and providing them with a constant point of reference in the years following the war. Soviet officials were aware of this juncture. Years after the war, when the Israeli poet Avraham Shlonski visited the Soviet Union, he was told by Aleksei Surkov, the secretary of the Union of Writers, that "[t]here were times when we thought that the process of Jewish assimilation was being intensified by dint of the historical logic of Soviet conditions, and that the Jewish problem was being solved by itself. Then came the war with its horrors, then the aftermath. All of a sudden Jews began to seek one another out and to cling to one another."[2] If Surkov is to be forgiven for some self-righteousness, he was not off the mark. From the early stages of the war, the Jewish community found itself pitted against the cornerstones of the Soviet ethos of the war, the twin institutions of hierarchical heroism and universal suffering. Whereas the various nations of the Soviet Union were ranked in a pyramid-like order based on their alleged contribution to the war effort, their suffering was undifferentiated, ruling out any ethnonational distinction, in spite of the awareness of the Nazis' own racial hierarchies and practices.

PONDERING THE UNTHINKABLE: RACIALIZED COMMUNISM?

It comes as no surprise that the totalization of Soviet practices in the quest for purity brought to the fore the inherent tension between the biological and the sociological categorization of the enemy within and consequently the inevitable comparison to Nazi Germany, the other totalitarian enterprise. Nowhere else was this issue exposed more clearly than in the Soviet policy toward its Jewish minority. Following the war and the trauma of the Holocaust, conducted extensively on Soviet soil with the implicit and often explicit approval of the local populace, as well as a wave of popular and official anti-Semitism in the immediate postwar era, ordinary Jewish citizens and activists began to ponder the unthinkable: was there a logical affinity between the two ideologies?

For some there certainly was. In the small town of Nemyriv, angry survivors of the genocide and returning partisans accused the local party leadership of deliberately impeding the evacuation of the Jewish community to the Soviet rear when the Germans were already at the outskirts and of actively collaborating and participating in the extermination of the local Jewish community. They concluded that the party's policy toward the Jews did not differ from that of the Germans.[3] Following a mass pogrom in Kiev on September 4, 1945, Jewish Red Army veterans complained to Stalin and Beria that the local Communist party consciously adapted German racist politics. The reference to the "new course" of the Communist Party unmistakably echoed the Nazi New Order. "This 'course'," wrote the four veterans, "has a lot in common with the one that originated earlier from the chancery of Goebbels, whose worthy transmitters turned out in the Central Committee and the Council of People's Commissars of Ukraine."[4]

This point was also laid out bluntly by Vasilii Grossman in his epic *Life and Fate*, which he started writing at this time. For Grossman there was nothing accidental or temporary about the barbarization of Bolshevism. It was ingrained in the core of the Bolshevik ethos, he argued. The war merely helped to bring this reality to the fore. Grossman chose none other than the triumphant moment and site of Stalingrad to underline the common ethos of the Nazi and Soviet enterprises:

> Suddenly, probably because of the war, he began to doubt whether there really was such a gulf between the legitimate Soviet question about social origin and the bloody, fateful question of nationality as posed by the Germans. . . . To me, a distinction based on social origin seems legitimate and moral. One thing I am certain of: it's terrible to kill someone simply because he's a Jew. They're people like any others—good, bad, gifted, stupid, stolid, cheerful, kind, sensitive, greedy . . . Hitler says none of that matters—all that matters is that they're Jewish. And I protest with my whole being. But then we have the same principle: what matters is whether or not you're the son of an aristocrat, the son of a merchant, the son of a kulak; and whether you're good-natured, wicked, gifted, kind, stupid, happy is neither here nor there. And we're not talking about the merchants, priests, and aristocrats themselves—but about their children and grandchildren. Does noble blood run in one's veins like Jewishness? Is one a priest or a merchant by heredity?[5]

Indeed, in the wake of the war, Soviet public representations increasingly identified Jews as inherently resistant to Soviet acculturation and, even more threateningly, as an undifferentiated entity. As early as December 1941, during a conversation with a visiting Polish delegation, Stalin found time to reflect on the martial qualities of the warring sides. The Slavs, observed the Soviet leader, are "the finest and bravest of all airmen. They react very quickly, for they are a young race which hasn't yet been worn out. . . . The Germans are strong, but the Slavs will defeat them." Jews, on the other hand, were repeatedly referred to as "poor and rotten soldiers."[6]

The core message of the anti-cosmopolitan campaign in the late 1940s was that the Jew remained a Jew, an eternal alien to the body national, no matter what the circumstances. As such, he had to be stripped of the false layers under which he deceptively wrapped himself. In early 1949, the Soviet press violated one of the taboos of Bolshevik revolutionary culture when it started disclosing pseudonyms. The birth names of assimilated Jewish figures in the arts were regularly attached to their assumed ones. And so the literary critic Il'ia Isaakovich Stebun learned, along with the readers of the republic's main newspaper, that at the end of the day, after honorable service at the front and a career of writing in the Ukrainian language, he was still Katsenelson. Similarly, the poet Lazar Samiilovych Sanov found out that his own work in the Ukrainian language and service as a war correspondent did not change the fact that he was still Smulson, just as Zhadanov was still Livshits and Han remained Kahan.[7]

When the anti-Semitic campaign was reaching its climax in early 1953, the alleged Jewish resistance to Soviet acculturation called for the use of uncompromising methods by the authorities. While exposing an accused Jewish embezzler in the town of Zhmerynka who, needless to say, had relatives abroad and managed to avoid the front during the Great Patriotic War ("he fell ill precisely at the end of June 1941"), the satirical magazine *Krokodil* posed a rhetorical question: "To tell you the truth, we became tired of reading your decisions scattered there: 'to reprimand, to point out, to suggest,' etc. Doesn't it seem to you, comrades, that you overestimate the educational significance of these resolutions of yours? And, anyway, who are you trying to reeducate? With such touching forbearance, too?"[8] The Jew, simply put, proved to be the anomaly in the Marxist premise of the primacy of nurture over nature. He was immune to reeducation. In early 1953, with the recent executions of the leadership of the Jewish Antifascist Committee, the unfolding Doctors' Plot (the fabricated charges against Jewish physicians accused of plotting to murder Soviet leaders), and rampant rumors about the inevitable mass deportation of Jews, the recommendation to transfer the case to the regional prosecutor, an office famed for meting out swift and harsh punishments, sent the unequivocal message that there was only one way to deal with such types.[9] As the living antithesis to the core Soviet myths of hard and honest socialist labor and the martyrdom of the recent war, the Jew was beyond redemption. His nature was immune even to the powerful acculturation of nearly four decades of Soviet life. Similarly, the portrayal of Jews in the press assumed an unambiguous racial character. In a biting feuilleton that could easily be mistaken for Nazi prose, the true physical and psychological traits of an exposed Jewish embezzler came to light once he was caught and brought to trial. Once "handsome, brown-haired, with a felt hat and well-cut overcoat," he turned into a physically repulsive creature. "His long, fleshy nose points mournfully downward, his puffy lips tremble with fear, his small rat-like eyes roam uneasily. He only comes to life when he tells how he bought gold and concealed diamonds." [10]

Uncovering the "real" Jew, however, was not confined to the Stalin era. Several years later, it was the turn of the de-Stalinizing Khrushchev to warn other Communists against the false hope of acculturating the Jew. While attending a session of the Central Committee of the Polish Communist Party, Khrushchev urged the Poles to correct the "abnormal composition of the leading cadres" as the Soviets successfully had done. Staring hard at the chairman of the meeting, Roman Zambrowski, who was born Zukerman, Khrushchev exclaimed: "Yes, you have many leaders with names ending in 'ski,' but an Abramovich remains an Abramovich. And you have too many Abramoviches in your leading cadres." [11] The meeting with a delegation of the Canadian Workers' Progressive Party on August 29, 1956, provided Khrushchev with a forum to articulate another "Jewish" trait, which he alleged he had discerned through his wartime experience: Jews' contempt for manual labor, coupled with their understanding that this was the domain of "the other." "I would like to tell you about one incident which I witnessed myself," Khrushchev told the delegation. "When the town of Chernivtsi was liberated during the course of Red Army offensive operations, it was extremely neglected and dirty. The town had to be cleaned. It should be mentioned that during the occupation period the Germans gave the town to the Rumanians and that's why its Jewish population escaped destruction. When we dealt with this issue, the Jewish population of the town declared to us that after the arrival of the Red Army, all the Ukrainians left for the villages, and so, they said, there was no one to clean the city." [12] Sometime later, while reflecting on the evident failure of the Jewish Autonomous Region of Birobidzhan to establish itself as a national homeland for Soviet Jewry, Khrushchev concluded that this was the result of historical conditions. Yet his description of the sociological was practically genealogical. "They [the Jews] do not like collective work, group discipline. They have always preferred to be dispersed. They are individualists," Khrushchev told *Le Figaro* in an interview in March 1958. Finally, in the crudest, officially ordained, anti-Semitic publication to emerge from the Soviet system, Trohym Kychko's *Iudaizm bez prikras* (Judaism without embellishment), Nazi-like vocabulary and illustrations drove home the message of alienation of everything distinctively Jewish from the tradition of progressive humanity in general, the Soviet family in particular, and, even more specifically, from the Ukrainian nation. Portrayed as speculators and hostile to manual labor, collaborators with the Nazis, and murderers of Symon Petliura, leader of the short-lived Ukrainian National Republic in 1918–19, Jews were entirely excluded from the October Revolution, the Great Patriotic War, and Ukrainian aspirations for independence—all subjects of core myths within the Soviet milieu.[13]

But this complete exclusion concealed a crucial difference between the Nazi and Soviet enterprises. The class-based Soviet theory and practices of social engineering seemed to present an ominous obstacle to the application of uniform social targeting. Classes, strata, and layers were neither faceless nor homogeneous. Rather, they were variegated and arranged in a hierarchical order based on the services their members had rendered to the Communist project. Responsibility and accountability were assessed on an individual's merit, even though this principle was often compromised in practice. Moreover, individuals maintained the right to appeal and often did so successfully and, after the initial deadly phases of deportations, throughout the 1930s and 1940s children were either spared the fate of their parents or won earlier rehabilitation.[14] Even when weakened and worn out, the social-class paradigm still allowed for the coexistence of humanistic allusions and the harshest repressions.

These acute differences between the biologically driven Nazi and the sociologically based Soviet cleansing policies came to the fore in the 1930s when Soviet terror was reaching a level that compelled the regime to address the inevitable comparison with the Nazis. No one could articulate this dilemma better than Stalin, and for good reason. In a series of speeches delivered as the terror approached its climax, Stalin explained the policy guidelines. Concluding his remarks to the plenary session of the Central Committee on March 5, 1937, Stalin warned the delegates not to confuse sworn and irredeemable enemies with those who recanted when they joined forces with the Bolsheviks in the anti-Trotskyite campaign or those "who, at one point happened to be walking along the street where this or that Trotskyite happened to be walking, too. . . . In this question, as in all other questions, *an individual, differentiated approach* is required. We must not treat all alike," concluded Stalin.[15] Three months later in a speech before the military council of the defense ministry on June 2, 1937, in the wake of the liq-

uidation of the military leadership, Stalin reflected on the tension arising from the Soviet search for the enemy within. Reminding his audience of Lenin's noble and Friedrich Engels's bourgeois origins on the
one hand, and of the proletarian origins of Serebriakov and Livshits
(former Central Committee secretary and Deputy People's Commissar
of Communications, respectively) who turned out to be bad apples on
the other, Stalin concluded:

> Not every person of a given class is capable of doing harm. Individual
> people among the nobles and the bourgeoisie worked for the working
> class and not badly. Out of a stratum such as the lawyers came many rev-
> olutionaries. Marx was the son of a lawyer, not a son of a *batrak* [agricul-
> tural laborer] or of a worker. Among these strata can always be found
> people who can serve the cause of the working class, no worse, [but]
> rather better, than pure-blooded proletarians. We consider Marxism not
> a biological science, but a sociological science. Hence this general stan-
> dard is absolutely correct with regard to estates, groups, strata, [but] it
> is not applicable to every individual who is not of proletarian or peasant
> origins.[16]

And indeed the Soviets persistently rejected the primacy of the biological over the sociological. The principle of human heredity and its
potential practices, whether exterminatory euthanasia or positive eugenics, were officially repudiated in the Soviet Union from the early
1930s on. What is more, the Soviet Union was practically alone among
the major countries in the 1930s in its rejection of euthanasia or sterilization of the mentally retarded, a practice that was embraced, often
enthusiastically, on both sides of the Atlantic. In such an atmosphere,
Alexis Carrel, the French-American physician who won the Nobel
Prize in medicine for his work on suturing blood vessels, transfusion,
and organ transplants, could call on modern societies to do away with
the mentally retarded and criminals who cost a fortune to maintain in
asylums and prisons. "Why do we preserve these useless and harmful
beings? Why should society not dispose of the criminals and the insane
in a more economic manner?" asked Carrel. The worst criminals (including the insane and people who misled the public in important matters), he concluded, "should be humanely and economically disposed
of in small euthanasic institutions supplied with proper gases. . . . Mod-

ern society should not hesitate to organize itself with reference to the normal individual. Philosophical systems and sentimental prejudices must give way before such a necessity." [17] In Nazi Germany, as several scholars have reminded us recently, euthanasia was a key element in ideology and practice, and the forerunner of the persecution of the Jews, "Gypsies," and homosexuals, in sharp contrast to the Soviet purification drive, which at no point was anchored in genocidal ideology. [18] Without it, the operation of industrialized killing—the aspect that set the Holocaust apart from other genocides—was inconceivable. [19]

The same applied to positive eugenics, the positive counterpart to euthanasia. In his 1935 *Out of the Night: A Biologist's View of the Future*, H. J. Muller, the chief advocate of eugenics in the Soviet Union, argued that with artificial insemination technology, "in the course of a paltry century or two . . . it would be possible for the majority of the population to become of the innate quality of such men as Lenin, Newton, Leonardo, Pasteur, Beethoven, Omar Khayyam, Pushkin, Sun Yat-Sen, Marx . . . or even to possess their varied faculties combined . . . which would offset the American prospects of a maximum number of Billy Sundays, Valentinos, Jack Dempseys, Babe Ruths, even Al Capones." [20] But when Muller forwarded a copy of his book to Stalin in May 1936 and assured him that "it is quite possible, by means of the technique of artificial insemination which has been developed in this country, to use for such purposes the reproductive material of the most transcendently superior individuals, of the one in 50,000, or one in 100,000, since this technique makes possible a multiplication of more than 50,000 times," he practically sealed his fate and the fate of eugenics in the Soviet Union for the next three decades. Stalin read the book, and although he did not respond in writing or verbally until June 1937, his actions spoke for themselves. Muller escaped the Soviet Union by the skin of his teeth, but his entire cohort was shot. The Institute of Medical Genetics was disbanded, and the era of Lysenkoism and its doctrine of acquired characteristics was ushered in. In the long process of constructing a socialist society, acculturation prevailed over biology as the means of both the expansion and purification of the polity.

And indeed, there was not, nor could there be, a highly placed Jew such as Lazar Kaganovich in the Nazi leadership; nearly half a million Jews could neither serve in the Wehrmacht nor become members of the National Socialist Party. Nor did it matter if they had excelled in the

ranks of the German army in the First World War. There was only one
Jew, and he could not be Nazified. The Jew was an enemy not because
of a role he played or a position he represented. He was evil incarnate,
irredeemable, unreconstructed, and, as such, had to be exterminated.
The extermination of the Jewish "lice" was based neither on religion
nor law, but on the racial bio-politics of genetic heredity.[21] That was not
the case in the Soviet Union. True, living by the motto "sons are not responsible for their fathers" proved difficult. Just two years after Stalin's
famous dictum, NKVD and party investigators started busily plunging
into the records of members of the Communist Party, resurrecting from
oblivion the original sin of the wrong social origin to destroy scores of
true believers and their families. In the wake of the Terror it appeared as
if the stain of bad social origin was permanent and incurable. It took the
war to realize and institutionalize Stalin's dictum in Soviet political life.
Nevertheless, even at the height of the officially endorsed anti-Semitic
campaign, there were hundreds of thousands of Jews in the ranks of the
party, the army, and scores of other political institutions. Restrictions on
the number of Jews in state institutions (*numerus clausus*) could and did
coexist side by side with Jewish high officers, Heroes of the Soviet
Union, and party activists.[22] The Nazi example was still a powerful deterrent, especially regarding the Jews. The United Nations draft resolution of the Genocide Convention on November 21, 1947, provided the
Soviets with the opportunity to elaborate their own definition of exci-
sionary and exterminatory ideologies and practices. In his comments on
the treaty, Aron Trainin, then the leading Soviet authority in international law, agreed with the prevailing notion of genocide as the extermination of national or racial collectives. His points of disagreement,
however, were telling. First, argued Trainin, however extreme the persecution of opponents based on political motives may be, it does not
constitute genocide.[23] Second, the definition of genocide should not be
confined to physical extermination but applied to the curtailment of
collective national-cultural rights as well. "Of course, in the land of the
Soviets, where the Leninist-Stalinist national politics triumphs and the
cooperation of nations is a political reality, there is no problem of national rights and national minorities," wrote Trainin. There was a problem, however, in the capitalist world, where class exploitation could be
identified with national oppression. Not only lynch trials but also a

dense net of national-cultural barriers separate Negroes in the United States from the white population, Trainin continued.

> Accordingly, international law should struggle against both lynch trials, as tools of physical extermination of Negroes, and the politics of national-cultural oppression. Therefore along with physical and biological genocide, the notion of national-cultural genocide must be advanced, a genocide that sets for itself the goal of undermining the existence and development of national and racial groups.[24]

In essence, these were the twin pillars of Soviet population policies: the application of state violence anchored in political rationale and the simultaneous cultivation of ethno-national particularism. Without them, one could hardly understand the simultaneous eradication of entire national elites and intelligentsias along with the persistent delineation of particularistic identities.[25] In this light, total excision in the Soviet polity was not necessarily exterminatory, nor did it operate by a racial and biological code. And this, in turn, shifts the focus of our discussion to another political arena within which the Soviet socio-ethnic body was delineated, the commemorative politics of cataclysmic events.

WHEN MEMORY COUNTS

Ironically, none other than Vasilii Grossman pointed to memory as key in shaping the postwar quest for purity. As the driving force behind the failed projects of the *Black Book* and the *Red Book,* the works celebrating Jewish martyrdom and heroism, respectively, which were never published in the Soviet Union, Grossman offered keen insight into a new mechanism for engineering the Soviet body social. The postwar construction of ethnic hierarchies of heroism and the simultaneous leveling of suffering underlined the power of commemoration in the shaping of an ideal-type community. This mechanism was fateful in particular for the Jews.

The refusal to recognize any distinctive Jewish traits pervaded all spheres of Soviet society, including the gulag. When toward the end of the war the head of a cultural-educational department in one of the camps drafted a working paper that advocated methods to redeem inmates, his exemplary cases included a Jewish inmate. Samuil Gold-shtein, whose ethnicity was not mentioned, was an exceptionally diffi-cult case, refusing to work regardless of the consequences. Yet, instead of resorting to harsh penalties as others advocated the author sum-moned Goldshtein for a talk about the war. "Do you know what goals the fascists pursue in the war against us?" Loginov asked Goldshtein. "I don't know," Goldhstein uttered quietly. "I explained to him who Hitler was and what his goals were. I showed him several pronouncements of the fascist bandits on world domination. I explained the essence of racial theory and the Hitlerite new order in Europe," wrote Loginov. In all likelihood, the NKVD man informed the Jewish inmate about the fate of the Jews under the Nazis, but in 1944 a spade was certainly not called a spade and the Jewish genocide was not mentioned explicitly. The tale, however, did not stop there. "The war will end. The happy life of our people will flourish once again. Every decent man will say: 'I shed blood and sweat fighting for this life.' What would you say? How would people look at you?" Loginov scolded the stubborn inmate and appeared to push his buttons. The conversation, claimed Loginov, was a turning point for Goldshtein, who after digesting the information turned into an exemplary worker in the camp and later volunteered for the front where he heroically sacrificed himself in battle. Back in the camp, his combat exploits and letters from the front were paraded be-fore the inmates. Loginov concluded with a dedication "in eternal memory of Samuil Goldshtein," but not the faithful son of the Soviet Jewish people, just one Goldshtein, a convict who redeemed himself by answering the motherland's call.[26]

Like the gulag, the rest of Soviet society would recognize neither unique Jewish suffering at the hands of the Nazis nor their distinct con-tribution in the war against the invaders. With the emergence of the war as the core legitimizing myth of the polity, Jews were separated as a *group* from the Soviet family. This incident outlined the twin institu-tions of hierarchical heroism and universal suffering, the cornerstones of the Soviet ethno-national ethos of the war. Whereas the various na-tions of the Soviet Union were ranked in a pyramid-like order based on their alleged contribution to the war effort, their suffering was undiffer-entiated. More so than with any other ethno-national community, these aspects of the Soviet ethos were evident with respect to the Jewish community. Jewish participation in the trials of combat service were ignored in public and denied in private. By the time Stalin addressed the commanders of the Red Army, Jews had disappeared from public representations of the war. The Holocaust was incorporated into the epic suffering of the entire Soviet population; its uniqueness for the Jews was ignored.

HIERARCHICAL HEROISM

Petrenko: "You grew up eating Russian bread, you received an education paid by the Russian people, and now you betray your motherland? For you and your whole people I fought at the front for four years."

Shcharansky: "My father also fought at the front. He spent four years there as a volunteer. Perhaps he did that for your son and your people?"

Petrenko: "Your father? In the army? What division was he in?"

Shcharansky: "Artillery."

Petrenko: "Artillery?" *He seemed genuinely amazed.* "I also fought in the artillery, but I didn't see your sort there. What front was he on?"[27]

This exchange took place at the Lefortovo prison in the course of the interrogation of Jewish dissident Anatoly Shcharansky by a KGB colonel named Petrenko in March 1977. This exchange might have looked surrealistic had it not engaged a core issue in the myth of war. Back then in a speech at the second meeting of the Jewish Antifascist Committee held in Moscow on February 20, 1943, Il'ia Ehrenburg limited himself to one burning issue: the need to publish a book that would detail Jewish heroism at the front. "Such a book is required," said Ehrenburg, "for the peace of mind of the Jewish soldiers at the front who received letters from their relatives in Uzbekistan or Kazakhstan telling them that people there say that the reason one does not see Jews at the front is because they don't fight." To illustrate this point, Ehrenburg told the attendants the following story:

I was paid a visit by an old Jew, the father of a famous pilot, whose heroism was celebrated in the entire military press. He was the only son of this man. He loved him very much. And he told me: "I spoke with a certain civilian official who said to me: 'Explain to me, please, why there are no Jews at the front. Why doesn't one see Jews in the war?' I did not answer him. I found it hard to speak. That was only four days after I had received from the commander the news of my son's death."[28]

What was the rationale behind these harsh and swift accusations? Such comments defied the evidence and contemporary official Soviet representations of the Jews in the war. Contemporary evidence and recognition of the participation of Jews in the war pointed in the opposite direction. A recent, conservative estimate points out that the number of Jews in active combat service during the war was proportional to their share in the general population and often exceeded it, especially among elite units, which bore the brunt of fierce fighting at the fronts. Even as the percentage of Jews declined with the influx of ethnic Ukrainians and Belorussians into the Red Army ranks after the liberation of the German-occupied territories, their overall share in the armed forces remained proportional to their share in the general population.[29]

Throughout the war the Jewish contribution to the combat effort was visible and rewarded publicly. Jewish soldiers and officers were not discriminated against in promotions or decorations in the fighting Red Army. Official publications that celebrated the friendships allegedly cemented under the trials of war allotted the Jews a respected place within the family of the fighting nationalities.[30] Early on, however, a certain pattern began to emerge. Breaking with the established pattern of mentioning the ethnicity of servicemen when celebrating their exploits in the mass media, official reports omitted the Jewishness of their subjects altogether even when their ethnicity was evident, as it was with General Iakov Kreizer, Hayim Fomin, and Yeidl Khaiat, to cite three of the most famous examples. And by the end of the war Jews were no longer marked as a separate group in either public presentations of war heroism or in confidential reports.

The paradox of a large Jewish presence at the front and the industrious denial of Jewish heroism invited several explanations. For one, the notion of Jewish avoidance of military service seemed to be deeply rooted in both pre-Revolutionary and prewar Soviet society, as was evident in both official reports in the First World War and in private deliberations during the interwar years. Second, the peculiarities of warfare on the Eastern Front further advanced the perception of "no Jews at the front." Jewish soldiers intentionally concealed their national identity, especially in combat units, as soon as it became clear that Jews faced summary execution by the Germans if taken prisoner. According to some historians, along with the progressive assimilation of Soviet Jewry, soldiers' denial of their Jewishness was a mass phenomenon.[31] The intensive Nazi propaganda at the front, which played on traditional prejudices, exacerbated the problem of the intentional concealing of identity. The consequences were bluntly conveyed by a Jewish colonel in a letter to Ehrenburg:

> We are all lying in the trenches. Soon I will have to give the command: "Attack—up and out!" And then those devils with the black crosses start to fly by one after the other—just like locusts. We bury ourselves in the trenches and wait. The bombs will drop soon and then we'll be in a really tight spot. But they keep flying and there are no bombs, only leaflets—a world of leaflets. Some of them made their way to me in the trenches. They contained only a few words, a message: "Look around you, soldiers. Are there any Abrahams or Israels around you?!" And that's all. And that was enough to make soldiers look around and, not knowing who was a Jew, come to the poisonous conclusion: "There are no Jews at the front-line."[32]

The popular perception that there were "no Jews at the front" was also based on the belief that Jews made up a relatively high percentage of the refugees and evacuees. This was due to large-scale flight because of fear of extermination, especially when reports and rumors about the German treatment of the Jews reached Jewish communities, as well as to the planned evacuation of industries and bureaucracies that employed many Jews.[33] This phenomenon, which saved the lives of hundreds of thousands of Soviet Jews, was not intentional, and many of the refugees and evacuees were eventually drafted into the Red Army. Nevertheless, it helped the proliferation of the notion of the "Tashkent Partisans," a derogatory term for those who had lived the war in the safety of the Soviet rear.

However, the denial of Jewish combat heroism pointed to some deeper concerns. The authorities fiercely resisted all attempts to carve out a particularistic Jewish space within the all-encompassing myth of the war. Jewish perceptions of the uniqueness of their wartime experience threatened to undermine the universality of suffering and the ethno-national hierarchy of heroism, the twin pillars of the ethos of the war. If the recollections of Jewish partisans are accepted at face value, then they went out of their way to exact a certain special revenge on the enemy. In the ongoing process of brutalization of public life, Jews appeared determined to present themselves as active perpetrators and not merely passive victims. "Among the [captured] Germans we also found Vlasovites," recalled Zalman Teitelman, a Jewish partisan in the Chechl'nyk district. "Granovskii, me, and several other Jews consulted with the partisans and decided that all Vlasovites should be executed. We staged a military trial on the spot, and we mowed down ten Vlasovites in the local dump, where the Jews were buried." [34] Probably of more political weight were the attempts to parade this particularistic urge in public. In his appearance before the Jewish Antifascist Committee in the summer of 1945, David Dragunskii, two-time Hero of the Soviet Union, described in detail the extermination of his entire family by the Germans in February 1942, his visit to Babi Yar and the concentration camps. The speech, however, was marked by Dragunskii's intense emphasis on the Jew's special reckoning with the Germans. "All of us hate the Germans!" Dragunskii told the audience,

> but I hate them doubly. Once because I am a Soviet man. Once because I am a Jew! I was filled with hate because I saw what the Germans had done to our people. . . . I yearned to get to Germany. I got to Germany. I did my duty as a son of our motherland. I fought for all Soviet people. I fought for all Jewish people. . . . The Germans knew that my brigade was headed by a Jew. They posted notices that they would flay me alive. They hated me twice over, for being a Russian and a Jew. That very night [in Berlin] we caught five hundred SS troops whose commander had posted that notice. We made shashlik and beef stroganoff of them all. We caught the colonel of the SS swine. He complained that someone had taken his watch. "Take care of his complaint," I commanded one of my men. The colonel is not around any more. [35]

Sometime later, a group of Jewish veterans set out to reverse the prevailing order in the hierarchy of heroism. The Jews, argued the veterans in a letter to Stalin, had a more than legitimate claim to share the glory of heroism with the rest of the Soviet people. After explaining the Jewish contribution to the October Revolution, in which the Jewish people "showed itself as the most revolutionary people," the veterans noted the Jewish contribution at the front, which they argued was exceptional. "During the Patriotic War tens of thousands of Jews fought heroically at the front. Many of them were killed in battles for their socialist motherland and many became heroes. The percentage of decorated Jews in the Patriotic War is very high," they noted with pride.[36]

Jews sought their own distinctive insignia. On May 19, 1947, *Dos Naye Lebn*, a Yiddish-language journal in Lódz, Poland, carried a short story by Itzik Kipnis, the Soviet-Jewish writer. In the story, entitled "On Khokhmes, On Kheshboynes," Kipnis intimated a personal wish "that all Jews walking the streets of Berlin with a sure, victorious step would wear bandannas with decorations and medals and also a small, pretty *Magen David* on their chests. It would be our shameful mark. Everyone would be able to see that this is a Jew, and my Jewish and human worth among loving citizens cannot be diminished."[37] The harsh reaction to Kipnis's story made it clear that as a symbol of Jewish heroism, the Star of David needed a different place.[38]

The response to Jewish attempts to set their agenda was telling. Taking on Il'ia Ehrenburg, the Jewish high priest of the Soviet anti-German hate campaign, Oleksandr Dovzhenko, the famous film director, entered in his diary a conversation alleged to have taken place among Soviet soldiers:

> When I read him or listen to him being read, I start to feel very sorry for him.
>
> Why is that?
>
> Because he's so full of hatred. A bottomless abyss of hatred.
>
> Where does he get it all? He's covered with hatred like a horse with mange.
>
> Maybe he's just afraid that we don't have enough of those poisonous feelings.
>
> That's what I think. He doesn't believe in our anger and intelligence and awareness of history.
>
> He has no pity for us. We've knocked off four hundred battles all the way to Berlin, and now we've got to find the strength to start a new life.
>
> Strength for our women, friends, and for starting families. He has no

pity for us, the living, only for the dead. That's why I don't want to read him. I have enough anger in myself and in all the pictures I've seen the last four years.

Never mind him. Let him write. It doesn't hurt us, but at least it annoys the Germans.[39]

Even at the very moment when all Soviet men appeared as one undifferentiated whole fighting a common enemy, the Jew remained alien. And it was not simply the additional devotion celebrated by Dragunskii and Ehrenburg. It was the Jew's vindictive nature and his mistrust of his own society that set him apart. Or maybe it was the enduring teachings of his dead religion with its pretense to superiority and utter lack of compassion that alienated his Christian comrades. Unfit for the tasks of war, the Jew did not have a place in the postwar milieu either.

All these representations of the motives behind the fighting spirit of the troops actually outlined various degrees of resilience and subsequent agendas within the Soviet family. The Jews possessed ulterior motives and agendas that were clearly out of step with the Soviet hierarchical order of heroism. In any case, Dragunskii's remarks could be related to his fellow Jews only in a closed gathering. By then, any effort to break with the hierarchy in public was bound to be curtailed as Ehrenburg learned in the summer of 1944. When Ehrenburg tried to promote the *Red Book* project, the second part of his planned trilogy on Jewish fate in the war against the Nazis which was supposed to tell the stories of Jewish soldiers and partisans, he was bluntly told by a top official in the *Sovinformburo* that "there is no need to mention the heroism of Jewish soldiers in the Red Army; this is bragging."[40]

UNIVERSAL SUFFERING

In the same vein, Soviet authorities had been fairly aware of how the Germans treated the Jews. Moreover, information on the Jewish genocide reached Moscow almost immediately. The regime pursued the punishment of perpetrators of anti-Jewish massacres from the moment of liberation until the disintegration of the Soviet Union. It also offered material help to Jewish survivors. Having learned about the obstacles put in the way of Jewish survivors in Ukraine, none other than Lavrentii Beria ordered the Ukrainian authorities to take the necessary measures to provide work and housing for Jews in the liberated territories "who were subjected to particular repressions by the German occupiers (concentration camps, ghetto, etc.)."[41]

Such actions, however, were kept out of the public eye. There were hardly any references to the Holocaust in the Soviet press, not even in the much-publicized reports of the Extraordinary State Committee for the Study of German-Fascist Arocities, where the Jewishness of victims was not specified even in testimonies on massacres that were directed solely against Jews.[42] When the veterans we encountered earlier complained to Stalin in the fall of 1945, the erasure of a distinct Jewish catastrophe was already a fait accompli. "No other people experienced as much sorrow and misfortune as did the Jewish people during the Patriotic War. [Yet] not a single article was devoted in the press or in print to their situation [or] their needs," lamented the veterans.[43] By then, the suffering of the civilian population at the hands of the invaders was universalized, ruling out any ethno-national distinction, in spite of the awareness of the Nazis' own racial hierarchies and practices. When space was allowed for the expression of ethno-national particularism, it was marginal, isolated, and hardly visible as in the tale of the Romanian occupation.

The Soviet authorities seemed much more troubled by the annual gatherings of Jews commemorating the extermination of their brethren, which they viewed as a pretext for stirring up separatist nationalist sentiments. "The NKVD seemed unaware of the effort of Zionist elements to organize in Kiev a mass demonstration of the Jewish population on the anniversary of the massacre by the Germans in Babyn Iar," charged the party officials.[44] When a survivor fixed the Star of David on an obelisk erected atop a mass grave the authorities threatened to bulldoze it unless it was replaced by the five-cornered Soviet star.[45] The reluctance to commemorate particularistic suffering was captured in Khrushchev's memorable retort to Il'ia Ehrenburg. When the latter appealed to Khrushchev to intervene and stop the construction of a marketplace on the site of the massacre in Babyn Iar, Khrushchev advised him "not to interfere in matters that do not concern you. You had better write good novels."[46]

The swan song of the attempt at public representations of particularistic ethno-national wartime suffering came in 1946 with the curtailment of the publication of the *Black Book*, edited by Il'ia Ehrenburg and Vasilii Grossman. Having read the preface, in which Grossman echoed the Nazi position that "the fascists placed the Jew in opposition to all peoples inhabiting the world,"[47] Georgii Aleksandrov, head of the agitprop department, shot back in a letter to Politburo member Andrei Zhdanov that the

> preface written by Grossman alleges that the destruction of the Jews was a particularistic provocative policy and that the Germans established some kind of hierarchy in their destruction of the peoples of the Soviet Union. In fact, the idea of some imaginary hierarchy is in itself incorrect. The documents of the Extraordinary State Committee convincingly demonstrate that the Hitlerites destroyed at one and the same time Russians, Jews, Belorussians, Ukrainians, Latvians, Lithuanians, and other peoples of the Soviet Union.[48]

"There are no Jews in Ukraine," lamented a horrified Grossman when he first encountered his liberated birthplace in 1943. "Nowhere—Poltava, Kharkov, Kremenchug, Borispol, Yagotin—in none of the cities, hundreds of towns, or thousands of villages will you see the black, tear-filled eyes of little girls; you will not hear the sad voices of an old woman; you will not see the dark face of a hungry baby. All is silence. Everything is still. A whole people has been brutally murdered."[49] True, soon after this lament, the Ukrainian terrain was filled again with returning Jews, albeit in significantly lower numbers and settling in fewer places. But already in 1943, Grossman's words rang true with regard to the future as well as to the recent past, and in a way he could not envision at the time. The invisibility of Jews in the Soviet Union in general, and in Ukraine in particular, was not because of lack of presence. The surviving Jews did indeed return but as a mythical antithesis, and into political invisibility.

At first glance, there seemed to be nothing unusual about an official nationality policy that envisioned as its final stage the merging (*sliianie*) of its various ethnic and national components into a single entity. Viewed in this light, the Jews were leading the Soviet camp in terms of historical development. But there was an ironic twist. Whereas other ethnic groups were supposed to cultivate ethnic particularism intensively as a step toward merger, in the wake of the war the Jews were to skip this stage. And since the date of the final merging remained as elusive as ever, the erasure of Jewish collective identity from the new legitimizing myth of the polity had grave consequences. In October 1946, merely two years after the liberation of the region, and equally important, two years before the establishment of the state of Israel, the Jewish community in the Soviet Ukrainian Republic joined their German and Polish minorities in political invisibility when Jewish national rural soviets were converted into Ukrainian soviets. At the same time official pressure for increased migration from Ukraine to Birobidzhan mounted.[50]

Deeply rooted popular anti-Semitism coincided with similar sentiments among the local and national leadership but, more crucially, these attitudes were articulated within the powerful Soviet ethos of a simultaneous search for harmony and purity. A barrage of popular novels portrayed Jewish characters as draft-dodgers who lived the war years in the safety of the rear—and off the blood—of their Soviet compatriots. It was only a short step from the exclusion of Jews from the Soviet fighting family to their exclusion from the Soviet family at large. The wartime stereotype of the Jewish draft-dodger occupied an increasingly central place in the anti-cosmopolitan campaign. This rootless cosmopolitanism was embodied by the worst anti-patriotic act of all, deliberate evasion of service at the front when the motherland needed the ultimate sacrifice of each and every one of its sons: the sons responded, except for the rootless cosmopolitans. Yet this did not prevent them from seeking medals for their "sacrifice" when the war ended.

In one of these novels, Vsevolod Kochetov's *Zhurbiny*, the beating of such a Jew (who happened to carry a copy of *The Wandering Jew* in his suitcase wherever he went) was portrayed as nothing less than a cathartic moment that transformed one worthless womanizer into a proud Soviet citizen. And how does the Party react to this recourse to violence? It is of two minds. The official mind views the incident as improper for modern Soviet society. "Comrade Skobelev," remarks the party organizer who deals with the incident, "the Stone Age was a good time. Primitive man picked up his club and went off to settle accounts with his neighbor." But then there is the more sympathetic private mind, between men. "You know," the party organizer intimates to Skobelev, "as a man, I understand you. Such people deserve a slap in the face."[51]

In a polity that associated military service with local, national, and supranational Soviet identities, and sacrifice on the battlefield with true patriotism, exclusion from the myth of the war amounted to exclusion from the Soviet family. A similar outcome, if only through a different practice, emerged from the commemoration of wartime suffering. The mass murder of Jews was never denied in Soviet representations of the war, but in the official accounts and artistic representations, memory of the Jewish catastrophe was subsumed by the larger Soviet tragedy, erasing the very distinction at the core of the Nazi pursuit of racial purity.

Such a policy certainly coincided with similar developments across the European continent. In the restored societies emerging from Nazi occupation, memories of defeat and victimization were set aside in favor of intensive, state-sponsored cults of heroism and resistance. In ravaged and humiliated societies burdened with the task of national revival, the mobilizing power of the myth of active heroism was undeniably greater than that of victimization. Above all, memories of victimization bore the troublesome particularism associated with the Jewish minority. Jewish particularistic suffering was integrated into an all-national paradigm of victimization and in some cases transformed into one of triumphant heroism.[52] The universality of the activist-triumphant myth was underscored by its predominance in the new Israeli state, where Zionism helped to reconstruct a series of cataclysmic defeats in Jewish history as redemptive triumphs, starting with the rebellions against the Romans in the first two centuries A.D. and culminating with the Holocaust. There, the official commemoration of the Holocaust had been incorporated into the epic struggle for an independent Jewish state.[53]

Such a dilemma and solution were all too familiar in Soviet society and for similarly compelling reasons. The wave of pogroms that swept Ukrainian cities in 1944–1945 marked a new development. For the first time in the Soviet era, violent anti-Semitism exploded as an open, urban phenomenon. In such a volatile environment and with the war still raging, identification with the traditionally resented minority was the last thing the returning Soviet power wanted. It was about this time that Khrushchev supposedly exclaimed: "Here is the Ukraine and it is not in our interest that the Ukrainians should associate the return of Soviet power with the return of the Jews."[54] Yet the wholesale deportations of alleged collaborationist minorities conveyed the message that the Soviet polity would not shy away from opening the Pandora's box of collaboration conceived in ethnic terms. This willingness to confront the ethnic face of wartime collaboration directly (which most multiethnic polities avoid doing), and the denial of the Jewish fate under the Nazis long after the rest of Europe recognized it, pointed to another motive, one which lay at the core of the revolutionary myth.[55]

The twentieth anniversary of the Great Patriotic War in 1965 marked the transformation of this cataclysmic event from a living to a historical memory, and a determined attempt to develop a commemorative canon and a sense of closure. The last vestiges of the socially alien element—the few remaining kulaks—were released and rehabilitated. Ethnic Germans deported en masse during the war received an official apology from the Supreme Soviet of the Soviet Union,[56] and, most notably, all limitations were removed on former leaders and members of underground nationalist movements, the last category to win rehabilitation (and among whom Ukrainian nationalists were the largest component). The reinstatement of the largest, best organized, and most persistent of the anti-Soviet separatist movements into the legitimate Ukrainian body politic only fifteen years after it was singled out for exclusion was indeed the most visible marker of reconciliation. By allowing them to return home, the government showed its confidence in the efficacy of the punitive system and in its redemptive power.

But no olive branch was extended to the Jewish community. On the contrary, Jews were branded as traitors. The community was handed a mass-circulation historical novel, *Tuchi and gorodom*, by Porfyrii Havrutto, which developed an earlier charge by Khrushchev about treason and the collaboration of a certain Jew-Judas who "betrayed the Kiev underground to the Germans, served as a translator for Field Marshal Paulus, cleaned his boots, helped interrogate Soviet prisoners of war, and even shot at his own compatriots." The readers were informed in the accompanying editorial note that the novel was actually a documentary. The Jew was not merely outside of the Soviet family. He was its living antithesis.[58]

At this time Stalin's daughter, Svetlana Allilueva, noted that already "with the expulsion of Trotsky and the extermination during the years of 'purges' of old party members, many of whom were Jews, anti-Semitism was reborn on new ground and first of all within the party itself."[59] Perhaps Allilueva got it right. The Bolshevik epic had to be purged of its association with the resented minority. By the eve of the war, the popular identification of the Revolution with the Jews had already found its echo inside the party ranks. In the early 1930s, peasant uprisings against forced collectivization were often directed against the "Jewish militia" and "Communist kikes." When the Party surveyed its rank and file throughout the prewar years, it found that Jews were perceived as the main beneficiaries of the October Revolution: holders of the best positions and jobs, owners of the apartments, and accomplished draft-dodgers.[60]

Victimization often breeds more victimization rather than empathy, and the pogroms of the summer of 1944 are a case in point. Several years after the war, a nationalist activist from Ukraine observed that, under the Germans, anti-Semitism had become racially rather than religiously based. The exposure to a lengthy, relentless barrage of Nazi anti-Semitic policies left unmistakable imprints on various segments of the local population. As the war progressed and the Nazi occupation became part of the local political scene, anti-Semitic expressions became ever more racialized. And so in the midst of the war, a rabid anti-Stalinist village poet could write this:

> O you, Stalin, the flayer,
> What have you done to us now?
> You expelled Ukrainians from their huts,
> And Jews became the rulers.
> We spend the nights under fences,
> We have no father, we have no mothers,
> Because you, Stalin, a cruel beast,
> Drove them as far as Siberia,
> And to the Jews you gave medals,
> So that they could torture us.[61]

The bestial metaphor was not limited to nationalist circles. The portrayal of the Jew as a parasite living off the blood of decent patriotic people could be found in the expressions of local Red Army servicemen as well. "There are five to seven thousand Jews [in the Ukrainian town of Vinnytsia]," wrote two officers to Khrushchev while they were on vacation in the summer of 1944. "They are like worms. A Jew controls the housing administration . . . In the military-trade store—a Jew. In the office—a Jew, that Kaminskii type. In other commercial establishments it is filthy."[62]

By the end of the war, Soviet society was not free of Jews. But it was a society that came to think of the "Jewish problem" as a legitimate one, and one to ponder in racial terms. The Jew was thought of as an inherently alien organism, which people wished to see removed from their midst. Soviet citizens may not have possessed the exterminatory intentions that made Nazi anti-Semitism unique, but they were open to its arguments. And this tension between arguments and the pursuit of their logic came to the fore with the "Doctors' Plot" in January 1953. By then, as the treatment of enemy nations and nationalist guerrillas indicated, the extension of guilt to entire collectives was the norm rather than the exception in the purification drive, conducted in a brutal and increasingly radical manner. Even one of Stalin's loyal lieutenants, Anastas Mikoyan, was shocked by this evolution of state terror. "Stalin's decision to deport entire nations had a depressing impact on me," recalled Mikoyan. "I did not understand how one can accuse entire nations of treason when they had party organizations, Communists, peasant masses, and Soviet intelligentsia! Many were mobilized into the army and fought at the front. Many representatives of these peoples were awarded medals as heroes of the Soviet Union! This was a deviation from the class approach to the solution of the nationality problem."[63]

Mikoyan may indeed have been shocked, and so were many Soviet citizens. Many others, however, had no qualms about the extending such charges to the entire community. In intimate settings and through anonymous leaflets, individuals stressed the elusive and beastly nature of this group ("they live like wolves," "this is not a people, but the anti-people called the 'kike.' They are not human beings, but traitors who sell innocent Soviet victims to America for dollars"). Moreover, the Jews were viewed by both believers and skeptics in light of the recent war. Recommending the deportation of the treacherous Jews from the southeastern and southwestern territories of the Soviet Union, one leaflet reminded the people of "[the parallel betrayal] of the Crimean Tatars during the war years, as well as that of the Chechens in the Northern Caucasus." Since all Jews were enemies and a fifth column, "they are like the Kalmyks, Ingushetians, and Crimean Tatars," another author charged. "They are American spies, our vilest enemies, there should be no forgiveness. Blood for blood! They deserve this, there is and there should be no mercy for them."[64] The reference to enemy nationalities deported during and after the war on charges of collective guilt underlined the internalization of the other pillar of the postwar purification drive: the abandonment of belief in the prospect for redemption of the enemy within. Ordinary citizens appear to accept not only the principle of elusive enemies in their midst, but also the worst charges against them. The treacherous wartime conduct of the Kalmyks and the Chechens was accepted at face value, and in the wake of the announcement of the arrest of the doctors, scores of people refused to be treated by Jewish physicians.[65]

Even more telling were the reactions to the April 4, 1953 announcement by the Ministry of Internal Affairs that the entire affair was a fabrication and that the doctors were fully rehabilitated. Issued only a month after Stalin's death, the laconic statement turned upside down nearly three months of relentless, ferocious announcements. But if the rehabilitation statement was meant as the first signal that the era of mass terror had come to an end, it did not land on fertile soil. If the admittedly limited number of letters to press and government organizations is indicative, the absolute majority was still receptive to the principle of elusive enemies and, more specifically, the identification of such enemies with the Soviet Jewish community. Once again, righteousness was judged in terms of one's wartime experience. Indeed, more than one letter expressed anger at the official admission of "impermissible investigation methods strictly forbidden by Soviet law." Yet even then, the legacy of the recent war bred skepticism. "Were they subjected to torture like those staunch and true patriots Zoia [Kosmodemianskaia] or Liza Chaikina?" cried one Savelev from Moscow in reference to the two young partisans who became symbols of martyrdom after being tortured and executed by the Germans. "Even terrible torture did not break the spirit of heroic *Komsomol* members and did not provide the fascists with the confessions they sought," wrote a group of students from Iaroslavl. "And what about our ordinary citizens who stood their ground when stars were being branded on their bodies or parts of their bodies were being amputated. They did not reveal anything," wrote another Moscovite.[66] Seen in this light, the Jews were not only guilty but, just as during the war, they once again "managed to get off scot-free." The basic Soviet view of the war was regenerated even when specific aspects were denounced. If the myth of the October Revolution was perceived as "Judaicized" beyond repair, then the new myth of the Great Patriotic War would not suffer the same fate.

Chapter Twelve

"An Aptitude for Being Unloved"

War and Memory in Japan

JOHN W. DOWER

In mid-June 1945, as World War II was reaching its denouement in Asia, a Japanese scholar of French literature named Watanabe Kazuo mused about Germany and Japan in his diary. While bombs fell on Tokyo, Watanabe, in his early forties at the time, was reading Romain Rolland's 1915 account of writings taken from the corpses of German soldiers in World War I. He was particularly struck by the observation of a Prussian officer that the Germans had an aptitude for being unloved. Was this not true, Watanabe wrote, of his own country and compatriots as well?

Watanabe, later esteemed as one of postwar Japan's most engaging "progressive intellectuals," deplored the war. His "diary of defeat," which beings in March 1945 and ends the following November (but was not published until fifty years later), is one of the more intimate and evocative lamentations about the insanity of their "holy war" that has come down to us from the Japanese side. Obviously, the murderous behavior of the odd couple of the Axis Alliance helped prompt Watanabe's observation of shared unlovable national personalities. In his view, however, there was more behind this than just militarism and atrocity. The

Japanese, he feared, alienated others because they had difficulty think-ing in terms of equality, and lacked any true sense of "responsibility." In January 1946, five months after the war ended, Watanabe devoted a short essay to this aptitude for being unloved, specifically relating it to the issue of "repentance" and his fear that Japanese comprehension of such matters remained superficial.[1]

Would Watanabe draw such an analogy about Germany and Japan today? Would we ourselves do so? Over half a century has passed since World War II ended, and it is surely fair to say that the former Axis partners have developed in ways that most of their non-Communist ad-versaries in 1945 only hoped and dreamed might be possible.[2] They have become fundamentally democratic societies. They have brought prosperity to a majority of their peoples. Although both have reemerged as great economic workshops, neither has menaced the peace of its neighbors.

And yet, where war and memory are concerned, it also seems fair to say that, in the eyes of most outsiders, Germany and Japan have gone separate ways. Deservedly or not, "the Germans" have been generally praised for confronting their Nazi past. "The Japanese," by contrast, are more usually castigated—not only by Americans and Europeans, but by Asian commentators as well—for sanitizing the war they waged in the emperor's name so many decades ago. Indeed, it is a commonplace of contemporary polemics to compare the Japanese unfavorably to the Germans when it comes to confronting war responsibility. On this par-ticular issue, the Japanese aptitude for being mistrusted and unloved is truly singular.

There are easy explanations for this. For all practical purposes, the Japanese cabinet and Diet (parliament) have been dominated by the same conservative political lineage since 1949 (it took the name Liberal Democratic Party in 1955). The electoral base of the conservatives lies in a constituency that still feels an intimate sense of bereavement for the two million Japanese soldiers and sailors who died in World War II. Such a constituency is, unsurprisingly, hostile to any blanket condem-nation of Japanese war crimes that denies honor and respect to those who died for their country.

This electorate, rather than outsiders, is the audience the conserva-tives most care about. This helps explain, at least in part, why official statements of war responsibility, repentance, and apology so often seem lukewarm to non-Japanese.[3] At the same time, the ranks of the conservatives do indeed include many die-hard nationalists who still subscribe to some of the propaganda under which imperial Japan was mobilized for war. In one form or another, they would argue that their country was engaged in a legitimate war of self-defense against the "Red Peril" of Communism and the "White Peril" of European and American imperialism and colonialism in Asia. Japan's war may have been ill advised, in this view, but neither in motive nor in conduct can it be fairly deemed to have been peculiarly criminal.

Until recently, it seemed possible to suggest (or at least hope) that much of the more intemperate nationalistic rhetoric that older conservative politicians continued to spout at regular intervals was simply the carryover of wartime indoctrination by a cohort of largely unrepentant patriots. Then Japan entered the twenty-first century with a new conservative leader who made it embarrassingly clear that this was not the case. In a widely publicized speech to an association of Shinto priests, Prime Minister Mori Yoshihiro, born in 1937, saw fit to evoke the most extreme and exclusionist nationalistic rhetoric of the militaristic past by referring to Japan as an "emperor-centered land of the gods" (*tennō o chūshin to suru kami no kuni*). On another occasion, addressing another purely domestic audience, he spoke of Japan's present-day mission in terms of defending the *kokutai*, or "national polity"—thereby resurrecting the central code word in prewar emperor-worship. In a trice, Japan's new leader had established himself as the international community's most notorious practitioner of rhetorical necrophilia. He became, overnight, the latest personification of the Japanese aptitude for being unloved.

The rub in all this, however, is that Mori's reactionary language (which he attempted to explain away, but did not retract) led him to be unloved by most of his compatriots as well. The media flayed him, and his personal approval rating plummeted to between 10 and 20 percent in opinion polls. More tellingly, his Liberal Democratic Party dropped from 271 to 229 seats in the House of Representatives in the general election of June 2000, maintaining but a narrow minority over a polyglot opposition. While factors such as Japan's continuing economic doldrums also contributed to this precipitous decline, the prime minister had clearly crossed the line where acceptable patriotic rhetoric is concerned. He misread the depth to which even a conservative electorate recalls the war years with horror.[4]

Non-Japanese, fixated as they usually are on the pronouncements of Japan's most bombastic nationalists, also tend to misread the tenor and complexity of popular Japanese recollections of World War II. Whereas Europeans commonly date the war from the German invasion of Poland in 1939, and Americans from the Japanese attack on Pearl Harbor in 1941, in Japan the war is usually dated from the Japanese invasion of Manchuria in 1931. In a name promoted by leftist scholars shortly after Japan's defeat, World War II in Asia is widely referred to as "the Fifteen-Year War."

Most Japanese now also acknowledge that this fifteen-year conflict was a war of aggression. To non-Japanese, this may seem surprising, for the litany of right-wing Japanese pronouncements that the foreign press highlights leaves little room for anticipating serious critical popular consciousness about the war. If Japanese were asked "Was Japan an 'Aggressor' in World War II?" most foreigners would probably predict that the response would be negative. In fact, this very question was posed to a random sample of people by the conservative *Yomiuri* newspaper in 1993. Fifty-three-point-one percent answered "Yes" and 24.8 percent "No," while the remainder had no response. Among the wartime generation itself (people over seventy), whom one might expect to be most firmly indoctrinated in the propaganda of the holy war, only 39.5 percent responded that Japan was *not* an aggressor (41.1 percent said it was, and the rest had no response). Among respondents in their twenties, 61.7 percent agreed Japan had been an aggressor, and only 17.1 percent disagreed with this label.[5]

This fracture of memory and perception accounts for much of the fervor of present-day nationalistic pronouncements in Japan. Whereas foreigners tend to isolate the most inflammatory right-wing utterances and interpret them as being representative of deep trends, the spokesmen for a new Japanese nationalism actually speak in almost apocalyptic terms of the *death* of patriotism in their country. Here, for example, is a representative passage from a pamphlet issued in 1998 by the Japanese Society for History Textbook Reform, one of the most influential associations of "revisionist" conservative academics:

When the young people of Japan were asked if they would defend their country if invaded by another nation, 10% of them answered "yes." Ninety percent replied that they would not. Over 70% of the world's young people say that they would defend their countries. When Americans and Koreans were asked if they would sacrifice their interests to serve their countries, 56.9% and 54.4% answered "yes," respectively. Only 5.5% of Japanese respondents answered that question in the affirmative. That figure is suggestive of what is at the depth of our national psychology. The foolish obsession with economic matters on the part of the Japanese, and their failure to contemplate the proper way for humans to live, have characterized the 50 years since World War II ended. The result is that the very future of our nation is in jeopardy. I am reminded of the last days of Carthage.

This is, indeed, alarmingly reactionary language. It suggests that serious engagement with "the proper way for humans to live" was lost in Japan only after the defeat in World War II, when the war was belittled and overt patriotism came to be viewed with deep and widespread skepticism. Such rhetoric is of a piece with Prime Minister Mori's suggestion that Japan's true identity is to be found elsewhere than in postwar professions of a commitment to peace and democracy. To escape this perceived crisis of national identity, those associated with the movement to create a "correct" national history have declared that the very purpose of historical writing and education is to instill pride in the nation. Professor Fujioka Nobukatsu, one of the best-known spokesmen for the movement, puts it this way: "It is precisely its way of teaching its modern history that is the crucial determinant of the constitution of a people as a nation. The people that does not have a history to be proud of cannot constitute itself as a nation."[6]

Such assertions are heard with increasing frequency as Japan enters a new century as perplexed and tormented as ever concerning its identity as a modern nation. At the same time, however, we should not loose sight of the panic that runs through these pronouncements: the near-hysterical perception, that is, that since their defeat the Japanese, and especially the younger generations, have become the *least* patriotic of contemporary peoples. How can one account for this? To individuals like those associated with the conservative "textbook reform" movement, the answer is clear. It is precisely because negative impressions of Japan as an aggressor in the wars of the mid-twentieth century run so deep that postwar Japanese have been unable to look upon their modern history and accomplishments with pride.

The interplay of war and memory in contemporary Japan is, in fact, even more complicated and convoluted than this dichotomy suggests. It is "kaleidoscopic" in the fullest sense, in that we can identify a great range of attitudes and opinions—and, with slight interpretive twists, make any number of patterns out of them. Five such patterns are singled out in the discussion that follows—five kinds of memory, as it were, that seem especially prominent in shaping the popular consciousness and public histories of Japan's war. They are [1] denial, [2] evocations of moral (or immoral) equivalence, [3] victim consciousness, [4] binational (U.S.–Japan) sanitizing of Japanese war crimes, and [5] popular discourses acknowledging guilt and responsibility.[7]

1. DENIAL

It is reasonable to speak of a collection of Japanese ranging from right-wing thugs through conservative politicians, bureaucrats, and businessmen to nationalistic journalists and academics and even cartoonists that is devoted to "denying" Japan's war crimes. But what, specifically, is being denied?

The answer varies. The most extreme position, as might be expected, simply counters the notion of Japan's grievous responsibility for engaging in militaristic aggression by resurrecting the propaganda of the war years. It argues, that is, that the emperor's loyal soldiers and sailors, fired by both love of country and pan-Asian idealism, were engaged in the mission of simultaneously defending their homeland and establishing a "Greater East Asia Co-Prosperity Sphere."

Japan, from this perspective, was driven to war by strategic, ideological, and economic threats that came from all directions: the Soviet Union in the north; Soviet-led "international" Communism spilling into China, Korea, and Japan itself; chaos and violation of Japan's treaty rights in China (including Manchuria); global economic depression, and the rise of anti-Japanese trade policies that followed in the wake of this; American and European opposition to the establishment of a Japanese-style "Monroe sphere" in Asia; unfair and destabilizing treatment by the United States and Great Britain in international naval arma-ments treaties in the 1930s; "economic strangulation" by the so-called ABCD powers (America, Britain, China, and the Dutch) as the crisis in Asia intensified; etc. In responding to these multiple threats, the argu-ment continues, imperial Japan's leaders did not just act in legitimate self-defense. They turned the crisis into a genuinely moral campaign to liberate all Asia from the oppressive Europeans and Americans, and to simultaneously create an impregnable bulwark against the rising tide of Communism. The "holy war" was thus both inescapable and altruistic.

Even among those who maintain that Japan was not an aggressor, however, relatively few subscribe to such undiluted jingoism. Here one encounters one of the more entertaining anomalies of the patriotic agenda. For whereas the heart and soul of old-fashioned Japanese-style nationalism lies in extolling the country's "peculiarly unique unique-ness" (as exemplified in Prime Minister Mori's archaic emperor-centered and Shinto-centered rhetoric), when it comes to the question of aggression and atrocity in World War II, uniqueness is more usually explicitly denied. In a world order that was collapsing into chaos every-where, and in a global conflict that witnessed unspeakable brutality in all theaters and on all sides, this more modulated mode of denial goes, it is absurd to single out the Japanese as sole bearers of responsibility for the outbreak of conflict in Asia, or as sole perpetuators of acts of bar-barism there. To do so amounts to simply perpetuating the victors' ver-sion of the war.

Those who deem it imperative to restore love of country by promot-ing a positive appreciation of Japan's twentieth-century experience are not concerned with merely downplaying or denying specific wartime horrors (such as the Rape of Nanking, abuse of POWs, or large-scale ex-ploitation of "comfort women" to service the imperial forces sexually). They are very precise in identifying what constitutes the "old" historiog-raphy that must be repudiated. It takes two forms. One is the Marxist analysis of modern Japanese history that had an enormous impact in scholarly, journalistic, and educational circles for several decades after the war (emphasizing the authoritarian emperor system, *zaibatsu*-led capitalist "dual structure," and other pernicious "feudal remnants" that all lay behind the domestic repression and overseas aggression of impe-rial Japan). The second target of revisionist ire is the outlook and values allegedly imposed on Japan during the post-surrender occupation by the American-led victors that lasted from 1945 to 1952. A target of particularly impassioned derision here is "the Tokyo War Crimes Trial view of history."[8]

This critical notion of "victor's history"—or victor's justice, or victor's double standards—entails a subtle turn in the kaleidoscope of war consciousness, amounting to an argument of moral relativism.

2. EVOCATIONS OF MORAL (OR IMMORAL) EQUIVALENCE

The Tokyo trial (formally, the International Military Tribunal for the Far East) is the great sitting duck of conservative Japanese revisionism, and for understandable reasons. These proceedings against accused "Class A" war criminals lasted almost three times as long as the counterpart Nuremberg trial of Nazi leaders; and when they limped to a close at the end of 1948, it already was apparent that the judgment imposed would not withstand the test of time very well. All twenty-five defendants were found guilty of war crimes, and seven were executed within a month after the courtroom proceedings came to an end. Even the Allied judges themselves, however, were unable to come to unanimous agreement. Thus, the decisive "majority judgment" of the tribunal (supported by eight of eleven justices) was accompanied by *five* separate opinions criticizing the proceedings and sentences from one perspective or another. The most detailed and dramatic of these separate opinions came from the Indian justice, Radhabinod Pal, who found the very premises of the trial unsound and acquitted all twenty-five defendants.

Pal's detailed dissent, which ran to many hundreds of pages, was published in Japanese in 1952 (as soon as the post-defeat Allied occupation ended), and has remained the bible for Japanese critics of "victor's justice" ever since. His critique is substantive. Pal challenged the juridical premises of the tribunal on the grounds that the defendants were being tried for ex post facto "crimes" (that is, offenses such as "crimes against peace" that did not exist in international law before the Nuremberg and Tokyo tribunals were convened). He rejected as absurd the basic argument on which the prosecution rested its case in Tokyo: namely, the charge that Japan's leaders had been engaged in a "conspiracy to commit aggression" that dated back to 1928 (which meant that the defendants could not argue that they were acting in accordance with their perception of legitimate self-defense, and that all military actions by the Japanese from 1928 on thereby constituted "murder"). And, good Indian nationalist that he was, Pal took seriously the defendants' arguments that they were intent on liberating Asia from Western colonialism (or, at least, the argument that Asia needed such liberation). Unsurprisingly, he managed to smuggle more than a few sharp comments about European and American hypocrisy into his dissenting opinion.

Justice Pal has proven a godsend to those who have devoted themselves to repudiating "the Tokyo War Crimes Trial view of history," for he gives their argument not merely a non-Japanese face (and, just as important, a non-Caucasian one), but also a dense theoretical scaffolding. They have used him sedulously, but not, in fact, fairly. The Tokyo trial was undeniably a poorly conceived affair; but what the deniers of grievous Japanese war responsibility have done is use this vulnerable exercise in victor's justice — and Pal's stinging technical dissent from its premises and conclusions — as a smokescreen for covering up the real war crimes and acts of aggression the Japanese did commit in the course of their fifteen-year war.[9] Repudiating the trial has become a synecdoche for implying that imperial Japan was, after all, an "innocent" participant in the cataclysmic breakdown of world order — or, at least, no more guilty than other nations, and no more brutal on the battlefield and in occupied areas than other combatants.

It is within this larger context of repudiating "victor's justice" that the denial of more discrete accusations of Japan's egregious acts of aggression and atrocity takes place. At a still grand level, and still within the framework of the war crimes trials, the revisionists vehemently reject the argument that imperial Japan was in any fundamental way comparable to its German ally. There was no Japanese counterpart to Hitler, they argue, or to the Nazi Party (which made charges of conspiracy more tenable at the Nuremberg trials). There was nothing comparable to the planned genocide we now speak of as the Holocaust. Thus, references to the 1937 Japanese massacre of civilians in Nanking as "the forgotten Holocaust of World War II" provoke especially emotional denials — which, again, become a smokescreen that obscures the terrible rape of the city that did occur, not to mention the systematic abuse of prisoners and civilians by the imperial forces in all theaters.[10]

In calling attention to the double standards of the victors who sat in judgment at Tokyo—and who still sit in judgment of Japan today—the revisionists, as might be anticipated, are able to move with near abandon from the nineteenth century through the war itself right up to the present day. Justice Pal set the pattern for some of this argumentation, and in ways beyond simply calling attention to the deep (and, as of the time of the trial, ongoing) history of Western imperialism and colonial oppression. He ridiculed the prosecution's repudiation of the "anti-Communism" defense offered by former war minister and prime minister Tōjō Hideki and his cohorts, pointing out that most of the governments represented on the bench at the Tokyo trial were at that very moment themselves obsessed by the need to contain Communism (Pal was himself strongly anti-Communist). He was less than impressed when white prosecutors accused the Japanese of racial prejudice. And, in one of his most controversial and frequently cited passages, Pal suggested that the closest counterpart to Nazi atrocities in the war in Asia may well have been the American use of the atomic bombs. Pal did acknowledge heinous behavior by the Japanese. His point was that they were not alone in this.

Japan's neo-nationalists deploy such arguments as another form of diversion, even as a kind of historiographic *cancellation* of immorality—as if the transgressions of others exonerate one's own crimes. In American, British, and Australian circles, for example, the strongest and most ineradicable "memory" of Japanese atrocity is surely the abuse of prisoners of war (coupled, in the American case, with the "treachery" and "infamy" of the attack on Pearl Harbor). It was estimated at the Tokyo trial that over one-quarter of the Anglo-American servicemen who fell into Japanese hands died in captivity—a vastly greater percentage than died under Japan's Axis allies on the Western Front. Japanese conservatives, in their turn, "cancel" this by emphasizing not merely the wanton killing of Japanese civilians in American air raids, but—a more exact counterthrust—the much greater number of Japanese prisoners who surrendered to the Soviets in the final week of the war and suffered prolonged incarceration and a massive death toll in the Siberian gulags. Unlike many Americans and Europeans, Japanese conservatives never forget that the Allied victors who stood in self-righteous judgment of Japan included the Soviet Union.[11]

This sense of victor's hypocrisy has grown stronger with the years.

Most of the nations that sat in judgment in Nuremberg and Tokyo were, even at the time of these trials, embroiled in their own acts of violence, aggression, and political and racial repression. Most engaged in subsequent mayhem and atrocity. None ever dreamed of allowing themselves to be held accountable to the new standards of international law that had ostensibly been established in the showcase trials in Germany and Japan. And—as our contemporary scrutiny of World War II "as history" reveals—all countries have engaged in the manipulation and obfuscation of public memory of their wartime conduct. Look at wartime anti-Semitism in the United States, for instance, and the vapid "Enola Gay" exhibition commemorating the atomic bomb that was installed in the Air and Space Museum of the Smithsonian Institution in 1995. Look at the exaggerated "myth of the Resistance" in collaborationist France, exposed so belatedly in the trials of Paul Touvier and Maurice Papon; the Nazi bank accounts in "neutral" Switzerland; the popularity of the xenophobic Jorg Haider in Austria; and the Vatican's sustained refusal to acknowledge Pope Pius XII's appeasement of Hitler. And in Germany itself, to give but one recent example, look at the public honoring of the historian Ernst Nolte as the new millennium opened, for his recognition of the "rational core" of Hitler's anti-Semitism and anti-Communism.

Why, in such a world, the neo-nationalist "revisionists" ask, are the Japanese still singled out for particular censure? Does this not reflect plain anti-Japanese racism more than any innate propensity for being unloved?

3. VICTIM CONSCIOUSNESS

The Japanese are hardly alone in their acute sense of victimization. Nor, where World War II is concerned, are they unique in conveying such victim consciousness through highly evocative, proper-name catchphrases. "Remember Hiroshima" has its obvious American analogue in "Remember Pearl Harbor" (or "Remember the Bataan Death March"). In British memory, "Singapore" and the "Burma-Thailand Railway" are comparable signatures of suffering from the war in Asia. For the Chinese, the encryption is "Nanking." For Filipinos, "Manila."

In Japan, however, postwar victim consciousness is inevitably coupled with the traumatic recollection of shattering defeat—with memory of futile death, that is, and the destruction in air raids of some sixty-six cities, culminating in Hiroshima and Nagasaki. All told, around three million Japanese, some 4 percent of the population, died in the war or as a result of it—leaving those who survived bereft of even the psychological consolation of ultimate victory. There could be no heroes for the losing side. It became commonplace to speak of the war dead themselves—and, indeed, of virtually all ordinary Japanese—as being "victims" and "sacrifices." [12]

The decisive period when the Japanese might have been expected to learn about and acknowledge the true nature of their "holy war" was, of course, during the American-led occupation that followed the defeat and lasted until April 1952. As in the Nuremberg trial of Nazis, one explicit purpose of the "Class A" Tokyo trial was heuristic: to establish a body of evidence and testimony that would persuasively demonstrate the extent to which Japan had waged an atrocious war of aggression. As long as the Tokyo trial lasted, the Americans used their control of the Japanese mass media to ensure that the details of such "war crimes" were well publicized.

Many Japanese at the time were in fact deeply shocked by the revelation of barbaric behavior on the part of their fighting men. (Atrocities against Chinese civilians, the Japanese rape of Manila in 1945, and reported incidents of cannibalism by members of the imperial forces appear to have made a particularly strong impression.) Indeed, in scenes that almost seem to foreshadow the plight a few decades later of U.S. servicemen who had served in Vietnam, demobilized Japanese soldiers and sailors often complained bitterly about returning to their homeland only to be reviled as criminals by their own compatriots. The impact of this early publicity about Japanese war crimes, however, was severely blunted by the hardship of everyday life that most Japanese continued to confront for many years after the surrender. The repatriation from overseas of millions of demoralized military men and civilians took years to complete, leaving many families at home in a state of enervating uncertainty. Those who made it back encountered, until around 1949, a country wracked by industrial stagnation, massive unemployment, hyperinflation, severe food shortages, and a ravenous black market.

In this milieu, the plight of Japan's Asian victims, even when acknowledged, seemed remote and abstract. And it was difficult even to imagine yesterday's Caucasian enemies as having been victims at all. On the contrary, the well-fed, splendidly equipped, victorious Americans who now occupied Japan (together with a small U.K. contingent) were obviously people to be *envied.*

The second circumstance that blunted development of a deeper Japanese sense of war responsibility was the Cold War. By the time the Korean War erupted in 1950 (and sparked Japanese economic recovery with a vigorous war boom), the Cold War had long since intervened to destroy not merely the old wartime Allied alliance but the old wartime enmities as well. Japan, like West Germany, became central to U.S. anti-Communist strategy militarily as well as economically; and, in this context, both forgetting the recent atrocities of the former Axis partners and *playing up* the danger of them becoming victimized by Soviet-led Communism served U.S. purposes. It is a bad joke, but Tōjō might well have been recruited as a ghostwriter for the new "Pacific partners."

Until the Cold War ended, the U.S.-Japan relationship provided Japan's conservative leaders with a clear, fixed, almost myopic sense of security and national identity. Tokyo's relationship with Washington was the great axis around which all of Japan's international activities revolved—to a much greater degree than was to be seen in the relationship between Germany and the United States. Whereas Germany was part of the larger NATO alliance, Japan took particular pride in being America's critical *bilateral* partner in Asia. And whereas Germany, over the decades, found it imperative to carefully build constructive relationships with its continental neighbors and former enemies, Japan's conservative governments followed a less independently creative course. Locked in the American embrace, their archipelago studded with U.S. military bases like a monstrous stationary battleship off the coast of Asia (the "battleship" metaphor is beloved of strategic planners), and their economy geared more to the United States and Europe than to Asia, they seem to have built more fragile bridges to their neighbors. Certainly, the end of the bipolar certainties of the Cold War, coupled with the dramatic rise of China as a formidable rival to Japan in the struggle for leadership in Asia, has created a mounting sense of insecurity in the last decade. The recent emergence of more strident nationalistic voices can be interpreted, at least in considerable part, as one manifestation of this new sense of vulnerability.

Even before the end of the Cold War, however, the peculiarly ingrown nature of the U.S.-Japan relationship had the paradoxical effect of enhancing Japanese victim consciousness even as it provided the security of strategic protection under the U.S. nuclear umbrella. The relationship has never been a genuinely equal one. (From the beginning, one mission of the U.S. military forces in Japan—almost never stated publicly—has been to ensure strategic control *of* Japan.) One can, of course, qualify this in various ways. Obviously, for instance, Japan has exercised considerable autonomy—considerable "economic nationalism," some would say—within the Pax Americana. Be that as it may, it is still difficult to deny the unusual degree to which the nation's status vis-à-vis the United States has been one of dependent, or subordinate, independence ever since the occupation ended in 1952. Even the zealous spokesmen for the "Pacific partnership" who deny this must acknowledge that many observers, both in and outside Japan, take it for granted that this is the case.

This is a wearying psychological situation under which to operate for so long. Nor is it the end of this complicated story. For even at the height of the Cold War, the peculiar imbalances in the bilateral relationship operated in ways that tended to turn the very phenomenon of "victim consciousness" itself into yet one more example of the double standards by which Japan tends to be judged. The American war in Indochina provides the most vivid example of this. It is not unreasonable to see this war, in its ferocity and futility, as a rough American counterpart to Japan's own atrocious lost war of several decades earlier. (U.S. planners in the 1960s even went so far as to study Japan's scorched-earth anti-Communist tactics in rural China in the 1930s and early 1940s for lessons pertinent to their own "pacification" campaign in Vietnam.) At the same time, it is obviously not politically acceptable to suggest such a comparison in the United States. The deep sense of suffering and victimization that defines mainstream American recollections and commemorations of this conflict is carved in stone in the Vietnam War Memorial in Washington. By the same token, visitors who come to pay their respects here are almost literally walled off from imagining the millions of Vietnamese and Cambodians and Laotians who also died in that tragedy. During the Gulf War, President George Bush went so far as to speak of there being a "statue of limitations" on self-recrimination where America's terrible war of a mere few decades earlier was concerned.

And so, Americans have their commemorative memorial, even for an atrocious and lost war, and the Japanese do not. Again, the point is not whether drawing such a parallel between Japan in World War II and the United States in the Indochina War is accurate in every respect. Rather, this is but one more example of how Americans (and others) are seen as holding the Japanese to standards they themselves do not in practice observe. The veneration of Confederate soldiers and battlefield sites in the United States—despite (or even because of) their pro-slavery cause—is another such example. All people honor their war dead, but it seems particularly difficult to do so publicly in Japan.

In one form or another, this issue has percolated through all the debates on war and memory that have taken place since 1945. It came to a boil in the 1990s, when individuals and interest groups across the ideological spectrum vigorously debated the construction of a national museum that appropriately addressed the World War II years as "public history." Powerful conservative lobbyists led by the Association of War-Bereaved Families (*Nihon Izokukai*) had long promoted such a museum as a vehicle for honoring the spirits of the Japanese war dead (*eirei*) and reminding younger generations of the hardship and sacrifices of these years. In opposition, Japanese associated with peace movements, the liberal media, and the academic left argued that any such facility must devote major attention to imperial Japan's aggression and atrocity. Names such as "Peace Prayer Hall" and "War Dead Peace Memorial Hall" were proposed as a way of turning such commemorative space into an overtly pacifist statement.

In the end, caution and conservatism prevailed. A multi-story "Shōwa Hall" (*Shōwa-kan*) opened its doors in Tokyo in 1999, with exhibits and programs designed to minimize controversial explicit interpretation of Japan's war and focus instead on the suffering of Japanese and non-Japanese alike.[13]

4. BINATIONAL (U.S.–JAPAN) SANITIZING OF JAPANESE WAR CRIMES

Even before the Cold War intruded to distort public memories of World War II, the United States had taken care to suppress certain aspects of Japan's war responsibility. This took place in the context of the Tokyo war crimes trial, and amounted to an exercise in "victor's justice" just the opposite of the anti-Japanese bias that Japanese nationalists decry. For purely expedient political reasons, the Americans concealed the true nature and full enormity of Japanese war crimes.

This unfinished business has come back to haunt Japan, and properly so. At the same time, however, non-Japanese usually approach this as but one more example of "Japanese" perfidy: the thoroughly binational nature of the cover-up does not play well outside Japan. The major issues and crimes the American-led prosecution chose to ignore and/or suppress were [1] the emperor's knowledge of and responsibility for his country's aggression and acts of atrocity; [2] lethal "medical" experiments conducted on at least 3,000 prisoners in Manchuria by the notorious "Unit 731"; [3] recruitment and virtual enslavement of many tens of thousands of so-called comfort women (ianfu) to service the emperor's soldiers and sailors sexually, the majority of them young Korean women; and [4] the full extent of Japan's use of chemical warfare in China. In the light of recent inquiries into the use of Caucasian and other POWs as slave labor in Japanese coal mines and other operations, it should be noted that the victors also formally decided to exclude any representatives of zaibatsu oligopolies from actual indictment for war crimes in the "Class A" trial in Tokyo. So substantial are these omissions that it does not seem too harsh to speak of criminal neglect, or even collusion, on the part of the prosecution itself.[14]

The most appalling of these cover-ups was the case of Unit 731, involving high-level officers and scientific researchers whose practice of official, institutionalized murder is comparable to the crimes of the "Nazi doctors." Unlike the German case, Japanese participants in these grotesque experiments on human subjects were granted secret immunity from prosecution in exchange for divulging their procedures and findings to the Americans. It naturally followed that the very existence of such practices within the formal structure of the Imperial Army had to be carefully suppressed by the Americans themselves thereafter.

Less sensational but more consequential where the question of popular Japanese consciousness of "war responsibility" is concerned was the exoneration of Emperor Hirohito from any responsibility whatsoever for the policies and actions undertaken in his name. Unlike Germany, where the Nazi regime was eliminated, there was no decisive break with the past in defeated Japan. Maintaining the same monarch on the throne under whom two decades of Japanese aggression had been carried out was but the crowning symbol of this institutional and even personal continuity.

This was a pragmatic decision on the part of the American victors, who deemed it expedient to use Emperor Hirohito to ensure popular acquiescence to the occupation. However reasonable this may have seemed at the time, the negative consequences of such a policy have been far-reaching. No serious investigation of the emperor's actual wartime role and responsibility was ever undertaken. Carefully choreographed pronouncements by both Japanese royalists and the American occupation command made clear that Hirohito did not even bear *moral* responsibility for whatever had been done in his name. In a remarkable act of collusive intrigue that brought together high occupation officers, court circles, members of both the prosecution and defense staffs in the Tokyo trial, the "Class A" defendants, and the emperor himself, the Tokyo trial was "fixed" from the very outset to exclude any possible testimony that might seem to incriminate the sovereign. As two of the separate critical opinions that emerged from the trial noted, the emperor's exemption made these judicial proceedings farcical.[15]

It is difficult to exaggerate how subtly but significantly this binational imperial cover-up impeded serious Japanese engagement with the issue of war responsibility, both at the time and in the decades that followed. Hirohito had been commander in chief of the imperial forces and the most exalted political figure in the nation. If *he* was deemed to have no responsibility whatsoever for the horrors and disasters that took place between his ascension to the throne in 1926 and the end of the war in 1945, why should ordinary Japanese even think of taking responsibility on themselves? Emperor Hirohito became postwar Japan's preeminent symbol, and facilitator, of non-responsibility and non-accountability.

This was compounded by his longevity. Hirohito outlived any of the other major national leaders of World War II by far, and remained on the throne until his death in 1989 at the age of eighty-nine. So long as he was alive, it was generally taboo to discuss his personal war responsibility in the mass media (though this did take place, often vigorously, in left-wing and certain liberal publications). When a journalist did make so bold as to ask Hirohito his thoughts about "war responsibility" in a famous press conference in 1975, following an unprecedented state visit to the United States, the emperor's response was revealing. "Concerning such a figure of speech," he said, "I have not done much study of these literary matters and so do not understand well and am unable to answer." Here was a sobering window not only on the emperor personally, but also on his country and the new "Pacific partnership" he was commemorating with his visit.

As the years passed and the emperor became an increasingly fragile and hollowed-out figure, it became understandably difficult for younger generations to associate his long "Shōwa" era (1926–1989) with anything but a kind of innocuous banality. War, peace, prosperity blurred into one — so thoroughly, in fact, that as Japan entered the present century conservative politicians introduced an astonishingly reactionary proposal to establish "Shōwa Day" (Shōwa no Hi) as a national holiday in commemoration of the late sovereign. Nothing of this sort has taken place in Germany, of course; and if contemporary Japan still maintains a peculiar "aptitude for being unloved," the binational imperial taboo must be factored in as a significant part of the explanation.[16]

The Cold War impact on *American* thinking about Japanese war crimes and war responsibility was openly apparent by 1948. Although hundreds of Japanese had been arrested as potential "Class A" war criminals between 1945 and 1946, only twenty-eight were actually indicted (two died during the trial, and one was excused on grounds of mental incompetence). By the time the Tokyo trial ended in November 1948, only a handful of the others still remained in jail. When the Tokyo judgment came down, that small number too was immediately exempted from prosecution. Unlike Germany, where the showcase Nuremberg trial was followed by ongoing prosecution of Nazi war criminals, there was no ongoing prosecution, or even investigation, of possible top-level Japanese war criminals. No indigenous Japanese system was ever established to pursue these issues.

Quite the opposite took place. By around 1949, former members of the imperial forces were being recruited by the Americans to assist in anti-Communist intelligence activity vis-à-vis China in particular. The outbreak of the Korean War in June 1950 prompted initiation of Japanese rearmament under the U.S. occupation forces — and with this, of course, a concerted binational campaign to *suppress* recollection of Japanese behavior in the "old" war that had ended (as of 1950) only a scant five years earlier. In the new imagery of the Cold War, "Red China" now replaced Japan as the truly threatening and atrocious menace in Asia.

The peace settlement under which Japan regained sovereignty in 1952 included most of the nations of the world but excluded the Soviet Union and the People's Republic of China. For these reasons, it was known at the time as a "separate" (as opposed to "overall") peace, and strongly criticized as such by left-wing elements within Japan. Where the issue of war responsibility is concerned, perhaps the most consequential aspect of the peace settlement lay in the handling of reparations.

In the immediate aftermath of Japan's defeat, the concept of reparations was essentially punitive. Existing industrial plants were to be transferred to other countries in Asia that had been ravaged by the Japanese war machine. Not only would this help compensate these countries for their losses, the argument went. It could also serve as a mechanism whereby a "leveling" of industrial productivity throughout Asia might be promoted. For technical as well as political reasons, these initial plans proved stillborn. And by 1951–1952, when the peace settlement was being finalized, U.S. planners, led by John Foster Dulles, had completely turned about the very purpose of reparations. Such compensation would now be taken out of current Japanese production, or in the form of financial arrangements, with the fundamental objective of promoting economic integration between Japan and the less developed anti-Communist nations of Asia. These state-to-state agreements were to be directed at rehabilitating Japan as the "workshop" of Asia (just as Germany was to become the workshop of Europe) and, at one and the same time, at strengthening Asian participation in the economic containment of China. The last thing anyone in Washington or Tokyo wished to see was a Japan left vulnerable to subsequent claims for compensation for its wartime abuses and atrocities.

Over the decade that followed, the Japanese government fulfilled its obligations under the 1952 peace treaty by negotiating bilateral "reparations" settlements with former enemy nations such as the Philippines, Burma, Indonesia, and South Vietnam. (The United States waived its right to reparations, as did the Kuomintang-led Republic of China on Taiwan, with which Japan had been forced to deal, rather than the Communist regime, at the time of the peace treaty.) Normalization of diplomatic relations with South Korea, delayed until 1965, was accompanied by a reparations agreement. (This rapprochement between Japan and the southern half of its former colony was promoted as part of the larger U.S. strategy of containment in Asia, coincident with the intensification of military engagement in Vietnam.) When Japan belatedly normalized relations with the People's Republic of China in 1972, on the other hand, the Chinese agreed not to pursue the issue of reparations. Through these various state-to-state transactions, all supported by the United States, Japan in theory formally addressed and resolved all outstanding war claims.[17]

The bilateral "Pacific partnership" that arose on the foundations of the 1952 peace settlement was characterized, on the Japanese side, by the consolidation of a conservative "iron triangle" of politicians, bureaucrats, and businessmen that has, for all practical purposes, maintained power to the present day. This coalition has always been racked with conflict and factionalism, and Japan scholars usually take care to repudiate the myth of a monolithic "Japan, Inc." Nonetheless, in yet another suggestive contrast to the situation in postwar Germany, it can still be said that the Japanese government has essentially been controlled by the same conservative political lineage since 1949. The creation of the misnamed Liberal Democratic Party in 1955 established a tradition of "one-party" dominance that carried through the Cold War and has continued, in somewhat bedraggled form, to the present day.

LDP prime ministers have usually, in one form or another, expressed generalized "regret" for Japanese behavior during the war years. Still, this is also the party that supported Kishi Nobusuke, an accused (but never indicted) "Class A" war criminal, as prime minister from 1957 to 1960. It is the party of former prime minister Nakasone Yasuhiro, who breached a long-standing taboo by officially visiting Yasukuni Shrine with his entire cabinet on the anniversary of the war's end in 1985, to pay homage to those who had died for the emperor in World War II. It is the LDP that secretly arranged for the seven defendants condemned to death in the Tokyo trial to be enshrined at Yasukuni; that has supported watered-down textbook treatments of the war; that time and again appoints cabinet ministers given to inflammatory statements such as the denial of the Rape of Nanking.

And it is the LDP that, for half a century and counting, has provided the United States with its "men in Japan"—staunch conservatives, virulent anti-Communists, loyal supporters of the U.S.-Japan security agreement, steadfast proponents of the necessity of gradually expanding Japan's military role under the Pax Americana. Their more extreme nationalistic statements have occasionally embarrassed their American patrons, but the larger *function* of their attempts to downplay the atrocious nature of Japanese behavior in World War II serves the perceived interests of both governments. For if the Japanese populace is to be persuaded to support greater and more diversified remilitarization under the bilateral security treaty—as both Washington and Tokyo desire—it remains necessary to dispel the critical perception of past Japanese militarism and "aggression" that remains so strong in popular consciousness.[18]

5. POPULAR DISCOURSES
ACKNOWLEDGING
GUILT AND RESPONSIBILITY

Why *is* "patriotism" still so suspect in Japan?

This question returns us to the phenomenon of victim consciousness and, more precisely, the manner in which this can be turned in positive and constructive directions. It also returns us to the Japan of half a century ago—not merely to defeat and occupation, but to the broader experience of war itself. To speak of having been victimized, or having been "sacrificed," was not merely a lament or rationalization or excuse. It opened up a world of interrogation.

It is difficult to exaggerate how bitter, heartfelt, and widespread such questioning was in the wake of the surrender, when it became possible to speak openly about such matters. Victimized, people asked, *by whom? Or by what? Sacrifices to what end?* And how, indeed, could one make atonement to the war dead so that their great sacrifice would not be in vain?

Being victims of the American air raids, or the atomic bombs, or the perceived double standards of the victorious powers was but one aspect of such consciousness. More potent and pervasive was a sense of having been victimized by war itself, by the stupidity of militarist leaders who had plunged the nation into the hopeless "holy war," and by the ignorance of the general populace for having allowed itself to be so brainwashed.

These attitudes were not imposed by the victors. They erupted from within, and quickly coalesced in a set of widely accepted articles of faith. The country must not become embroiled in war in the future.

The way to avoid being deceived again was to create a more rational and open society. To create such a society, committed to "peace and democracy," was not only the path through which to regain national pride and international respect. It was also the only conceivable way by which the living could assure the dead that they had not perished in vain.

Such sentiments found expression at all levels. Teachers and scholars who had failed to speak out against the war experienced deep feelings of guilt for having thereby contributed to the deaths of kin and compatriots and, perhaps most poignantly, former students. Almost instinctively, many of them came together in what the influential political scientist Maruyama Masao later described as a "community of remorse" (*kaikon kyōdōtai*). More than a few academics turned to one form or another of Marxism to explain not merely the structural dynamics that had propelled Japan to war, but also the false consciousness that had led most Japanese to go along with the militarists. The Communist Party, legalized under the occupation, made strong inroads into the ranks of organized labor, including the national teachers' union. Socialists, feminists, "old liberals," religious leaders, academics, literary figures, media people in radio, journalism, and filmmaking who had chafed under the wartime censorship—all joined in a chorus of criticism and self-criticism.

Contempt for the militarists who had led the country to destruction was quite extraordinary in the half year or more that preceded the convening of the Tokyo trial in June 1946. It is striking to return to the public record of these years. Political cartoonists ridiculed yesterday's honorable leaders. Editorials and letters to the press complained that the victors were not arresting *more* top-level individuals. People expressed regret that the Japanese themselves had been excluded from participating directly in the investigation and prosecution of war criminals.

There were certainly elements of superficiality and outright deceit in this—"repainting signs," as one of the cynical sayings of the time put it. The unregenerate did not speak their minds in public, and much sincere early criticism and self-criticism faded under the sheer pressures of daily life, the new fashions of the Cold War, and the accumulating sense of victor's double standards. Still, there have also been notable countertrends to the dilution of critical consciousness. In the years and decades that followed, engagement with issues of war memory and responsibility has been kept alive through a number of domestic controversies and confrontations. Notable among these are seemingly interminable debates concerning constitutional revision, the content of nationally certified textbooks, proper language for official "apologies" for imperial Japan's depredations, and the appropriate mission of the nation's still benignly labeled "self-defense forces." To these has been added, in the last decade, the question of redress or reparations to individuals such as "comfort women," prisoners of war, and civilians in occupied areas who were personally victimized by Japan's "crimes against humanity."

These topics, all deserving of extended treatment, constitute a kind of "contested institutionalized memory" that has kept critical consciousness of World War II just as alive in Japan as the "triumphal" consciousness and mythologizing of that same conflict is kept alive in the United States. Heated clashes over revising the decidedly pacifistic provisions of the "no war" constitution, for example, have continued ever since the occupation ended in 1952. Invariably, these provoke evocation of the horrors of war in general and the irresponsibility of the prewar Japanese military machine in particular.[19] In much the same way, the textbook controversies that have drawn strong criticism from abroad since the mid-1960s do indeed reflect official attempts to downplay the "dark" aspects of Japan's modern history. At the same time, however, the cyclical nature of textbook certification—and the snail's-pace court cases deriving from legal challenges to the government's position—have served as an ongoing domestic education in the clash between orthodoxy and its critics.[20]

These contentious forms of institutionalized memory, running like a leitmotiv through postwar political discourse, have been given emphatic counterpoint by discrete incidents and occasions that likewise force war and peace issues to the forefront of popular consciousness. The end of the occupation in 1952, for instance, was accompanied by shocking "Bloody May Day" demonstrations protesting the Cold War nature of the peace settlement, with its attendant remilitarization of Japan and demonization of China. The mid-1950s witnessed the emergence of a broad-based antinuclear movement (sparked by the 1954 "Bikini incident," in which Japanese fishermen were irradiated by fallout from a U.S. hydrogen-bomb test on the Bikini atoll). In 1959–60, pending renewal of the bilateral U.S.–Japan security treaty provoked

massive protests in Tokyo, in which the issue of Japan's accelerated remilitarization under the eagle's wing was again dramatically called in
question. (Prime Minister Kishi Nobusuke, America's "man in Japan"
on this occasion, was one of the accused "Class A" war criminals who
escaped indictment in the Tokyo trial and was released from prison in
its immediate wake.)[21]

In the latter half of the 1960s, war and peace issues were com-
pellingly reformulated in the context of nationwide protests against
Japan's complicity in U.S. aggression in Indochina. Spearheaded by the
highly articulate and media-savvy League for Peace in Vietnam (Be-
heiren), this New Left movement entailed not only placing U.S. behavior in the mirror of Japan's own atrocious war a quarter century earlier,
but also reexamining the very notions of "victim" and "victimizer" (and
the possibility, for Japanese then and now, of being simultaneously
both).[22] Hard on the heels of this, Japan's opening to China in the early
1970s paved the way for a truly wrenching confrontation with the de-
baucheries of imperial forces in the now resurrected China War. From
this time on, a cadre of prolific scholars and journalists has continued to
produce detailed accounts of Japanese war crimes, including the Rape
of Nanking and the activities of Unit 731—materials that tend to pass
under the radar of most non-Japanese observers and popular commentators.[23] In some circles, it is true, the lingering presence of Emperor Hirohito on the throne continued to put a damper on forthright discussion
of Japanese war responsibility. Ironically enough, the emperor's death
in 1989 simultaneously rang the death knell for this particular royalist
taboo. His passing was followed by the appearance of a number of hitherto repressed diaries and memoirs from the war years, and, once again,
gave new impetus to public discussion of the issue of Japanese war responsibility.[24]

Can we draw some kind of "balance sheet" based on all this? Perhaps,
but it is risky business. Watanabe Kazuo's despondent observation concerning Japan's peculiar "aptitude for being unloved" does seem as ap-
posite now as it did in 1945, but why this is so where the issue of
repentance is concerned is not easily explained. Watanabe's own explanation—that Japanese have difficulty thinking in terms of equality and
lack a genuinely deep sense of responsibility—is not very persuasive. To

our ears today, such a note of cultural determinism sounds very much like a self-referential, self-deprecating sort of Orientalism. Watanabe himself was not trapped in such a world. Many of his compatriots escaped it as well, as the persistence of postwar discourses of responsibility and repentance attests. Or, to take an entirely different tack, can it not be said that most nations, states, peoples, collectivities fall short when it comes to thinking in terms of equality and assuming a sense of responsibility for historical transgressions? Wherever we turn, "repentance" rarely holds a candle to self-righteousness or victim consciousness or parochial loyalties or, indeed, indifference to the sins of the past. The situation in Japan, on either side of the ledger, does not really seem exceptional.

Within Japan, it is fair to speak of other kinds of balance sheets. One must certainly look to the general public rather than to the conservative tripod of ruling party, bureaucracy, and big business for genuine engagement with the issue of war responsibility—that "figure of speech" Emperor Hirohito found too literary for his tastes. Japan's deeply entrenched elites have proven steadfastly disinclined to seriously open either their minds or their archives on these matters; and where their pocketbooks are concerned, they remain wedded to the narrowest technical notions of reparations and redress. Here again, opinion polls suggest a public far readier than its leaders to acknowledge past wrongdoings, and to attend to them. A 1994 survey, for example, found that 80 percent of Japanese polled agreed that the government "has not adequately compensated the people of countries Japan invaded or colonized."[25]

It is precisely this general receptivity to such "unpatriotic" notions that has given a desperate edge to the rise of a new wave of reactive neo-nationalism in the last decade, spearheaded by conservative academics who have learned to use the mass media quite masterfully. They have also learned to play the racial card adroitly—against Americans, Chinese, and Koreans in particular, whom they unsurprisingly portray as being prejudiced against the Japanese. There is an ominous circularity in all this—and, to outsiders, a certain perverse reinforcement of Watanabe's old notion of an aptitude for being unloved.

Chapter Thirteen

An Incident at No Gun Ri

MARILYN B. YOUNG

In *Remembering to Forget: Holocaust Memory through the Camera's Eye*, Barbie Zelizer argues that World War II Holocaust photographs came, over time, to stand for war atrocity as such. Contemporary photographs of Cambodia, Bosnia, and Rwanda consciously invoke familiar concentration camp images. "The recycling of photos from the past not only dulls our response to them," Zelizer argues, "but potentially undermines the immediacy and depth of our response to contemporary instances of brutality, discounting them as somehow already known to us."[1] This is in part because the context in which atrocities are perceived is that of other atrocities, rather than the particular situation depicted. The original Holocaust photographs forced the viewer to bear witness; later such photographs have become a way of labeling, a superficial remembering serving a deeper forgetting. Zelizer's focus is the photography of atrocity, the visual evidence of its having taken place. Making people witness past horrors, she reflects, "is becoming the *acte imaginaire* of the twentieth century." The overuse of visual representations of atrocities "may create a situation in which much of the public is content *not* to see—looking so as not to see, and remembering so as to forget."[2] I am going to borrow this notion of remembering in order to forget to discuss the recent uncovering of a massacre committed by American troops during the Korean War.

There were no photographs of the events at No Gun Ri and there did not have to be. They were taken years later in Vietnam and then projected backward, with one major difference. The American public had grown accustomed, with whatever discomfort, to the notion that very bad things happened during the Vietnam War—though for the entire fifteen-year period, only one bad thing, My Lai, was accorded the label "atrocity." The war in Korea, which the U.S. public has had difficulty knowing how to remember (and which historians routinely designate "forgotten"), was thought of—when thought about at all—as a coda to World War II rather than a prologue to the Vietnam War—on the whole a necessary war and perhaps even a just one.

The Korean War itself began in images made familiar by the recent past. On June 25, 1950, North Korean tanks surged (or, in other newspapers accounts, swept) across the 38th parallel to fall upon an unsuspecting South Korea in an act that melded the Nazi blitzkrieg in Poland with Japanese perfidy in Pearl Harbor. In quick succession, President Harry S. Truman ordered naval and air units to support South Korean troops, placed the Seventh Fleet in the Taiwan Straits to block any Chinese move against Taiwan and, on January 27, won approval for a United Nations Security Council resolution condemning North Korean aggression and agreeing to a joint effort to repel the invasion and restore peace.

After an initial and predictable rallying of the public around the flag, the Korean War steadily lost popular support, with poll levels rarely rising above 40 percent for its entire course. What had begun as the apparently simple task of restoring the status quo ante against an inferior enemy developed first into a rout of American forces and then, as reinforcements arrived in ever-growing numbers, into a U.S.-led drive to destroy the North Korean government and unify the country under American auspices. Chinese intervention ended these ambitions and, along with it, American public support for the entire enterprise.

For a month or so, the war was reported as a civil war, the continuation of years of border conflict between North and South Korea. And not only a civil war between the two halves of an artificially divided country, but a civil war *within* the South, with the surviving elements of an earlier guerrilla movement, repressed in 1947–49, reemerging. This history, however, quickly disappeared from the contemporary press and from subsequent histories in favor of a version of the conflict which cast it entirely within a Cold War framework: Communist expansion versus free-world containment. Truce talks, begun in the summer of 1951, were concluded two years later and the war ended where it had begun — South Korea saved for the free world, North Korea properly chastised, the Chinese contained within their borders. Not quite a victory, perhaps, but not a defeat either and, as rapidly as could be, the war, which in the main was attended to only by Americans who had relatives fighting there, was filed away. American casualties were over 100,000 (with more than 33,000 dead); a total of about 3 million Koreans and 1 million Chinese had died.

Unlike the Vietnam War, the unpopularity of the Korean War was forgotten except by the politicians who drew from it a specific and limited lesson for the future: avoid Chinese Communist intervention. In its aftermath, the received wisdom on the war was that the country had appropriately responded to an aggressive Communist challenge: the entry of North Korean troops into South Korea. Things got a little murky later on in the war, after U.S. forces had driven the North Koreans back where they came from only to find themselves facing a new and more menacing enemy, the Chinese Communists. There were lingering issues — particularly the alleged collaboration of large numbers of American prisoners of war with their captors — but few wondered why the war had occurred or doubted its necessity.

The only atrocities associated with it were attributed to North Korean and Chinese troops. This is not unusual. As one expert in military law put it: "Battlefield war crimes committed by one's own forces are almost never charged as such. Instead, they are simply alleged as the Uniform Code of Military Justice offenses of murder, rape, or aggravated assault. . . . They are denominated war crimes only if committed by enemy nationals."[3] (No one at My Lai, for example, was charged with having committed a war crime.) And then suddenly one fall day in 1999, the *New York Times* published on its front page an Associated Press story about what had taken place under a railroad bridge in South Korea in July 1950.

For years Korean survivors of what they claimed was an American massacre of innocent civilian refugees had fruitlessly and, given the nature of the political repression in Korea at the time, fearlessly, petitioned their government for redress. In July 1994, the group petitioned the U.S. Armed Forces Claims Service asking for an apology and compensation. The judge advocate, Major John G. Warthen, informed them that the United States government was not liable to claims "resulting from an act of the Armed Forces of the United States in combat." Three years later, the petitioners renewed their effort, this time addressing their appeal to President Clinton and insisting that "the massacre occurred before the arrival of the North Korean army." In 1998, the U.S. National Council of Churches wrote to the Pentagon on behalf of the petitioners and the Army Center of Military History finally reviewed the complaint but found "no information to substantiate the claim . . ."[4] But when a team of AP reporters, Sang-hun Choe, Charles J. Hanley, and Martha Mendoza, revealed that American veterans confirmed the petitioners' story and, in addition, cited declassified army documents as further evidence, the story at last commanded national attention.

I want to reflect on how people learn to forget by looking at the way in which what was quickly dubbed an "incident" was reported. All except historians of the Korean War were taken by surprise. Here was a massacre of noncombatants, testified to by those who had participated in it. Korean refugees, strafed by U.S. planes as they fled the fighting, were then herded, by U.S. soldiers, under a railroad bridge and fired upon, in some accounts over a three-day period, as they huddled there. The number of dead remains in dispute, though it is likely to have been several hundred and perhaps as many as 400. It seemed initially an unassimilable story, misplaced in the wrong war.

News stories of what happened under the bridge incorporated in their accounts a set of extenuating circumstances. First, the civilians had given cause, since North Korean soldiers were known to infiltrate refugee columns in order to get behind U.S. lines. Second, the soldiers themselves did not really represent the U.S. military—they were soft, untrained troops suddenly catapulted into combat from comfortable occupation duty in Japan. Third, the circumstances were particularly fraught: U.S. troops were in chaotic retreat, confusion reigned, there was a danger of being wiped out entirely. The *Los Angeles Times* elaborated: the troops at No Gun Ri were equipped with old World War II ordnance; they relied on old Rand McNally maps; the troops were in retreat, were unaccustomed to nighttime operations, had lost weapons and men, were struggling "against oppressive heat, rugged terrain, and inadequate supplies of water, as well as pursuing North Korean units." They were, as the military historian Allan R. Millett reflected, "all scared to death . . . Add to that anxiety, ignorance, horror stories of atrocities committed by the North Koreans and you have troops in a condition not to exercise very good judgment."[5] The relationship between these factors and the mass death under the railroad bridge is left implicit. Some accounts offered the circumstances first and only then turned to the events themselves; others reversed the order, but none made any effort to restrict the discussion to the decision of senior officers to stop refugees attempting to cross U.S. lines by any means necessary and only one raised the problem that distinctions between "friend" and "foe" were difficult to make in Korea, as they were to be again in Vietnam.

James Webb, a Vietnam veteran, novelist and former Secretary of the Navy, has written a short essay about No Gun Ri which I think provides a model of the way remembering can become simultaneous with forgetting. Webb begins this way: "I do not know what happened to the civilians at the bridge near the village of No Gun Ri, although it seems clear from recent AP reports that many of them died in the early days of the Korean War as their country was being ripped apart by a communist invasion and the U.S. Army was thrown into disarray." Webb has laid out the terms: probably civilians died, but in the mitigating context of enemy invasion and American helplessness. Next he suggests the questions that will be asked as the Army investigates: "Did the refugees die from American bombs and bullets? If so, were the deaths deliberate? If they were, were they the result of battlefield realities that left them caught in the middle?" As the American reader moves through the list, each successive question answers the preceding one, so that by the end it is logical to conclude that yes, civilian refugees were killed by Americans, perhaps deliberately, but the deaths were the result of "battlefield realities." Webb follows this opening set of questions with another: "Were the American soldiers ordered to keep refugees off the road and away from the bridge so that a retreating army could move south before it was annihilated? Were the refugees attempting to move, by day or night, into the American perimeter? Or were the American soldiers simply having a little target practice, shooting off precious ammunition to see if they might kill a woman here and a kid there as the world was falling down upon their heads?" Now the battlefield realities become more real to the reader: this was an American army in danger not so much of defeat as of annihilation; they were under orders to keep the bridge clear so the army could move south and save itself; the refugees may have been trying to move inside American lines. Once Webb has established this persuasive scene, the notion that the deaths were wanton cannot be taken seriously.[6]

Finally, Webb suggests that perhaps raking up No Gun Ri is only about "some team of lawyers trying to squeeze millions out of a long-ago tragedy of the sort that seems always to accompany battles fought where other people live." Now the reader knows whom to blame for the unwelcome knowledge of American wrongdoing: lawyers making money out of war, a new variety of war profiteer. In the last phrase about the sort of tragedies that occur when battles are fought "where other people live," Webb takes a chance. Some readers might pause to wonder what Americans were doing fighting their battles in someone else's country?

Throughout the essay Webb repeats the sequence of acknowledgment and extenuation. Sometimes, as in the opening sentence, the two occur in the same sentence; elsewhere in the essay, they are sequential. But a bald statement of a possible American wrong never stands alone. The sentences and paragraphs seem to tense and then relax, and the reader is encouraged to do likewise: clench against an unwanted revelation, breathe when it is explained. The explanations explain away. Thus, he observes that the Korean War was more brutal than Vietnam, with a civilian death toll of some 2 million Koreans, 70 percent of the total. This is followed by a return to the immediate situation in July 1950: a massive invasion from the north "which flattened every major city, threw hundreds of thousands of refugees onto the roads, and left little time for American and South Korean forces to reconstruct firm lines of defense." The role of the U.S. Air Force in flattening the cities and generating refugees is not denied but folded into the passive voice of war being waged. The implication of this way of summarizing the history of the Korean War is that North Koreans were responsible for the 2 million civilian deaths.

The heart of Webb's argument is his discussion of the "Hobson's choice of combat: Do I protect my men and lose my innocence? Or do I keep my innocence and lose my men?" The question insists on an absolute fault line, in Webb's words, the "thin unbreachable line" separat-

ing those who have gone to war and those who stayed home. Easy
enough to contemplate the actions of the soldiers in the 100 degree heat
of summer at No Gun Ri from the comfort of air-conditioned offices,
sipping "herbal tea or Snapple." But suppose you had been there?
Webb goes on to write a combat scenario as charged as any in his Vietnam novel *Field of Fire*. What standard should be set "for those who had
little hope of even seeing tomorrow when the world turned suddenly
ugly and they pressed their faces far into the dirt while the mortars
twirled overhead and the bullets kicked up dust in their eyes?"[7] Webb
invites readers to test themselves and sets the terms: "Your men are
dying. [The reader is, apparently, a junior officer.] The lines are shrink-
ing. You are running out of food and even ammunition. . . . Civilians
are everywhere, thousands upon thousands of them. They are starving
and they are afraid and some of them are in fact not civilians. . . . They
want to sleep inside your perimeter. They need your food. They dream
of your protection. But the only true protection you can give them is to
defeat the invading enemy. If you take even 10, you will be unable to
care for your own people. And if you take 10, you will be besieged by
10,000. You have a mission to perform. But they are desperate and you
cannot speak their language. They are going to swarm your perimeter.
When they come, what do you do?"

Rather than answer the question, Webb shifts ground. Is the deliberate killing of civilians a war crime? And if so, what about "death delivered by a bomb" which earns the pilot "an air medal, while, when it
comes to the end of a gun, it earns one a trip to jail." A good debater's
point, but Webb cannot afford to linger on it, lest it impugn the modern
way of warfare as such. Still, the U.S. is a nation "founded on Judeo-
Christian principles that we proudly carry to the battlefield." Killing
prisoners of war, or indeed anyone "under one's actual control" is a
crime. Hence, the prosecution of the perpetrators of My Lai, "despite
the unassailable fact that most of the villagers killed . . . were part of a
highly organized Communist cadre." Since "they were under the physical control of the soldiers who killed them," those soldiers should indeed answer to criminal charges. Once again, Webb takes away as he
gives: the villagers at My Lai were not really innocent at all, but killing
them was wrong. However, had those same women and children ignored the "rigid protocols of war understood by both sides, such as mov-

ing near an American perimeter at night, running from a combat patrol or signaling with lamps after dark, they would have been killed with impunity." And perhaps this was the case at No Gun Ri.

The reward for Vietnam veterans struggling with these terrible moral distinctions, Webb concludes, was the "same vitriol that is now being directed at the soldiers who fought at No Gun Ri." The essay ends with a resounding non sequitur: ". . . the only lessons seem to be: Make sure you fight in a popular war. Make sure you use bombs instead of bullets. And make sure you win."

Returning to No Gun Ri itself, this is what Webb read in the original AP report: On July 26, 660 men of the 1st Division of the 7th Cavalry Regiment were dug in by a railroad bridge near several villages. Some troops had been operating in the area for several days and, according to survivors of the massacre, had ordered the inhabitants of two villages near the bridge out of their homes, warning them that the North Koreans were coming. As the refugees approached the railroad bridge, soldiers ordered them off the road and onto a parallel railroad track so that U.S. military vehicles could pass. The group rested there and then suddenly came under strafing attack by U.S. planes. Running for their lives, dragging their children, abandoning the dead and dying, people took shelter in a culvert beneath the tracks. One Korean survivor told a *Washington Post* reporter that American soldiers then walked among the wounded, "checking every wounded person and shooting them if they moved."[8]

It is possible the strafing attack was a mistake, although after-mission reports filed by fighter-bomber pilots in this period frequently mention strafing people who "appeared to be evacuees," people "wearing white clothing," and "refugees." Several Americans were caught in the strafing run and took shelter with the villagers in the culvert. Then, a veteran named Delos Flint remembered "somebody, maybe our guys, was shooting in at us." Flint and his friends escaped and hundreds of the refugees ran for the safety of a nearby railroad bridge. One Korean survivor told an American reporter that he and his family, along with perhaps 300 others, had been ordered into the underpass by U.S. soldiers. Anyone who tried to leave was shot down. The orders from headquarters were explicit: "No refugees to cross the front line. Fire everyone trying to cross lines. Use discretion in case of women and children." Similar orders were issued by Major General William Kean, commander of the 25th Infantry Division: "All civilians seen in this area are to be considered as enemy and action taken accordingly."[9]

Not everyone followed orders. A first lieutenant, Robert M. Carroll, didn't think there were any enemy soldiers about and ordered a cease-fire in his sector. He then led a young boy to presumed safety under the double arches of the bridge. Other Americans also led refugees into the underpasses. After dark, however, the firing began. One captain, Melbourne Chandler, checked with his superior officers before ordering machine gunners in his heavy weapons company to "set up near the tunnel mouths and open fire." "We didn't know if they were North or South Koreans," one veteran told the AP reporter. "We were there only a couple of days and we didn't know them from a load of coal," Eugene Hesselman recalled. "The hell with all those people," he remembers his captain telling him. "Let's get rid of all of them." According to another veteran, Norman Tinkler, "We just annihilated them."[10] Many soldiers disobeyed orders. Delos Flint told *Time* magazine that he, along with perhaps half of the troops around him, refused to fire at the refugees: "I couldn't see killing kids, even if they were infiltrators."[11]

There have been a number of follow-up stories on No Gun Ri. Both AP and some of the networks contacted veterans and sent reporters to search the archives. Lester Todd told CBS that he had been part of "Operation Killer," a 1951 campaign in which he had orders to kill "everything in front of us, including women and children. We killed anything that walked."[12] This was not an easy task, as an evaluation report sent to the commanding officer of the 38th Infantry at the time made clear: "The 8th Army directive that civilians be turned away from the front lines by artillery and/or small arms fire was difficult to carry out, due to the hesitancy on the part of the younger soldiers to fire directly upon groups of old men, women and children."[13] Charles Hanley, of the AP, turned up a classified report by the commander of the 1st Cavalry Division, Maj. Gen. Hobart R. Gay, vividly describing the destruction of one of the bridges over the Naktong River in August 1950 while it was still crowded with refugees.

> By nightfall of 2d August all troops were across the Naktong except the rear guard of the 1st Battalion of the 8th Cavalry. Orders were to blow both the railroad and the footbridge. . . . At dusk, thousands upon thou-

sands of refugees were on the west side of the Naktong and as the rear guard of the 8th Cavalry would start across the bridge, they would follow them. The Division Commander [Gay] ordered the rear guard to go back to the west side and hold back the refugees and when all was set they would run across the bridge to the east side so it could be blown. This scene was repeated several times but each time the refugees were on the heels of the rear guard. Finally it was nearly dark. There was nothing else to be done. The Division Commander gave the order to blow the bridge. It was a tough decision because up in the air with the bridge went hundreds of refugees.[14]

Not all such incidents were reported. At the Tuksong-dong bridge, former sergeant Carroll F. Kinsman recounted, there were streams of women, children, old men, ox carts. "We stayed up all that night and searched them," Kinsman said, but found no infiltrators. At 7 A.M., Company A, of the 14th Combat Engineers Battalion, was told to blow up the bridge. The explosion, Kinsman remembered, "lifted up [the bridge] and turned it sideways and it was full of refugees end to end." The report of the 14th Engineers recorded the destruction of the bridge laconically: "Results, excellent." The day before the bridge was blown, retreating American soldiers had been followed by a group of some eighty refugees. One veteran claims that suddenly five North Koreans dressed in white peasant clothing opened fire on the Americans. Another disagrees—they had surrendered peacefully.[15]

The destruction of the bridges did not stop the flow of refugees. Duane E. 'Bud' Biteman was patrolling the Naktong River in an F-51 that steamy August day. To an admiring interviewer, Jennie Ethell Chancey, he described the moral dilemma he faced, a dilemma "for which my years of air force training had neglected to prepare me and that violently contradicted my Christian upbringing. Could I bring myself to fire my machine guns at those refugees in order to keep them from crossing the Naktong River?" Biteman does not recall receiving any orders, nor even "firm guidelines," but North Koreans soldiers had infiltrated refugee groups in the past and no one knew how many infiltrators were among the thousands trying to cross the river. Instead of orders there was a "sort of general unspoken consensus" that the refugees must be stopped. "No one would take the responsibility to issue a specific instruction on just how the refugees were to be stopped." So Biteman flew ten feet above the heads of "hundreds upon hundreds of white-robed men, women, and children standing in the middle of the river." He remembers how they ducked as his fighter wing swooped over them, then scrambled forward again as the planes flew by to make another pass. Biteman fired in front of those who had stopped midstream, which drove them back—but only for a moment. "The mental anguish of those couple of hours, sitting alone in my cockpit as I played 'God' to those thousands of homeless, defenseless dregs of humanity, was the heaviest burden I had ever been forced to bear—or ever would." He prayed for a clear challenge that would justify his strafing, searched his conscience for "moral justification to pull the trigger on them." But the reader never learns how it all came out. Instead, at once remembering and forgetting, Biteman ends his account of the early years of the war by noting that 1950 and 1951 were "vintage years for courage, valor and heroism."[16]

Biteman may not have remembered specific orders with respect to strafing, but Colonel Turner C. Rogers, Deputy Air Force Commander in Korea, seems nevertheless to have been operating under them. On July 25, 1950, he wrote an agitated memorandum to his commanding officer on the problems posed by the policy of strafing civilian refugees. The memorandum, neatly organized in roman numerals, first poses "The Problem," which is to "determine the policy for guidance of all Fifth Air Force units in regard to strafing of civilian refugees on the highways." "Facts Bearing on the Problem" include reports that "large groups of civilians, either composed of or controlled by North Korean soldiers, are infiltrating U.S. positions." The army requested that "all civilian refugee parties . . . approaching our positions" be strafed, and this had been done. But Colonel Rogers worried that the policy might well "cause embarrassment to the U.S. Air Force and to the U.S. government in its relation with the United Nations." Was strafing civilian refugees really the best use of the Air Force? Besides, why wasn't the army doing its own dirty work, "screening such personnel or shooting them as they came through if they desire such action"? Rogers recommended that for "the protection of the Air Force," henceforth attacks on groups of civilians would be confined to those "definitely known to contain North Korean soldiers or commit hostile acts."[17]

Reporters discovered yet more instances of wanton killing. On Janu-

ary 20, 1951, Cho Bong-won told the AP, four U.S. planes dropped napalm at the entrance of a cave 90 miles southeast of Seoul, in which
some 300 refugees had sought shelter from U.S. bombing. That same
week, according to Kim In-tae, a survivor, 300 South Koreans died in an
American bombing raid as they took shelter in a storage house. Hong
Won-ki, survivor of an attack close to Seoul, described being strafed repeatedly. As the low-flying planes approached, Hong remembered, the
refugees held their bundles of belongings over their heads "to show that
we were just refugees," but they were strafed anyway. Three days later,
planes returned to the same refugee-packed village to strafe and drop
napalm.[18]

Eight months after the first revelation of the massacre, questions
were raised as to whether it had ever occurred. Edward Daily, a veteran
whose description of the killing at No Gun Ri was especially powerful,
confessed that he had not been there.[19] Joseph L. Galloway, writing for
U.S. News and World Report, breathed a sigh of relief. It is clear, he
wrote, that "something terrible *did* happen [at No Gun Ri] — in the confusion of war, some refugees were shot by American soldiers."[20] "Some
refugees" is far less than a massacre. For Galloway and, I suspect, a good
many Americans, Daily's recantation was sufficient to cast doubt on the
testimony of all the surviving South Koreans, the documentary evidence, and the accounts of other veterans. Daily's behavior, like that of
Vietnam veterans who confess to crimes of war they did not commit, is
a matter for psychologists to unravel. But, as one forensic psychiatrist reflected, "It is not uncommon when a serious murder occurs for a couple
of folks to drop by and say, 'I did it.' "[21] Like others who falsely confess to
crimes they did not commit, Daily had made up a true story.

The form of Galloway's debunking story, much like Webb's dramatic
narrative, furthers the process of remembering to forget. He begins by
noting that the original AP account admitted the veterans were incon-
sistent in their stories and blames the tremendous attention the story received on the way other news organizations, in their reporting of AP's
findings, had "failed to reflect the ambiguities in the AP story. Assertions
. . . took on the air of hard fact; the narrative line became more dramatic." That said, however, Galloway leans to the other side of the ambiguities, so to speak, making the narrative line dramatic by focusing on
Ed Daily's recantation, taking as hard fact anxious second thoughts by

some of the veterans, and failing to reflect on the evidence offered by another set of witnesses—the Korean survivors—or the documents cited in the original AP story.

The narrative form which concedes some things in the service of a larger denial is hardly unique to the reporting on No Gun Ri. Indeed, it marks one of the earliest contemporary reports concerning the disturbing nature of the Korean War, an account close to the one Hanley and his colleagues unearthed in 1999. Reporting for *Time* and *Life* in August 1950, John Osborne's distress at the savagery of what he was witnessing is evident. "This is a story that no American should ever have to write," he begins. "It is the ugly story of an ugly war." In a familiar manner, Osborne does not immediately go on to talk about why it's so bad. Rather, he writes that just because it's such a "sorrowful and sickening" story, he will begin with "a few good and heartening things" that can be said about it. First, the soldiers are terrific. They may have been raw when they arrived in June and even abandoned positions they should have held, but "in a land and among a people that most of them dislike, in a war that all too few of them understand and none of them want, they became strong men and good soldiers—fast." Second, U.S. firepower and the ability to coordinate and use it is "thrilling." That's the good news.

The bad news is that in Korea, these same fine soldiers were having forced upon them "acts and attitudes of the utmost savagery." By this Osborne means not the "inevitable savagery of combat in the field, but savagery in detail—the blotting out of villages where the enemy *may* be hiding; the shooting and shelling of refugees who *may* include [the enemy] or who *may* be screening an enemy march upon our positions." Even harder to witness was the "savagery by proxy, the savagery of [our ally]. . . . They murder to save themselves the trouble of escorting prisoners to the rear; they murder civilians simply to get them out of the way or to avoid the trouble of searching and cross-examining them. And they extort information . . . by means so brutal that they cannot be described."

Osborne is told that American soldiers have seen North Korean soldiers change out of their uniforms into ordinary Korean peasant garb, so their suspicion of refugees is not surprising and "every time they see a column of peasants coming toward them they reach for their guns, and sometimes they use their guns." He is present at a particularly tense moment when a call comes through to the regimental command post that a column of three to four hundred refugees is moving right into the lines of a company of U.S. soldiers. "Don't let them through," the major in command orders the regimental commanders. And if they won't go back, a staff officer asks? Then fire over their heads, comes the answer. And then? "Well, then, fire into them if you have to. *If you have to,* I said." Osborne does not inform us of what happened next. But later the same day a report comes in that troops at an advanced post have fired into a group of refugees. "From the command post," Osborne writes, "an urgent and remonstrating voice speaks over the wire into the hills. 'My God, John. It's gone too far when we are shooting at children.' " And then in response to the unheard voice from the outpost, the same officer says, "Watch it, John, watch it! But don't take any chances." And they *do* have to watch it, Osborne hastens to add.

The general point Osborne wants to make is that Korea is a different sort of war, one fought, as he puts it, "amongst and to some extent by the population of the country." A purely military approach cannot work; the problem has to be engaged at a political level. Otherwise, Osborne warns, the U.S. effort is doomed and along with it, the American soldier, who has then to fight in ways Osborne cannot bear to describe in too great detail. Because he explicitly blames the behavior of American troops on the way they were being *forced* to fight, because he stresses the fact of infiltration rather than the possibility of checking refugees before shooting them, because he assigns the worst cases of brutality to the South Koreans, without discussing the relationship of U.S. authority to them, the ordinary reader of *Time* or *Life* is protected from the fullest implications of the story he has just read: that in Korea, the American army is behaving in ways Americans had been taught only its enemies did.

Webb, Galloway and indeed Osborne himself root the behavior of troops in what Webb called "battlefield realities." These can be stated succinctly: in July 1950, American troops, sent to Korea to help the South Korean army repel a North Korean invasion, were on the run. Their movements were often hampered by fleeing South Korean civilians, among whom there were said to be North Korean infiltrators. Standing orders were to prevent refugees from crossing American lines. At this level, probably in all armies, there will always be soldiers who fire their weapons at unarmed civilians when ordered to do so, and those who refuse. And in all countries, some portion of the public which will justify such actions and another which will condemn them.

But the full historical context is more complicated than a single battlefield and it would be useful, at this point, to recall it. A powerful movement against the government installed in South Korea by the United States, including a guerrilla insurgency, had gripped many parts of South Korea in 1947 and 1948. In several areas, the government of Sygmann Rhee had conducted a war of extermination with the full knowledge of the U.S. occupation. Local guerrillas, with little or no connection to North Korea, continued to operate in the early months of the Korean War itself. In short, the Korean civil war, waged both politically and militarily inside South Korea and in constant border incidents, was being fought for a good two years before the North Koreans attempted to resolve it militarily and the Americans moved in to block them on behalf of the government it had created in Seoul. It is in this context that civilian refugees became the enemy and, from the air, the entire peninsula became a free fire zone.[22]

This is the war, under-reported but still visible, that the American public both rejected and refused to think about. The initial Pentagon response to the AP story was flatly to deny the charges. Then, as more evidence emerged, the Pentagon assured survivors they would look into the matter carefully as "a tribute to the shared sacrifices of the Korean and American people during the Korean War." A statement issued by survivors after they met with Pentagon officials put it a little differently, employing the language of World War II and human rights: "No Gun Ri Holocaust is the massacre of innocent people, committed by the U.S. military forces who pursued only efficiency of their military operation, totally ignoring human rights."[23]

The final army report, released in January 2001, follows Webb, Galloway and Osborne in its artful acceptance and denial of what happened that summer day fifty years ago.[24] The report acknowledges that "an unknown number of Korean civilians were killed or injured" at No Gun Ri but insists that "what befell civilians . . . was a tragic and deeply regrettable accompaniment to a war forced upon unprepared U.S. and ROK forces."[25] Rumors of North Korean infiltrators, fearful and untrained American soldiers, and the confusion of combat were sufficient to explain the deaths at No Gun Ri. Charles Cragin, the deputy assistant secretary of defense, told a reporter that the U.S. team found nothing in the record that "rose to the level of criminality." "Unfortunately, in the fog of war," he explained, "and in war, innocent civilians die."[26]

The army report cast doubt on the memories of those veterans who claimed to have received orders to fire, but accepted the reliability of those who did not remember having received orders. The documents AP reporters had found in the archives were either not mentioned or selectively quoted.[27] President Clinton expressed his personal regret that "Korean civilians lost their lives at No Gun Ri" and drew a general lesson: "The intensive, yearlong investigation . . . has served as a painful reminder of the tragedies of war and the scars they leave behind on people and on nations." It had proven impossible to determine exactly what had occurred but a joint South Korean–U.S. Statement of Mutual Understanding concluded that "an unconfirmed number of innocent Korean refugees were killed or injured" and to them Clinton offered his condolences. More obscurely, Clinton referred to the many Americans who had "experienced the anguish of innocent casualties of war" and were thus able to "understand and sympathize with the sense of loss and sorrow that remains even after a half a century has passed." But "pain is not the only legacy of the Korean War," Clinton declared. "Americans and Korean veterans fought shoulder to shoulder . . . for the cause of freedom, and they prevailed." Korea's vibrant democracy and the "closeness of our two peoples today" was a testament "to the sacrifices made by both of our nations fifty years ago." The civilians gunned down at No Gun Ri, it turns out, had contributed to the future of South Korea. Compensation to the victims, in such circumstances, was out of the question, but symbolic gestures were in order. "I sincerely hope that the memorial the United States will construct to these and all other innocent Korean civilians killed during the war will bring a measure of solace and closure." Not only a memorial, but a scholarship fund as a "living tribute" to their memory.[28]

Asked why he had used the language of regret rather than apology, Clinton explained: "I think the findings were—I think [President Kim Dae-jung] knows that 'regret' and 'apology' both mean the same thing, in terms of being profoundly sorry for what happened. But I believe that the people who looked into it could not conclude that there was a deliberate act, decided at a high enough level in the military hierarchy, to acknowledge that, in effect, the government had participated in something terrible."[29]

Not everyone was convinced. "Any final report that does not deal with the responsibility of commanders," a representative of the survivors declared, "has a serious defect. It can't be construed as anything other than a Pentagon attempt to whitewash the massacre." There has been some talk among survivors of bringing the case before the International Court of Justice in The Hague.[30] Whatever the level of dissatisfaction in Korea, however, the incident at No Gun Ri is now closed as far as the United States is concerned. No one is responsible for what happened at No Gun Ri, not even the soldiers who fired into groups of unarmed civilians. Such things happen in the "fog of war."[31] Atrocities arise unbidden; no one orders them. The *particular* war in which the United States was engaged from 1950 to 1953 remained submerged. The atrocity at No Gun Ri was briefly remembered but not the war that made that atrocity if not inevitable then at least more than likely. Like pictures of the Holocaust, atrocity stories have become only another way of forgetting.

Notes

Introduction

1 Hamburger Institut für Sozialforschung (ed.), *Vernichtungskrieg, Verbrechen der Wehrmacht 1941 bis 1944* (Hamburg, 1996).

2 Hamburger Institut für Sozialforschung (ed.), *Besucher einer Ausstellung: Die Ausstellung "Vernichtungskrieg, Verbrechen der Wehrmacht 1941 bis 1944" in Interview und Gespräch* (Hamburg, 1998).

3 Bogdan Musial, "Bilder einer Ausstellung. Kritische Anmerkungen zur Wanderausstellung 'Vernichtungskrieg. Verbrechen der Wehrmacht 1941 bis 1944,'" in *Vierteljahrshefte für Zeitgeschichte* 47 (1999): 563–91; Krisztián Ungváry, "Echte Bilder—problematische Aussagen. Eine quantitative und qualitative Analyse des Bildmaterials der Ausstellung 'Vernichtungskrieg. Verbrechen der Wehrmacht 1941 bis 1944,'" in *Geschichte in Wissenschaft und Unterricht* 10 (1999): 584–95; Dieter Schmidt-Neuhaus, "Die Tarnopol-Stellwand der Wanderausstellung 'Vernichtungskrieg. Verbrechen der Wehrmacht 1941 bis 1944.' Eine Falluntersuchung zur Verwendung von Bildquellen," in *Geschichte in Wissenschaft und Unterricht* 10 (1999): 596–603.

4 Hamburg Institute for Social Research (ed.), *The German Army and Genocide: Crimes Against War Prisoners, Jews and Other Civilians, 1939–1944* (New York, 1999).

5 István Deák, Jan T. Gross, and Tony Judt (eds.), *The Politics of Retribution in Europe: World War II and Its Aftermath* (Princeton, N.J., 2000); Roy Gutman and David Rieff (eds.), *Crimes of War: What the Public Should Know* (New York, 1999).

6 Michael Ignatief, "Lemkin's Word," in *The New Republic* (February 26, 2001): 26.

7 For a history of the politics of human rights, see, for example, Geoffrey

Robertson, *Crimes Against Humanity: The Struggle for Global Justice* (New York, 1999). See also Gary Jonathan Bass, *Stay the Hand of Vengeance: The Politics of War Crimes Tribunals* (Princeton, N.J., 2000); Howard Ball, *Prosecuting War Crimes and Genocide: The Twentieth-Century Experience* (Lawrence, Kan., 1999); Carla Hesse and Robert Post (eds.), *Human Rights in Political Transitions: Gettysburg to Bosnia* (New York, 1999); Aryeh Neier, *War Crimes: Brutality, Genocide, Terror, and the Struggle for Justice* (New York, 1998); Martha Minow, *Between Vengeance and Forgiveness: Facing History after Genocide and Mass Violence* (Boston, 1998). For a general discussion of definitions of genocide and the relevant literature, see Frank Chalk and Kurt Jonassohn, *The History and Sociology of Genocide: Analyses and Case Studies* (New Haven, Conn., 1990), pp. 8–27. See also Leo Kuper, *Genocide: Its Political Use in the Twentieth Century* (New Haven, Conn., 1981). For a review of the most recent works, see Aryeh Neier, "The Quest for Justice," in *The New York Review of Books* vol. XLVIII, Nr. 4 (March 8, 2001).

8 See the chapter by Robert G. Moeller in this volume. See also his *War Stories: The Search for a Usable Past in the Federal Republic of Germany* (Berkeley, Calif., 2001), p. 25.

9 For a general historiographical background, see Omer Bartov, "German Soldiers and the Holocaust: Historiography, Research and Implications," in *History & Memory* 9 (Fall 1997): 162–88. See also his *Hitler's Army: Soldiers, Nazis, and War in the Third Reich* (New York, 1992) and *The Eastern Front, 1941–45: German Troops and the Barbarisation of Warfare* (New York, 1986).

10 For differing perspectives on the impact of the exhibition, see Omer Bartov's and Bernd Boll's chapters in this volume.

11 On the evolution of the representation of World War II and the gradual introduction of the Holocaust to its historiography, see Omer Bartov, "Germany's Unforgettable War: The Twisted Road from Berlin to Moscow and Back," in *Diplomatic History* 25:3 (Summer 2001): 405–23. Interestingly, such vastly different books on the Holocaust and the concentration camp system as Daniel Jonah Goldhagen, *Hitler's Willing Executioners: Ordinary Germans and the Holocaust* (New York, 1996); Dieter Pohl, *Nationalsozialistische Judenvernichtung in Ostgalizien, 1941–1944. Organisation und Durchführung eines staatlichen Massenverbrechens* (Munich, 1996); and Ulrich Herbert, Karin Orth, and Christoph Dieckmann (eds.), *Die nationalsozialistischen Konzentrationslager: Entwicklung und Struktur*, 2 vols. (Göttingen, 1998), have little to say on the context of total war in which genocide and mass incarceration were taking place. Conversely, Michael Burleigh, *The Third Reich: A New History* (New York, 2000), successfully integrates the two events.

12 Vahakn N. Dadrian, *The History of the Armenian Genocide: Ethnic Con-

flict from the Balkans to Anatolia to the Caucasus, 3d rev. ed. (Providence, R.I., 1997); Ben Kiernan (ed.), *Genocide and Democracy in Cambodia: The Khmer Rouge, the United Nations and the International Community* (New Haven, Conn., 1993); Philip Gourevitch, *We Wish to Inform You That Tomorrow We Will Be Killed with Our Families: Stories from Rwanda* (New York, 1998); David Rieff, *Slaughterhouse: Bosnia and the Failure of the West* (New York, 1996).

13 On March 30, 1941, Hitler gave a two-and-a-half hour speech to some 250 senior Wehrmacht officers, the content of which was summarized by Chief of the General Staff Colonel-General Franz Halder. He noted that this would be "a struggle between two ideologies. . . . We must move away from the viewpoint of soldierly comradeship. The Communist was never and will never be a comrade in arms. This is a battle of extermination." Christian Streit, *Keine Kameraden: Die Wehrmacht und die sowjetischen Kriegsgefangenen, 1941–1945*, 2d ed. (Bonn, 1991), p. 34.

14 On ethnic cleansing and "population policies," see Norman M. Naimark, *Fires of Hatred: Ethnic Cleansing in Twentieth-Century Europe* (Cambridge, Mass., 2001); Amir Weiner (ed.), *Modernity, Revolution, and Population Management in the Twentieth Century* (Stanford, Calif., forthcoming). On state criminality and utopian schemes, see Yves Ternon, *L'État criminel: Les Génocides au XXᵉ siècle* (Paris, 1995); James C. Scott, *Seeing Like a State: How Certain Schemes to Improve the Human Condition Have Failed* (New Haven, Conn., 1998). For a theory on the cultural and psychological preconditions of genocide, see Ervin Staub, *The Roots of Evil: The Origins of Genocide and Other Group Violence* (Cambridge, 1989). On genocide and modernity, see Zygmunt Bauman, *Modernity and the Holocaust* (Ithaca, N.Y., 1991); Mihran Dabag and Kristin Platt (eds.), *Genozid und Moderne*, vol. I: *Strukturen kollektiver Gewalt im 20. Jahrhundert* (Opladen, 1998). On collective violence and political religion, see Hans Maier (ed.), *Wege in die Gewalt: Die modernen politischen Religionen* (Frankfurt am Main, 2000). On colonial violence, see Sven Lindqvist, *"Exterminate All the Brutes,"* trans. Joan Tate (New York, 1996).

15 On perceptions of German soldiers in the immediate aftermath of World War II in West Germany, see Moeller, *War Stories*; Frank Biess, "Survivors of Totalitarianism: Returning POWs and the Reconstruction of Masculine Citizenship in West Germany, 1945–1955," in Hanna Schissler (ed.), *The Miracle Years: A Cultural History of West Germany, 1949–1968* (Princeton, N.J., 2001), pp. 57–82.

16 This criticism was made recently by Aleksa Djilas at a panel discussion with Misha Glenny about the former Yugoslavia, held at Brown University on March 14, 2001.

17 Geoffrey H. Hartman (ed.), *Bitburg in Moral and Political Perspective*

(Bloomington, Ind., 1986). For a chronology of the Enola Gay controversy see *www.afa.org/enolagay/home.html*.

18 See Marianne Hirsch's chapter, in this volume. See also her book *Family Frames: Photography, Narrative and Postmemory* (Cambridge, Mass., 1997).

19 One sensational example is Binjamin Wilkomirski's 1995 text *Fragments: Memories of a Wartime Childhood* (New York, 1996). See Stefan Maechler, *The Wilkomirski Affair: A Study in Biographical Truth* (New York, 2000); Philip Gourevitch, "The Memory Thief," in *The New Yorker* (June 14, 1999); 48–68; Elena Lappin, "The Man with Two Heads," in *Granta* 66 (Summer 1999): 9–65. An earlier case concerned Jerzy Kosinski's *The Painted Bird* (New York, 1965). See, for example, J. P. Sloan, "Kosinski's War," in *The New Yorker* (October 10, 1994): 46–53.

20 Jeffrey Herf, *Divided Memory: The Nazi Past in the Two Germanys* (Cambridge, Mass., 1997); Norbert Frei, *Vergangenheitspolitik: Die Anfänge der Bundesrepublik und die NS-Vergangenheit* (Munich, 1996).

21 Moeller, *War Stories*.

22 Stéphane Courtois, Nicolas Werth, Jean-Louis Panné, Andrzej Paczkowski, Karel Bartošek, Jean-Louis Margolin, *The Black Book of Communism: Crimes, Terror, Repression*, trans. Jonathan Murphy and Mark Kramer (Cambridge, Mass., 1999). See also François Furet, *The Passing of an Illusion: The Idea of Communism in the Twentieth Century*, trans. Deborah Furet (Chicago, 1999); Abbott Gleason, *Totalitarianism: The Inner History of the Cold War* (New York, 1995). A recent history of Nazi Germany that makes a case for similarity with the Soviet system is Michael Burleigh's *The Third Reich: A New History* (New York, 2000). For a comparison of personalities see Alan Bullock, *Hitler and Stalin: Parallel Lives* (New York, 1992) and of systems, Ian Kershaw and Moshe Lewin (eds.), *Stalinism and Nazism: Dictatorships in Comparison* (Cambridge, 1997). Different opinions on the usefulness of the concept of totalitarianism can be found in Krzytof Pomian, "Totalitarisme," in *Vingtième Siècle* 47 (July–September 1995): 4–23; Klaus-Dietmar Henke, "Die Verführungskraft des Totalitären," in Hannah Arendt Institut für Totalitarismusforschung, *Berichte und Studien* 12 (Dresden, 1997); Ian Kershaw, "Nazisme et stalinisme: Limites d'une comparaison," *Le Débat* 89 (March–April 1996): 177–89; Henry Rousso (ed.), *Stalinisme et nazisme: Histoire et mémoire comparées* (Brussels, 1999).

23 Most recently, see the debate over Jan T. Gross, *Neighbors: The Destruction of the Jewish Community in Jedwabne, Poland* (Princeton, N.J., 2001). See, for example, Associated Press [AP], "Polish Face Truth of Jedwabne," in *The New York Times* [NYT] (March 12, 2001); Peter Finn, "Painful Truth in Poland's Mirror: Book on 1941 Massacre of Jews Shifts Blame from Nazis to Neighbors," in *The Washington Post* (March 14, 2001); AP, "Poles Accept Blame for 1941 Massacre of Jews," in *The Jerusalem Post*

(March 15, 2001); Adam Michnik, "Poles and the Jews: How Deep the Guilt?" in *NYT* (March 17, 2001) A15, A17; Steven Erlanger, "Soul-Searching at Another Polish Massacre Site," in *NYT* (April 19, 2001) A3. See the debate in the pages of the *Times Literary Supplement* [*TLS*] following the review by Abraham Brumberg, "Murder Most Foul: Polish Responsibility for the Massacre at Jedwabne," *TLS* (March 2, 2001): 8–9, in letters to the editor by Jan Nowak, Czeslaw Karkowski, Norman Davis, Werner Cohn, Tony Judt, and others, in *TLS* issues of March 16, 23, 30, and April 6, 2001.

24 Victor Klemperer, *I Will Bear Witness*, 2 vols. trans. Martin Chalmers (trans.) (New York, 1999); Daniel Jonah Goldhagen, *Hitler's Willing Executioners: Ordinary Germans and the Holocaust* (New York, 1996). On responses to German memory debates, see, most recently, Geoff Eley (ed.), *"The Goldhagen Effect": History, Memory, Nazism — Facing the German Past* (Ann Arbor, Mich., 2000) and Mary Nolan, "The Politics of Memory in the Berlin Republic," in *Radical History Review* (Fall 2001). See also Robert R. Shandley (ed.), *Unwilling Germans? The Goldhagen Debate* (Minneapolis, Minn., 1998); Norman G. Finkelstein and Ruth Bettina Birn, *A Nation on Trial: The Goldhagen Thesis and Historical Truth* (New York, 1998); Julius H. Schoeps (ed.), *Ein Volk von Mördern? Die Dokumentation zur Goldhagen-Kontroverse um die Rolle der Deutschen im Holocaust* (Hamburg, 1996). On the Berlin memorial see James E. Young, "Germany's Memorial Question: Memory, Counter-Memory, and the End of the Monument," in *The South Atlantic Quarterly* 96:4 (Fall 1997): 853–80; Caroline Wiedmer, *The Claims of Memory: Representations of the Holocaust in Contemporary Germany and France* (Ithaca, N.Y., 1999), pp. 140–64.

25 On memorial debates in Berlin, see Brian Ladd, *The Ghosts of Berlin: Confronting German History in the Urban Landscape* (Chicago, 1997), pp. 217–35.

26 Tzvetan Todorov, "In Search of Lost Crimes," in *The New Republic* 4, 489 (January 29, 2001).

27 Elazar Barkan, *The Guilt of Nations: Restitution and Negotiating Historical Injustices* (New York, 2000). On trials and tribunals, see also Mark Osiel, *Mass Atrocity, Collective Memory, and the Law* (New Brunswick, N.J., 1997).

28 See Priscilla Hayner, "Fifteen Truth Commissions — 1974–1994: A Comparative Study," in *Human Rights Quarterly* 16: 597–655.

29 Barbie Zelizer, *Remembering to Forget: Holocaust Memory through the Camera's Eye* (Chicago, 1998).

30 See Marilyn Young's chapter in this volume and the recent publicity about New School University President and former Senator Bob Kerrey's role in a 1969 massacre in Thanh Phong in Vietnam. See especially Gregory L.

Vistica, "What Happened in Thanh Phong?" in *The New York Times Magazine* (April 29, 2001): 50–57, 66–68, 133. See also Daniel Jonah Goldhagen and Samantha Power, "Kerrey Should Be Investigated," in *The Boston Globe* (May 3, 2001).

31 Moeller, *War Stories*. For a good example, see Andreas Hillgruber, *Zweierlei Untergang: Die Zerschlagung des Deutschen Reiches und das Ende des europäischen Judentums* (Berlin, 1986). See also Omer Bartov, "Historians on the Eastern Front: Andreas Hillgruber and Germany's Tragedy," in Bartov, *Murder in Our Midst: The Holocaust, Industrial Killing, and Representation* (New York, 1996), pp. 71–88.

32 On the globalization of Holocaust memory, see Andreas Huyssen, "Present Pasts: Media, Politics, Amnesia," in *Public Culture* 12 (1): 21–38.

33 Todorov, "In Search of Lost Crimes," p. 30. See further in Omer Bartov, *Mirrors of Destruction: War, Genocide, and Modern Identity* (New York, 2000).

34 James Knowlton and Truett Cates (ed.), *Forever in the Shadow of Hitler? Original Documents of the Historikerstreit, the Controversy Concerning the Singularity of the Holocaust* (Atlantic Highlands, N.J., 1993); Charles S. Maier, *The Unmasterable Past: History, Holocaust, and German Nationalism* (Cambridge, Mass., 1988); Richard Evans, *In Hitler's Shadow: West German Historians and the Attempt to Escape from the Nazi Past* (New York, 1989); Peter Baldwin (ed.), *Reworking the Past: Hitler, the Holocaust, and the Historians' Debate* (Boston, 1990).

35 Amir Weiner, *Making Sense of War: The Second World War and the Fate of the Bolshevik Revolution* (Princeton, N.J., 2000) and his "Nature, Nurture, and Memory in a Socialist Utopia: Delineating the Soviet Socio-Ethnic Body in the Age of Socialism," in *American Historical Review* 104 (October 1999): 1114–55.

36 See, for example, Lindqvist, *"Exterminate All the Brutes"*; Tilman Dedering, " 'A Certain Rigorous Treatment of All Parts of the Nation': The Annihilation of the Hero in German South West Africa, 1904," in Mark Levene and Penny Roberts (eds.), *The Massacre in History* (New York, 1999), pp. 205–22; Helmut Walser Smith, "The Talk of Genocide, the Rhetoric of Miscegenation: Notes on Debates in the German Reichstag Concerning Southwest Africa, 1904–14," in Sara Friedrichsmeyer, Sara Lennox, and Susanne Zantop (eds.), *The Imperialist Imagination: German Colonialism and Its Legacy* (Ann Arbor, Mich., 1998), pp. 107–23; Frantz Fanon, *The Wretched of the Earth*, trans. Constance Farrington (New York, 1963).

37 Misha Glenny, *The Fall of Yugoslavia: The Third Balkan War*, 3d rev. ed. (New York, 1996); David Rieff, *Slaughterhouse: Bosnia and the Failure of the West* (New York, 1996); Michael A. Sells, *The Bridge Betrayed: Religion and Genocide in Bosnia* (Berkeley, Calif., 1998); Michael Ignatief, *Virtual War: Kosovo and Beyond* (New York, 2000).

38 Eric A. Johnson, *Nazi Terror: The Gestapo, Jews, and Ordinary Germans*
    (New York, 1999). For a somewhat different view that stresses the complic-
    ity of the German population in Gestapo activities by means of widespread
    denunciations, see Robert Gellately, *The Gestapo and German Society:
    Enforcing Racial Policy, 1933–1945* (Oxford, 1990).

39 See also Walter Manoschek, *"Serbien ist judenfrei": Militärische Be-
    satzungspolitik und Judenvernichtung in Serbien 1941/42* (Munich, 1995);
    Guenter Lewy, *The Nazi Persecution of the Gypsies* (New York, 2000).

40 See Dieter Pohl's highly critical review of Bogdan Musial's book *Konter-
    revolutionäre Elemente sind zu erschiessen: Die Brutalisierung des deutsch-
    sowjetischen Krieges im Sommer 1941* (Berlin/Munich, 2000) on
    H-SOZ-U-KULT@H-NET.MSU.EDU, April 27; 2001.

41 See Moeller, *War Stories*; Robert G. Moeller (ed.), *West Germany under
    Construction: Politics, Society, and Culture in the Adenauer Era* (Ann
    Arbor, Mich., 1997), especially essays there by Atina Grossmann and
    Frank Stern. See also articles in Schissler, *Miracle Years*, especially
    Part I.

42 Deák et al., *The Politics of Retribution.*

43 Vasily Grossman, *Life and Fate*, trans. Robert Chandler (New York, 1985).

War and War Crimes: A Brief History

1 John Keegan, *The First World War* (New York, 1998), p. 8.

2 House of Commons Debate (June 21, 1938).

On War Crimes

1 Das deutsche Volk . . . hat sich fast widerstandslos, ja zum Teil mit Begeis-
   terung gleichschalten lassen. Darin liegt seine Schuld. Im Übrigen hat
   man aber auch gewusst . . . dass die Gestapo, unsere ss und zum Teil auch
   unsere Truppen in Polen und Russland mit beispiellosen Grausamkeiten
   gegen die Zivilbevölkerung vorgingen. . . . Man kann also wirklich nicht
   behaupten, dass die Öffentlichkeit nicht gewusst habe, dass die nationalsozialistische Regierung und die Heeresleitung ständig aus Grundsatz
   gegen das Naturrecht, gegen die Haager Konvention und gegen die ein-
   fachsten Gebote der Menschlichkeit verstiessen. (Konrad Adenauer:
   Briefe 1945–1947, bearb. v. Hans Peter Mensiny. Berlin 1983, S.172).

2 "Obwohl der Gerichtshof der Meinung ist, daß die im Artikel 9 enthaltene
   Bezeichnung 'Gruppe' mehr enthalten muß, als eine Anhäufung, von Of-
   fizieren, ist ihm doch viel Beweisstoff über die Teilnahme dieser Offiziere
   an der Planung und Führung des Angriffskrieges und an der Begehung von
   Kriegsverbrechen und Verbrechen gegen die Menschlichkeit vorgelegt
   worden. Dieses Beweisergebnis ist gegen viele von ihnen klar und über-

zeugend. Sie sind in großem Maße verantwortlich gewesen für die Leiden und Nöte, die über Millionen Männer, Frauen und Kinder gekommen sind. Sie sind ein Schandfleck für das ehrenhafte Waffenhandwerk geworden. Ohne ihre militärische Führung wären die Angriffsgelüste Hitlers und seiner Nazi-Kumpane akademisch und ohne Folgen geblieben. Wenn diese Offiziere auch nicht eine Gruppe nach dem Wortlaut des Statuts bildeten, so waren sie doch sicher eine rücksichtslose militärische Kaste (. . .) Viele dieser Männer haben mit dem Soldateneid des Gehorsams gegenüber militärischen Befehlen ihren Spott getrieben. Wenn es ihrer Verteidigung zweckdienlich ist, so sagen sie, sie hatten zu gehorchen; hält man ihnen Hitlers brutale Verbrechen vor, deren allgemeine Kenntnis ihnen nachgewiesen wurde, so sagen sie, sie hätten den Gehorsam verweigert. Die Wahrheit ist, daß sie an all diesen Verbrechen rege teilgenommen haben oder in schweigender Zustimmung verharrten, wenn vor ihren Augen größer angelegte und empörendere Verbrechen begangen wurden, als die Welt je zu sehen das Unglück hatte (. . .) Wo es der Sachverhalt rechtfertigt, sollen diese Leute vor Gericht gestellt werden, damit jene unter ihnen, die dieser Verbrechen schuldig sind, ihrer Bestrafung nicht entgehen" (Der Nürnberger Prozeß: Urteil, S. 277. Digitale Bibliothek Band 20: Der Nürnberger Prozeß, S. 914–16 [vgl. NP Bd. 1, S. 313–14]). (Source: The Avalon Project at the Yale Law School: Judgement of the International Military Tribunal for the Trial of German Major War Criminals: The Accused Organizations: General Staff and High Command http://www.yale.edu/lawweb/avalon/imt/proc/judorg.htm#staff.)

The Wehrmacht, German Society, and the Knowledge of Mass Extermination

1 About the operation of Sonderkommando 4a and of its subunits, see, among others, Helmut Krausnick, *Hitlers Einsatzgruppen: Die Truppe des Weltanschauungskrieges 1938–1942* (Frankfurt am Main, 1993), p. 163.

2 See mainly Helmuth Groscurth, *Tagebücher eines Abwehroffiziers 1938–1940*, Helmut Krausnick and Harold C. Deutsch (eds.) (Stuttgart, 1970), pp. 534 ff. The main documents relating to these events are available in English translation in Ernst Klee, Willi Dressen, and Volker Riess (eds.), *"The Good Old Days": The Holocaust as Seen by Its Perpetrators and Bystanders*, (New York, 1991), pp. 137 ff.; Michael Burleigh, *The Third Reich: A New History*, (New York, 2000), pp. 617–19.

3 Klee et al., *"The Good Old Days,"* p. 138.

4 *Ibid.*

5 *Ibid.*

6 *Ibid.*, p. 149.

7 Bernd Boll and Hans Safrian, "Auf dem Weg nach Stalingrad: Die 6.

Armee 1941/42," in Hannes Heer and Klaus Naumann (eds.), *Vernichtungskrieg. Verbrechen der Wehrmacht 1941 bis 1944*, (Hamburg, 1995), p. 277.

8 Klee et al., *"The Good Old Days,"* p. 141.

9 Herr and Naumann, *Vernichtungskrieg*, p. 271.

10 Christian Gerlach, "Deutsche Wirtschaftsinteressen, Besatzungspolitik und der Mord an den Juden in Weissrussland 1941–1943," in Ulrich Herbert (ed.), *Nationalsozialistische Vernichtungspolitik, 1939–1945* (Frankfurt, 1998), pp. 281–82.

11 The English translation is quoted in Omer Bartov, *Hitler's Army: Soldiers, Nazis and War in the Third Reich* (New York, 1991), p. 130.

12 *Ibid.*

13 *Ibid.*, pp. 130–31.

14 Klee et al., *"The Good Old Days,"* p. 32.

15 Walter Manoschek (ed.), *"Es gibt nur eines für das Judentum: Vernichtung." Das Judenbild in deutschen Soldatenbriefen 1939–1944* (Hamburg, 1995).

16 On this topic see Saul Friedländer, *Nazi Germany and the Jews* (New York, 1997).

17 Alexander B. Rossino, "Destructive Impulses: German Soldiers and the Conquest of Poland," in *Holocaust and Genocide Studies*, vol. 7, no 3 (Winter 1997).

18 Georg Meyer (ed.), *Generalfeldmarschall Wilhelm Ritter von Leeb: Tagebuchaufzeichnungen und Lagebeurteilungen aus zwei Weltkriegen* (Stuttgart, 1976), p. 288, quoted in Jürgen Förster, "The Wehrmacht and the War of Extermination Against the Soviet Union," *Yad Vashem Studies*, vol. 14 (1981), pp. 7 ff.

19 Jonathan Steinberg, *All or Nothing: The Axis and the Holocaust, 1941–1943* (London, 1990), p. 98.

20 Klee et al., *"The Good Old Days,"* p. 141.

21 Christian Gerlach, "Männer des 20. Juli und der Krieg gegen die Sowjetunion," in *Vernichtungskrieg*, p. 434.

22 For more about Groscurth's personality, see the detailed introduction to the *Tagebuch*. For Groscurth's reference to Heydrich, see *Tagebuch*, p. 130.

23 Klee et al., *"The Good Old Days,"* p. 150.

24 *Ibid.*, p. 149.

25 *Ibid.*, pp. 150–51.

26 Martin Broszat, "A Social and Historical Typology of the German Opposition to Hitler" in D. C. Large, *Contending with Hitler: Varieties of Resistance in the Third Reich* (New York, 1991), p. 30.

27 For the reports of Swiss diplomatic representatives, see Daniel Bourgeois, *Business Helvètique et Troisième Reich* (Lausanne, 1998), pp. 197 ff.

28   Walter Laqueur, *The Terrible Secret* (London, 1980), p. 26.

29   "Einstellung der Bevölkerung zur Evakuierung der Juden," SD Aussenstelle Minden, 6.12.1941, M18/11 Bestand: Preussische Regierung Minden/SD Abschnitt Bielefeld, Nordrhein Westfälisches Staatsarchiv Detmold.

30   Ludwig Volk (ed.), *Akten deutscher Bischöfe über die Lage der Kirche 1933–1945*, vol. 5 (Mainz, 1983), p. 675n.

31   *Ibid.*

32   Yaakov Lozowick, "Documentation: 'Judenspediteur,' Deportation Trains," in *Holocaust and Genocide Studies*, vol. 6, no. 3 (1991), pp. 286 ff.

33   Mihail Sebastian, *Journal 1935–1944* (Chicago, 2000), p. 397.

34   Victor Klemperer, *I Will Bear Witness* (New York, 2000).

35   Elisabeth Freund, "Waiting," in Mark Anderson, *Hitler's Exiles* (New York, 1998) p. 123.

36   Michael Phayer, *The Catholic Church and the Holocaust, 1930–1965* (Bloomington, 2000) pp. 73 ff.

37   Otto Ogermann, *Bis zum letzten Atemzug*, (Leutesdorf, 1985), quoted in Hilberg, *Perpetrators, Victims, Bystanders* (New York, 1992), p. 268.

38   Christian Gerlach, "Männer," p. 434.

39   David Bankier, *The Germans and the Final Solution* (London, 1992), p. 156.

40   Hans Mommsen, "The Realization of the Unthinkable" in his *From Weimar to Auschwitz* (Princeton, 1991), p. 252.

41   SD Aussenstelle Minden, 6.12.1941.

42   Inge Scholl, *The White Rose: Munich 1942–1943* (Middletown, 1983), p. 78.

43   Sybille Steinbacher, *"Musterstadt" Auschwitz. Germanisierungspolitik und Judenmord in Ostoberschlesien* (Munich, 2000).

44   Frank Bajohr, *"Arisierung" in Hamburg. Die Verdrängung der Jüdischen Unternehmer* (Hamburg, 1997).

45   Klee et al., *"The Good Old Days,"* p. 154.

The Wehrmacht in Serbia Revisited

1   For previous studies, see Christopher R. Browning, "Wehrmacht Reprisal Policy and the Mass Murder of the Jews in Serbia," *Militärgeschichtliche Mitteilungen*, 1/83, pp. 31–47, and "Harald Turner und die Militärverwaltung in Serbien," *Verwaltung contra Menschenführung im Staat Hitlers*, ed. Dieter Rebentisch and Karl Teppe (Göttingen, 1986), pp. 351–73, and "Germans and Serbs: The Emergence of Nazi Antipartisan Policies in 1941," *A Mosaic of Victims: Non-Jews Persecuted and Murdered by the Nazis*, ed. Michael Berenbaum (New York, 1990), pp. 64–73; and Walter

Manoschek, *"Serbien ist judenfrei": Militärische Besatzungspolitik und Judenvernichtung in Serbien 1941–42* (Munich, 1993).

2 Immanuel Geiss, *July 1914* (New York, 1969), p. 183.

3 American Military Tribunal, case 7 [hereafter cited as AMT 7], transcript, pp. 3427–28 [List testimony].

4 Bundesarchiv-Militärarchiv Freiburg [hereafter cited as BA-MA], RW 40/7, Turner situation report, October 6, 1941. The army archivist Wisshaupt made a similar formulation. See Paul Hehn, *The German Struggle Against Yugoslav Guerrillas in World War II. German Counter-Insurgency in Yugoslavia 1941–1943* (New York, 1979), p. 28.

5 Jevrejski Isotrijski Muzej Belgrade, 21-1-1/20, "Verordnung betreffend die Juden und Zigeuner," May 30, 1941, issued by the Militärbefehlshaber in Serbien.

6 BA-MA, RW 40/4, entry of July 5, 1941; and Attachment 33, report of July 23, 1941 (NOKW-1091); RW 40/5, Attachment 1, Commanding General in Serbia, Ia, to Military Commander Southeast, Ic, August 2, 1941 (NOKW-1128).

7 BA-MA, RH 26-104/8, Attachment 156, Verfügung über Vorbeugungs- und Sühnemassnahmen, Militärbefhlshaber in Serbien, Verwaltungs- stab, July 1941.

8 BA-MA, RW 40/4, Attachment 61, Ehrmann report, August 1, 1941; Politisches Archiv des Auswärtigen Amtes [hereafter PA-AA], Staatssekretär Jugoslawien, vol. 3, Benzler to Foreign Office, August 1, 1941.

9 BA-MA, RW 40/4, entries of July 22, 24, and 29, 1941; Attachment 33, Gravenhorst to 65th Corps, July 21, 1941; Attachment 35, Kiessel to List, July 23, 1941; and Attachment 48, List to Danckelmann, July 29, 1941. PA-AA, Staatssekretär Jugoslawien, vol. 3, Benzler to Foreign Office, July 23, 1941

10 BA-MA, RW 40/5, entry of August 9, 1941; RH 25-104/9, Attachment 180, Stobbe to 704th Division, August 7, 1941; RH 26-114/3, August summary; 40411/7, Bader to List, August 28, 1941.

11 BA-MA, 40411/7, Bader to List, July 28, 1941.

12 Hehn, *The German Struggle*, pp. 28–29. PA-AA, Staatssekretär Jugoslaw- ien, vol. 3, Benzler to Foreign Office, July 23 and August 1, 1941; Inland IIg 401, Benzler to Foreign Office, August 8, 1941. BA-MA, RW 40/5, At- tachment 59, Ic, Picht's report for July; 14 749/18, reports of Wehrmacht liaison officer, July 31 and August 1, 1941 (NOWK-1114); 40411/6, Bader report, August 23, 1941.

13 BA-MA: 14 729/4, Attachment 17, Turner to Böhme, September 21, 1941 (NOKW-892); Attachment 20, Böhme order of September 9, 1941 (NOKW-183); Attachment 22, Böhme order of September 23, 1941 (NOKW-194); Attachment 17, Pemsel to Turner and 342nd Division,

September 27, 1941 (NOKW-193); Attachment 31, Böhme order and message to the troops, September 25, 1941 (NOKW-1048).

14 For the records of the 342nd Division, see BA-MA, 15 365.

15 BA-MA: 15 365.8, ten-day report of October 20, 1941.

16 BA-MA: 17729/2, entries of October 2 and 3, 1941; RH 26-114/2, October summary. AMT 7, transcript, 8433-4 (testimony of Topola survivor Johann Koerbler). Manoshek, "*Serbien ist Judenfrei,*" pp. 79–83.

17 BA-MA, 17 729/9, Attachment 48, Keitel order, September 16, 1941 (NOKW-258).

18 BA-MA, 17 729/8, Attachment 24, Faulmüller draft order to Turner and 342nd Division, October 4, 1941 (NOKW-192). NOKW-5810, Turner to Hildebrant, October 17, 1941.

19 BA-MA, 17 729/8, Attachment 49, Böhme order, October 10, 1941 (NOKW-891 and 557).

20 BA-MA: RH 26-117/3, entries of October 15–17 1941; RH 26-104/16, Attachment 486c, König report, October 27, 1941 (NOKW-904); RW 40/12, Bischofhausen report, October 20, 1941 (NOKW-387).

21 BA-MA, 15 365.9, Hinghofer to Böhme, November 14, 1941.

22 BA-MA, 17 729.9, Attachments 80 and 81, Faulmüller to Infantry Regiment 749, October 21, 1941, and Pemsel to 65th Corps, October 22, 1941; 17 729.2, entry of October 22, 1941.

23 BA-MA, 17 729.8, Attachment 28, List to Böhme, October 4, 1941 (NOKW-203).

24 BA-MA, 17 729.9, Böhme order, October 25, 1941. NOKW-802, Turner to FK and KK, October 22, 1941.

25 BA-MA, RW 40/23, Memo of December 20, 1941 (NOKW-474).

26 BA-MA, RW 40/14, Attachment 26, Supplement No. 3 to ten-day report of December 20, 1941, and Attachment 29, Bader to Verwaltungsstab, 22.12.41.

The Wehrmacht Exhibition Controversy: The Politics of Evidence

1 For a sampling of the debate in the media see Heribert Seifert, "Gefährliches Spiel mit der Bildermacht," *Neue Zürcher Zeitung,* November 12, 1999; Fritz Göttler, "Bilder einer Einstellung," *Süddeutsche Zeitung* [SZ], November 9, 1999; Götz Aly, "Machtbeflissene Verharmlosung," *Berliner Zeitung* [BZ], November 8, 1999; " 'Geschrei ist unangebracht.' Wolfgang Benz zum Streit über die Wehrmachtsausstellung," SZ, November 8, 1999; Krisztián Ungváry, "Reemtsmas Legenden," *Frankfurter Allgemeine Zeitung* [FAZ], November 5, 1999; Omer Bartov, "Eine Frage der Ehre," *Die Woche* November 5, 1999; Bernhard R. Kroener, "Die Deformation des Menschen im Krieg," *Die Welt,* November 4, 1999; Volker Ullrich, "Von Bildern und Legenden," *Die Zeit* October 28, 1999;

Jost Nolte, "Wahre Bilder, falsche Bilder—welche Bilder?" *Die Welt*, October 27, 1999; "Fotos der Wehrmachtsausstellung falsch zugeordnet," *FAZ*, October 20, 1999.

2 Omer Bartov, Cornelia Brink, Gerhard Hirschfeld, Friedrich P. Kahlenberg, Manfred Messerschmidt, Reinhard Rürup, Christian Streit, Hans-Ulrich Thamer, *Bericht der Kommission zur Überprüfung der Ausstellung "Vernichtungskrieg. Verbrechen der Wehrmacht 1941 bis 1944"* (November 2000), pp. 79, 85. Report made available by the Institute for Social Research, Hamburg, Germany.

3 Bogdan Musial, "Bilder einer Ausstellung. Kritische Anmerkungen zur Wanderausstellung 'Vernichtungskrieg. Verbrechen der Wehrmacht 1941 bis 1944,'" in *Vierteljahrshefte für Zeitgeschichte* 47 (1999): 563–91; Krisztián Ungváry, "Echte Bilder—problematische Aussagen. Eine quantitative und qualitative Analyse des Bildmaterials der Ausstellung 'Vernichtungskrieg. Verbrechen der Wehrmacht 1941 bis 1944,'" in *Geschichte in Wissenschaft und Unterricht* 10 (1999): 584–95; Dieter Schmidt-Neuhaus, "Die Tarnopol-Stellwand der Wanderausstellung 'Vernichtungskrieg. Verbrechen der Wehrmacht 1941 bis 1944.' Eine Falluntersuchung zur Verwendung von Bildquellen," in *Geschichte in Wissenschaft und Unterricht* 10 (1999): 596–603.

4 Markus Krischer and Robert Vernier, " 'Es geht nicht um die Wahrheit.' Horst Möller, Leiter des Münchner Instituts für Zeitgeschichte, über die Fehler und den wissenschaftlichen Gehalt der Wehrmachtsausstellung," *Focus*, October 25, 1999; Michael Stürmer, "Tod, Trauer und Tabu," *Die Welt*, October 28, 1999; Jörg Friedrich, "Die 6. Armee im Kessel der Denunziation," *BZ*, October 30, 1999; Philipp Blom, "Hungry for Evidence of Wickedness," *Financial Times*, November 13/14, 1999; Jörg Friedrich, "Der Hamburger Bilderschau zur Wehrmacht ging es nicht um historische Aufklärung," *Die Welt*, November 11, 1999; Gerhard Spörl and Klaus Wiegrefe " 'Gegen Kritik immun.' Der Potsdamer Historiker Rolf-Dieter Müller über die Wehrmacht im Zweiten Weltkrieg und die Thesen des Hamburger Instituts für Sozialforschung," *Der Spiegel*, No. 23, November 11, 1999.

5 Bartov et al., *Bericht der Kommission*, p. 79.

6 "Goldes Wert," *Der Spiegel*, No. 16, April 13, 1981, pp. 74–80, cited in Omer Bartov, "The Barbarisation of Warfare: German Officers and Men on the Eastern Front, 1941–1945," in *Jahrbuch des Instituts für Deutsche Geschichte*, XIII (1984): 305–39 (citation on p. 305).

7 Andreas Hillgruber, "Erschreckende Beteiligung des Heeres an den Verbrechen," *FAZ*, April 29, 1981, p. 10, cited in Bartov, "The Barbarisation of Warfare," pp. 305–306.

8 Andreas Hillgruber, *Zweierlei Untergang: Die Zerschlagung des Deutschen Reiches und das Ende des europäischen Judentums* (Berlin, 1986); Ernst

Nolte, "The Past That Will Not Pass: A Speech That Could Be Written but Not Delivered," in *Forever in the Shadow of Hitler? Original Documents of the Historikerstreit, the Controversy Concerning the Singularity of the Holocaust*, trans. James Knowlton and Truett Cates (Atlantic Highland, NJ, 1993), pp. 18–23, originally published in the *FAZ*, June 6, 1986. See also Omer Bartov, "Historians on the Eastern Front: Andreas Hillgruber and Germany's Tragedy," in Bartov, *Murder in Our Midst: The Holocaust, Industrial Killing, and Representation* (New York, 1996), pp. 71–88.

9   For a brief survey of the literature, see Omer Bartov, "German Soldiers and the Holocaust: Historiography, Research, and Implications," *History & Memory* 9/1–2 (Fall 1997): 162–88; a shorter version of this essay is Bartov, "Introduction," in Hamburg Institute for Social Research (ed.), *The German Army and Genocide: Crimes Against War Prisoners, Jews, and Other Civilians, 1939–1944* (New York, 1999), pp. 10–17.

10 Spörl et al., " 'Gegen Kritik immun.' " In this interview with the historian Rolf-Dieter Müller by the weekly magazine *Der Spiegel* Müller estimated that only 5 percent of German soldiers fighting in Italy were involved in war crimes and that, consequently, the percentage on the Eastern Front was even lower. The interviewer asked whether that meant that there could be no general indictment (*Generalverdacht*) of Wehrmacht soldiers. Müller's reply is instructive: "No, especially not against those who are still alive today. The majority were in their early twenties as they came out of the war. The organizers of the exhibition obviously expect them to declare themselves now as a guilty generation. This is unfair and also arrogant, considering that this generation built the Federal Republic." One could have put it differently, of course. It is a troubling thought that the generation that built the Federal Republic was deeply implicated in a murderous and criminal war, and has never faced up to its guilt.

11 Compare, for instance, Omer Bartov, *The Eastern Front, 1941–45: German Troops and the Barbarisation of Warfare* (London, 1985); Stephen G. Fritz, *Frontsoldaten: The German Soldier in World War II* (Lexington, Ky, 1995); Wolfram Wette (ed.), *Deserteure der Wehrmacht: Feiglinge—Opfer —Hoffnungsträger? Dokumentation eines Meinungswandels* (Essen, 1995); Norbert Haase and Gerhard Paul (eds.), *Die anderen Soldaten: Wehrkraftzersetzung, Gehorsamsverweigerung und Fahnenflucht im Zweiten Weltkrieg* (Frankfurt am Main, 1995).

12 For a longer discussion, see Bartov, "Historians on the Eastern Front."

13 This argument was subsequently developed in Bogdan Musial, *"Konterrevolutionäre Elemente sind zu erschiessen." Die Brutalisierung des deutsch-sowjetischen Krieges im Sommer 1941* (Berlin, 2000).

14 Norbert Frei, *FAZ*, November 2, 1999, Feuilleton Kommentar; Christian Gerlach, "In der Steppe versickert. Es geht nicht bloss um Fotos, es geht um die Wehrmacht," *Frankfurter Rundschau* [FR], November 30, 1999;

Johannes Klotz, "Kurzer Atem. Resignierten die Macher zu schnell? —
Eine Kritik der Kritiker der Wehrmachtsausstellung," *FR*, November 26,
1999 (this article cites the unpublished paper by the prominent Wehrmacht historian Christian Streit "Die Kontroverse um die sogenannte
Wehrmachtsausstellung," [unpublished ms.], November 1999).

15 Thomas Urban, "Wehrmachtsausstellung: Der Historiker, der den
Fehlern auf den Grund ging," *SZ*, November 11, 1999; and Krisztián
Ungváry, "Verbrechen und Haftung," *SZ*, November 16, 1999.

16 Pieter Lagrou, "Utopia, Violence, Resistance: The Legacy of Nazi Occupation in Western Europe" (unpublished paper, 1999). See also Lagrou,
*The Legacy of Nazi Occupation: Patriotic Memory and National Recovery
in Western Europe, 1945–1965* (Cambridge, UK, 2000); and Jay M. Winter, *The Great War and the British People* (Cambridge, MA, 1986),
pp. 66–76.

17 See the essays in Ulrich Herbert (ed.), *National Socialist Extermination
Policies: Contemporary German Perspectives and Controversies* (New York,
2000).

18 For the best two histories of this region under German occupation, see
Dieter Pohl, *Nationalsozialistische Judenverfolgung in Ostgalizien
1941–1944. Organisation und Durchführung eines staatlichen Massenverbrechens* (Munich, 1996); Thomas Sandkühler, *"Endlösung" in Galizien.
Der Judenmord in Ostpolen und die Rettungsinitiativen von Berthold Beitz,
1941–1944* (Bonn, 1996).

19 See, most recently, Amir Weiner, "Nature, Nurture, and Memory in a Socialist Utopia: Delineating the Soviet Socio-Ethnic Body in the Age of Socialism," *American Historical Review* 104 (October 1999): 1114–55.

20 See note 2, above, and Musial, *Konterrevolutionäre Elemente*. For some reactions in the German media to Musial's book, see Klaus Wiegrefe, "Aus
dem Hinterland," *Der Spiegel*, No. 32, August 7, 2000, p. 41; Peter Lon-
gerich, "Inspirierte Gewalt," *FR*, August 11, 2000; Johannes Hürter, "Ver-
scharrt und aufgestapelt," *FAZ*, August 16, 2000; Berthold Seewald,
"Können Opfer auch Täter sein?" *Die Welt*, August 18, 2000; Bogdan Musial, "Stalins willige Helfer," interview by Adelbert Reif, *Rheinischer
Merkur*, August 25, 2000; Daniel Brössler, "Der Enthüller stellt sich
bloss," *SZ*, August 26, 2000; Wolfgang Wippermann, "Ein Nolte aus
Polen," *Jüdische Allgemeine Wochenzeitung*, August 31, 2000; Wolfram
Wette, "Opfer zu Tätern gemacht," *Die Zeit*, August 31, 2000. Curiously,
having made his reputation by criticizing the Wehrmacht exhibition for
mislabeling photographs, the photographs in Musial's own book bear only
scant indication of their source in the last page of the book without any reference to their problematic labeling.

21 Martin Dean, *Collaboration in the Holocaust: Crimes of the Local Police in
Belorussia and Ukraine, 1941–44* (New York, 2000); Bernhard Chiari, *All-*

tag hinter der Front. Besatzung, Kollaboration und Widerstand in Weiss-russland 1941–1944 (Dusseldorf, 1998).

22 On the terrible destruction of the population of Belorussia, see Christian Gerlach, *Kalkulierte Morde. Die deutsche Wirtschafts- und Vernichtungs-politik in Weissrussland 1941 bis 1944* (Hamburg, 1999).

23 See, for example, Dean, *Collaboration in the Holocaust,* pp. 1–16.

24 Omer Bartov, *Hitler's Army: Soldiers, Nazis, and War in the Third Reich* (New York, 1991), pp. 106–78.

25 Musial, "Bilder einer Ausstellung," pp. 565–67. Hamburg Institute for Social Research (ed.), *Vernichtungskrieg. Verbrechen der Wehrmacht 1941 bis 1944,* 4th rev. ed. (Hamburg, May 1999), p. 208. Musial's article, however, refers to the third edition of the catalogue, issued in April 1997.

26 Irene and Carl Horowitz, *Of Human Agony* (New York, 1992), p. 82.

27 Musial, "Bilder einer Ausstellung," pp. 567–78; Hamburg Institute, *Vernichtungskrieg,* pp. 204–5.

28 *Ibid.,* p. 577.

29 Bernd Boll, "Das Grab in der Zitadelle: Der Judenmord in Złoczów vom Juli 1941 und die Rolle der deutschen Wehrmacht. Eine historische Analyse," *FR,* August 14, 1999.

30 Streit, "Die Kontroverse," citing documents from the Bundesarchiv-Militärarchiv in Freiburg, Germany. See also Klaus Wiegrefe, "Leichen im Obstgarten," *Der Spiegel,* No. 4, 1999, pp. 52–53.

31 Musial, "Bilder einer Ausstellung," p. 568. In this context, see also Michael C. Steinlauf, *Bondage to the Dead: Poland and the Memory of the Holocaust* (Syracuse, N.Y., 1997).

32 Ilona Karmel, *An Estate of Memory* (Boston, 1969); Ilona Karmel, *Stephania* (Boston, 1953). The following story was told separately to me and some other friends in summer/fall 2000. Karmel passed away on the last day of November 2000, shortly after she told me this story.

33 Musial, "Bilder einer Ausstellung," pp. 578–79.

34 Hamburg Institute, *Vernichtungskrieg,* p. 69.

35 Ungváry, "Echte Bilder," p. 587; Schmidt-Neuhaus, "Die Tarnopol-Stellwand"; Bartov et al., *Bericht der Kommission,* pp. 44–45.

36 Ungváry, "Echte Bilder," p. 587, 590, 593.

37 Bartov et al., *Bericht der Kommission,* p. 79.

38 For the exceptions, see note 14, above. For the orders, see Christian Streit, *Keine Kameraden: Die Wehrmacht und die sowjetischen Kriegsgefangenen, 1941–1945,* 2d ed. (Bonn, 1991), pp. 28–61.

39 Ulrich von Hassell, *Die Hassell-Tagebücher 1938–1944. Aufzeichnungen vom Andern Deutschland,* ed. Friedrich Freiherr Hiller von Gärtringen (Berlin, 1988), p. 248. I wish to thank Christian Streit for this citation.

40 Bartov et al., *Bericht der Kommission,* p. 53.

41 Cited in Bartov, *Hitler's Army,* pp. 129–30.

42 For examples, see *ibid.*, pp. 129–32; Streit, *Keine Kameraden*, pp. 115–19.

43 Krischer et al., " 'Es geht nicht um die Wahrheit.' " (n. 4, above).

44 For a recent study on the "antipartisan campaign" see Truman Anderson, "Incident at Baranivka: German Reprisals and the Soviet Partisan Movement in Ukraine, October–December 1941," *Journal of Modern History* 71, no. 3 (September 1999): 601–602. One example cited by Truman is the case of the 62nd Infantry Division. Operating under the command of the Sixth Army in the Poltava region of the Ukraine in the fall of 1941, this formation was directly involved in the killing of hundreds of Jews, the majority of whom were women, old men, and especially children, as "reprisals" for minor partisan activities and because of the "need" to do so.

45 Ahlrich Meyer, *Der Blick des Besatzers: Propagandaphotographie der Wehrmacht aus Marseille 1942–1944* (Bremen, 1999); Daniel Uziel, " ' . . . Demands from German Propaganda: Increased Struggle Against Jewry . . . ' The Wehrmacht's Propaganda Units and the Jews," *Yad Vashem Studies* 29 (2001). I would like to thank Friedrich P. Kahlenberg for drawing my attention to the Koblenz collection.

46 For some interesting work on this see Barbie Zelizer, *Remembering to Forget: Holocaust Memory Through the Camera's Eye* (Chicago, 1998); Dagmar Barnouw, *Germany 1945: Views of War and Violence* (Bloomington, Ind., 1996); Cornelia Brink, *Ikonen der Vernichtung. Öffentlicher Gebrauch von Fotografien aus nationalsozialistischen Konzentrationslagern nach 1945* (Berlin, 1998).

47 See, for example, Jaroslaw M. Rymkiewicz, *The Final Station: Umschlagplatz*, trans. Nina Taylor (New York, 1994); Henri Raczymow, *Writing the Book of Esther*, trans. Dori Katz (New York, 1995).

Złoczów, July 1941:

The Wehrmacht and the Beginning of the Holocaust in Galicia

1 Press release of the Hamburg Institute for Social Research, November 4, 1999; Michael Z. Wise: "The German Army and Genocide: Bitterness Stalks an Exhibition," *The New York Times*, November 6, 1999.

 2 Bogdan Musial, "Bilder einer Ausstellung. Kritische Anmerkungen zur Wehrmachtsausstelllung," in *Vierteljahreshefte für Zeitgeschichte*, vol. 4 (1999); pp. 563–91; Dieter Schmidt-Neuhaus, "Die Tarnopol Stellwand der Wanderausstellung, 'Vernichtungskrieg: Verbrechen der Wehrmacht', 1941 bis 1944; Eine Falluntersuchung zur Verwendung von Bildquellen, in *Geschichte in Wissenschaft und Unterricht*, vol. 10, (1999) pp. 596–603); Krisztián Ungváry, Echte Bilder — Problematische Aussagen. Eine quantitative und qualitative Foto analyse der ausstellung Vernichtungskrieg. Vebrechen der Wehrmacht 1941 bis 1944,"in *Geschichte in Wissenschaft und Unterricht*, Vol. 10 (1999): pp. 584–95.

3 Katyn was the site of a mass execution of some 15,000 Polish military officers murdered by the Soviets in 1940 after the Red Army occupied eastern
   Poland in accordance with the Ribbentrop-Molotov pact. Discovered by
   the Germans in April 1943, and initially blamed by the Soviets on the Germans, it is now clear that this atrocity was committed by the NKVD. "Die
   Spitze eines Eisbergs; Der polnische Historiker Bogdan Musial, hält
   die Wehrmachtsausstellung in ihrer heutigen Form für unseriös," in *Die
   Welt*, October 24, 1999; Bogdan Musial, "Die Gerechten und die Selbst-
   gerechten," *Süddeutsche Zeitung*, November 25, 1999; "Es geht nicht um
   die Wahrheit"; Horst Möller, director of Munich's Institute for Contemporary History, about errors and scientific contents of the Wehrmacht Exhibit, *Focus*, No. 43 (1999), pp. 44–46.

4 Meinrad von Ow, "Wehrmachtsausstellung mit falschen Bildern?"
   Rheinischer Merkur, September 19, 1997; "Leichen im Obstgarten," *Der
   Spiegel* 4 (1999), pp. 51–53.

5 Barbara Just-Dahlmann, *Simon* (Stuttgart, 1980), pp. 9–11; Eliezer
   Boneh, "Introduction," in I. M. Lask (ed.), *The City of Złoczów* (New York,
   1967), Part 1 of B. Kora (ed.), *Sefer Kehilat Złoczów* (Tel Aviv, 1967), col.
   11–13.

6 Just-Dahlmann, *Simon*, p. 11, 59f; Boneh, "Introduction," col. 12.

7 Samuel Lipa Tennenbaum, *Złoczów Memoir* (New York, 1986), p. 99;
   Frank Golczewski, "Die Ukraine im Zweiten Weltkrieg" in *Geschichte
   Der Ukraine* (Göttingen, 1993), p. 243.

8 Golczewski, "Ukraine," p. 244ff.

9 Tennenbaum, *Złoczów Memoir*, pp. 114, 153f.

10 *Ibid.*, pp. 161ff.

11 Bogdan Musial, "*Konterrevolutionäre Elemente sind zu erschieben*," *Die
   Brutalisierung des deutsch-sowjetischen Krieges im Sommer 1941* (Berlin
   and Munich 2000), pp. 98–101.

12 Wladislaw A. Serczyk, "Die sowjetische und die 'polnische' Ukraine zwischen den Weltkriegen" in Golczewski, *Geschichte Der Ukraine*, pp. 99–
   109; Golczewski, "Die Ukraine," p. 243.

13 For the following, see John A. Armstrong, *Ukrainian Nationalism*, 2d ed.
   (New York and London, 1963), pp. 37–45

14 Ryszard Torzecki, "Die Rolle der Zusammenarbeit mit der deutschen
   Besatzungsmacht in der Ukraine für deren Okkupationspolitik," in *Okku-
   pation und Kollaboration (1938–1945)* (Berlin and Heidelberg, 1994),
   p. 246f.

15 Armstrong, *Nationalism*, pp. 55–62; Torzecki, Zusammenarbeit, p. 247.

16 Torzecki, "Zusammenarbeit," p. 124.

17 Armstrong, *Nationalism*, pp. 75–83.

18 Document USSR-231: IMT Vol. 7, p. 303; cf. Dieter Pohl, *Nationalsozialistische Judenverfolgung in Ostgalizien 1941–1944. Organisation*

und Durchführung eines staatlichen Massenverbrechens, 2nd ed. (Munich, 1997), p. 57.

19 Pohl, *Judenverfolgung*, p. 57.

20 Report by Group GFP 711, July 7, 1941; BA/MA RH 26-454/48.

21 Cited in Pohl, *Judenverfolgung*, p. 57.

22 Cited in *ibid.*, p. 62.

23 Cited in *ibid.*, p. 58.

24 The head of the *Sicherheitspolizei* and SD: Activity Report USSR (hereafter quoted as EM) no. 24, July 16, 1941; BA R 58/214.

25 Shlomo Wolkowicz, *Das Grab bei Złoczów; Geschichte meines Überlebens, Galizieu 1939–45* (Berlin, 1996), p. 40; Tennenbaum, *Złoczów Memoir*, p. 164ff.

26 EM no. 14, July 6, 1941; BA R 58/214.

27 Just-Dahlmann, *Simon*, pp. 64–65.

28 Tennenbaum, *Złoczów Memoir*, pp. 167ff.

29 *Ibid.*, p. 169.

30 Musial, *Konterrevolutionäre Elemente*, p. 162.

31 This is the number of victims according to Pohl, *Judenverfolgung*, p. 62; EM no. 24 of July 16, 1941, mentions 700 prisoners murdered by the NKVD; BAK R 58/214, p. 193 f. Musial's estimate of 2,000 to 3,000 murdered prisoners is based on statements by the Polish historian Krysztof Popilński (Musial, *Konterrevolutionäre Elemente*, p. 138).

32 Tennenbaum, *Złoczów Memoir*, p. 174. The town commander's orders regarding special measures against Jews are not recorded in the German military files. According to Altman they were not issued until July 15. He recalls that children under twelve did not have to wear the Jewish star. However, Altman's reminiscences are generally less accurate than those of other contemporary witnesses (S. Altman, "Haunting Memories," in Lask, *The City of Złoczów*, col. 44).

33 Wolkowicz, *Das Grab bei Złoczów*, p. 43.

34 Just-Dahlmann, *Simon*, p. 68.

35 Wolcowicz, *Das Grab bei Złoczów*, pp. 35–40.

36 *Ibid.*, pp. 44ff.

37 Testimony of Katarzyna D., January 8, 1991, at the OKL (District commission investigating crimes against the Polish people in Łodz. The document is signed OKL, p. 5/91/NK); cited in Musial, *Konterrevolutionäre Elemente*, p. 163.

38 Musial, *Konterrevolutionäre Elemente*, p. 163.

39 Wolkowicz, *Das Grab bei Złoczów*, p. 45.

40 *Ibid.*, p. 47.

41 295.ID/1c, Report on Activities, July 3, 1941, BA/MA RH 26-295/16.

42 IV.Ak Morning Report, July 5, 1941, BA/MA RH 20-17/277.

43 Philipp-Christian Wachs, *Der Fall Theodor Oberländer (1905–1998)*.

Ein Lehrstück deutscher Geschichte (Frankfurt and New York, 2000), p. 291.

44 295. ID/KTB Ia, July 3, 1941. BA/MA RH 26–295/3.

45 Otto Korfes, typewritten manuscript with handwritten corrections, [April 1960]. Testimony before the highest court [in the GDR during the trial in absentia against Theodor Oberländer] in BA Pots, 90K10, estate of Otto Korfes, no. 99 pp. 25–29. Cited in Sigrid Wegner-Korfes, *Weimar, Stalingrad, Berlin; Das Leben des deutschen Generals Otto Korfes* (Berlin, 1994), pp. 90f.

46 Wolkowicz, *Das Grab bei Złoczów*, pp. 49–60.

47 Morning report by the IV Ak July 5, 1941, BA/MA RH 20–17/277.

48 Wegner-Korfes, *Weimar*, p. 91.

49 *Ibid.*, p. 91.

50 Testimony by Otto Korfes in *Der Oberländer Prozess*, p. 107f. Most of the material from the in absentia trial of Theodor Oberländer, Minister for Refugees, concerning war crimes in the Soviet Union, in Berlin/GDR, 1960), was politically biased and should be handled with care. However, there is no reason to doubt Korfes since he exonerates Oberländer. His testimony gave so little support to the prosecution that he was censored by the court. Cf. Wachs, *Der Fall Theodor Oberländer*, p. 291.

51 Testimony of Dietfried Müller-Hegemann in *Der Oberländer Prozeb*, p. 109.

52 *Ibid.*

53 A report by the Jewish Self-Help mentions a population loss of 2,000 Jews by April 1, 1942 — the result of pogroms and the murder of members of the intelligentsia by the Security Police, as quoted in Pohl, *Judenverfolgung*, note 130, p. 63. Just-Dahlmann (*Simon*, p. 68) puts the number of victims at 2,400; Altman (*Haunting Memories*, col. 42/43) at 2,500. Tennenbaum (*Złoczów Memoir*, p. 178) gives a higher figure, "at least three thousand people," which does not include those Jewish victims who fled the occupied teritory but had not been registered. Wolkowicz (*Das Grab bei Złoczow*, p. 42), speaks of "more than 3,000 Jews." Musial (*Konterrevolutionäre Elemente*, p. 185 and p. 324, note 33) contests those figures and concedes merely a few hundred "with certainty," since the numbers quoted by the Jewish Self-Help include the victims of the NKVD, several hundred Jews who had fled with the Red Army, Jews who had been drafted after June 22, 1941, and 300 members of the intelligentsia shot by the military police on July 10, 1941. Musial, however, tends to quantify vague assumptions to suit his purpose; besides, he simply ignores the unregistered refugees. Therefore we must presume that the figures for pogrom victims lie closer to a few thousand than several hundred, especially as Musial tends to round up recorded figures when it comes to the victims of the NKVD, but downwards in the case of murdered Jews.

54 Pohl, *Judenverfolgung*, p. 67.

55 EM no. 24, July 16, 1941; BA R 58/214, p. 194.

56 IV.A.K. Morning Report 1a, July 5, 1941: BAMA RH 20–17/277; Testimony of Korfes and Müller-Hegeman, in *Der Oberländer Prozess*, p. 108.

57 Telex from Heydrich to the *Einsatzgruppen* commanders (*Einsatzbefehl* no. 1), June 29, 1941. Cited in Peter Klein (ed.), *Die Einsatzgruppen in der besetzten Sowjetunion 1941/42; Die Tätigkeits- und Lageberichte des Chefs der Sicherheitspolizeí und des SD* (Berlin, 1987), p. 318f.

58 EM no. 10, July 2, 1941; BA R 58/214.

59 *Einsatzbefehl* no. 1 cited in Klein, *Einsatzgruppen*, pp. 320ff.

60 EM no. 14, June 6, 1941; BA R58/214.

61 Ralf Ogorrek, *Die Einsatzgruppen und die "Genesis der Endlösung"* (Berlin, 1996), pp. 136–41.

62 EM no. 24, July 16, 1941.

63 AOK 17/ChefGenSt. by telephone to IV.AK/1a July 3, 1941 10:50 A.M., BAMA RH 20–17/46; IV AK/KTB Ia, July 3, 1941 10:55 A.M; BAMA RH 24–4/38, p. 136.

64 KTB IV.AK, July 2, 1941; BAMA RH 24–4/38.

65 Testimony by Korfes, in *Der Oberländer Prozeb*, pp. 108, 189.

66 Testimony by Korfes, ibid., p. 189.

67 Killings by the SD are not recorded until July 8, 1941. *Einsatz-Kommando* 6, having replaced *Sonderkommando* 4b, reports the execution of "16 communist functionaries and informers, including 3 Jewesses." EM no. 19, July 11, 1941; BAK R 58/214. p. 127.

68 Christian Streit, "Angehörige des Militärischen Widerstand und der Genozid an den Juden in Südabschnitt der Ostfront," in Gerd R. Ueberschär (ed.), *NS-Verbrechen und der militärische Widerstand gegen Hitler* (Darmstadt, 2000), p. 97.

69 Otto Korfes confirms this in Wegner-Korfes, *Weimar*, p. 91.

70 Compare Friedrich-Christian Stahl, "General Karl-Heinrich von Stülpnagel," in Gerd R. Ueberschär (ed.), *Hitlers Militärische Elite*, vol. 1, pp. 240–47.

71 Helmut Krausnick, *Hitler's Einsatzgruppen. Die Truppen des Weltanschauungskrieges 1938–1942* (Frankfurt, 1989), pp. 191ff.

72 AOK 17/1c/AO, Activity Report July 7, 1941; BAM RH 20–17/768.

73 IV.AK/1a, Telex to AOK 17, July 2, 1941, 9:45 am; BAMA RH 24 4/39, encl. 103; IV.AK/KTB 1a, July 2, 1941, 9:45 am; BAMA RH 24–4/38.

74 Jürgen Förster, "Die Sicherung des Lebensraums," in Horst Boog, Jürgen Förster, Joachim Hoffmann, Ernst Kling, Rolf-Dieter Müller, and Gerd R. Ueberschär, eds., *Der Angriff auf die Sowjetunion*, (Frankfurt/M., 1991), p. 1237.

75 Raul Hilberg, Die Vernichtung der europäischen Juden, (Frankfurt/M. 1994), vol. 2, p. 316

76 Streit, "Angehörige," p. 95. But Musial erroneously describes the mass murders at Złoczów as a spontaneously pogrom. He completely ignores the part played by the OUN, the SD, the SS "Viking," and the Wehrmacht and their collaboration in order to buttress this undocumented interpretation (Musial, *Konterrevolutionäre Elemente*, pp. 180, 277).

77 Pohl, *Judenverfolgung*, pp. 67ff.

78 Cited in *ibid.*, p. 60.

79 Wartime memoir of Infantry General Karl von Roques about the early days of the eastern campaign, 1941 (Part I: BA/MA NS 152/10, p. 9f). I am obliged to Peter Steinkamp, Freiburg, for drawing my attention to this document.

80 But members of the Red Army who were captured after August 8, having lost contact with their units, were to be shot as irregulars. Berück Süd/Ic.no.1125/41, confidential; July 29, 1941, BAMA RH 22/5.

81 Commander of the Army, Group Rear Area South AZ III no. 3/41 conf. Sept.1, 1941; NOKW-2594, cited in Christian Streit, *"Keine Kameraden." Die Wehrmacht und die sowjetischen Kriegsgefangenen 1941–1945* (Bonn, 1991), pp. 122ff.

82 Among the observers standing close to the civilians who are chasing and hitting Jews with clubs, numerous Wehrmacht soldiers can be seen taking in the spectacle. The dead were thrown on top of each other; in one scene of the film, the same mountain of corpses is shown as the one seen in two of the exhibit's photos. The scenes were used in Jochen Trautmann and Tina Mendelschn, Der Skandal und die Wehrmachtsfotos. Auf den Spuven einer umstrittenen Ausstellung (Südwestdeutscher Rundfunk, 2000; first broadcast on SWR 3, June 19, 2000).

83 Guido Knopp, *"Der verdammte Krieg. Das 'Unternehmen Barbarossa,'"* 2d ed (Munich, 1991), p. 130.

84 295. ID/1c to the officer in charge of censorship at Deputy Corps Headquarters. XI.AK, Hanover, July 8, 1941; BA/MA RH 26–295/22.

85 Press release "Die zwei Seiten des Vormarschs" signed, Wittke, Gefr.: BA/MA RH 26–295/22.

86 Willy Kahlert, war correspondent, PK 666, "Die Schandtaten von Z . . .": BA/MA RH 26–295/22.

87 295. ID/1c to the censorship officer at Deputy Corps Headquarters XI.AK, Hanover, July 8, 1941; BA/MA rh 26–295/22.

88 Cf. "Wacht im Osten," July 8, 9, and 12, 1941; BAMA RHD 69/26.

89 Altman, *Haunting Memories*, col. 42.

90 Regarding the propagandistic exploitation of the NKVD massacres by the German propaganda machine, see also Blanka Pietros-Ennker, "Die Sowjetunion in der Propaganda des Dritten Reiches: Das Beispiel der Wochenschau," in *Militärgeschichtliche Mitteilungen* 2 (1989): pp. 79–120.

91 Ralf Georg Reuth (ed.), *Joseph Goebbels: Tagebücher* (Munich, 1992), vol 4, p. 1622 (July 6, 1941).

92 Heinz Boberach (ed.), *Meldungen aus dem Reich 1938–1945. Die geheimen Lageberichte des Sicherheitsdienstes der SS*, vol. 7 (Herrsching, 1984), pp. 2535–36 (July 7, 1941).

93 *Ibid.*, p. 2596 (July 31, 1941).

94 Excerpts from Instructions for the Press, V.I. no. 170/41 of July 5, 1941 (confid.); BA Kob, Sammlung Oberheitsmann, Zsg.109/23.

95 BA, RMVP, R 55/1308; pp. 290–303; reprinted in Wolfgang Diewerge (ed.), *Feldpostbriefe aus dem Osten. Deutsche Soldaten sehen die Sowjetunion* (Berlin, 1941), pp. 41–42.

96 Reuth, *Goebbels: Tagebücher*, vol. 4, p. 1626 (July 9, 1941).

97 Hamburg Institute for Social Research (ed), *German Army and Genocide: Crimes Against War Prisoners, Jews and Other Civilians, 1939–1944* (New York, 1999). p. 195. ill. 28–34.

98 Heinz Bergschicker, *Deutsche Chronik 1933–1945. Alltag im Faschismus* (Berlin, 1983).

99 Ernst Klee, Willi Dressen, and Volker Riess, *"Schöne Zeiten" Der Judenmord aus der Sicht der Täter und Gaffer*, 5th ed. (Frankfurt, 1988).

100 Musial, *Bilder*, pp. 568ff.

101 Musial (*Bilder*, p. 578) implies that the exhibit organizers recognized certain murdered Jews in the photos reprinted in Wegner-Korfes, pp. 96ff. In actual fact, it was this, as yet unpublished, picture from which we made the identification. This implication is another attempt at bolstering the thesis that the Złoczów photos all show victims of the NKVD.

102 Musial, *Bilder*, p. 575.

103 Musial, *Konterrevolutionäre Elemente*, unnumbered plate (no. 16) following p. 176. The caption indicates that only the rows of corpses in the foreground are important: "Exhumierte Opfer im Innenhof der Zitadelle von Złoczów." Musial ignores the activities of the people in the background and does not put them in context with the exhibition photos or the written documents. The fact that this picture was twice published in Poland as "Exhumation of NKVD victims, Summer 1941," as Musial reports in *Bilder*, p. 575, does not prove that the attribution is correct.

104 Musial asserts that the photos 29 and 31 also show victims of the NKVD. To be sure, he cannot explain why the corpses are piled on top of each other. If they are Jews, he implies, they must have been buried first and subsequently dug up and piled on top of each other (*Bilder*, pp. 564f.). That would indeed be an absurd explanation. But Musial himself makes an equally improbable assumption in order to explain why not all NKVD victims had been laid out in rows. He bases his theory on a "comparison photograph" in a Polish archive: "The comparison photo must have been taken later than photos 29 and 31, for in the latter pictures the exhumed

corpses are laid out in rows in the inner courtyard" (*Bilder*, p. 576). If you follow the logic of this explanation, then the corpses of NKVD victims were first piled on top of each other and later laid out in rows. This is highly improbable when you consider that—according to eyewitnesses— the corpses were in a state of advanced decay. Musial (*Konterrevolutionäre Elemente*, p. 212) quotes from an autobiographical novel (Bruno Brehm, *Aus der Reitschul* (Graz, 1951), p. 290) in which victims of the NKVD, laid out for identification, are described from the viewpoint of a German soldier: "Thousands of flies buzzed above the eight or ten long rows of corpses that were laid out here. Between them, women crept along, bent over, looking for their husbands and sons among the dead [my translation]." But Musial deliberately refrains from quoting a short passage on the next page of the same book, which would have contradicted his argument. The next day, when the protagonist wants to show the corpses to his general, they have been cleared away. In their place, they observe the following scene: "A big stack was piled up in a corner of the courtyard. A chain of women kept taking things from that pile and passing them along. It was dusk. One had to move closer to see. The women were Jewish. What they kept passing from hand to hand were corpses. The dead, piled on top of each other—those were the Jews of Złoczów." (Brehm, pp. 290 and 291, my translation). Although both of these citations have been taken from a novel, the author should be taken quite seriously as an eyewitness: Bruno Brehm, already a well-known author at that time, was an officer with the Fourtieth Army Corps. On July 5, 1941, he arrived at the Ninth Tank Division, which was then quartered in Tarnopol. There he discussed the "publication of descriptions of combat with the Intelligence Section." 9th Armored Div. Intelligence, Activity Report, July 5, 1941: BAMA RH 27-9/81, p. 3.

105 Ungváry, *Echte Bilder*, p. 590.

106 Schmidt-Neuhaus, *Tarnopol-Stellwand*, p. 602.

107 Musial, *Bilder*, p. 590.

108 *Ibid.*

109 The same desire for a "normalized" history motivated Martin Walser's speech in the fall of 1998 in Frankfurt's Paulskirche—which led to the controversy with Ignaz Bubis.

110 Rolf-Dieter Müller, "Die Wehrmacht—Historische Last und Verantwortung. Die Historiograpie im Spannungsfeld von Wissenschaft und Vergangenheitsbewältigung," in Rolf-Dieter Müller and Hans-Erich Volkmann (eds.), *Die Wehrmacht. Mythos und Realität*, commissioned by the Office for Research of Military History (Munich, 1999), p. 22.

111 Müller, "Wehrmacht," p. 30.

112 Musial, "*Konterrevolutionäre Elemente*," p. 20.

113 Musial, "Täter und Tabu," in *Frankfurter Rundschau*, October 6, 2000.

114 Reviewer dl in: *Soldat und Technik* 8 (1999).

115 Klaus W. Wippermann, in *Informationen für die Truppe* (September/ October, 1999).

116 Meinrad von Ow, "Seit sechs Monaten läuft Überarbeitung," in *Kölnische Rundschau*, May 12, 2000.

117 Meinrad von Ow, "Zur Ausstellung 'Vernichtungskrieg. Verbrechen der Wehrmacht 1941–1944. Können 8 Gutachter ihr Glaubwürdigkeit verleihen?" *konservativ.de/wma/ow.doku1.htm* and *konservativ.de/wma/ow. doku2.htm*.

118 Thomas Medicus, deputy editor in chief for cultural affairs at the *Frankfurter Rundschau*, hails the dismissal of Hannes Heer from the Institute as the dawn of a new era for dealing with National Socialism: "Złoczów could become a symbolic place for a new approach to history by the Hamburg Institute for Social Research, for a new interpretation that will throw the old Federal Republic's cult of remembrance and self-accusation overboard and clears the way for a debate about neototalitarianism that has emancipated itself from the usual kind of self-exoneration" (Thomas Medicus, "Schatten. Hannes Heer muss gehen," in *Frankfurter Rundschau*, August 15, 2000).

Nazi Photographs in Post-Holocaust Art:
Gender as an Idiom of Memorialization

1 Primo Levi, "The Chemical Examination," *Survival in Auschwitz: The Nazi Assault on Humanity*, trans. Stuart Woolf (New York, 1960), pp. 105, 106.

2 Sybil Milton, "Photography as Evidence of the Holocaust," *History of Photography* 23, no. 4 (Winter 1999): 303–12.

3 In a related article, I briefly discuss this image as one of a number of images of children that have frequently been seen and reproduced in works of Holocaust memory: "Projected Memory: Holocaust Photographs in Personal and Public Fantasy," in Mieke Bal, Jonathan Crewe, and Leo Spitzer, eds., *Acts of Memory: Cultural Recall in the Present* (Hanover, N.H., 1999).

4 Lawrence Langer, *Preempting the Holocaust* (New Haven, Conn., 1998).

5 Stewart Justman, ed. *The Jewish Holocaust for Beginners* (London, 1995); Götz Aly, *'Final Solution': Nazi Population Policy and the Murder of the European Jews* (London, 1999); *Lest We Forget: A History of the Holocaust* (Oak Harbor, WA, 1998).

6 Jaroslaw M. Rymkiewicz, *The Final Station: Umschlagplatz*, trans. Nina Taylor (New York, 1994).

7 Jürgen Stroop, *The Stroop Report: The Jewish Quarter of Warsaw Is No More!*, trans. Sybil Milton (New York, 1979).

8 In the latter two cases, I have chosen not to reproduce the actual images themselves, but the contemporary works that incorporate them. Even though I will argue that these works to some degree retain and perpetuate the power of the Nazi gaze, I would feel that I am myself contributing to the problem I identify in this essay were I to expose these archival images to further viewing.

9 For a similar approach to the images of atrocity taken by the liberating armies, see Barbie Zelizer, "Gender and Atrocity: Women in Holocaust Photographs," in Barbie Zelizer, ed., *Visual Culture and the Holocaust* (New Brunswick, N.J., 2001). Zelizer argues that in liberator images, there is either a surplus or an absence of gender in the representations of women, indicating the inability of visual discourses to accommodate a nuanced or differentiated representation of gender.

10 See Judith Stacey, "Is Academic Feminism an Oxymoron?" *Signs: Journal of Women in Culture and Society* 25, no. 4 (Summer 2000): 1189–94.

11 See my discussion of the co-implication of these two kinds of Holocaust photographs in Marianne Hirsch, *Family Frames: Photography, Narrative and Postmemory* (Cambridge, Mass., 1997), pp. 20, 21. See also Cornelia Brink's response to and elaboration of my argument, "How to Bridge the Gap: Überlegungen zu einer fotographischen Sprache des Gedenkens," in Insa Eschebach, Sigrid Jacobeit, and Susanne Lanwerd, eds., *Die Sprache des Gedenkens: Zur Geschichte der Gedenkstätte Ravensbrück* (Berlin, 1999).

12 Marianne Hirsch, "Surviving Images: Holocaust Photographs and the Work of Postmemory," in Zelizer, *Visual Culture and the Holocaust*, and in *Yale Journal of Criticism* 14 (Spring, 2001), 5–37

13 See in particular Christian Metz's contention that a monocular and thus inherently violent perspective rules the field of vision in "Photography and Fetish," in Carol Squiers, ed. *The Critical Image: Essays on Contemporary Photography* (Seattle, 1990). Theorists have profoundly contested Metz's notion as they have identified a visual field in which power is shared in more complicated ways. But here, disturbingly, this equation between camera and weapon reemerges with new force. See Hirsch, "Surviving Images."

14 For other useful analyses of Nazi photographic practices, see Sybil Milton; Judith Levin, and Daniel Uziel, "Ordinary Men, Extraordinary Photos," *Yad Vashem Studies* 26 (1998); Bernd Hüppauf, "Emptying the Gaze: Framing Violence through the Viewfinder," *New German Critique* 72 (Fall 1997): 3–44; Alexander B. Rossino, "Eastern Europe through German Eyes: Soldiers' Photographs 1939–42," *History of Photography* 23, no. 4 (Winter 1999), 313–21; Daniel Jonah Goldhagen, *Hitler's Willing Executioners: Ordinary Germans and the Holocaust* (New York, 1996), pp. 245–47, 405–6. While there is considerable disagreement among these

writers about how Nazi photographic acts are to be interpreted, they all attest to the importance of a careful contextual analysis.

15 Susan Sontag, *On Photography* (New York, 1989), p. 15.

16 See Roland Barthes's moving discussion of this photographic temporality in *Camera Lucida: Reflections on Photography,* trans. Richard Howard (New York, 1981), esp. pp. 76, 77, 80, 81.

17 For the distinction between gaze, look, and screen see Jacques Lacan, *Four Fundamental Concepts of Psychoanalysis,* trans. Alan Sheridan (New York, 1978), and Kaja Silverman, *Threshold of the Visible World* (New York, 1996).

18 See Lawrence Langer's discussion of Samuel Bak in *Preempting the Holocaust.*

19 Aleksandar Tisma, "Mein Photo des Jahrhunderts" *Die Zeit* (October 14, 1999).

20 Geoffrey Hartman, *The Longest Shadow: In the Aftermath of the Holocaust* (Bloomington, Ind., 1996), p. 131.

21 Froma Zeitlin, "The Vicarious Witness: Belated Memory and Authorial Presence in Recent Holocaust Literature," *History & Memory* 10, no. 2 (Fall 1998): 5–42.

22 See my discussion of this more triangulated exchange in "Projected Memory," and further reflections of identification and postmemory in "Marked by Memory: Feminist Reflections on Trauma and Transmission," in Nancy K. Miller and Jason Tougaw, eds., *Extremities: Trauma, Testimony and Community* (Urbana, Ill., 2002).

23 Judy Chicago, *Holocaust Project: From Darkness into Light* (New York, 1993).

24 I am grateful to Sidra Ezrahi for calling this play to my attention. See her discussion of this moment in "Revisioning the Past: The Changing Legacy of the Holocaust in Hebrew Literature," *Salmagundi* no. 68–69 (Fall 1985–Winter 1986): 245–70.

25 David Levinthal, *Mein Kampf* (Santa Fe, 1996).

26 James Young, *At Memory's Edge: After-Images of the Holocaust in Contemporary Art and Architecture* (New Haven, Conn., 2000), p. 44.

27 Young, *At Memory's Edge*, p.51.

28 Young, *At Memory's Edge*, p.55.

29 See Yitzhak Arad, Shmuel Krakowski, Shmuel Spector, eds., *The Einsatzgruppen Reports: Selections from the Dispatches of the Nazi Death Squad's Campaign Against the Jews, July 1941–January 1943* (New York, 1989); Chirstopher Browning, *Ordinary Men: Reserve Police Batallion 101 and the Final Solution in Poland* (New York, 1992); and Goldhagen, *Hitler's Willing Executioners.*

30 Ruth Klüger, *Von hoher und niedriger Literatur* (Bonn, 1996); Silke Wenk, "Pornografisierungen—Einrahmungen des Blicks auf die NS Vergangen-

heit" in *Geschlecht und Gedächtnis*, ed. Insa Eschebach, Silke Wenk (Frankfurt am Main, forthcoming).

31 For a discussion of these photographs, see Nechama Tec and Daniel Weiss, "The Heroine of Minsk: Eight Photographs of an Execution," *History of Photography* 23, no. 4 (Winter 1999): 322–30.

32 This installation was first shown at the 1993 Whitney Biennial. See John Bird, Jo Anna Isaak, and Sylvère Lotringer, *Nancy Spero* (London, 1996).

"During Total War, We Girls Want to Be Where We Can Really Accomplish Something": What Women Do in Wartime

1 Elizabeth D. Heineman, *What Difference Does a Husband Make? Women and Marital Status in Nazi and Postwar Germany* (Berkeley, 1999), p. 71.

2 Atina Grossmann provides an excellent overview in "Feminist Debates about Women and National Socialism," in *Gender & History* 3, no. 3 (1991), 350–58.

3 Claudia Koonz, *Mothers in the Fatherland: Women, the Family and Nazi Politics* (New York, 1988).

4 Gisela Bock, "Die Frauen und der Nationalsozialismus. Bemerkungen zu einem Buch von Claudia Koonz," in *Geschichte und Gesellschaft* 4 (1989), 563–79.

5 Gisela Bock, "Ordinary Women in Nazi Germany: Perpetrators, Victims, Followers, and Bystanders," in Dalia Ofer and Leonore J. Weitzman, eds., *Women in the Holocaust* (New Haven, Conn., 1998), 85–100.

6 I refer to children as being accepted as German if they were in possession of an *Ahnenpass*, which proved that they had no Jewish ancestors. Only these children were accepted for membership in the Hitler Youth. Without this proof of German "blood," children and young people were deprived of opportunities to develop and participate in public life; they became outcasts whose property was confiscated, and they were stigmatized, deported, and ultimately murdered. The *Ahnenpass* was the ticket needed to embark on any educational, professional, political, or military career. This fact is often denied by many former members of the Hitler Youth and the BDM, who thereby fail to acknowledge the privileges they enjoyed. Being a racially pure German was a criterion of normality, a prerequisite for those young people mobilized for Hitler's Germany. Since, however, this criterion was not a matter of personal merit, it was accepted all the more readily and seen as a kind of sign of nobility.

7 Melitta Maschmann, *Fazit. Mein Weg in die Hitler-Jugend* (Frankfurt 1979) and Eva Sternheim-Peters, *Die Zeit der grossen Täuschungen. Mädchenleben im Faschismus* (Bielefeld, 1992).

8 Sibylle Hübner-Funk, *Loyalität und Verblendung. Hitlers Garanten der Zukunft als Träger der zweiten deutschen Demokratie* (Potsdam, 1998), p. 272.

9 Renate Finckh, *Mit uns zieht die neue Zeit. Die Geschichte einer Jugend* (Baden-Baden, 1979), p. 3.

10 Gisela Miller-Kipp, " 'Wir wollen dass dieses Volk treu ist.' Weibliche Jugend im Dritten Reich: Der Bund Deutscher Mädel in der Hitler-Jugend," in *Frankfurter Rundschau*, March 12, 1998, ZB5.

11 Clifford Kirkpatrick, *Nazi Germany: Its Women and Family Life* (1938; reprint, New York, 1981), p. 98.

12 Heineman, *What Difference . . . ?* , p. 45.

13 Gudrun Schwarz and Gaby Zipfel, "Die halbierte Gesellschaft. Anmerkungen zu einem soziologischen Problem," in *Mittelweg*-36-7, no. 1 (1998): 78–88; and Franka Maubach, "Verdrängte Bilder. Frauen in der Wehrmacht. Rekonstruktion des Werdegangs von Nachrichten- und Stabshelferinnen und ihres Einsatzes in den besetzten sowjetischen Gebieten" (Master's Thesis, University of Freiburg, 2000).

14 Gudrun Schwarz, "Verdrängte Täterinnen. Frauen im Apparat der SS (1939–1945)," in Theresa Wobbe, ed., *Nach Osten. Verdeckte Spuren nationalsozialistischer Herrschaft* (Frankfurt, am Main, 1992), 197–227.

15 Gertrud Herr, "Inhaltsreiche Jahre," in *Kritik. Die Stimme des Volkes* 63 (1985), 59.

16 See Anna Spieckerman's "Als Flakhelferin im Einsatz 1944/45. Ein Bericht," in *Feministische Studien* 3, no. 2 (1984), 27–38.

17 See Elizabeth Harvey, " 'Soon We Forgot All Jews and Poles': German Women and the 'Ethnic Struggle' in Nazi-Occupied Poland" (paper presented at the Berkshire Conference on the History of Women, 1999); Elizabeth Harvey, "Die deutsche Frau im Osten," in *Archiv für Sozialgeschichte* 38 (1998), 191–214; Gerhard Rempel, *Hitler's Children. The Hitler Youth and the SS* (Chapel Hill: 1989); Dagmar Reese. "Bund Deutscher Mädel–Zur Geschichte der weiblichen deutschen Jugend im Dritten Reich," in Frauengruppe Faschismusforschung, ed., *Mutterkreuz und Arbeitsbuch. Zur Geschichte der Frauen in der Weimarer Republik und im Nationalsozialismus* (Frankfurt am Main, 1981), pp. 163–87.

18 Gudrun Schwarz, *Nationalsozialistische Lager*, rev. ed. (Frankfurt am Main, 1996), pp. 126ff.

19 See Hilde Munske, ed., *Mädel—eure Welt! Das Jahrbuch der Deutschen Mädel* (Munich, 1942). This yearbook is replete with reports and photos from operations in the East.

20 Bundesarchiv Berlin, NS 2/46, vol. 10, 185.

21 Maschmann, *Fazit*. (Frankfurt am Main, 1979), p. 127.

22 Harvey, " 'Soon we forgot . . . ' " p. 18. In her paper, Harvey provides much more information about such "normal" behavior.

23 Gerhard Rempel, *Hitler's Children*, pp. 152 ff.

24 Maschmann, *Fazit*, p. 117.

25 Internationaler Gerichtshof Nürnberg, ed., "Geheimbericht der Dienststelle des *Hauptbannführer* Nickel vom 19. Oktober 1944 an Rosenberg über die Rekrutierung von baltischen und russischen Jugendlichen als Helfer für die Deutsche Wehrmacht," in *Der Prozess gegen die Hauptkriegsverbrecher vor dem Internationalen Gerichtshof Nürnberg, Amtlicher Wortlaut in deutscher Sprache*, vol. XXVII, doc. no. 1137-PS (Nuremburg, 1947–1949), 12 ff. This report states that a total of 28,117 youths from the occupied eastern territories were to be "made available to" the Luftwaffe and the armaments industry "by way of the office under the leadership of the Hitler Youth. This group included 500 girls who were to man Luftwaffe search light stations and 2,000 girls for constructing field fortifications along the Baltic Sea, directed by BDM leaders."

26 Report of BDM *Hauptmädelführerin* G.K. from Frankfurt am Main, September/October 1943, cited in Bernhard Chiari, *Alltag hinter der Front. Kollaboration und Widerstand in Weissrussland 1941–1944* (Düsseldorf, 1998), p. 72.

27 US National Archives, roll A 3343-SF-A-0049-0068-0178; see also A-0023-2870-3004.

28 US National Archives, roll A 3343-SF-B0034-2386-2374.

29 Internationaler Gerichtshof Nürnberg, *Der Prozess gegen die Hauptkriegsverbrecher*, vol. XXXIX, doc. no. 397-USSR (Nürnberg, 1947–49), 501–2.

30 Ina Seidel, "Frauen im Dienste des Heeres," in *Die Heeresverwaltung* 8, no. 2 (1943), 31.

31 Ursula Gersdorff, *Frauen im Kriegsdienst 1914–1945* (Stuttgart, 1969), p. 74.

32 See Gudrun Schwarz, "Frauen in der SS: Sippenverband und Frauenkorps," in Kirsten Heinsohn, Barbara Vogel, and Ulrike Weckel, eds., *Zwischen Karriere und Verfolgung. Handlungsräume von Frauen im nationalsozialistischen Deutschland* (Frankfurt am Main, 1997), pp. 223–80.

33 See Kurt W. Böhme, "Zum Schicksal der weiblichen Kriegsgefangenen," in Erich Maschke, ed., *Die deutschen Kriegsgefangenen des Zweiten Weltkrieges. Eine Zusammenfassung* (Bielefeld, 1974), pp. 322 ff.

34 Internationaler Gerichtshof Nürnberg, "Affidavit SD-69," in *Der Prozess gegen die Hauptkriegsverbrecher*, vol. XXVI, doc. no. 471.

35 Adolf Rübe was found guilty of murder and of manslaughter in twenty-six cases by the state court of Karlsruhe on December 15, 1949. He was sentenced to life in prison and deprived of his civic rights for the rest of his life. This court decision was confirmed on November 7, 1951, by the jury court of the state court of Karlsruhe. See Adelheid L. Rüter-Ehlermann, *Justiz und NS-Verbrechen. Sammlung deutscher Strafurteile wegen national-*

sozialistischer Tötungsverbrechen 1945–1966, vol. 9 (Amsterdam, 1968–81), p. 3.

36 Hartmut Lenhard, *"Lebensraum im Osten." Deutsche in Belorussland 1941–1944* (Düsseldorf, 1991), pp. 131 ff.

37 Christian Gerlach, *Kalkulierte Morde. Die deutsche Wirtschafts- und Vernichtungspolitik in Weissrussland 1941 bis 1944* (Hamburg, 1999), p. 1157.

38 Ilse Schmidt, *Die Mitläuferin. Erinnerungen einer Wehrmachtsangehörigen* (Berlin, 1999), p. 75.

39 *Ibid.*, p. 62.

40 *Ibid.*, p. 63.

41 Internationaler Gerichtshof Nürnberg, "Affidavit from Hermann Friedrich Graebe, November 10, 1945," in *Der Prozess gegen die Hauptkriegsverbrecher*, vol. XXXI, doc. no. 2992-PS, 443 ff.

42 Zentrale Stelle der Landes-Justizverwaltung, 141 Js 4534/60, Bd. 6, Bl. 202–208. The questioning took place in 1959.

43 Gerlach, *Kalkulierte Morde*, p. 680.

44 Bundesarchiv Koblenz, Best. R 58/1002, Bl. 107–206, here 197 ff.

45 Gerlach, *Kalkulierte Morde*, p. 266.

46 See US National Archives, RG 242 (roll A3343-RS-D509) RuSHA-Akte Landau, biography of Gertrud Segel from March 31, 3, 1943.

47 Testimony of Marjan Nadel from August 18, 1959 published in Tuviah Friedmann, *Die SS- und Polizeiführer in Radom 1939–1945. Die SS- und Gestapo-Offiziere, die in Radom-Polen 1939–1945 bei der Vernichtung der Juden direkt aktiv beteiligt waren und vor Gericht in Hamburg standen. Eine dokumentarische Sammlung von SS-Dokumenten* (Haifa, 1995).

48 *Ibid.*

49 *Der Regenbogen*, vol. 1, no. 1, April 1, 1946.

Between Amnesty and Anti-Communism:
The West German *Kameradenschinder* Trials, 1948–1960.

1 "Schmitz fand seine Richter," *Der Sozialdemokrat*, July 16, 1949, ASD, 044, 1949.

2 Case of Oskar S., Staatsanwaltschaft Wuppertal, 24 Js 57/50, NRWHStA, Rep.92/60.

3 On the use of German POWs for camp administration and on political reeducation efforts in captivity, see Andreas Hilger, *Deutsche Kriegsgefangene in der Sowjetunion, 1941–1956. Kriegsgefangenenpolitik, Lageralltag und Erinnerung* (Essen, 2000), pp. 119–24, 220–54.

4 "Zusammenstellung der im Bundesjustizministerium bekannten Fälle rechtskräftiger Verurteilungen von Heimkehrern wegen Kameradenmisshandlungen," BAK, B150/7123b. This essay is based on forty cases primar-

ily from the North Rhine–Westphalian Archive in Düsseldorf-Kalkum. Ten of these cases ended with a conviction.

5 See the contributions in Tony Judt, Istvan Deak, and Jan Gross, eds., *The Politics of Retribution: World War II and its Aftermath* (Princeton, N.J., 2000).

6 On this function of the rule of law with respect to Nazi trials, see Peter Steinbach, *Nationalsozialistische Gewaltverbrechen. Die Diskussion in der westdeutschen Öffentlichkeit* (Berlin, 1981), p. 41.

7 One of the so-called Nuremberg successor trials targeted sixteen leading Nazi judges and prosecutors, of whom fourteen were convicted; see Heinz Wrobel, *Verurteilt zur Demokratie. Justiz und Justizpolitik in Deutschland, 1945–1949* (Heidelberg, 1989), pp. 169–91.

8 On the reconstruction of the judiciary in the British zone, see Wolfgang Heilbronn, "Der Aufbau der nordrhein-westfälischen Justiz in der Zeit von 1945 bis 1948/49," in *Juristische Zeitgeschichte* 5 (1996): 1–59, and Hans Eckhard Niermann, "Zwischen Amnestie und Anpassung: Die Entnazifizierung der Richter und Staatsanwälte des Oberlandesbezirksgerichts Hamm 1945 bis 1950," in *ibid.*, pp. 61–94. See also Wrobel, *Verurteilt zur Demokratie*, pp. 139–151, and Ingo Müller, *Furchtbare Juristen. Die unbewältigte Vergangenheit unserer Justiz* (Munich, 1987), pp. 210–21. Figures are cited according to Niermann, "Zwischen Amnestie und Anpassung," p. 65, and Wrobel, *Verurteilt zur Demokratie*, p. 149.

9 Bernd Diestelkamp/Susanne Jung, "Die Justiz in den Westzonen und der frühen Bundesrepublik," *Aus Parlament und Zeitgeschichte* 39 (1989): 19–29.

10 Adalbert Rückerl, *NS-Verbrechen vor Gericht. Versuch einer Vergangenheitsbewältigung* (Heidelberg, 1984), p. 127; Steinbach, *Nationalsozialistische Gewaltverbrechen*, pp. 21–30. For the occupation period, see Martin Broszat, "Siegerjustiz' oder strafrechtliche 'Selbstreinigung.' Aspekte der Vergangenheitsbewältigung der deutschen Justiz während der Besatzungszeit 1945–1949," *Vierteljahreshefte für Zeitgeschichte* 29 (1981): 477–544

11 Robert Moeller, "War Stories. The Search for a Usable Past in the Federal Republic of Germany," *American Historical Review* 101 (1996): 1008–48, and Robert Moeller, *War Stories: The Search for a Usable Past in the Federal Republic* (Berkeley, 2001).

12 Trial of Willy K., Verdict, April 19, 1951, Staatsanwaltschaft Köln, 24 Kls 8/51 NRWHStA, Rep. 231/393, 519.

13 For charges of "crimes against humanity," see Strafanzeige gegen den Heimkehrer Gerd T. wegen Verbrechen gegen die Menschlichkeit, 12 October 1949, 6 Js 1030/49 Staatsanwaltschaft Krefeld, Rep 8/211, 1–2; Amtsgericht Gelsenkirchen an Oberstaatsanwalt in Köln, November 8, 1949, Strafsache gegen K. wegen Verbrechens gegen die Menschlichkeit, Staat-

sanwaltschaft Köln, 24 Js 660/49, NRWHStA, Rep.231/333, 4; Strafanzeige gegen Konrad S. wegen Verbrechen gegen die Menschlichkeit, Staatsanwaltschaft Köln, 24 Js 57/50, NRWHStA, Rep.231/363, 2. For verdicts, see the case of Frieder G., Verdict, September 21, 1953, Staatsanwaltschaft Kleve, 8 Kms 6/50, NRWHStA, Rep.224/39, 41 and the case of Hans O., Verdict, June 1, 1950, Staatsanwaltschaft Kleve, 8 Ks 3/49, NRWHStA, Rep.107/52. 111. In the North Rhine–Westphalian archives, the *Kameradenschinder* cases are stored together with Nazi trials under the common category of "crimes against humanity."

14 Case of Oskar E., Staatsanwaltschaft Köln, 24 Js 403/56, NRWHStA, Rep.231/813, 113. See also "In der Heimat, in der Heimat," *Der Spiegel* 3/29 (1949): 6.

15 Trial of Helmut K., Verdict, Staatsanwaltschaft Mönchengladbach, 6 Kms 8/51, NRWHStA, Rep.72/23, 93.

16 "Schmitz fand seine Richter," *Der Sozialdemokrat*, July 16, 1949, ASD O44 (1949).

17 *Christ und Welt* 18 (1950), cited in *Der Heimkehrer* 2, no. 1 (1951): 2.

18 "Schmitz fand seine Richter."

19 Statement of Hans P., 27 April 1950, Staatsanwaltschaft Kleve, 8 Kms 20/50, NRWHStA, Rep. 238/67, 13–16; Statement of Oskar S., November 11, 1948, Staatsanwaltschaft Wuppertal, 24 Js 57/50, NRWHStA, Rep.92/60, 16 and *Der Spiegel* 3/29 (1949): 5; Statement of Fritz K., January 29, 1957, Staatsanwaltschaft Köln, 24Kls3/57, NRWHStA, Rep.231/1006, 55–58.

20 Steinbach, *Nationalsozialistische Gewaltverbrechen*, 71–72.

21 See, for example, the case of Ewald F., Staatsanwaltschaft Köln, 24 Js 87/50, Verfügung, June 24, 1950, NRWHStA, Rep.231/364, 89–90 and case of Frieder G., Staatsanwaltschaft Kleve 8 Kms 6/50, Verdict, September 21, 1953, NRWHStA, Rep.224/41, 55–57.

22 Quotation from case of Hermann Josef K., Verdict, Staatsanwaltschaft Mönchengladbach; case of Horst R. Verfügung, January 17, 1951, 24 Js 225/50, Staatsanwaltschaft Köln, NRWHStA Rep.231/373.

23 See case of Werner K., Verdict, Staatsanwaltschaft Köln, 24 Kls 8/51, NRWHStA Rep.231/395, 519–20, 553. In this case, the court also justified the conviction of a former German camp commandant to two and a half years in prison because of the possibility that the verdicts might become known in existing Soviet POW camps, thus easing the lot of German POWs, i.e., camp officials would be discouraged from violence against their fellow POWs. In fact, German camp officials did not have any disciplinary powers while in Soviet captivity; see Hilger, *Deutsche Kriegsgefangene in der Sowjetunion*.

24 BGH Verdict, 12 July 1951, in Lindenmaier-Möhring, 1950–1985, §54, No. 1.

25 See the case of Rolf S., Beauftratger der Arbeitsgemeinschaft der Heim-
    kehrer Verbände an Oberstaatsanwalt Bonn, November 13, 1949, Staat-
    sanwaltschaft Köln, 24 Js 26/50, NRWHStA, Rep.231/361, 1; Ober-
    staatsanwalt Bonn an den Verband der Heimkehrer, March 18, 1953,
    Nr.37 15/51–33 Kameradenmisshandlungen, VdH Archive. The associa-
    tion then used its own publications to search for witnesses. See Verband
    der Heimkehrer, Rundschreiben 17/55, 17 February 1955, "Kameraden
    als Zeugen gesucht," Nr.37, 15/51–33 Kameradenmisshandlungen, VdH
    Archive. In some cases, however, charges were also filed by former Com-
    munists. See for example the case of Rolf T. who was charged by Jakob M.,
    a former KPD member and survivor of the Dachau and Auschwitz con-
    centration camps: Jakob M. an Amtsgericht Reichenhall, January 18,
    1950, NRWHStA, Rep.231/399, 2.

26 See *Der Heimkehrer* No. 6/7 1(1950): 8, and No.3 2(1951): 5.

27 Oberstaatsanwalt Kaiserslautern an VdH, July 27, 1957; Staatsanwalt-
    schaft Stuttgart an VdH, 7 October 1954; Untersuchungsrichter beim
    Landgericht Regensburg an VdH München, November 4, 1954; Nr.37
    15/51–33, Kameradenmisshandlungen, VdH Archive.

28 See, for example, Werner Kiessling an Oberstaatsanwalt Verden/Aller,
    7 March 1955, Nr.37, 15/51–33, Kameradenmisshandlungen, VdH
    Archive.

29 On this campaign, see Norbert Frei, *Vergangenheitspolitik. Die An-
    fänge der Bundesrepublik und die NS-Vergangenheit* (Munich, 1996),
    pp. 133–306.

30 Rückerl, *NS Verbrechen vor Gericht*, p. 282.

31 On leniency toward Nazi perpetrators, see Steinbach, *Nationalsozialistis-
    che Gewaltverbrechen*, pp. 69–70.

32 The Kemmna trial was the first trial of concentration camp personnel be-
    fore a West German court. See Peter Steinbach, "NS-Prozesse nach 1945.
    Auseinandersetzung mit der Vergangenheit–Konfrontation mit der Wirk-
    lichkeit," *Dachauer Hefte* 13 (1997): 15.

33 Case of Oskar S., Vorstand der Strafanstalt an Herrn Oberstaatsanwalt in
    Wuppertal, 10 June 1955, NRWHStA, Rep.92/60.

34 Der Hessische Minister des Inneren, Schneider, an den Hessischen Min-
    isterpräsidenten Dr. August Georg Zinn, June 22, 1956, HHStA,
    502/1003; see also Chapter V of my dissertation, "The Protracted War: Re-
    turning POWs and the Making of East and West German Citizens,
    1945–1955," (Ph.D. diss., Brown University, 2000), pp. 378–79.

35 On these trials, see Manfred Zeidler, *Stalinjustiz contra NS-Verbrechen.
    Die Kriegsverbrecherprozesse gegen deutsche Kriegsgefangene in der UdSSR
    in den Jahren 1943–1955. Kenntnisstand und Forschungsprobleme* (Dres-
    den, 1996) and Hilger, *Deutsche Kriegsgefangene in der Sowjetunion*,
    pp. 255–302.

36 Broszat, " 'Siegerjustiz' oder strafrechtliche 'Selbstreinigung'," p. 533. On denunciations during the Third Reich, see Robert Gellately, *The Gestapo and German Society. Enforcing Racial Policy, 1933–1945* (Oxford, 1990), 130–58.

37 Lindenmeier-Möhring, *Nachschlagwerk des Bundesgerichtshofs, 1950–1985*, Band 57, Nr.2, § 3 StGB.

38 On denunciations and comradeship, see Thomas Kühne, "Zwischen Männerbund und Volksgemeinschaft. Hitlers Soldaten und der Mythos der Kameradschaft," *Archiv für Sozialgeschichte* 38 (1998): 165–89, and Thomas Kühne "Kameradschaft—'das Beste im Leben eines Mannes,'" *Geschichte und Gesellschaft* 22 (1996):504–29; on military justice, see Norbert Haase, "Wehrmachtsangehörige vor dem Kriegsgericht," in Rolf-Dieter Müller and Hans Erich Volkmann, *Die Wehrmacht. Mythos und Realität* (Munich, 1999) pp. 474–86.

39 In my view, this is also how the evidence in the following source needs to be read: Hannes Heer, *'Stets zu erschiessen sind die Frauen, die in der Roten Armee dienen.' Geständnisse deutscher Kriegsgefangener über ihren Einsatz an der Ostfront* (Hamburg, 1995). The quotation is from Hilger, *Deutsche Kriegsgefangene in der Sowjetunion*, p. 300.

40 On the armed SS, see Bernd Wegner, *Die Waffen SS 1933–1945. Hitlers Politische Soldaten. Studien zu Leitbild, Struktur und Funktion einer nationalsozialistischen Elite* (Paderborn, 1982).

41 Case of Fritz K., Verdict, Staatsanwaltschaft Köln, 24Kls 3/57, NRWHStA, Rep. 231/1006, 94–98.

42 Case of Heinz S., Vernehmungsprotokoll, August 10, 1954, Staatsanwaltschaft Frankfurt, 4 KLs 9/58, Hessisches Hauptstaatsarchiv (HHStA), Abt. 461/Nr.33147.

43 Case of Heinz S., Verdict Bundesgerichtshof, January 29, 1960, HHStA, Abt.461/Nr.33147.

44 Case of Theo B., Staatsanwaltschaft Köln, 24 Js 443/56, NRWHStA, Rep.231/814.

45 See Bernd Boll, "Wehrmacht vor Gericht. Kriegsverbrecherprozesse der Vier Mächte nach 1945," *Geschichte und Gesellschaft* 24 (1998): 570–94.

46 Case of Rolf S., Staatsanwaltschaft Köln, 24 Js 26/50, NRWHStA, Rep.231/361.

47 West German courts did have, in principal, jurisdiction for such offenses. See Ruth Bettina Birn, "Wehrmacht und Wehrmachtsangehörige in den deutschen Nachkriegsprozessen," in Müller and Volkmann, eds., *Die Wehrmacht*, pp. 1081–99.

48 Hilger, *Deutsche Kriegsgefangene in der Sowjetunion*, p. 300.

49 On comradeship as facilitating participation in genocidal warfare, see Kühne, "Zwischen Männerbund und Volksgemeinschaft," and Christo-

pher Browning, *Ordinary Men: Reserve Police Battalion 101 and the Final Solution in Poland* (New York, 1992).

50 Case of Rolf T., Verdict, NRWHStA, Rep.231/40, 448.

51 On the myth of the clean Wehrmacht see Friedrich Gerstenberger, "Strategische Erinnerungen. Die Memoiren deutscher Offiziere," in Hannes Heer and Klaus Naumann, eds., *Vernichtungskrieg. Verbrechen der Wehrmacht 1941 bis 1944* (Hamburg, 1995), pp. 620–29; Michael Schornstheimer, " 'Harmlose Idealisten und draufgängerische Soldaten.' Militär und Krieg in den Illustriertenromanen der fünziger Jahre," in *ibid.*, pp. 634–50; and Gabriele Rosenthal, "Vom Krieg erzählen, von den Verbrechen schweigen," in *ibid.*, pp. 651–63.

52 Case of Theo B., Verfügung, NRWHStA, Rep.231/814, 48.

53 *Ibid.*, p. 52.

54 On West German political justice, see Patrick Major, *The Death of the KPD. Communism and Anti-Communism in West Germany, 1945–1956* (Oxford, 1997), pp. 277–83; Rolf Gössner, *Die vergessenen Justizopfer des Kalten Krieges. Verdrängung im Westen—Abrechnung im Osten?* (Berlin, 1998).

55 Alexander Griebel, "Zu den Strafprozessen gegen Heimkehrer," *Juristenzeitung* 6 (1951): 362–63.

56 Steinbach, "NS-Prozesse nach 1945," p. 20.

57 Case of Rolf T., Staatsanwaltschaft Bonn 24 Kls 23/51, Anklageschrift, Staatsanwaltschaft Köln, NRWHStA, Rep. 231/400, 224.

58 Case of Rolf T., Verdict, NRWHStA, Rep. 231/401, 407.

59 In the case of Werner K., for example, the court interrogated more than seventy witnesses. See case of Werner K., Verdict, NRWHStA, Rep. 231/393, 516–17.

60 Case of Rolf T., Verdict, NRWHStA, Rep. 231/401, 409.

61 See case of Hermann Josef K., Verdict, Staatsanwaltschaft Mönchengladbach 6 Kms 8/51, NRWHStA, Rep. 72/23, 93.

62 On the ways "healthy public sensibilities" was only superficially replaced by the term "reprehensible" in West German law, see Müller, *Furchtbare Juristen*, p. 232.

63 Michael Stolleis, *The Law under the Swastika. Studies on Legal History in Nazi Germany* (Chicago, 1998), p. 176. On depoliticization, see also Wrobel, *Verurteilt zur Demokratie*, pp. 225–30.

64 This tendency toward depoliticization also manifested itself in West German responses to other forms of "deviant" behavior, such as adolescents' infatuation with American popular culture, and reflected a more widespread move into what Uta Poiger has called "Cold War liberalism." See Uta Poiger, *Jazz, Rock, and Rebels: Cold War Politics and American Culture in a Divided Germany* (Berkeley, 2000).

65 Case of Oskar S., Verdict, 8 July 1949, NRWHStA, Rep. 92/60, 252; case of Rolf T., Verdict, NRWHStA, Rep.231/399, 409.

66 Quotations from case of Hermann, Josef K., Beschluss June 27, 1951, NR-WHStA, Rep.72/23, 118 and case of Fritz K., Verdict, NRWHStA, Rep.231/1006, 98.

67 See case of Rolf T., Verdict, NRWHStA, Rep.231/401, 404, 408.

68 Case of Rolf T., Anklageschrift, NRWHStA, Rep.231/400, 233. He was ultimately cleared of these charges.

69 *Ibid.*, p. 404.

70 On the persistence of soldierly ideals of masculinity in the treatment of returning POWs from the Soviet Union, see Svenja Goltermann, "Die Beherrschung der Männlichkeit. Zur Deutung psychischer Leiden bei den Heimkehrern des Zweiten Weltkrieges 1945–1956," in *Feministische Studien* 18 (2000): 7–19.

71 Case of Oskar S., Verdict, NRWHStA, Rep.92/60, 252. In another trial, the court considered it detrimental to one POW's preparation for his job as a German camp official that he had not experienced "the daily worries of the ordinary front soldier" during the war. See case of Werner K., Verdict, NRWHStA. Rep.231/393, 534.

72 Case of Oskar S., Verdict, NRWHStA, Rep.92/60, 252.

73 Case of Hans Peter T., Staatsanwaltschaft Wuppertal, 12 Kls 1/57, NR-WHStA Rep.240/155–162.

74 Dr.med. Fritz Wawersik an Untersuchungsrichter beim Landgericht W-Elberfeld, May 28, 1955, NRWHStA, Rep. 240/158, 36.

75 "Tallarek konnte nicht aus seiner Haut," *Westdeutsche Rundschau*, December 4, 1957, NRWHStA, Rep.240/162.

76 On military reform, see David Clay Large, *Germans to the Front: West German Rearmament in the Adenauer Era* (Chapel Hill, N.C., 1996), pp. 176–204. On ways that these ideals of the "citizen in uniform" were projected onto returning POWs, see Robert Moeller, "The 'Last Soldiers of the Great War' and Tales of Family Reunions in the Federal Republic of Germany," *Signs* 24 (1998): 129–45, and Moeller, *War Stories*, p. 119.

77 Ministry of Expellees to *Dienststelle Blank*, "Ehemalige kriegsgefangene Offiziere im Dienst der Sowjetunion (Entwurf)," BAK-B150/156; "Vertraulich: Zweite Liste an die Dienststelle Blank," January 29, 1953, BAK-B150/156.

78 A. Helling, March 19, 1953; A. Helling to Herr Albert, March 19, 1953, BAK, B150/156.

79 See Wurm, "Schuld und Niederlage der Antifa," *Neues Abendland* 7 (1982), p. 414. There is some evidence that former Nazis were indeed more likely to collaborate with Soviet authorities, probably because they faced greater risks of reprisals and prosecution; see, for example, the case of

the former National Socialist Leadership Officer (NSFO) Oskar E., who later became an antifascist activist in Soviet captivity (case of Oskar E., NRWHStA, Rep.231/813).

80 Valentin Gorges, "Man muss leben! Ein Beitrag zur Psychologie der Kameradenschinder," *Deutsche Rundschau* 78 (1952): 599–604.

81 On this process, see Omer Bartov, "Defining Enemies, Making Victims," in *American Historical Review* 103 (1998): 771–816, and Omer Bartov, *Mirrors of Destruction: War, Genocide, and Modern Identity* (New York, 2000). Quotations are from Gorges, "Man muss leben," (1982), p. 602. On the nature of West German anti-Communism, see also Major, *The Death of the KPD*.

82 Gorges, "Man muss leben!," p. 604.

83 See H. H. Wubben, "American Prisoners of War in Korea: A Second Look at the 'Something New in History' Theme," *American Quarterly* 22 (1970): 3–19; Adam Zweiback, "The 21 'Turncoat GIs': Nonrepatriation and the Political Culture of the Korean War," *Historian* 60 (1998): 345–63. My thanks to Michael Parrish for alerting me to these sources.

84 Zweiback, "The 21 'Turncoat GIs' "

85 On returning POWs' reception in East Germany, see Frank Biess, "Pioneers of a New Germany: Returning POWs and the Making of East German Citizens, 1945–1950," *Central European History* 32 (1999): 143–80.

86 Bericht über die westdeutschen Provokationsprozesse im Zusammenhang mit der Rückkehr von aus sowjetischer Strafhaft Entlassenen, Anlage No. 5 zum Protokoll No. 39/55, August 23, 1955, BA-SAPMO, DY 30/J IV2/2/436; also cited in Beate Ihme-Tuchel, "Die Entlassung der deutschen Kriegsgefangenen im Herbst 1955 im Spiegel der Diskussion zwischen SED und KPdSU," *Militärgeschichtliche Mitteilungen* 54 (1994): 449–65.

87 Norbert Frei discusses how Cold War Germany fostered increasingly rigid memories of the Nazi past in "NS Vergangenheit unter Ulbricht und Adenauer," in Jürgen Danyel, ed., *Die geteilte Vergangenheit. Zum Umgang mit Nationalsozialismus und Widerstand in beiden deutschen Staaten* (Berlin, 1995), pp. 125–32.

88 Case of Gustav J. Staatsanwaltschaft Bonn 8 Js 389/54, Interrogation of Hans S., November 14, 1953, NRWHStA, Rep.104/82, 5–8.

89 Gustav J. an das Polizeipräsidium Bonn, NRWHStA, May 7, 1955, Rep.104/83, 315–25.

90 Case of Gustav J., Vermerk, November 11, 1955, NRWHStA, Rep.104/83, 372–81.

91 See Peter Steinbach and Gerd Überschär, "Die Geschichtsschreibung zum NKFD und BdO in der Bundesrepublik und in den westlichen Ländern," in Gerd Überschär, ed., *Das Nationalkommittee 'Freies Deutschland' und der 'Bund Deutscher Offiziere'* (Frankfurt, 1996), pp. 141–60.

92 See case of Gustav T., 6 Js 1030/49, NRWHStA, Rep. 8/211; case of Ewald F., 24 Js 87/50, NRWHStA, Rep.231/364; case of Oskar E., 24 Js 403/56, NRWHStA, Rep. 213/813.

93 Frei, *Vergangenheitspolitik*, pp. 29–53.

94 Case of Fritz G., Staatsanwaltschaft Kleve, 8 Kms 6/50, NRWHStA, Rep.224/41; case of Fritz M., Staatsanwaltschaft Wuppertal, 5 Kms 2/51, NRWHStA, Rep.191/166.

95 Case of Werner K., BGH Verdict, May 16, 1952, NRWHStA, Rep.231/393, pp. 746–47.

96 On the tendency to refrain from prosecution of Nazi crimes during the early 1950s, see Rückerl, *NS Verbrechen vor Gericht*, pp. 123–139.

97 On the East German purges of West POWs, see Biess, "The Protracted War," pp. 262–72, and Catherine Epstein, "The Last Revolutionaries: The Old Communists of East Germany, 1945–1989" (Ph.D. diss., Harvard University, 1998), pp. 161–92.

98 Charles Maier, *Dissolution: The Crisis of Communism and the End of East Germany* (Princeton, N.J., 1997), p. 20.

"In a Thousand Years, Every German Will Speak of This Battle": Celluloid Memories of Stalingrad

1 Rüdiger Overmans, "Das andere Gesicht des Krieges: Leben und Sterben der 6. Armee," in *Stalingrad: Ereignis—Wirkung—Symbol*, ed. Jürgen Förster (Munich, 1992), pp. 444–46; Manfred Hettling, "Täter und Opfer? Die deutschen Soldaten in Stalingrad," *Archiv für Sozialgeschichte* 35 (1995): 524; and Antony Beevor, *Stalingrad* (New York, 1998), 434–40.

2 See G. F. Krivosheev, et al., *Soviet Casualties and Combat Losses in the Twentieth Century* (London, 1997), p. 127; and David M. Glantz and Jonathan M. House, *When Titans Clashed: How the Red Army Stopped Hitler* (Lawrence, Kans., 1995), pp. 141–42.

3 Jens Ebert, ed., *Stalingrad: Eine deutsche Legende* (Reinbek bei Hamburg, 1992); Hettling, "Täter und Opfer?" pp. 515–16; Wolfram Wette, "Das Massensterben als 'Heldenepos,'" in *Stalingrad: Mythos und Wirklichkeit einer Schlacht*, ed. Wolfram Wette and Gerd R. Ueberschär (Frankfurt am Main, 1992), pp. 43–60; Jay Baird, "The Myth of Stalingrad," *Journal of Contemporary History* 4 (1969): 187–204; Insa Eschebach, "Das Opfer deutscher Männer," *SOWI* 22 (1993): 37–41; and Michael Kumpfmüller, *Die Schlacht von Stalingrad: Metamorphosen eines deutschen Mythos* (Munich, 1995), pp. 445–48. See also the useful discussion of the meanings of *Opfer* in Helmut Dubiel, *Niemand ist frei von der Geschichte: Die nationalsozialistische Herrschaft in den Debatten des Deutschen Bundestags* (Munich, 1995), p. 74.

4 "Reichsmarschall Görings Appell an die Wehrmacht: Unerschütterliche

Härte bis zum Sieg im Kampf gegen den Bolschewismus, Stalingrad—der grösste Heroenkampf unserer Geschichte," *Völkischer Beobachter* February 2, 1943, reprinted in Ebert, 36, 37.

5 Fritz Wöss, *Hunde, wollt ihr ewig leben?* (Hamburg, 1958). For an English translation, see *Dogs, Do You Want to Live Forever?*, trans. Sonja Rosenzweig (Vienna, 1991). A video of the movie is readily available for purchase from the German Language Video Center in Indianapolis, Indiana (*www.germanvideo.com*)

6 See, for example, Hans Wagener, "Der Fall 'Stalingrad': Zufall, Schuld oder geschichtliche Logik? Zur Interpretation einiger deutscher Kriegsromane," in *Elemente der Literatur: Beiträge zur Stoff-, Motiv- und Themenforschung. Elisabeth Frenzel zum 65. Geburtstag*, [vol. II], ed. Adam J. Bisanz and Raymond Trousson (Stuttgart, 1980), pp. 149–58; Ebert, *Stalingrad*; Gerd R. Ueberschär, "Die Schlacht von Stalingrad in der deutschen Historiographie," in *Stalingrad: Mythos und Wirklichkeit einer Schlacht*, pp. 192–204; Manfred Kehrig, "Stalingrad im Spiegel der Memoiren deutscher Generale," in *ibid.*, pp. 204–13; Ulrich Baron, "Stalingrad als Thema der deutschsprachigen Literatur," in *ibid.*, pp. 226–32; Kumpfmüller, *Die Schlacht von Stalingrad*, pp. 226–37, and in Wöss; Jürgen Schäfer, " 'Alle fluchten, alle funktionierten': Die Schlacht um Stalingrad in deutschen Romanen der Nachkriegszeit," *SOWI* 22 (1993): pp. 42–49; Stefanie Carp, *Kriegsgeschichten: Zum Werk Alexander Kluges* (Munich, 1987), pp. 102–4; and in general, Jochen Pfeifer, *Der deutsche Kriegsroman, 1945–1960: Ein Versuch zur Vermittlung von Literatur und Sozialgeschichte* (Königstein/Ts., 1981), esp. pp. 48–49; Hans Wagener, "Soldaten zwischen Gehorsam und Gewissen: Kriegsromane und -tagebücher," *Gegenwartsliteratur und Drittes Reich: Deutsche Autoren in der Auseinandersetzung mit der Vergangenheit*, ed. Hans Wagener (Stuttgart, 1977), p. 241; and Jost Hermand, "Darstellungen des Zweiten Weltkrieges," in *Literatur nach 1945*, vol. I, *Politische und regionale Aspekte* (Wiesbaden, 1979), pp. 29–32. The war in the East also figured in the trilogy by Hans Hellmut Kirst, *Zero Eight Fifteen: The Strange Mutiny of Gunner Asch*, trans. Robert Kee (London, 1955); Hans Hellmut Kirst, *Gunner Asch Goes to War: Zero Eight Fifteen II*, trans. Robert Kee (London, 1956); and Hans Hellmut Kirst, *The Return of Gunner Asch: Zero Eight Fifteen III*, trans. Robert Kee (London, 1957). On the second installment of the movie version that followed Gunner Asch to the war in Russia, see Friedrich A. Wagner, "Null-acht-fünfzehn im russischen Winter," *Frankfurter Allgemeine Zeitung*, August 20, 1955; and Herbert Hohenemser, ". . . übrig bleibt brüllendes Vergnügen," *Münchener Merkur*, August 28, 1955. And in Heinz G. Konsalik, *Der Artz von Stalingrad* (Munich, 1997), the focus shifts to the fate of those taken captive after surrender.

7 Interview in "Frank Wisbar hasst den Krieg," *Stuttgarter Zeitung*, January

30, 1959. See also Karl Kurt Ziegler, "Der Wahrheit zu dienen!" *Westfälische Rundschau*, April 21, 1959. Movie reviews cited here and subsequently come from the extraordinary collection of the Deutsches Filminstitut in Frankfurt am Main.

8 Vitus B. Dröscher, "Der Barde des zweiten Weltkriegs: Frank Wisbar," *Bonner Rundschau*, November 26, 1960.

9 Frank Wisbar, "Filme sind Leitartikel," *Die Kultur*, November 1, 1958.

10 Heide Fehrenbach, *Cinema in Democratizing Germany: Reconstructing National Identity after Hitler* (Chapel Hill, N.C., 1995), pp. 211–13.

11 See Linda Schulte-Sasse, *Entertaining the Third Reich: Illusions of Wholeness in Nazi Cinema* (Durham, N.C., 1996), p. 31. In general, see also Fehrenbach, whose *Cinema in Democratizing Germany* is the essential starting point for anyone interested in the West German films of the 1950s.

12 Unless otherwise indicated, all translations are my own. I have not been able to locate a screenplay for *Hunde*. Quotations are from my own transcription of the dialogue of the movie.

13 Michael Burleigh and Wolfgang Wippermann, *The Racial State: Germany 1933–1945* (New York, 1991), pp. 217–18.

14 See Fehrenbach's discussion of these movies in *Cinema in Democratizing Germany*, pp. 152–55, 159–61. See also Robert G. Moeller, *War Stories: The Search for a Usable Past in the Federal Republic of Germany* (Berkeley, 2001), 128–43.

15 " 'Goldene Schale' und 150000 DM für 'Helden,' " *General-Anzeiger*, June 29, 1959.

16 Quotations from "So hart wie der Titel?" *Telegraf*, February 1, 1959; Hans Hellmut Kirst, "Filmunternehmen Stalingrad," *Münchener Merkur*, May 14, 1959. See also "Keine Zeit für Heldentum," *Westfälische Rundschau*, March 19, 1959; Will Fischer, "Hunde, wollt ihr ewig leben?", *Rhein-Neckarzeitung* April 30, 1959; also "Hundewollt ihr ewig leben?", *Abendzeitung*, May 13, 1959; Henning Harmssen, "Keine Zeit für Heldentum, *Mannheimer Morgen*, February 28, 1959.

17 "Hunde, wollt ihr ewig leben?" *Düsseldorfer Nachrichten*, April 11, 1959.

18 "Frei nach Schiller," *Der Spiegel*, April 15, 1959; also Peter Miska, "Der Wahrheit dienen," *Frankfurter Rundschau*, April 4, 1959.

19 Quotations are from Frank Wisbar, "Ein Wort zu meinem Stalingrad-Film," *Stuttgarter Zeitung*, April 3, 1959; "Frei nach Schiller;" and "Frank Wisbar hasst den Krieg." See also the judgment of Hans-Dieter Roos, "Hunde, wollt ihr ewig leben?" *Süddeutsche Zeitung*, May 15, 1959.

20 See the background story on Wisbar and the making of the film in Peter Miska, "Frank Wisbars Stalingrad-Film: 'Hunde, wollt ihr ewig leben?' " *Frankfurter Rundschau*, April 4, 1959.

21 Wolfgang Bartsch, "Die 'verheitzte' Armee," *Frankfurter Rundschau*, April 23, 1959.

22 Alfred Streim, "Saubere Wehrmacht? Die Verfolgung von Kriegs- und NS-Verbrechen in der Bundesrepublik und in der DDR," in *Vernichtungskrieg: Verbrechen der Wehrmacht 1941–1944*, ed. Hannes Heer and Klaus Naumann (Hamburg, 1995), pp. 569–97; and Klaus Naumann, "Die 'saubere' Wehrmacht: Gesellschaftsgeschichte einer Legende," *Mittelweg 36*, 4 (1998): 8–18. See also James M. Diehl, *The Thanks of the Fatherland: German Veterans after the Second World War* (Chapel Hill, N.C., 1993).

23 Quoted in Donald Abenheim, *Reforging the Iron Cross: The Search for Tradition in the West German Armed Forces* (Princeton, N.J., 1988), p. 70.

24 Quoted in *ibid.*; see also David Clay Large, *Germans to the Front: West German Rearmament in the Adenauer Era* (Chapel Hill, N.C., 1996), pp. 114–17; Ulrich Brochhagen, *Nach Nürnberg: Vergangenheitsbewältigung und Westintegration in der Ära Adenauer* (Hamburg, 1994), p. 197; Gerhard Wettig, *Entmilitarisierung und Wiederbewaffnung in Deutschland 1943–1955: Internationale Auseinandersetzung um die Rolle der Deutschen in Europa* (Munich, 1967), pp. 400–401; and on the background in the late 1940s, Roland G. Foerster, "Innenpolitische Aspekte der Sicherheit Westdeutschlands (1947–1950)," in *Von der Kapitulation bis zum Pleven-Plan*, by Roland G. Foerster et al., vol. I of *Anfänge westdeutscher Sicherheitspolitik, 1945–1956*, edited by Militärgeschichtliches Forschungsamt (Munich, 1982), p. 403; and Georg Meyer, "Zur Situation der deutschen militärischen Führungsschicht im Vorfeld des westdeutschen Verteidigungsbeitrages 1945–1950/51," in *ibid.*, pp. 652–55; Hans-Jürgen Rautenberg, "Zur Standortbestimmung für künftige deutsche Streitkräfte," in *ibid.*, p. 803.

25 Thomas Alan Schwartz, "John J. McCloy and the Landsberg Cases," in *American Policy and the Reconstruction of West Germany, 1945–1955*, ed. Jeffry M. Diefendorf, Axel Frohn, and Hermann-Josef Rupieper (New York, 1993), p. 450; also Thomas Alan Schwartz, *America's Germany: John J. McCloy and the Federal Republic of Germany* (Cambridge, Mass., 1991), pp. 157–75; and Brochhagen, *Nach Nürnberg*, pp. 44–51.

26 "Hunde, wollt ihr ewig leben?" *Abendzeitung*, May 13, 1959.

27 See Michael Schornstheimer, " 'Harmlose Idealisten und draufgängerische Soldaten': Militär und Krieg in den Illustriertenromanen der fünfziger Jahre," in *Vernichtungskrieg*, pp. 634–50; Michael Schornstheimer, *Die leuchtenden Augen der Frontsoldaten: Nationalsozialismus und Krieg in den Illustriertenromanen der fünfziger Jahre* (Berlin, 1995); and Klaus F. Geiger, *Kriegsromanhefte in der BRD: Inhalte und Funktionen* (Tübingen, 1974).

28 "Hunde, wollt ihr ewig leben?" *Abendzeitung*.

29 Quotations in "Frei nach Schiller."

30 *Verhandlungen des deutschen Bundestags*, 3 Wahlperiode, 70. Sitzung, June 3, 1959.

31 Joachim Weiner, "Der letzte Sinn des grossen Opfers," *Hannoversche Rundschau*, April 8, 1959.

32 "Schicksal an der Volga," *Telegraf*, May 7, 1959.

33 Quoted in "Frei nach Schiller."

34 Karl-Heinz Frieser, *Krieg hinter Stacheldraht: Die deutschen Kriegsgefangenen in der Sowjetunion und das Nationalkomitee "Freies Deutschland"* (Mainz, 1981); and Bodo Scheurig, *Free Germany: The National Committee and the League of German Officers*, trans. Herbert Arnold (Middletown, Conn., 1969).

35 Review by Hannes Schmidt in *Neue Rhein Zeitung*, April 9, 1959.

36 Abenheim, *Reforging the Iron Cross*, pp. 102–3; and in general, on rearmament, Large, *Germans to the Front*; and Detlef Bald, *Militär und Gesellschaft, 1945–1990* (Baden-Baden, 1994); Detlef Bald, " 'Bürger in Uniform': Tradition und Neuanfang des Militärs in Westdeutschland," in *Modernisierung im Wiederaufbau: Die westdeutsche Gesellschaft der 50er Jahre*, ed. Axel Schildt and Arnold Sywottek (Bonn, 1993), pp. 392–402; Rautenberg, "Zur Standortbestimmung für künftige deutsche Streitkräfte," p. 747, p. 872, p. 879; Hans-Adolf Jacobsen, "Zur Rolle der öffentlichen Meinung bei der Debatte um die Wiederbewaffnung 1950–1955," in *Aspekte der deutschen Wiederbewaffnung bis 1955*, ed. Militärgeschichtliches Forschungsamt (Boppard am Rhein, 1975), pp. 70–89; Meyer, "Innenpolitische Voraussetzungen," pp. 31–44.

37 Friedrich Sieburg, "Der schönste Mann im Staate," *Die Zeit*, July 28, 1955. A public opinion poll revealed that 77 percent of men and 76 percent of women preferred to see men in civilian clothing: "Was steht ihrer Meinung nach einem Mann Besser—ein Zivilanzug oder eine Uniform?" *Der Spiegel*, October 5, 1955. Joachim Besser, "Nicht alle tragen Uniform . . . ," *Die Welt*, October 20, 1955.

38 Wolfgang Bartsch, "Die 'verheizte' Armee," *Frankfurter Rundschau*, April 23, 1959.

39 Josef Schmidt, "Stalingrad—für die Kinoleinwand," *Süddeutsche Zeitung*, January 21, 1959, also Friedrich A. Wagner, "Die Wolga war ihr Schicksal," *Frankfurter Allgemeine Zeitung*, April 13, 1959.

40 Horst Oberstrass, "Fettschicht," *Velberter Zeitung*, April 11, 1959.

41 Alexander Mitscherlich, "Der geteilte Vater: Generationskonflikte in der modernen Welt," *Der Tagesspiegel*, November 13, 1955. Mitscherlich developed these arguments at length in *Auf dem Wege zur vaterlosen Gesellschaft: Ideen zur Sozialpsychologie* (1963; reprint, Munich, 1973), translated as *Society without the Father: A Contribution to Social Psychology*, trans. Eric Mosbacher (New York, 1969); and Alexander Mitscher-

lich, "Der unsichtbare Vater: Ein Problem für Psychoanalyse und Soziologie," *Kölner Zeitschrift für Soziologie und Sozialpsychologie* 7 (1955):
188–201.

42 See the review of "Die Saat der Gewalt," *Der Abend*, November 3, 1955;
also Hans Steinitz, "Amerikas 'Krankheit der Jugend': Eine Folge von
Wohlleben und Bequemlichkeit?" *Die Welt*, November 3, 1955; and the
ad for the movie *Die Saat der Gewalt*, which located the film "in the cross-
fire of protest and enthusiasm," *Die Welt*, November 18, 1955. And, in
general, Uta G. Poiger, *Jazz, Rock, and Rebels: Cold War Politics and
American Culture in a Divided Germany* (Berkeley, 2000); Uta G. Poiger,
"A New, 'Western' Hero? Reconstructing German Masculinity in the
1950s," *Signs* 24 (1998): 147–62; Uta G. Poiger, "Rebels with a Cause?
American Popular Culture, the 1956 Youth Riots, and New Conceptions
of Masculinity in East and West Germany," in *The American Impact on
Postwar Germany*, ed. Reiner Pommerin (Providence, R.I., 1995), pp.
93–124; and Uta G. Poiger, "Rock 'n' Roll, Female Sexuality, and the Cold
War Battle over German Identities," in *West Germany Under Construc-
tion: Politics, Society, and Culture in the Adenauer Era*, ed. Robert G.
Moeller (Ann Arbor, Mich., 1997), pp. 373–410.

43 On the debate over the Americanization of youth culture in West (and
East) Germany in the 1950s, see the pathbreaking study by Poiger, *Jazz,
Rock, and Rebels*.

44 *Verhandlungen des deutschen Bundestages*, 3 Wahlperiode, March 20,
1958, p. 880, quoted in Marc Cioc, *Pax Atomica: The Nuclear Defense Debate in West Germany During the Adenauer Era* (New York, 1988), p. 62.

45 Schmidt, "Stalingrad—für die Kinoleinwand;" also Karl Kurt Ziegler,
"Stalingrad: Symbol und Mahnung," *Westfälische Rundschau*, April 12,
1959; "Film-Menetekel aus Stalingrad," *Hamburger Echo*, April 17, 1959;
Heinz Bruegger, "Nicht im Interesse der Bundeswehr?" *Andere Zeitung*,
April 29, 1959; and review in *Allgemeine Zeitung*, May 1, 1959.

46 W. Bittermann, "Verzweiflung mit Feuerpausen," *Rheinischer Merkur*,
May 22, 1959.

47 Klaus Theweleit, *Male Fantasies*, vol. 1, *Women, Floods, Bodies, History*,
trans. Stephen Conway in collaboration with Erica Carter and Chris
Turner (Minneapolis, 1987), pp. 70–79.

48 See Gottfried Niedhardt and Normen Altmann, "Zwischen Beurteilung
und Verurteilung: Die Sowjetunion im Urteil Konrad Adenauers," in *Adenauer und die deutsche Frage*, ed. Josef Foschepoth (Göttingen, 1988), pp.
99–117.

49 Robert G. Moeller, " 'The Last Soldiers of the Great War' and Tales of
Family Reunions in the Federal Republic of Germany," *Signs* 24 (1998):
129–46.

50 Letter of 5 February 1957 to Adenauer, published in *Pravda*, February 12,

1957 and reprinted in *Moskau-Bonn: Die Beziehungen zwischen der Sow-jetunion und der Bundesrepublik Deutschland, 1955–1963*, vol. 3, part 1, ed. Boris Meissner (Cologne, 1975), p. 234.

51 Marc Trachtenberg, *A Constructed Peace: The Making of the European Settlement, 1945–1963* (Princeton, N.J., 1999), pp. 252–82.

52 Joachim Weiner, "Der letzte Sinn des grossen Opfers."

53 Uwe Kuckei, "Ein ewig Suchender fand Heim nach Deutschland," *Der neue Film*, September 7, 1959.

54 Clemens Riemenschneider in *Die Tat*, May 2, 1959.

55 "Ewig lebt am längsten," *Vorwärts*, April 17, 1959.

56 Hans-Dieter Roos in *Süddeutsche Zeitung*, May 15, 1959.

57 "So ging die 6. Armee zugrunde," *Hamburger Abendblatt*, April 18, 1959.

58 Friedrich A. Wagner, "Die Wolga war ihr Schicksal," *Frankfurter Allgemeine Zeitung*, April 13, 1959; see also Bartsch, "Die 'verheizte' Armee." Bartsch refers to the "unbewältigte historische Schock" of Stalingrad; and Wilhelm Mogge, "Gipfel der deutschen Tragödie," *Bonner Rundschau*, April 11, 1959.

59 "Kritikerpreis für Adorno und Wisbar," *Abendzeitung*, August 17, 1959. See also the discussion of the movie in Bärbel Westermann, *Nationale Identität im Spielfilm der fünfziger Jahre* (Frankfurt am Main, 1990), pp. 67–84.

60 Theodor W. Adorno, in "What Does Coming to Terms with the Past Mean?" *Bitburg in Moral and Political Perspective*, ed. Geoffrey H. Hartman (Bloomington, Ind. 1986), p. 116.

61 *Ibid.*

62 "So hart wie der Titel," *Telegraf*, February 1, 1959.

63 Weiner, "Der letzte Sinn."

64 "Ewig lebt am längsten."

65 Quotations from Gert Koegel, "Kerls, wollt ihr niemals lernen? Diskussion um den Stalingrad-Film: Mit schamhaften Verschweigen ist nichts getan," *Vorwärts*, May 8, 1959; and Paul Fr. Weber, "Hunde, wollt ihr ewig leben?" *Frankfurter Nachtausgabe*, April 23, 1959.

66 "So ging die 6. Armee zugrunde."

67 "Stalingrad auf Leinwand," *Christ und Welt*, April 16, 1959.

68 Review by Heinz Linnerz, *Hamburger Abendblatt*, April 18, 1959.

69 Adenauer's remarks to the Bundestag are republished in *Deutschlands Weg nach Israel: Eine Dokumentation mit einem Geleitwort von Konrad Adenauer*, ed. Rolf Vogel (Stuttgart, 1967), p. 36.

70 Wisbar's formulation, quoted in "Keine Zeit für Heldentum," *Westfälische Rundschau*, March 19, 1959.

71 Harold Marcuse, *Legacies of Dachau: The Uses and Abuses of a Concentration Camp, 1933–2001* (Cambridge, 2001); Harold Marcuse, "The Revival of Holocaust Awareness in West Germany, Israel, and the United

States," in *1968: The World Transformed*, ed. Carole Fink, Philipp Gassert, and Detlef Junker (New York, 1998), pp. 421–38; and Alvin H. Rosenfeld, "Popularization and Memory: The Case of Anne Frank," in *Lessons and Legacies: The Meaning of the Holocaust in a Changing World*, ed. Peter Hayes (Evanston, Ill., 1991), pp. 243–78.

72 Werner Bergmann, "Antisemitismus als politisches Ereignis," in *Antisemitismus in der politischen Kultur nach 1945*, ed. Werner Bergmann and Rainer Erb (Opladen, 1990), pp. 253–75, particularly pp. 254–55; Hans Gathmann, "Der latente Antisemitismus: Prozesse und Fälle in der Bundesrepublik," *Politische Meinung* 4 (1961): pp. 61–72; and Klaus Harpprecht, "Im Keller der Gefühle: Gibt es noch einen deutschen Antisemitismus?" *Der Monat* 11 (1958/59): 13–20.

73 Marcuse, *Legacies of Dachau*, pp. 206–210; see also *KZ-Verbrechen vor deutschen Gerichten: Dokumente aus den Prozesssen gegen Sommer (KZ Buchenwald), Sorge, Schubert (KZ Sachsenhausen), Unkelbach (Ghetto in Czenstochau)*, ed. H.G. van Dam and Ralph Giordano (Frankfurt am Main, 1962), pp. 152–510; Reinhard Henkys, *Die nationalsozialistischen Gewaltverbrechen: Geschichte und Gericht* (Stuttgart, 1964), pp. 55–58; *Narben, Spuren, Zeugen: 15 Jahre Allgemeine Wochzeitung der Juden in Deutschland*, ed. Ralph Giordano (Düsseldorf, 1961), pp. 394–413; also Brochhagen, *Nach Nürnberg*, p. 250.

74 Quotation from "Heimkehrer ohne Namen," *General-Anzeiger für Bonn und Umgegend*, January 16, 1956; also Hans Ulrich Kersten, "Heimkehr ins Gefängnis: SED-Propaganda auf Hochtouren—Sühne ohne Schuldbeweis," *Bremer Nachrichten*, December 21, 1955. In general, on the reception of returning POWs in East and West, see Frank Biess's excellent study *The Protracted War: Returning POWs and the Making of East and West German Citizens, 1945–1955* (Ph.D. diss. Brown University, 2000); also Moeller, *War Stories*, 88–122.

75 "Ein deutsches Requiem," *Telegraf*, May 7, 1959.

76 Wilfried von Bredow, "Filmpropaganda für Wehrbereitschaft: Kriegsfilme in der Bundesrepublik," in *Film und Gesellschaft in Deutschland: Dokumente und Materialien*, ed. Wilfried von Bredow and Rolf Zurek (Hamburg, 1975), pp. 316–26; Westermann, 30–95.

77 Erich Kuby, *Mein ärgerliches Vaterland* (Munich, 1989), p. 210; see also Irmgard Wilharm, "Krieg in den deutschen Nachkriegsspielfilmen," in *Lernen aus dem Krieg? Deutsche Nachkriegszeiten 1918 und 1945*, ed. Gottfried Niedhart and Dieter Riesenberger (Munich, 1992), pp. 281–99; and Bredow, "Filmpropaganda."

78 Kuby, *Mein ärgerliches Vaterland*, p. 210.

79 Large, p. 189, citing Adelbert Weinstein, *Armee ohne Pathos: Die deutsche Wiederbewaffnung im Urteil ehemaliger Soldaten* (Bonn, 1951).

80 My thought on these subjects is particularly influenced by Anton Kaes,

From Hitler to Heimat: The Return of History as Film (Cambridge, Mass., 1989).

81 See Carp, *Kreigsgeschichten.*

82 Alexander Kluge, *Die Patriotin: Texte/Bilder 1–6* (Frankfurt am Main, 1979), p. 59. See also Alexander Kluge, *The Battle,* trans. Leila Vennewitz (New York, 1967), a translation of the 1964 version of *Schlachtbeschreibung.* See also Carp, *Kriegsgeschichten.*

83 Kluge, *Die Patriotin,* pp. 54–58. See also "Herrlicher Quatsch," *Der Spiegel,* December 17, 1979; Volker Bauer, "Das Knie und die Weltgeschichte," *Der Tagesspiegel,* December 21, 1979; Wolfram Schütte, "Lichte Tiefen auf Bohrgelände," *Frankfurter Rundschau,* December 9, 1979; and H. G. Pflaum, "Das Knie des Obergefreiten Wieland," *Süddeutsche Zeitung,* December 15, 1979.

84 Wolfgang Borchert, *The Man Outside: Prose Works of Wolfgang Borchert,* trans. David Porter, intro. by Stephen Spender (Norfolk, Conn., 1952), pp. 77–78. A paperback edition was published by Rowohlt in 1956. By 1957, it was in a third printing and 100,000 copies were in circulation. By 1970, the number was 878,000. Wolfgang Borchert, *Draussen vor der Tür und ausgewählte Erzählungen* (1956; reprint, Hamburg, 1970).

85 Kaes, p. 133; Marcuse, "The Revival of Holocaust Awareness," p. 422; see also Omer Bartov, *Murder in Our Midst: The Holocaust, Industrial Killing, and Representation,* pp. 139–52; and the otherwise highly favorable reflections of Stefanie Carp, "Schlachtbeschreibungen: Ein Blick auf Walter Kempowski und Alexander Kluge," in Herr and Naumann, *Vernichtungskrieg,* p. 677.

86 See the review by Kenneth Turan, *Los Angeles Times,* April 26, 1996. See also Louis Menashe, "Stalingrad," *Cineaste* 23 (1997): 50–51; Stanley Kaufmann, "Stalingrad," *New Republic,* June 5, 1995, 32–33; and Julian Graffy, "Stalingrad," *Sight and Sound* 4 (1994): 55–56.

87 "Remarks of President Ronald Reagan to Regional Editors, White House, April 18, 1985," in *Bitburg in Moral and Political Perspective,* p. 240.

88 Andreas Hillgruber, *Zweierlei Untergang: Die Zerschlagung des Deutschen Reiches und das Ende des europäischen Judentums* (Berlin, 1986).

89 Stephen Kinzer, "The War Memorial: To Embrace the Guilty, Too?" *New York Times,* November 15, 1993; *Im Irrgarten deutscher Geschichte: Die neue Wache 1818 bis 1993,* eds. Daniela Büchten and Anja Frey (Berlin, 1993); Peter Reichel, *Politik mit der Erinnerung: Gedächtnisorte im Streit um die nationalsozialistische Vergangenheit* (Munich, 1995), pp. 231–46; and Mariatte C. Denman, "Visualizing the Nation: Madonnas and Mourning Mothers in Postwar Germany," in *Gender and Germanness: Cultural Production of Nation,* ed. Patricia Herminghouse and Magda Mueller (Providence, R.I., 1997), pp. 189–201.

90 Andreas Kilb, "Warten, bis Spielberg kommt," *Die Zeit,* January 28, 1994;

and on the continuing difficulties of balancing German and Soviet losses, Timothy W. Ryback, "Stalingrad: Letters from the Dead," *New Yorker*, February 1, 1993, 58–71.

91 Bernd Boll and Hans Safrian, "Auf dem Weg nach Stalingrad: Die 6. Armee 1941/42," in *Vernichtungskrieg*, pp. 262–63.

92 Bogdan Musial, "Bilder einer Ausstellung: Kritische Anmerkungen zur Wanderausstellung 'Vernichtungskrieg: Verbrechen der Wehrmacht 1941 bis 1944,' " *Vierteljahrshefte für Zeitgeschichte* 47 (1999): 563–91.

93 In general, see Moeller, *War Stories*; also Gabriele Rosenthal, "Vom Krieg erzählen, von den Verbrechen schweigen," in *Vernichtungskrieg*, pp. 651–63.

94 Alexander and Margarete Mitscherlich, *Die Unfähigkeit zu trauern: Grundlagen kollektiven Verhaltens* (Munich, 1967), p. 19. See also Hartmut Berghoff, "Zwischen Verdrändung und Aufarbeitung," *Geschichte in Wissenschaft und Unterricht* 49 (1998): 96–114; and Eric L. Santner, *Stranded Objects: Mourning, Memory, and Film in Postwar Germany* (Ithaca, N.Y., 1990), pp. 1–6.

95 Hermann Lübbe, "Der Nationalsozialismus im politischen Bewusstsein der Gegenwart," in *Deutschlands Weg in die Diktatur: Internationale Konferenz zur nationalsozialistischen Machtübernahme im Reichstagsgebäude zu Berlin*, ed. Martin Broszat (Berlin, 1983), pp. 329–49, esp. pp. 334–35.

96 Jeffrey Herf, *Divided Memory: The Nazi Past in the Two Germanys* (Cambridge, Mass, 1997), p. 225. My thoughts on this topic have been greatly influenced by discussions with Frank Biess. See Biess's insightful review of Herf's book in *German Politics and Society* 17 (1999): 144–51.

97 Here my analysis diverges from the thoughtful comments of Michael Geyer, "The Place of the Second World War in German Memory and History," *New German Critique* 71 (1997): 17.

98 Iwona Irwin-Zarecka, *Frames of Remembrance: The Dynamics of Collective Memory* (New Brunswick, N.J., 1994), pp. 47–65. See also Ulrich Herbert, " 'Die guten und die schlechten Zeiten': Überlegungen zur diachronen Analyse lebensgeschichtlicher Interviews," in *"Die Jahre weiss man nicht, wo man die heute hinsetzen soll": Faschismus-Erfahrungen im Ruhrgebiet*, ed. Lutz Niethammer (Berlin, 1983), pp. 67–96; and Gabriele Rosenthal, "Vom Krieg erzählen," pp. 651–63.

99 See, e.g., Dubiel, *Niemand ist frei von der Geschichte*, pp. 22–33.

100 Vasily Grossman, "The Murder of Jews in Berdichev," in *The Black Book: The Ruthless Murder of Jews by German Fascist Invaders throughout the Temporarily Occupied Regions of the Soviet Union and in the Death Camps of Poland during the War of 1941–1945*, ed. Ilya Ehrenburg and Vasily Grossman, trans. John Glad and James S. Levine (New York, 1981), pp. 13–24.

101 John Garrard and Carol Garrard, *The Bones of Berdichev: The Life and Fate of Vasily Grossman* (New York, 1996), pp. 5–6, 20–21, 30, 229–62; Frank Ellis, *Vasily Grossman: The Genesis and Evolution of a Russian Heretic* (Oxford, 1994), pp. 10–16; and Vasily Grossman, *Life and Fate: A Novel*, trans. Robert Chandler (New York, 1985).

102 Jürgen Habermas, "A Kind of Settlement of Damages (Apologetic Tendencies)," *New German Critique* 44 (1988): 26.

103 Hettling, "Täter und Opfer?" Beevor's book offers a starting point for such an account.

104 See also Helmut Kohl, "Jedem einzelnen Schicksal schulden wir Achtung," *Frankfurter Allgemeine Zeitung*, May 6, 1995.

105 See *Geschichtswissenschaft und Öffentlichkeit: Der Streit um Daniel J. Goldhagen*, eds. Johannes Heil and Rainer Erb (Frankfurt am Main, 1998); *The "Goldhagen Effect": History, Memory, Nazism—Facing the German Past*, ed. Geoff Eley (Ann Arbor, Mich. 2000); and *Unwilling Germans: The Goldhagen Debate*, Robert R. Shandley, ed., and trans. by Jeremiah Riemer (Minneapolis, 1998).

106 Stephen Kinzer, "Germans More Willing to Confront Nazi Crimes," *New York Times*, May 1, 1995; and "Lust am Erinnern," *Der Spiegel*, April 24, 1995, 18–21. In general, see the interesting analysis of press accounts in Klaus Naumann, *Der Krieg als Text: Das Jahr 1945 im kulturellen Gedächtnis der Presse* (Hamburg, 1998).

107 Ryback, "Stalingrad: Letters from the Dead."

When Memory Counts: War, Genocide, and Postwar Soviet Jewry

1 On the impact of the war on Soviet purification campaigns, see Amir Weiner, *Making Sense of War: The Second World War and the Fate of the Bolshevik Revolution* (Princeton, N.J., 2000), pp. 21–39, 129–90.

2 Yehoshua A. Gilboa, *The Black Years of Soviet Jewry, 1939–1953* (Boston, 1971), p. 88.

3 Partiinyi arkhiv Vinnyts'koi oblasti (PAVO), f.136, op. 13, d. 186, II. 224, 228–31, 236–39.

4 Tsentral'nyi derzhavnyi arkhiv hromads'kykh ob'iednan Ukrainy (TsDA-HOU), f.1, op. 23, d. 2366, II. 25, 27–28.

5 Vasilii Grossman, *Zhizn' i sud'ba* (Moscow, 1988), pp. 542–43. In his letter to Khrushchev on February 23, 1962, pleading for the publication of his novel, Grossman noted that he had started writing it during Stalin's life. [*Istochnik* 3 (1997): 133.]

6 Stanislaw Kot, *Conversations with the Kremlin and Dispatches from Russia* (Oxford, 1963), p. 153; Wladyslaw Anders, *Bez ostatniego rozdzialu: wspomnenia z lat 1939–1946* (Newtown, Wales, 1950), pp. 118, 124–25.

7 "Do kantsa razgromit kosmopolitov-antipatriotov!" *Pravda Ukrainy*,

March 6, 1949; "Bezridni kosmopolity—nailiutishi vorohy radians'koi kul'tury," *Naddnistrians'ka zirka*, March 27, 1949.

8 Vasilii Ardamatskii, "Pinia iz Zhmerinki," *Krokodil* 8 (March 20, 1953): 13.

9 In his memoirs, Aleksandr Nekrich claimed that he knew "for certain" of a brochure written by Dmitrii Chesnokov explaining the need for deporting the Jews. The brochure was ready for distribution when Stalin died. Nekrich, *Otreshis ot strakha: Vospominaniia istorika* (London, 1979), p. 114. Nekrich's allegation was recently corroborated by Iakov Etinger, a former professor at the Institute of World Economics and International Relations at the Russian Academy of Sciences. According to Etinger, the book by Chesnokov argued that the Jews proved to be "unreceptive" to socialism. Iakov Etinger, "The Doctors' Plot: Stalin's Solution to the Jewish Question," in Yaacov Ro'i, ed., *Jews and Jewish Life in Russia and the Soviet Union* (Portland, 1995), p. 118. Throughout the Soviet Union, the secret police recorded the private conversations of both Jewish and non-Jewish citizens in which the deportation of the Jews was accepted as a fait accompli. See the documents assembled by Mordechai Altschuler, "More about Public Reaction to the Doctors' Plot," *Jews in Eastern Europe* (Fall 1996): 34, 45, 52, 55, 56–57.

10 *Komsomol'skaia pravda*, February 15, 1953.

11 Joseph B. Schechtman, *Star in Eclipse* (New York, 1961), p. 81. According to Benjamin Pinkus, this statement was authenticated by Jewish immigrants to Israel who held important posts in the Polish Communist Party and government. [Pinkus, *The Soviet Government and the Jews 1948–1967: A Documented Study* (Cambridge, Eng., 1984), 487, n. 38.]

12 *Istochnik* 3 (1994): 97–98.

13 Trohym Kychko, *Iudaizm bez prikras* (Kiev, 1963), pp. 160–61, 164–66. The book appeared in mass publication (12,000 copies) and was endorsed by the Academy of Sciences of the Soviet Ukrainian Republic. Worst of all, such accusations came from one whose own wartime record was marred by allegations of collaboration. In his memoirs, the emigré journalist Leonid Vladimirov tells of his shock when he learned about the content of Kychko's book and the fact that a person accused of collaboration with the Germans rose to such academic status. When Vladimirov asked a friend, a prominent author in Kiev, the latter told him that the "colorful past of the rogue Kychko was well known in Kiev to all the proper people. However, there are services in Russia for which even collaborators are pardoned. Kychko understood this well, and already long ago, immediately after the war, 'devoted himself' to anti-Semitic scientific research." Leonid Vladimirov, *Rossiia bez prikras i umoichanii*, (Frankfurt am Main, 1973), pp. 279–81. The fact that the Kychko affair was not accidental was demonstrated by the belated Soviet reaction after the public storm had subsided. In 1968 the Supreme Soviet of the Ukraine awarded Kychko the Diploma

of Honor "for his work on atheist propaganda," which followed the earlier reward of the Order of Lenin. Nora Levin, *The Jews in the Soviet Union Since 1917: The Paradox of Survival* (New York, 1988), vol. 2, p. 621; Moshe Decter, "Judaism without Embellishment," in Ronald Rubin, ed., *The Unredeemed: Anti-Semitism in the Soviet Union* (Chicago, 1968), p. 135.

14 Weiner, *Making Sense of War*, pp. 201–2.

15 "Zakliuchitel'noe slovo tovarishcha Stalina na plenume TsK VKP (b) 5 marta 1937 g.," *Bol'shevik* 7 (1937): 19.

16 "Rech' I.V. Stalina v Narkomate oborony, 2 iiunia 1937 g.," *Istochnik* 3 (1994): 73–74, italics added. In this light, and without underestimating Stalin's anti-Semitism, Lenin could be recognized as a scion of the aristocracy but not as the grandson of the Jew Moishe Itskovich Blank. When Lenin's eldest sister, Anna Elizarova, reminded Stalin in 1932–33 of their grandfather's Jewishness, her reasons ran against the grain of the Marxist ethos. Lenin's Jewish origins "are further confirmation of the exceptional abilities of the Semitic tribe," she wrote Stalin in 1932. In another letter, a year later, Anna wrote Stalin that "in the Lenin Institute, as well as in the Institute of the Brain . . . they have long recognized the gifts of this nation and the extremely beneficial effects of its blood on mixed marriages." Stalin's refusal to publish a word about the matter became the rule for years to come. Dmitrii Volkogonov, *Lenin* (New York, 1994), pp. 8–9.

17 Alexis Carell, *Man the Unknown* (London, 1935), pp. 318–19. On the wide approval of the sterilization of the mentally ill in interwar Europe and the United States, see Henry Friedlander, *The Origins of the Nazi Genocide: From Euthanasia to the Final Solution* (Chapel Hill, 1995), pp. 7–9.

18 Michael Burleigh, *Death and Deliverance: "Euthanasia" in Germany 1900–1945* (Cambridge, Eng., 1994); Friedlander, *The Origins of Nazi Genocide*. There was, however, a single incident that accentuated the rule. In early 1938, about 170 invalid prisoners in the Moscow oblast, who had already been tried and convicted for petty crimes such as theft and vagrancy, were tried again for the same charges, only this time they were sentenced to death. The operation was run by a special troika of the Moscow NKVD (the body that reviewed cases and passed sentences during the Terror). The idea behind the execution was to make room for the arrival of deported Germans, Poles, Latvians, and other ethnic groups. The chairman of the troika, Mikhail Ilich Semenov, was himself tried and executed in the summer of 1939. *Soprotivlenie v Gulage; Vospominaniia. Pis'ma. Dokumenty* (Moscow, 1992), pp. 114–27.

19 Ironically, Grossman, who insisted on the similarity of the Soviet and Nazi polities, was also the first observer to recognize that "conveyor belt execution" was the distinguishing feature of Nazi exterminatory practices. See

his description of Treblinka in Vasilii Grossman and Il'ia Ehrenburg, eds., *Hasefer Hashahor* (The black book) (Tel Aviv, 1991), pp. 495–515, esp. p. 507.

20 Mark B. Adams, "Eugenics in Russia, 1900–1940," in Adams, ed., *The Wellborn Science: Eugenics in Germany, France, Brazil, and Russia* (New York, 1990), pp. 194–95.

21 Georgio Agamben, *Homo Sacer: Sovereign Power and Bare Life* (Stanford, Calif., 1998), pp. 114, 146–47. In this sense, Saul Friedländer's recent introduction of "redemptive anti-Semitism" as the guiding logic of Nazi attitudes toward the Jews requires some modification. Redemption implies a linear concept of historical time and a certain finality, alien both to the Nazis' nihilistic violence and their cyclical view of history, one filled with nightmares of a possible defeat at the hands of the Jews. Saul Friedländer, *Nazi Germany and the Jews*, vol. 1, *The Years of Persecution, 1933–1939* (New York, 1997), pp. 73–112. For a lucid analysis of the place of the Jew within the Nazi racial hierarchy in theory and practice see John Connelly, "Nazis and Slavs: From Racial Theory to Racial Practice," *Central European History* 32, no. 1 (1999): 1–33.

22 A rare admission by a Soviet official of a de facto *numerus clausus* for Jews was offered by Ekaterina Furtseva, a Central Committee Secretary, during an interview with the *National Guardian*, June 25, 1956. "The government had found in some of its departments a heavy concentration of Jewish people, upwards of 50 percent of the staff," said Furtseva. "Steps were taken to transfer them to other enterprises, giving them equally good positions and without jeopardizing their rights." These steps were misinterpreted as anti-Semitic, Furtseva told the interviewer. Pinkus, *The Soviet Government and the Jews*, pp. 58–59.

23 Eventually, the Soviets and their allies succeeded in omitting the category of political groups from the draft, in a deviation from an earlier resolution of the General Assembly. Nehemiah Robinson, *The Genocide Convention: Its Origins and Interpretation* (New York, 1949), p. 15.

24 Aron Naumovich Trainin, "Bor'ba s genotsidom kak mezhdunarodnym prestupleniem," *Sovetskoe gosudarstvo i pravo* 5 (May 1948): 4, 6. The official amendment offered by the Soviet delegation called for the extension of the definition of genocide to "national-cultural genocide," which included "a) ban on or limitation of the use of national language in public and private life; ban on instruction in the national language in schools; b) the liquidation or ban on printing and distribution of books and other publications in national languages; c) the liquidation of historical or religious monuments, museums, libraries and other monuments and objects of national culture (or religious) cult" (ibid., p. 14).

25 For a stimulating discussion of this duality in Soviet nationality policy, see Yuri Slezkine, "The USSR as a Communal Apartment, or How a Socialist

State Promoted Ethnic Particularism," *Slavic Review* 53 (Summer 1994): 414–52.

26 Gosudarstvennyi arkhiv Rossiiskoi Federatsii (GARF), f. 9414, op. 4, d. 145, II. 11–12b.

27 Anatoly Shcharansky, *Fear No Evil* (New York, 1988), pp. 10–11.

28 *Eynikayt*, March 15, 1943.

29 Mordechai Altshuler, "Antisemitism in Ukraine toward the End of the Second World War," *Jews in Eastern Europe* 3 (Winter 1993): 49–50, n. 29.

30 "Druzhba narodov SSSR—moguchii faktor pobedy nad vragom," *Bol'shevik* 23–24 (December 1944): 6. Overall, 160,722 Jews won military awards, the fourth largest group to do so, after the Russians, Ukrainians, and Belorussians. These figures should be compared with the data from the 1939 population census that placed the Jews as the seventh largest ethnic group in the Soviet Union. Yossef Guri, "Yehudei Brit-Hamoatsot Bamilhama Neged Hanazim," in *Lohamin Yehudim Bamilhama neged Hanazim* (Tel Aviv, 1971), p. 41.

31 Some cases indicated that this phenomenon was helped by Jews' own internalization of traditional stereotypes. "True, in my unit they did not know that I was a Jew. I am strong and tall, a worker," wrote Mikhail Shakerman to Ehrenburg and Khrushchev. PAVO, f. 136, op. 13, d. 184, I. 93.

32 Hersh Smolar, *Vu Bistu Haver Sidorov?* (Tel Aviv, 1975), pp. 257–58.

33 Mordechai Altshuler, "Escape and Evacuation of Soviet Jews at the Time of the Nazi Invasion: Policies and Realities," in Lucjan Dobroszycki and Jeffrey S. Gurock, eds., *The Holocaust in the Soviet Union: Studies and Sources on the Destruction of the Jews in the Nazi-Occupied Territories of the USSR, 1941–1945* (New York, 1993), pp. 77–104.

34 Yad Vashem Archive (YVA), the testimony of Zalman Teitelman, #03-3446, p. 20.

35 Raymond Arthur Davies, *Odyssey Through Hell* (New York, 1946), pp. 206–7.

36 TsDAHOU, f. 1, op. 23, d. 2366, II. 23–24.

37 Significantly, Kipnis did not include this paragraph in a shorter version of the story, which he published in June 1945 in Kiev under the title *Libshaft*.

38 Kipnis was subjected to harsh criticism for the blasphemous idea of placing the Star of David, the Zionist symbol, side by side with the Soviet star, an "idea that is incompatible for a Soviet writer," as the secretary of the Ukrainian Union of Writers concluded. *Literaturna Hazeta*, September 25, 1947; Haim Loytsker, "Far ideyisher reynkeyt fun undzer literatur," *Der Shtern* (Kiev, 1948): 105–12. Kipnis's writings appeared to embody the dual sin of the Jewish subversion of the Soviet myth of the war, namely Jewish particularistic heroism and suffering. This could be traced back to his writings in the 1920s. In 1926 Kipnis published a novel, *Khadoshim un teg* (Months and Days), that focused on the recent pogroms in the

Ukraine, a fact that was not lost upon Loytsker. "Kipnis, so it turns out, has not forgotten his former *Khadoshim un teg*, although many years have passed. And he has learnt nothing in all these years of Soviet rule," exclaimed Loytsker. [Here, 112.]

39 Notebooks, Entrance on November 30, 1945 in Marco Carrynyk, ed., *Alexander Dovzhenko: The Poet as Filmmaker* (Cambridge, Mass., 1973), p. 137.

40 Il'ia Ehrenburg, *Sobranie Sochineniia*, (*Liudi, Gody, Zhizn'*), vol. 9 (Moscow, 1967), p. 377.

41 TsDAHOU, f. 1, op. 23, d. 3851, ll. 3–5.

42 See, for example, the report by the Vinnytsia region branch of the committee in Tsentral'nyi derzhavnyi arkhiv vyshchykh orhaniv vlady ta upravlinnia Ukrainy (TsDAVOVU) f. 4620, op. 3, d. 253.

43 TsDAHOU, f. 1, op. 23, d. 2366, l. 26.

44 *Ibid.*, l. 16.

45 YVA, the testimony of Hanna Schwartzman, #03–6401, pp. 15–16.

46 Abraham Sutzkever, "Il'ia Ehrenburg (A Kapital Zikhronot fon di Yaren 1944–1946)," *Di Goldene Keit* 61 (1967): 30.

47 Grossman and Ehrenburg, *Hasefer Hashahor*, p. 17.

48 Bossiiskii gosudarstvennyi arkhiv sotsial'no-politicheskoi istorii (RGASPI), f. 17, op. 125, r. 1442, d. 438, l. 216.

49 Vasilii Grossman, "Ukraina bez evreev," in Shimon Markish, *Vasilii Grossman. Na evreiskie temy*, vol. 2 (Jerusalem, 1985), pp. 333–40; here, pp. 334–35. This is a translation back to Russian of the Yiddish version, which appeared in *Eynikayt*, November 25 and December 2, 1943. The original version in the Russian language was apparently rejected by *Krasnaia zvezda*.

50 PAVO, f. 136, op. 13, d. 208, ll. 1–7. On the migration to Birobidzhan, see GARF, f. 814, op. 1, d. 8, l. 59; and Pinkus, *Soviet Government and the Jews*, 378. One may recall Khrushchev's alleged retort a few years earlier that "it would be advisable for Ukrainian Jews who have survived Nazi extermination not to return to the Ukraine. They would do better in Birobidzhan." Leon Leneman, *La Tragedie des juifs en URSS* (Paris, 1959), pp. 178–79.

51 Vsevolod Kochefov, *Zhurbiny* (Leningrad, 1952), pp. 225, 328–29, 335, 347, 349–50. The first edition of *Zhurbiny* alone enjoyed a circulation of 45,000 and was supplemented by subsequent editions.

52 See Pieter Lagrou, "Victims of Genocide and National Memory: Belgium, France and the Netherlands 1945–1965," *Past & Present* 154 (February 1997): 191–222.

53 Omer Bartov, "Defining Enemies, Making Victims: Germans, Jews, and the Holocaust," *American Historical Review* 103 (June 1998): 771–816; Tom Segev, *The Seventh Million: The Israelis and the Holocaust* (New

York, 1993); James Young, *The Texture of Memory: Holocaust Memorials and Meaning* (New Haven, Conn., 1993), part 3; Yael Zerubavel, *Recovered Roots: Collective Memory and the Making of Israeli National Tradition* (Chicago, 1995).

54 Leon Leneman, *La tragedie des Juifs en U.R.S.S.*, p. 179.

55 For the shift in Western European discourse on the Holocaust in the mid-1960s see Lagrou, "Victims of Genocide," pp. 215–20.

56 For the decree of August 28, 1964, by the Presidium of the Supreme Soviet, see *Tak Eto Bylo* 1993, vol. 1, pp. 246–47.

57 The rehabilitation was enacted in two resolutions of the Presidium of the Supreme Soviet, December 6, 1963, and April 29, 1964. GARF, f. 7523, op. 109, d. 195, II. 38–39.

58 Porfirii Gavrutto [Porfyrii Havrutto], *Tuchi nad gorodom* (Moscow, 1968), 165–66. For an extensive documentation of the affair, including Khrushchev's speech and the rebuttal by Moisei Kogan, the falsely accused Jew, see Pinkus, *Soviet Government and the Jews*, pp. 76, 127–33, 493, nn. 113–14.

59 Svetlana Allilueva, *Only One Year* (New York, 1969), pp. 153. Ironically, this was also the view in Berlin in early 1937. "Again, a show trial in Moscow," Goebbels noted in his diary on January 25, 1937. "This time again exclusively against Jews. Radek, etc. The Führer still in doubt whether there isn't after all a hidden anti-Semitic tendency. Maybe Stalin does want to smoke the Jews out. The military is also supposedly strongly anti-Semitic." Cited in Friedländer, *Nazi Germany and the Jews*, pp. 185–86.

60 Iurii Larin, *Evrei i antisemitizm v SSSR* (Moscow, 1929), 241–44; PAVO, f. 136, op. 1, d. 96, II. 25–26; op. 3, d. 219, I. 26.

61 TsDAHOU, f. 57, op. 4, d. 356, I. 186.

62 TsDAHOU, f. 1, op. 23, d. 1385, II. 4–5.

63 Anastas Mikoyan, *Tak bylo: razmyshleniia o minuvshem* (Moscow, 1999), p. 514.

64 Altshuler, "More About Public Reaction to the Doctors' Plot," pp. 29, 39–40, 45, 56–57.

65 *Ibid.*, p. 33.

66 Aleksandr Lokshin, "Delo vrachei": "otkliki trudiashchikhsia," *Vestnik evreiskogo universiteta v Moskve* 1, no. 5 (1994): 56–62.

"An Aptitude for Being Unloved": War and Memory in Japan

1 Watanabe Kazuo, *Haisen Nikki* (Diary of defeat), ed. Kushida Magoichi and Ninomiya Atsushi (Tokyo: Hakubunkan Shinsha, 1995), pp. 36–38, 56–58, 77. The passage in question appeared in Romain Rolland's *Au-dessus de la melée*, and the original German phrase that Rolland

quoted and Watanabe rendered as "aptitude for being unloved" (*aisareenu nōryoku; aisarenai nōryoku*) was *Unbeliebtheit*. The 1946 essay is reprinted in *ibid.*, pp. 143–48. In 1970, Watanabe added a very brief "postscript" to this essay expressing concern that Japanese pride in emerging as an industrial power was but one more reflection of the superficiality that caused his compatriots to be so unloved.

2 By "Germany," I refer primarily to the former "West Germany" here.

3 High Japanese government officials have in fact made numerous public statements of "regret" and "apology" concerning imperial Japan's acts of colonialism (especially in Korea) and belligerency and atrocity in World War II. Some of these statements have been quite forthright, but few have attracted widespread media attention outside of Japan. None has been praised for being a statesman-like, *emblematic* utterance comparable to the famous speech delivered by Germany's former president Richard von Weizsacker on May 8, 1985, the fortieth anniversary of Germany's surrender. It is noteworthy, and hardly a coincidence, that the two most unequivocal statements acknowledging Japan's war responsibility were delivered by prime ministers who headed short-lived coalition cabinets and were not affiliated with the Liberal Democratic Party: Hosokawa Morihiro in 1993 and Murayama Tomiichi on the occasion of the fiftieth anniversary of the end of the war in 1995. For a detailed critical summary of official Japanese statements on the war, see Wakamiya Yoshibumi, *The Postwar Conservative View of Asia: How the Political Right Has Delayed Japan's Coming to Terms with Its History of Aggression in Asia* (Tokyo, 1998). Wakamiya is an editor at the *Asahi* newspaper, and this volume is a translation of his 1995 book *Sengo Hoshu no Ajia Kan*. Ian Buruma offers a comparative study of German and Japanese recollections of the war in *The Wages of Guilt: Memories of War in Germany and Japan* (New York, 1994). See also Thomas U. Berger, *Cultures of Antimilitarism: National Security in Germany and Japan* (Baltimore, 1998). For a comparative study focusing on textbooks, see Laura Hein and Mark Selden, eds., *Censoring History: Citizenship and Memory in Japan, Germany, and the United States* (Armonk, N.Y., 2000). The issue of massaging official statements of apology for the war so as not to besmirch the memory of Japan's own war dead emerged vividly in 1995, when the Diet debated (and watered down) a formal statement on the fiftieth anniversary of the end of the war. For a selection of translated documents from this debate, see John W. Dower, "Japan Addresses Its War Responsibility," *ii: The Journal of the International Institute* (newsletter of the International Institute, University of Michigan) 3.1 (Autumn 1995), 8–11.

4 Mori was forced to step down as party head and prime minister in April 2001, after merely a year in office. The manner in which his "land of the gods" comment triggered a critical public debate on national identity is ex-

emplified by a series of guest essays initiated in August 2000 in the influential daily newspaper *Asahi Shimbun* under the topical title "Land of the Gods, Land of the People" (*Kami no Kuni, Hito no Kuni*). The general thrust of the series was to demonstrate in detail how reactionary and anachronistic Mori's rhetoric was. At the same time, however, non-Japanese—and Americans in particular—should keep in mind how *typical* Mori's rhetoric is of conservative nationalism in general. To give but one recent example, in the U.S. presidential campaign of 2000, the Democratic vice-presidential candidate called the United States "the most religious country in the world" and spoke of all Americans as being "children of the same awesome God," while the Republican presidential candidate was proclaiming that "Our nation is chosen by God and commissioned by history to be a model to the world of justice and inclusion and diversity without division," (*New York Times*, August 29, 2000).

5 The *Yomiuri* poll, based on a random sample of 3,000 individuals, was published on October 5, 1993, and is reproduced in the October 1993 issue of the Japanese government publication *Japan Views* (p. 10). The full poll results are as follows:

WAS JAPAN AN 'AGGRESSOR'?

	Agree (%)	Disagree (%)	No Response (%)
TOTAL	53.1	24.8	22.1
Age over 70	41.1	39.5	19.5
60s	49.1	33.6	17.3
50s	48.4	27.6	24.0
40s	56.0	21.5	22.5
30s	57.4	15.4	27.3
20s	61.7	17.1	21.2

6 The "Carthage" quote appears in an essay by Namikawa Eita in Japanese Society for History Textbook Reform, *The Restoration of a National History: Why Was the Japanese Society for History Textbook Reform Established, and What Are Its Goals?* (Tokyo, 1998), p. 15. This pamphlet, published in English, was widely distributed among English-speaking Japan specialists. The society (whose slightly differently named Japanese parent group is the Atarashii Rekishi Kyōkasho o Tsukuru Kai) is one of two influential organizations founded in the mid-1990s by Fujioka Nobukatsu, a professor of education at the University of Tokyo. The other organization is the misleadingly named Liberal View of History Study Group (Jiyūshugi Shikan Kenkyūkai). Numerous books and countless articles have been promoted by these organizations, including a huge (775 pages) new "History of the Japanese People" (*Kokumin no Rekishi*) written

by Professor Nishio Kanji (a specialist in German literature at Electro-Communications University), and published in 1999 by Sankei Shimbunsha (publisher of the conservative national newspaper *Sankei*, a major mouthpiece for the revisionist position). Nishio's book became an immediate best-seller. For an incisive introduction to these groups and activities, see Gavan McCormack's essay on "The Japanese Movement to 'Correct' History" in Hein and Selden, op. cit.

7 These "typologies" are, of course, open-ended. Space permitting, it would have been fruitful to explore at least two other "kinds of memory" here. One is the manner in which "national memory" is *doubly* mediated and manipulated by others (how Chinese and Americans, for example, tend to set simplistic negative renderings of the situation in Japan against equally selective positive constructions of their own history and contemporary collective mind-set). The other might be called, in the Japanese case, "legally suffocated memory" (referring specifically to the manner in which official fears of costly lawsuits have prompted the Japanese government to dismiss current individual claims for redress and reparations). For a recent study of war memory sensitive to the approaches of contemporary critical theory, see Yoshiyuki Igarashi, *Bodies of Memory: Narratives of War in Postwar Japanese Culture, 1945–1970* (Princeton, N.J., 2000). I have addressed the multiple memories associated with just the atomic-bomb experience in "The Bombed: Hiroshimas and Nagasakis in Japanese Memory," *Diplomatic History* 19, no. 2 (Spring 1995): 275–95.

8 A high point in the revisionist campaign to promote a "correct" view of history occurred in early 2001, when the conservative activists succeeded in gaining certification of a middle-school history textbook reflecting their position. To gain such certification, the publisher and authors agreed to some 137 large and small changes. Among the more revealing of these was a passage in the epilogue that originally read as follows: "After the war (in which as many as 700,000 civilians were killed in indiscriminate bombing, culminating in the atomic bombs), the direction the country should take was determined by the Occupation force, and Japan has remained under this influence to the present day. . . . Regrettably, the scars of defeat have not healed after more than fifty years. Because of this, the Japanese are on the verge of losing their independent spirit." In the version approved by the central government, this was revised as follows: "As many as 700,000 civilians were killed in indiscriminate bombing, culminating in the atomic bombs. After the war, the Japanese people, through great effort, achieved economic recovery and attained a position among the world leaders, but in spite of this they still lack self-confidence. . . . Regrettably, the scars of defeat have not healed." The controversy concerning this textbook (and a companion "civics" volume) is covered in considerable detail in *Asahi Shimbun*, April 4, 2001.

9 I have discussed the problems of the Tokyo trial at length in chapter 15 of my *Embracing Defeat: Japan in the Wake of World War Two* (New York, 1999). The most dramatic recent use of Pal's dissenting opinion by the conservative revisionists took the form of a slick 1998 feature film titled *Pride: The Fatal Moment* (*Puraido: Unmei no Toki*). Conceived and promoted by prominent conservatives, and funded by a nationalistic entrepreneur, this was a courtroom drama that re-created the physical setting and *defense* arguments of the Tokyo trial with considerable skill. Although former general and prime minister Tōjō Hideki, the trial's best-known defendant, emerges as a flawed leader but humane and sincere victim of "victor's justice," the elegant and irreproachable hero of the film is Justice Pal himself. *Pride* is a dishonest film (its treatment of atrocities such as the Rape of Nanking, for example, is reprehensible), but its presentation of half-stories and half-truths is exceedingly clever.

10 "The Forgotten Holocaust of World War II" is the subtitle of Iris Chang's phenomenal international best-seller, *The Rape of Nanking* (New York, 1997). In Japan, such rhetoric and the broader flawed analogies that lie behind it (compounded by a number of petty factual errors in this particular case) has turned what could have been a persuasive indictment of Japanese war behavior into a perfect straw man for those who argue that Japan's critics have no interest in even getting the facts straight. Substantial rightwing money has been poured into attempts to counter Chang's indictment in English-language publications distributed gratis outside Japan. See, for example, Takemoto Tadao and Ohara Yasuo, *The Alleged 'Nanking Massacre': Japan's Rebuttal to China's Forged Claims* (Tokyo, 2000); Tanaka Masaaki, *What Really Happened in Nanking: The Refutation of a Common Myth* (Tokyo, 2000); and Hata Ikuhiko, "Nanking: Setting the Record Straight," *Japan Echo* 25, no. 4 (August 1998).

11 At the Tokyo tribunal, the prosecution calculated that a total of 9,348 U.S. and U.K. servicemen died at the hands of the Germans and Italians, out of a total of 235,473 prisoners. The corresponding figures given for the Pacific theater were 35,756 deaths out of 132,134 prisoners taken by the Japanese; see Dower, *Embracing Defeat*, 625 (n. 4). The official estimate of the number of Japanese prisoners who died in the hands of the Soviet Union is 55,000. Soviet sources, however, suggest that as many as 113,000 POWs may well have perished in the gulags between 1945 and 1956; see Philip West, Steven I. Levine, and Jackie Hiltz, eds., *America's Wars in Asia: A Cultural Approach to History and Memory* (Armonk, N.Y., 1998), p. 232. The Soviet Union was one of the eleven Allied nations represented on the bench at the Tokyo trial, having entered the war in Asia at the last moment, in violation of its neutrality pact with Japan. This (a perfect example of the "double standards" argument, since the Tokyo tribunal found Japan's leaders guilty of violating international agreements), *plus* atrocities

committed by the Soviet military against Japanese civilians and soldiers in Manchuria at the end of the war, *plus* the abusive years-long imprisonment of over a half million prisoners in Siberia, has understandably drawn particularly outraged attention from Japanese conservatives. The tactic of arguing that "nothing we may have done was as bad as the horrors perpetuated by the Soviets and Communists" is to be found, of course, among German conservatives as well.

12 It is impossible to give exact figures for Japanese fatalities in World War II (or, by the same token, for any other peoples or nations). The confusion of the times made precise enumeration difficult if not impossible. Beyond this, however, whole categories of deaths sometimes are excluded from conventional calculations. Estimates of the number of Japanese killed in the air raids and by the atomic bombs vary, for example, while figures for the number of civilians slaughtered in ferocious battles such as Saipan and, most devastatingly, Okinawa often are neglected. Little attention has been given to civilian deaths attributable to the collapse of the home front (such as more numerous deaths of mothers and infants in childbirth, as well as rising mortality from malnutrition, infectious diseases such as tuberculosis, etc.). War-related deaths that occurred after Japan's surrender are also difficult to tally. These would include prisoners who died in the hands of their captors (especially, but not exclusively, the Soviets), as well as those who died of war-related wounds or illness in the immediate or longer-term wake of the defeat. It would also include a truly forgotten category of Japanese war victims: the many tens of thousands of civilian men, women, and children who perished attempting to make their way home from Manchuria and other parts of China.

I attempted to examine the confusing available numbers in a 1986 publication; see Dower, *War Without Mercy: Race and Power in the Pacific War* (New York), 293–301. The most recent "official" estimate given by the Japanese is a total of 3.1 million war dead (2.3 million servicemen and 800,000 civilians); see *Asahi Shimbun*, August 16, 2000. The total number of U.S. fatalities from all theaters of World War II was roughly 400,000. The number of Chinese war dead was at least four or five times that of the Japanese, possibly more. The point to keep in mind where Japanese war memories are concerned, in any case, is not the precise number of deaths but rather the intimate impact of these large numbers in strengthening the "victim consciousness" of virtually all who survived.

13 At a very particular level of comparison, the "context-less" nature of the Vietnam War Memorial invites comparison to the atomic-bomb memorials in Hiroshima and Nagasaki. Until recently, visitors to the latter sites could be excused for emerging with the impression that the war began in August 1945 and consisted primarily of innocent Japanese being slaughtered with nuclear weapons. Non-Japanese commentators routinely dwell

on this as a typical example of Japan's peculiar "historical amnesia," when in fact it is better understood as being typical not of Japan but of victim consciousness more generally.

14 On the exclusion of Emperor Hirohito from war responsibility, see Dower, *Embracing Defeat*, chapters 9 through 11; also Herbert P. Bix, *Hirohito and the Making of Modern Japan* (New York, 2000) especially chapter 15. The deplorable cover-up of the activities of Unit 731 is addressed in depth in Peter Williams and David Wallace, *Unit 731: Japan's Secret Biological Warfare in World War II* (New York, 1989). The major research-based critical Japanese study of the *ianfu*, by Yoshimi Yoshiaki, is now available in English under the title *Comfort Women: Sexual Slavery in the Japanese Military During World War II* (New York, 2000). On chemical warfare, see Yuki Tanaka, "Poison Gas: The Story Japan Would Like to Forget," *Bulletin of the Atomic Scientists* (October 1988): 10–19.

15 The extraordinary American-Japanese collusion not only to keep the emperor out of the Tokyo trial, but also to ensure that no imputation whatsoever of his possible war responsibility be introduced into the proceedings, emerges vividly in the 1961 testimony given by Shiohara Tokisaburo, a former defense attorney at the trial, to representatives of Yasukuni Jinja, the shrine dedicated to the memory of those who died for the emperor. (The archival citation is "Kyokutō Kokusai Saiban Gunji Saiban kankei Chōshu Shiryō," in Shozō Inoue Tadao Shiryō, Yasukuni Kaikō Bunko, July 4, 1961. I am indebted to Professor Yoshida Yutaka for sharing a copy of this document, which was unknown to me when I wrote *Embracing Defeat*.)

The neo-nationalist "revisionists" who have so vigorously attacked "the Tokyo War Crimes Trial view of history" have been surprisingly reticent, to date, on the emperor issue—in sharp contrast to the more thuggish element in the Right. In some cases (such as the feature film mentioned in note 9), they have even used the emperor's exemption from the trials to *reinforce* their argument that defendants like Tōjō were not ultimately responsible for the crimes with which they were charged.

16 The transcript of the press conference appears in Takahashi Hiroshi, *Heika, Otazune Mōshiagemasu: Kisha Kaiken Zenkiroku to Ningen Tennō no Kiseki* (Tokyo: Bunshun Bunko, 1988), pp. 226–27. The *gengo* system, by which the years are measured in accordance with the reign of the emperor (1945 was thus "Shōwa 20"), is a modern practice, dating back only to the nineteenth century. Its political and ideological ramifications are particularly pernicious in the case of Hirohito's "Shōwa" era. Not only does this highlight Japan's emperor-centered "uniqueness" as the key to postwar and contemporary national identity. Simultaneously, it dilutes popular consciousness of the horrors of the 1930s and 1940s by essentially pouring these years into a larger brew of postwar peace and prosperity. The

"Shōwa Day" proposal was shelved following the adverse public reaction to Prime Minister Mori's definition of Japan as an "emperor-centered land of the gods." The Imperial Household Agency controls all private materials pertaining to Emperor Hirohito (and his predecessors), and vigilantly guards these against outside scrutiny. The general taboo on serious discussion of the emperor as a political actor while he was still living extended to withholding from publication personal accounts by persons who had been close to him.

17 For an overview of the claims for "individual" reparations from Japan that have proliferated since the mid 1990s, see Laura Hein, "Claiming Humanity and Legal Standing: Contemporary Demands for Redress from Japan for Its World War II Policies," in John Torpey, ed., *Politics and the Past: On Repairing Historical Injustices* (Lanham, Md., 2001).

18 If the phenomenon of "binational sanitizing of Japanese war crimes" were pursued in more detail, it undoubtedly would be found that Americans in general, at both official and media levels, became more critical of Japan's failure to address its "war responsibility" beginning in the early 1970s. The explanation for this seems obvious. This is when the exaggerated perception of Japan as an "economic superpower" threatening U.S. hegemony became voguish—and, with this, the resurrection of martial rhetoric and imagery (Japanese "treachery," "economic war," "a financial Pearl Harbor," etc.). Coincident with this, the reopening of U.S. relations with China—and the rather heady and uncritical Sinophilism that accompanied this—made it politically acceptable and even fashionable for Americans to once again think sympathetically about China and its "suffering."

19 For the constitutional debates at the start of the new century, see Glen D. Hook and Gavan McCormack, eds., *Japan's Contested Constitution* (London, 2001). I have tried to sketch out the broader milieu of postwar political and ideological contention—a topic that runs against the grain of popular stereotypes of Japan as a peculiarly harmonious and "consensual" society—in "Peace and Democracy in Two Systems: External Policy and Internal Conflict," in Andrew Gordon, ed., *Postwar Japan As History* (Berkeley, 1993), pp. 3–33.

20 The famous "Ienaga textbook case," involving a legal challenge to the Ministry of Education's certification process, was initiated in 1965 and dragged through the courts for some three decades. The case attracted a strong cadre of activist supporters, and the media publicity that accompanied the protracted process of appeal and reappeal made Ienaga's position far more widely known than would have been the case if his textbook had just been allowed to pass into the system of approved texts. For a recent intimate account, see Ienaga Saburo, *Japan's Past, Japan's Future: One Historian's Odyssey*, translated and introduced by Richard H. Minear (Lanham, Md., 2001).

21 The best English source on the security treaty struggle is George R. Packard III, *Protest in Tokyo: The Security Treaty Crisis of 1960* (Princeton, NJ., 1966).

22 These "New Left" protests are well treated in Thomas R. H. Havens, *Fire Across the Sea: The Vietnam War and Japan, 1965–1975* (Princeton, NJ., 1987).

23 For a belated English-language sample of popular writings on war crimes in China beginning in the early 1970s, see Honda Katsuichi, *The Nanjing Massacre: A Japanese Journalist Confronts Japan's National Shame* (Armonk, N.Y., 1999). Historians affiliated with Marxist-oriented research organizations such as the large and influential Rekishigaku Kenkyūkai turned attention to these issues soon after the defeat, and have consistently played an important role in uncovering basic archival materials. In 1993, these research activities were elevated to a new level with the establishment of Japan's War Responsibility Data Center (Nihon no Sensō Sekinin Shiryō Sentā), publisher of an invaluable quarterly titled *Sensō Sekinin Kenkyū* (The report on Japan's war responsibility).

24 Bix's study of Hirohito, cited in note 14, draws extensively on primary as well as secondary materials that became available after the emperor's death. It is perhaps a sign of changing times that the Japanese translation of his prize-winning study was picked up by Kodansha, one of Japan's largest mainstream publishing houses.

25 *New York Times*, March 6, 1995; cited in Mark Osiel, *Mass Atrocity, Collective Memory, and the Law* (New Brunswick, NJ, and London, 1997), pp. 183, 189.

An Incident at No Gun Ri

1 Barbie Zelizer, *Remembering to Forget: Holocaust Memory through the Camera's Eye* (Chicago, 1998), p. 15. The author wishes to thank Myra Jehlen, Robert Moeller and the editors of this volume for their helpful comments, and the John Simon Guggenheim Foundation and the American Council of Learned Societies for their support.

 2 *Ibid.*, pp. 211, 212.

 3 Gary Solis and Edwin H. Simmons, *Son Thang: An American War Crime* (Annapolis, MD., 1997), p. 108.

 4 Documents included in "Bridge at No Gun Ri," an Associated Press Special Report by Sang-Hun Choe, Charles J. Hanley, and Martha Mendoza, December 21, 1999. Since the writing of this essay, Charles Hanley, Sang-Hun Choe, and Martha Mendoza have written a powerful full-length account, which readers are strongly urged to consult: *The Bridge at No Gun Ri: A Hidden Nightmare from the Korean War* (New York, 2001).

 5 *Los Angeles Times*, October 5, 1999.

6 James Webb, "The Bridges at No Gun Ri," *Wall Street Journal*, October 6, 1999, p. 22.

7 The wish to see tomorrow may be a reference to a famous David Duncan photograph of the Korean War. When Duncan asks a weary soldier what he wants for Christmas, the man replies that he wants only to "see tomorrow." Duncan, David Douglas, *This War! A Photo-Narrative in Three Parts* (New York, 1951), no page numbers.

8 Douglas Strick, "Airing an Ugly Secret," *Washington Post*, October 27, 1999, pp. 24, 28.

9 "GI's Tell of a U.S. Massacre in Korean War," *New York Times*, September 30, 1999, pp. 1, 16.

10 *Ibid.*

11 *Time*, October 11, 1999, p. 42.

12 *CBS Evening News*, October 12, 1999.

13 "S-2 Evaluation, May 1951," Headquarters, 38th Infantry, from Capt. Rizalito Abanto to Commanding Officer, 38th Infantry. I want to thank Bob Port, currently a reporter for the *New York Daily News*, for this document.

14 Charles Hanley, AP dispatch, October 13, 1999.

15 *Ibid.*

16 *Hot Shots: An Oral History of the Air Force Combat Pilots of the Korean War*, ed. Jennie Ethell Chancey and William R. Fortschen (New York, 2000), pp. 28–32.

17 Memo to General Timberlake, Advance Headquarters, Fifth Air Force, July 25, 1950, from Turner C. Rogers, Colonel, USAF, D C/S Operations; the text was reprinted in full by *New York Newsday* and discussed in a report by its Washington Bureau correspondent, Patrick J. Sloyan ("New Account of No Gun Ri," January 19, 2001).

18 Sang-Hun Choe, Charles J. Hanley, and Martha Mendoza, "Korea Air War, Korea Documents, Korea Strafings," December 28, 1999.

19 For a survey of press opinion on Daily and related issues, see Felicity Barringer, "A Press Divided: Disputed Accounts of a Korean War Massacre," *New York Times*, May 22, 2000.

20 Joseph L. Galloway, "Doubts about a Korean 'Massacre,' " *U.S. News & World Report* (online), May 12, 2000. In addition to *U.S. News & World Report*, the *Baltimore Sun* and the military Web site *stripes.com* have been particularly assiduous in fact-checking the original AP story.

21 Michael Moss, "The Story behind a Soldier's Story," *New York Times*, May 31, 2000, p. 1, 22.

22 John Osborne, "This Savage War," *Time*, August 21, 1950.

23 "Koreans Recount Massacre by U.S. Seeking Justice for Alleged Slayings," AP dispatch in *Newsday*, November 13, 1999.

24 The complete text is available online at *www.army.mil/nogunri/*

25 Robert Burns, "Army Says U.S. Soldiers Killed South Korean Civilians, Clinton Expresses Regret," AP, January 12, 2001.

26 Sue Pleming, "Clinton Expresses Regret Over Korean War," Reuters, January 11, 2001.

27 For a critique of the report, see Charles Hanley, "No Gun Ri: Unanswered Questions Remain: Where's the Log? Who Knew? Who Was Responsible?" AP January 13, 2001; "Korean Massacre Probe Needs Independent Investigation," *FAIR*, January 23, 2001 (*www.fair.org*).

28 Press release, US Newswire, January 11, 2001.

29 "Interview of the President," Reuters, January 12, 2001.

30 Richard Pyle, "Survivors Denounce Army's No Gun Ri Report," January 12, 2001. *http://wire.ap.org.*

31 For its part, the Korean government, while politely disagreeing with the Americans over the likely number of victims at No Gun Ri, had other issues in mind as well. In the Korean translation of documents, interviews, and statements, the word "massacre" was systematically deleted, in an effort, according to Elizabeth Becker, "to ensure that Japan could not compare its war crimes with events at No Gun Ri." [Elizabeth Becker, "Army Confirms G.I.'s in Korea Killed Civilians," *New York Times*, January 12, 2001.]

About the Authors

OMER BARTOV is the John P. Birkelund Distinguished Professor of European History at Brown University. His books include *The Eastern Front 1941–45: German Troops and the Barbarisation of Warfare* (1985), *Hitler's Army: Soldiers, Nazis, and War in the Third Reich* (1991), *Murder in Our Midst: The Holocaust, Industrial Killing, and Representation* (1996), *Mirrors of Destruction: War, Genocide, and Modern Identity* (2000), and the edited volumes *The Holocaust: Origins, Implementation, Aftermath* (2000) and (with Phyllis Mack) *In God's Name: Genocide and Religion in the Twentieth Century* (2001).

FRANK BIESS teaches at the University of California–San Diego, and is currently working on a book on returning POWs in East and West Germany.

BERND BOLL, a historian and specialist in museum pedagogy, was a research fellow for the exhibition "*Vernichtungskrieg. Verbrechen der Wehrmacht 1941 bis 1944*" organized by the Hamburg Institute for Social Research. He has published " . . . *das wird man nie mehr los." Ausländische Zwangsarbeiter in der Offenburger Kriegswirtschaft 1939–1945* (1994) and, in collaboration with Ursula Huggle, *Die Industrie- und Handelskammer Südlicher Oberrhein. Geschichte und Wirkungsfeld der Kammern Lahr und Freiburg* (1998).

CHRISTOPHER R. BROWNING is the Frank Porter Graham Professor of History at the University of North Carolina at Chapel Hill. Among his publications are *Ordinary Men: Police Battalion 101 and the Final Solution in Poland* (1992) and *Nazi Policy, Jewish Workers, German Killers* (2000).

JOHN W. DOWER, the Elting E. Morison Professor of History at the Massachusetts Institute of Technology, is author of the prize-winning 1986 study *War without Mercy: Race and Power in the Pacific War*. His most recent book, *Embracing Defeat: Japan in the Wake of World War Two*, also won many awards, including both the Pulitzer Prize and National Book Award in general nonfiction, the Bancroft Prize in U.S. history, the John Fairbank Prize in Asian studies, and the *Los Angeles Times* Book Award in history.

SAUL FRIEDLÄNDER is professor of history at the University of California, Los Angeles. His most recent book is *Nazi Germany and the Jews*, vol I, *The Years of Persecution, 1933–1939* (1997).

ATINA GROSSMANN is associate professor of history in the Faculty of Humanities at The Cooper Union for the Advancement of Science and Art in New York City. Her publications include *Reforming Sex: The German Movement for Birth Control and Abortion Reform 1920–1950* (1995, 1997), *When Biology Became Destiny: Women in Weimar and Nazi Germany* (co-editor, 1984), and articles on gender and modernity in interwar Germany and Germans and Jews in postwar Germany. She is currently working on "Victims, Victors, and Survivors: Germans, Allies, and Jews in Occupied Postwar Germany, 1945–1949."

MARIANNE HIRSCH is professor of French and comparative literature at Dartmouth College. Her recent books are *The Mother/Daughter Plot: Narrative, Psychoanalysis, Feminism* (1989) and *Family Frames: Photography, Narrative and Postmemory* (1997). She is also the editor of *The Familial Gaze* (1998). She is currently writing a book with Leo Spitzer, *Czernowitz Album: Four Jewish Families and the Idea of a City Before, During and After the Holocaust*.

ROBERT G. MOELLER teaches German and European history at the University of California, Irvine. He is the author of *Protecting Mother-*

hood: *Women and the Family in the Politics of Postwar West Germany* (1993), *War Stories: The Search for a Usable Past in the Federal Republic of Germany* (2001), and numerous articles on the social and political history of Germany in the twentieth century.

ARYEH NEIER is the president of the Open Society Institute and the Soros Foundation. He spent twelve years as executive director of Human Rights Watch, of which he was a founder. He is the author of five books: *Dossier* (1975), *Crime and Punishment: A Radical Solution* (1976), *Defending My Enemy* (1979), *Only Judgment* (1982), and *War Crimes: Brutality, Genocide, Terror and the Struggle for Justice* (1998). He has been a frequent contributor to the *New York Review of Books* and the *Nation*.

MARY NOLAN is professor of history at New York University. She is the author of *Social Democracy and Society: Working-Class Radicalism in Düsseldorf, 1890–1914* (1980) and *Visions of Modernity: American Business and the Modernization of Germany* (1994). Her recent articles include "The Politics of Memory in the Berlin Republic," "America in the German Imagination," and "Work, Gender and Everyday Life: Reflections on Continuity, Normality and Agency in Twentieth-Century Germany."

JAN PHILIPP REEMTSMA is the founder and director of the Hamburg Institute for Social Research. He is a member of the board of curators of the Cultural Foundation of the German Federal States (*Kulturstiftung der Länder*) and the spokesperson of its Working Group on Literature, Libraries, Archives and Cultural History. Reemtsma's extensive list of publications includes essays and academic works focusing on a wide range of topics from the areas of literature, history, politics, cultural studies, and philosophy.

GUDRUN SCHWARZ is a sociologist and a member of the research staff in the research unit Theory and History of Violence at the Hamburg Institute for Social Research. She is the author of *Eine Frau an seiner Seite: Ehefrauen in der SS-Sippengemeinschaft* (1997). She is currently working on a study of women in the SS order and in the SS apparatus.

AMIR WEINER teaches in the Department of History at Stanford University. He is the author of *Making Sense of War: The Second World War and the Fate of the Bolshevik Revolution* (2000).

MARILYN B. YOUNG teaches the history of U.S. foreign policy in Asia at New York University. She is currently the director of the Cold War Project at the International Center for Advanced Study at NYU. Her previous published work focused on Vietnam and China. With the support of Guggenheim and ACLS fellowships, she is now working on a book about the Korean War.

INDEX

Note: Page numbers in italics refer to illustrations.